Thematic Guide
to
American Poetry

Thematic Guide
to
American Poetry

Allan Burns

GREENWOOD PRESS
Westport, Connecticut • London

Library of Congress Cataloging-in-Publication Data

Burns, Allan (Allan Douglas)
   Thematic guide to American poetry / Allan Burns.
      p.   cm.
   Includes bibliographical references and index.
   ISBN 0–313–31462–4 (alk. paper)
      1. American poetry—Bibliography—Indexes.   2. American poetry—Themes,
   motives—Indexes.   I. Title.
   Z1231.P7B87   2002
   [PS303]
   016.811009—dc21   2001058646

British Library Cataloguing in Publication Data is available.

Library of Congress Catalog Card Number: 2001058646
ISBN: 0–313–31462–4

First published in 2002

Greenwood Press, 88 Post Road West, Westport, CT 06881
An imprint of Greenwood Publishing Group, Inc.
www.greenwood.com

Printed in the United States of America

The paper used in this book complies with the
Permanent Paper Standard issued by the National
Information Standards Organization (Z39.48–1984).

10 9 8 7 6 5 4 3 2 1

For Theresa

Contents

Contents

Introduction

❦

A "theme" is the central idea or unifying concept stated or implied by a poem. It is usually an abstraction made immediate and particular by concrete representation. Often, one can distinguish between a poem's abstract theme and its concrete subject. An example will help to clarify this distinction. In Philip Freneau's well-known poem "The Wild Honey Suckle," the subject is the wild honeysuckle itself (titles often indicate subjects). The theme, or main idea of the poem, on the other hand, is the transience of life, which the concrete honeysuckle illustrates.

Not all poems, of course, present such straightforward illustrations. In some cases, even careful, informed readers may disagree on the question of what a poem is "really" about. So, from a theoretical standpoint, it is useful to conceptualize the theme less as an intrinsic part of the poem and more as part of a reader's interpretation of a poem. When we pose the question, What is the theme of this particular poem? (which is identical to the question, What is this poem really about?), we are beginning to interpret the poem. The validity of any interpretation, however, will have to be supported by evidence and argument based on close reading—that is, careful consideration of all the poem's details and overall design. In addition, knowledge of the poet's life, times, viewpoint, and other poems is indispensable to one's understanding of what a poem says and means.

This *Thematic Guide* offers 250 interpretations, representing the work of 86 poets, divided into 21 thematic categories. The categories are organized alphabetically, and within each category, the individual explications are arranged chronologically, to emphasize the evolution of a particular theme over time. Chronology has been violated in a few instances to discuss multiple poems by a single author as a group or to effect smoother transitions. The book draws upon the full range of American poetry, including the work of a large number of contemporary poets.

In order, however, to trace a relatively coherent history of thematic connections, the meaning of "American poetry" has been limited to "poetry of the United States." In other words, the guide does not include poems from the colonial period or from other countries of North and South America. Individual sections typically begin with the groundbreaking work of poets such as Philip Freneau, Ralph Waldo Emerson, and Walt Whitman, all of whom helped to establish a more-or-less distinctive and self-consciously "American" poetic tradition. The quality of a poem, its relative availability in standard anthologies, and the degree to which it lends itself to a thematic approach were important selection criteria. Limitations of time and space necessitated some difficult choices. Not every notable poem, obviously, could be included for discussion; the aim has merely been to provide analysis of a cross-section of high-quality American poems. If readers lament the exclusion of certain poems, perhaps they will be compensated by having their attention directed to worthy poems that had previously escaped their notice.

No definitive list of the total number of possible themes exists, nor are there necessarily absolute boundaries between one theme and another. Any given theme simply functions as a conceptual tool that allows an interpreter to make connections between human experience and poetry and between one poem and others. Reading for themes is one strategy readers have for organizing their literary experience. A consideration of how a theme is handled differently through time will inevitably lead one to contemplate not only the diverse temperaments of individual authors but also the ideas, values, and assumptions that have informed their works.

The guide does not purport to offer complete explications of individual poems. A theme, after all, though extremely important, is only one part of a poem; further, great poems are sometimes more remarkable for the *way* they say something than for simply *what* they say. Certainly, attention can and should also be paid to genre, structure, style, tropes, archetypes, syntax, sound, meter, etc. Here, however, these other aspects of poetry have only been brought into the discussion when they directly help to illuminate our understanding of a poem's theme. The aim of this book is simply to help students better understand what poems are saying, specifically against the wider backdrop of American poetic traditions. Individual discussions of poems typically provide an analytical paraphrase, with the assumption that the reader will follow along with the text of the poem itself. Paraphrase, of course, is never an adequate substitute for what the poems themselves say in their far richer manner; it is simply one tool of critical explication, which may help the reader better grasp the full significance of a poem. The author does not expect that readers will assent to all his analytical observations. They are offered not as definitive interpretations but as provocations to further reflection and study. There are always more things to be said about good poems and new ways to look at them. As interpretation is a provisional process always open to revision and refinement, critical commentators know only too well that, with the passage of time and the accumulation of experience, insight, and further information, it is quite possible that they may well end up disagreeing with even their own conclusions.

Studying poetry is an exacting but also enlightening and pleasurable exercise of the mind. The author's greatest hope is that students who read this book—and we are all lifelong students—will find new poems to treasure and will be stimulated to read poetry with care, thoughtfulness, and enthusiasm.

BIBLIOGRAPHICAL NOTE

In order to assist students, teachers, and librarians in locating the texts of each poem, the poems are listed in the order discussed at the end of each chapter, each one followed by codes that correspond to the "List of Anthologies" in *The Columbia Granger's Index to Poetry in Anthologies* (11th ed., Columbia University Press). For anthologies not listed in *Granger's*—such as anthologies of American literature rather than those strictly of American poetry—the author has invented codes of his own.

Anthologies of American Poetry and Abbreviations Used

ᗡᐯᐯᗡ

HAL-1   *The Harper American Literature.* Vol. 1. Donald McQuade et al., eds. 2nd ed. Harper Collins, 1993.

HAL-2   *The Harper American Literature.* Vol. 2. Donald McQuade et al., eds. 2nd ed. Harper Collins, 1993.

HCAP   *The Harvard Book of Contemporary American Poetry.* Helen Vendler, ed. Belknap Press, 1985.

HoAL-1   *Heritage of American Literature.* Vol. 1. James E. Miller, Jr. Harcourt Brace Jovanovich, 1991.

HoAL-2   *Heritage of American Literature.* Vol. 2. James E. Miller, Jr. Harcourt Brace Jovanovich, 1991.

LPTT   *Lyric Poems on Twelve Themes.* Charles H. Kegel and William J. Shanahan, eds. Scott, Foresman and Co., 1970.

MAP   *Anthology of Modern American Poetry.* Cary Nelson, ed. Oxford University Press, 2000.

NAL-1   *The Norton Anthology of American Literature.* Vol. 1. Nina Baym et al., eds. 5th ed. W. W. Norton, 1998.

NAL-2   *The Norton Anthology of American Literature.* Vol. 2. Nina Baym et al., eds. 5th ed. W. W. Norton, 1998.

NoAM   *The Norton Anthology of Modern Poetry.* Richard Ellman and Robert O'Clair, eds. 2nd ed. W. W. Norton, 1988.

NOBA   *The New Oxford Book of American Verse.* Richard Ellman, ed. Oxford University Press, 1976.

NoP-4   *The Norton Anthology of Poetry.* Margaret Ferguson et al., eds. 4th ed. W. W. Norton, 1996.

OxBA   *The Oxford Book of American Verse.* F. O. Matthiessen, ed. Oxford University Press, 1950.

RA   *Rebel Angels: 25 Poets of the New Formalism.* Mark Jarman and David Mason, eds. Story Line Press, 1998.

SoSe-9   *Perrine's Sound and Sense: An Introduction to Poetry.* Thomas R. Arp, ed. 9th ed. Harcourt Brace, 1997.

TFi   *The Top 500 Poems.* William Harmon, ed. Columbia University Press, 1992.

VCAP   *The Vintage Book of Contemporary American Poetry.* J. D. McClatchy, ed. Vintage Books, 1990.

VGW   *The Voice That Is Great within Us.* Hayden Carruth, ed. Bantam Books, 1970.

WeW-4   *Western Wind: An Introduction to Poetry.* John Frederick Nims and David Mason, eds. 4th ed. McGraw-Hill, 2000.

Art and Beauty

❦

> It is art that *makes* life, makes interest, makes importance . . . and I
> know of no substitute whatever for the force and beauty of its proc-
> ess.
>
> Henry James, letter to H. G. Wells

Art and beauty are not, of course, synonymous: one can easily think of
many art works that deliberately eschew beauty in order to pursue some
other ideal or effect. In the twentieth century, the breakdown of traditional aesthetic forms and belief systems, coarsened industrial cityscapes,
and the horrors of human behavior—most notably in the two world
wars—contributed further to the dissociation of art and beauty. Many
artists came to feel that to pursue beauty was not to be true to experience.
It seemed a superficial quality, the epitome of sheltered, bourgeois notions of what art should be. Beauty is probably not the principal quality
that comes to mind when we think of the paintings of Picasso, the music
of Stravinsky, or the poetry of T. S. Eliot. Nor is it the central quality one
would associate with many powerful artists of previous centuries, including Dante, Michelangelo, Beethoven, and Goya.

Nonetheless, in many times and places and in many artistic traditions
and forms, the creation of beauty has been a paramount concern. In the
nineteenth century in particular, many poets, such as Keats, Poe, Tennyson, and Swinburne, strove, above all, to create beautiful effects in
their poetry. (Another way of understanding the prevalent twentieth-
century rejection of beauty in art is as a reaction to an overemphasis on
this virtue in nineteenth-century art.) Poetry, with its resources of rhythm
and sound and imagery, perhaps more readily lends itself to the creation
of beauty than does any other art form besides music. Because of this,

some poets have been tempted to equate poetry with beauty itself. Much nineteenth-century American poetry and poetic theory exemplifies such a tendency. Edgar Allan Poe, for example, defined poetry as *"The Rhythmical Creation of Beauty,"* and Ralph Waldo Emerson, called the poet "the man of Beauty." Both Poe and Emerson also wrote significant poems about the nature of beauty itself.

"To Helen" (1831, rev. 1845), one of Poe's most famous lyrics, was inspired by the mother of one of Poe's friends, Jane Stanard, who died insane in 1824 at the age of twenty-eight. Poe transforms Stanard into an idealized, inspiring muse, who returns the poet to pure classical ideals. Simply by addressing Stanard as Helen, Poe evokes Grecian antiquity, for in Greek mythology, Helen was the most beautiful of mortals. A daughter of Zeus and the wife of Menelaus, king of Sparta, she was kidnapped by Paris, an event that touched off the Trojan War; thus, according to Christopher Marlowe's Faustus, she possessed "the face that launched a thousand ships." In Poe's poem, the classical beauty of Helen, which in a knowing nod to Marlowe is likened to a ship, conveys the speaker, metaphorically, to his "native shore," or personal aesthetic ideals. Helen has brought him back—in the poem's most famous lines— "To the glory that was Greece, / And the grandeur that was Rome." (The 1831 version of the poem included the much inferior lines "To the beauty of fair Greece, / And the grandeur of old Rome." One weakness of the original is that Greece was far older than Rome, which makes the adjective "old" seem imprecise in this context. The revision offers greater precision as well as memorable alliteration.) The third stanza, more difficult than the preceding two, transforms the idealized woman-figure into a work of art: she becomes "statue-like." Further transformations change the woman's name from Helen to Psyche (the soul, or the goddess of the soul) and "native land" to "Holy-Land." The woman's inspiring influence has been fully internalized by the poet. Beauty, an abstraction that lives in the imagination beyond the death of any particular mortal, becomes an ideal that ushers the poet not to the actual classical world itself, long since gone, but rather into the "Holy-Land" of artistic creation. The classical ideal of beauty can thus be reborn in the poet's own work.

In contrast with Poe's inwardly focused vision, Emerson's "Each and All" (1847) takes a holistic view of beautiful objects in relation to their context. The opening of the poem (lines 1–12) explores the unexpected interconnectedness of things, particularly how the things that provide aesthetic delight to an observer often do so unintentionally. Emerson develops an abstract argument from his examples—"All are needed by each one; / Nothing is fair or good alone." (Following ancient philosophical precedent, Emerson conflates the good with the beautiful, which helps explain why he includes the example of the "neighbor's creed" along with the more strictly aesthetic instances of unintended influence.) He then moves on to three specific examples, each of which illustrates how removing a thing from its context tends to diminish its beauty. The examples of the sparrow, the seashells, and the maid all seek to enforce the idea that beauty is not so much the property of an object as the property of the relations between objects, which are integrated by the sensory perception of an observer. By removing an object from its context, you do not, according to Emerson, isolate its beauty but rather destroy it. The poem's speaker, confronted with this evidence, initially disparages beauty as a childish quality, inferior to truth; but he comes into a full appreciation of beauty once again when instead of collecting specimens, he confronts the whole of nature. "I yielded myself to the perfect whole," he writes in the poem's memorable climactic line, a generous gesture of self-abnegation. The poem aptly summarizes Emerson's transcendental belief in the interconnectedness of all things.

A related poem by Emerson, "The Rhodora" (1847) belongs to the early American tradition of symbolic flower poetry, which also includes Philip Freneau's "The Wild Honey Suckle," William Cullen Bryant's "The Yellow Violet" and "The Fringed Gentian," and James Russell Lowell's "To the Dandelion." Thematically, however, Emerson's poem more resembles Bryant's "To a Waterfowl" (discussed under "Skepticism & Belief"), in that the poet intuits a higher "Power" by observing another life form. The first half of the poem is principally descriptive: Emerson finds the flower in the May woods, where its purple petals, which outshine a cardinal's feathers, have fallen into a pool. Apostrophe follows in the second half: Emerson admonishes the flower to answer those who wonder why its charm "is wasted on the earth and sky"—which recalls the concluding lines from the celebrated fourteenth quatrain of Thomas Gray's "Elegy Written in a Country Churchyard": "Full many a flower is born to blush unseen, / And waste its sweetness on the desert air." The answer the rhodora is to provide is that "Beauty is its own excuse for being." Emerson rejects reductive accounts of beauty, instead favoring the notion that beauty is an end in and of itself. The poem does not have an answer for the question "whence?" from the subtitle; instead, it expresses a naive faith in a "Power" that fatefully brought both poet and flower together. Emerson's task in this poem is not to explain the origin of things but rather to celebrate the beauty of what exists.

Herman Melville's brief poem "Art" (1891) illustrates one of the major nineteenth-century ideas about great art: that it results from the reconciliation of opposites. Melville took this idea from the vastly influential English poet and critic Samuel Taylor Coleridge, who had derived it from the German philosopher F. W. J. Schelling. Dreaming about creating art, the poem asserts, is relatively easy; the difficulty involves embodying one's idea in a specific form. Art is, thus, the reconciliation of two opposing principles: fantasy and form. The middle portion of Melville's poem lists further pairs of opposites—e.g. "Sad patience—joyous energies"—that must meet and "mate" if true art is to be created. At the conclusion of the poem, Melville invokes the figure of Jacob wrestling with the angel (from Genesis 32) as an analog for the artist's difficulties in the struggle to create. For the author of *Moby-Dick*, art was clearly an immense undertaking, requiring the utmost of one's mental and emotional resources. Readers should note that Melville's poem does not once mention beauty. For Melville, unlike Poe, art was not principally the creation of beauty (or some other effect) but rather a titanic and paradoxical struggle to reconcile opposites.

Whereas Melville's "Art" focuses on art without mentioning beauty, Edna St. Vincent Millay's "Euclid Alone Has Looked on Beauty Bare" (1920) and Elinor Wylie's "Beauty" (1921) focus on beauty without mentioning art. Millay's sonnet stresses the elusive nature of beauty, personified as a kind of aloof goddess in sandals. The poem scoffs at those who would idly speak of "her" without genuine understanding: they are likened to noisy, self-absorbed geese, whose clamor prevents them from discerning anything significant about the beauty of the world. By contrast, Millay holds up the example of Euclid, the Alexandrian mathematician whose work still serves as the basis for much of what we understand about geometry. By making liberating use of his intellect, Euclid immeasurably enriched our understanding of beauty's abstract laws. The poem would seem to equate looking on beauty not so much with examining particulars, as a poet typically does, but with discerning underlying patterns and postulates. The poem concludes by reasserting that Euclid alone has looked directly on naked beauty, but then adds that those who have even once heard her tread at a distance (i.e., those who are dimly aware of her presence) are fortunate. For Millay, the perception of beauty is not a given, but results from disciplined inquiry.

Wylie, in three succinct quatrains, also personifies her subject, again as a female entity. Instead of stressing the elusiveness of beauty, Wylie emphasizes her amoral (but not immoral) character. The poem's structure could almost be described in the dialectical terms of thesis, antithesis, and synthesis. The first quatrain establishes that beauty is not good, the second that she is not evil, and the third that she is neither, but instead "innocent and wild." For Wylie, beauty is an amoral concept and therefore both decadent and insufficient. Wylie warns the would-be aesthete not to love beauty too much, for that betokens an even graver failing than asserting her immorality. Another danger is to enshrine her, for she must be allowed to exercise her wildness freely. Two symbolic images encapsulate Wylie's conception of beauty: the gull of the opening stanza and the child of the final stanza, both of which simultaneously represent innocence and wildness. The child image, shorn of any sentimentality that might ordinarily cling to it by the emphasis placed on the "hard heart," indicates that innocence does not automatically imply compassion any more than beauty implies goodness.

John Crowe Ransom examines the nature of mortal beauty in "Blue Girls" (1924), a lyric less given to abstraction than those of Millay and Wylie. The poem exhorts the college-age girls it addresses to seize the moment of their youth and beauty and to make the most of it, all very much in the tradition of the seventeenth-century English poet Robert Herrick (whose work includes such celebrated lyrics as "To the Virgins, to Make Much of Time"). Ransom endorses an almost animal-like existence, given neither to intellectuality nor self-conscious speculation about the future. The reasons for these preferences emerge as the poem's tone darkens. The turning point comes in the first rhyme of the third stanza: "before it [beauty] fail . . . It is so frail." This pair ("fail"/"frail") intensifies what has already been suggested by line 6: "And think no more of what will come to pass." What will come to pass, is that beauty will fade. The fourth stanza exemplifies this notion with reference to a story that the poet says he could relate to the girls (which implies a second audience for the poem beyond the girls themselves). Ransom speaks of an old woman with bleary eyes and "a terrible tongue," who was once more beautiful even than any of the "blue girls." Now, all her "perfections" are "tarnished." The implication is clear: the "blue girls" will themselves one day decline just as this allegedly greater beauty has. Throughout, Ransom develops the theme of beauty's fragility and inevitable decline with reference to the color blue. Blue, which evokes the sky and therefore freshness and purity, is the color of the girls' skirts and of the bluebirds to which the poet compares the girls. Ransom relates beauty's decline to the eyes of the old woman, which have "fallen from blue." By the end, blue's other conventional and antithetical association—sorrow—has come into play, reminding us of the duality of an imperfect world, in which beautiful girls all too quickly become "tarnished" old women.

Robinson Jeffers considers the persistence of artistic creation in "To the Stone-Cutters" (1924) and finds that mortality of the type Ransom contemplates lords over all creation. The immortality of art had long been a conventional notion, inherited from Horace and the Renaissance writers. Art, in contrast with life, was conceived of as enduring through the ages; one could "immortalize" a subject (particularly a loved one) with a painting or a poem, thereby transcending the "tarnished" fate of all mortals. Shakespeare provides supreme examples of this idea in many of his sonnets, notably #18 ("Shall I compare thee to a summer's day?") and #65 ("Since brass, nor stone, nor earth, nor boundless sea"). Jeffers, in light of the picture of the universe developed by modern science—that is, a universe constrained by entropy—turns this conventional notion on its head. Artists, he asserts, have become merely "foredefeated / Challengers of oblivion." Sculptors, for example, are unable to meet the challenge of time even on the scale of recorded history. Their creations may survive in tact for many generations, but eventually, unless very special precautions are taken, they wear out, fall apart, and erode away. Nor are they unique in this respect. On a cosmic scale of time, even the poet labors in vain. Poems, which do not directly depend on perishable materials, may be transmitted through the ages much more safely than sculptures, architecture, or paintings; but even they depend on the existence of humanity and human culture and language, and none of these things is exempt from the ravages of time. One day, as Jeffers points out, the sun itself will burn out. All things are mortal—even, as the law of entropy tells us, the universe itself—so the boasts of those who claim to "immortalize" anything through art are ultimately empty. Jeffers, however, does not end the poem on this pessimistic note. Instead, he offers a more realistic and relativistic appraisal of art's value. It does not immortalize anything, but it does offer consolation, illumination, and delight across many generations and even ages. Temporally, its value is relative, but still highly significant in human terms.

If art works are not immortal, they still enjoy a vastly greater durability than individual lives—a proposition Marianne Moore explores in the brief, seemingly enigmatic poem "No Swan So Fine" (1932). The poem begins with a sentence fragment concerning the fountains at Versailles (the magnificent palace outside Paris built by Louis XIV in the seventeenth century), culled from an article by Percy Phillip in the *New York Times Magazine*. (Moore loved to incorporate "found" statements such as this one into her poetry.) The fragment describes the fountains as "dead," which introduces the poem's central contrast between inanimate and animate objects. The remainder of the first stanza consists of an original fragment, modeled on Phillip's, that develops the poem's main idea by contrasting a china swan at Versailles with a live one. Moore finds the artificial swan "more fine" than its living counterpart, a judgment that enforces the view that art, with its selective perfection and durability, is, in certain ways, superior to life. The second stanza, roughly parallel to the first, consists of two sentences. The first, much longer sentence describes the china swan further, with particular attention to its gaudy, artificial surroundings. The final sentence, terse and initially puzzling, reads simply, "The king is dead." At first, this ending may seem as abruptly out of place as that of James Wright's "Lying in a Hammock at William Duffy's Farm in Pine Island, Minnesota" (discussed under "Thought & Perception"); however, a moment's reflection will undoubtedly allow the reader to connect the final "dead" back to the "dead fountains" of the second line. But there is a significant difference between the meaning of the two adjectives: the first means simply still, whereas the latter means "perished"; thus, Moore has developed the contrast between inanimate and animate by skillfully suggesting the difference that inheres within seeming similarities. "Dead" differs from "dead" just as the fake swan differs from the live one. The king in question (Louis XV) has, despite his pomp and grandeur, perished, as the mortal swan and all mortal beings must. The king had owned the china bird, but whereas he has died, it still stands, giving pleasure to an observer centuries later. The living have the privilege to own art works and to enjoy them, but the art works themselves persist in defiance of both time and ownership. Moore's poem twits the pretensions of kings and acknowledges the superiority of art over life in terms of duration—but at the same time, it subtly suggests that the only value art possesses eventuates from its relation to a living, appreciating observer.

In the poem "Juggler" (1950), Richard Wilbur explores yet another aspect of art: the way in which it transfigures the commonplace. The poem's eponymous hero stands as Wilbur's representative artist figure, whose task it is to deliver the world from precisely those blind forces of negation Jeffers had identified. The poem's opening stanza describes how gravity robs a ball of its inertia, an image of diminishment against which the poem counterpoises the juggler's work. In the second stanza, Wilbur writes that the juggler shakes "our gravity up," punning on two meanings of "gravity" as both the physical force and an audience's solemnity. The juggler demonstrates his skill at preventing balls from falling, but then creates new and greater difficulties for himself by trading in the balls for three mundane objects: a table, a broom, and a plate. The juggler's skill at animating and transforming reality becomes fully apparent as he spins the table with a toe, balances the broom on his nose, and whirls the plate on the end of the broom. Although at the conclusion of the performance the juggler has tired and knows that his quotidian objects will soon be returned to their homely stations, the artistic victory has been won. The audience claps fervently, for the juggler has accomplished something truly remarkable: he has overcome—if but momentarily—"the world's weight." A celebration (as well as a demonstration) of artistic skill, the poem shows us how art transcends the ordinary and adds something not strictly necessary yet altogether worthwhile—even, as line fourteen suggests, redemptive—to the world.

Wilbur turns his attention to spontaneous and un-self-conscious beauty in another poem, "Piazza di Spagna, Early Morning" (1956). Inspired by a memory of how the poet watched a girl gracefully descend the long, curved stairway of the Piazza di Spagna (a plaza in Rome), the poem sets out to capture something of the girl's grace for itself. The first stanza describes the girl's movements as she pirouettes and dances down to where the soft white noise of a fountain quiets the plaza. The second stanza then provides a close-up of her face, marked by impersonal loneliness. She seems not to be a girl at all but rather "a reverie" of the place, its embodied genius whose traits of grace and beauty mirror and distill those of the plaza. Wilbur then summarizes the girl's motion, underscoring its grace with a repetition of the "l" sound (often regarded as the most beautiful phoneme in the language): it is "A called-for falling glide and whirl." The final stanza develops an extended simile, comparing the girl's motions to those of a delicate object, such as a leaf, petal, or wood chip, riding over a waterfall. The comparison introduces the same idea that Emerson explored at the beginning of "Each and All": that beauty often exists simply for itself and without any awareness of the pleasure it may bring to an observer. As with "The Juggler," the poem exhibits the traits of what it describes. Wilbur does not merely commemorate grace and beauty; he skillfully exemplifies them.

Adrienne Rich, a more politically inclined poet, examines in "Aunt Jennifer's Tigers" (1951) how the creation of art can redeem a life oppressed by circumstances. Overtly feminist in its stance, Rich's poem describes Aunt Jennifer's needlework. The tigers she creates do not fear men with guns, for they are safe from masculine violence, outside of time, as are the figures on Keats's Grecian urn. The poem's full effect depends on suggestive diction and—much like Wilbur's "Juggler"—on clever wordplay. The reference to predatory men in the first stanza resonates with the image of the weighty wedding band in the second to convey a definite impression of male oppressiveness, manifest both in the practice of hunting and in the institution of marriage. Simultaneously, Rich metamorphoses the "tigers" of line one into the "fingers" of line five; the parallel phrasing calls attention to the phonetic similarity of the two words and reminds us that Aunt Jennifer's fingers created the tigers of the needlework. In the third stanza, Rich plays off the image of the wedding band (also directly associated with the fingers) when she depicts Aunt Jennifer's dead hands, "Still ringed with ordeals she was mastered by." The noun "ring" has now become the verb "ringed": clearly, marriage was the decisive burden of Aunt Jennifer's existence. But if her life had been a failure, her needlework remains a triumph. Although the hands that created the tigers may have been "terrified," the proud tigers themselves still prance, transcendently "unafraid." This final antithesis asserts the redemptive power of art to rise above circumstance and to inspire later generations to confront sources of oppression. The tigers, ultimately, become a feminist symbol of moral and unvanquished defiance. Rich's poem invites us to contemplate the various purposes art may serve. It also forecasts both the feminist movement and Rich's pivotal role within that movement.

Cathy Song's "Beauty and Sadness" (1983) brings the consideration of art and beauty full circle, for it fuses these central concepts back together. Her poem concerns the works of Kitagawa Utamaro (1753–1806), a Japanese printmaker who specialized in sensuous portraits of beautiful women. The poem describes the artist, his models, and his works; it also meditates on how art transforms impermanent things into something enduring. Song characterizes Utamaro himself as a quick and nimble man, whose presence seems as delicate as the "skinlike paper" of his prints. The poem's last glimpse of him at the very end (lines 53–56) indicates that the artist was himself—"dwarfed and bespectacled"—practically the opposite of the beauty he devoted his life to capturing. His eye is described as "inconsolable" (line 42), intimating that his thirst for beauty could not be quenched. This interpretation would seem to account for Utamaro's prolificacy (he drew hundreds of women, as the first line tells us) and for the word "Sadness" in the title (which also would seem to refer to the "melancholy" of the models). The models themselves came from various walks of life—waitresses, actresses, prostitutes, maids, and geishas (or professional singing and dancing girls in Japan). All, in other words, were entertainers or menials whose principal task, in life as in the prints, was to serve or provide pleasure for men. Song implicitly makes but chooses not to dwell on this point. She focuses instead on the way that Utamaro "absorbed" these lives into his work, much like the speaker of Poe's "To Helen." We see the women principally as they appear in the prints, transfigured by art—notably in the marvelous description that occupies the entire second stanza. In the poem's fourth and final section, the prints are likened to ash-winged moths that the Japanese venerate as reincarnated ancestors. The beauty of the actual women, long since dead, has been reincarnated in the enduring prints. Returning to the theme that Jeffers had interrogated, Song claims that Utamaro has immortalized the women. As is the case in many of Shakespeare's sonnets, Song's poem meditates on art's transcendent ability to capture the beauty of transitory things.

❦

"To Helen," Edgar Allan Poe

AAL-1; APN-1; ATL-1; ColAP; HAL-1; HoAL-1; NAL-1; NOBA; NoP-4; OxBA; TFi; WeW-4

"Each and All," Ralph Waldo Emerson

AAL-1; APN-1; ATL-1; ColAP; HAL-1; HoAL-1; NAL-1; NOBA; OxBA

"The Rhodora," Ralph Waldo Emerson

AAL-1; APN-1; ATL-1; HAL-1; HoAL-1; NAL-1; NOBA; NoP-4; OxBA; TFi

"Art," Herman Melville
AAL-1; APN-2; ATL-1; ColAP; HAL-1; HoAL-1; NOBA
"Euclid Alone Has Looked on Beauty Bare," Edna St. Vincent Millay
APT-1; HAL-2; HoAL-2; NoP-4
"Beauty," Elinor Wylie
APT-1; OxBA
"Blue Girls," John Crowe Ransom
AAL-2; APT-1; ATL-2; ColAP; NoAM; NoP-4; VGW; WeW-4
"To the Stone-Cutters," Robinson Jeffers
ATL-2; ColAP; HoAL-2; NAL-2; NOBA; NoP-4; OxBA
"No Swan So Fine," Marianne Moore
AAL-2; ATL-2; HAL-2; HoAL-2; MAP; NoP-4; OxBA
"Juggler," Richard Wilbur
AAL-2
"Piazza di Spagna, Early Morning," Richard Wilbur
NoP-4; VGW
"Aunt Jennifer's Tigers," Adrienne Rich
ATL-2; CAPP-6; ColAP; HoAL-2; MAP; NoAM; NoP-4; SoSe-9
"Beauty and Sadness," Cathy Song
ATL-2; HAL-2; NAL-2; NoAM

Civilization

༺∿༒∿༻

Civilization is the lamb's skin in which barbarism masquerades.
Thomas Bailey Aldrich, *Ponkapog Papers*

American poets have always had an uneasy relationship with American civilization at large. On the one hand, poets have extolled American liberty, democracy, possibility, prosperity, and ingenuity; on the other, they have lamented and excoriated American materialism, vulgarity, greed, corruption, hypocrisy, and imperialism. Poems in both praise and blame of America are numerous. That the more critical tend also to be the more memorable and the more widely anthologized perhaps simply indicates what a spur to creative response the idealist's pang at seeing the world fall short of its promise is. Some readers might wish our poets tempered their views with a more "realistic" appraisal of human limitation and the drawbacks of other civilizations, past and present; but the poets themselves, quite justifiably, allow little time for self-congratulation while self-improvement remains a possibility. Perhaps, too, poets are prone to a certain vitriol simply by virtue of their marginalized position within a utilitarian, business-driven society that assigns little value to literary pursuits. Undoubtedly, the rise in the twentieth century of the mass electronic media, particularly television, has further diminished the position of poets within America. The prestige and recognition enjoyed by even our finest contemporary poets dwindles to nothing beside that accorded to media celebrities.

That, however, has not deterred the poets from speaking their minds—or prevented their words from stubbornly enduring. When one thinks of poets critical of American civilization, Robinson Jeffers, Robert Lowell, and Allen Ginsberg might immediately come to mind; but even before them there was Walt Whitman. Often—and justifiably—regarded as the great celebrant of American democracy, freedom, and diversity, Whitman could also be quite acerbic on occasion about America's shortcomings, his statements of disappointment sharpened by the very intensity of his love and hope for the nation. Whitman often felt an acute gap between the ideal of America and the reality. Nothing made that gap more apparent than the political situation of the 1850s. Whitman's "To the States" (1860), subtitled "To Identify the 16th, 17th, or 18th Presidentiad," excoriates the politics of Washington, which then, as now, seemed to be designed to suffocate idealism. To understand the subtitle, one has to realize that by counting "Presidentiads," Whitman meant the number of four-year terms rather than the number of persons who had served as president. In other words, he counted the two-term presidents (Washington, Jefferson, Madison, Monroe, and Jackson) twice and the presidents who died in office along with their successors (Harrison and Tyler, Taylor and Fillmore) only once. Taylor and Fillmore thus served the sixteenth presidentiad (as opposed to Abraham Lincoln, who would later become the sixteenth president), Pierce served the seventeenth, and Buchanan the eighteenth. What strikes Whitman about these presidentiads is the degree to which they indicate a lack of vigilance on the part of himself and the American public.

He asks: "why myself and all drowsing?" In other words, Americans had to have been asleep, at least metaphorically, to allow such rulers—who stand for things so far away from the supposed beliefs of the democracy—to have taken power. Public life has become a kind of nightmare (to continue the trope of sleep), in which the politicians play the part of "bats and night-dogs." Whitman pulls no punches and minces no words: "What a filthy Presidentiad!" (In his pamphlet *The Eighteenth Presidency!* Whitman went even further, making claims such as that Pierce "eats dirt and excrement for his daily meals, likes it, and tries to force it on The States.") What irked Whitman, in particular, about the presidents of the 1850s was his feeling that they were corrupt nonentities elected by special interest groups, who did nothing to remedy the problems of slavery and growing sectional differences that would result in the Civil War. Confronted with the reality of American politics, Whitman stands astonished: "Are those really Congressmen? are those the great Judges? is that the President?" Many readers will no doubt find that Whitman's incredulity seems only too familiar. For his part, Whitman can only cautiously retreat and await the great awakening that must, he feels, eventually come to the American people. One day, Americans would demand a true and honest democracy and take the government out of the hands of corrupt, shortsighted politicians. Perhaps we are still waiting?

The poets who followed immediately after Whitman were somewhat more likely to write about civilization in regional rather than national terms. After the Civil War, "regionalism" became a major movement in American literature. It explicitly acknowledged the heterogeneous character of American civilization and therefore tended to avoid the kind of sweeping generalizations and indictments in which Whitman indulged. Regionalism in poetry can be represented by Carl Sandburg, who wrote of the burgeoning civilization of the Midwest, and by Edwin Arlington Robinson and E. E. Cummings, who produced ironic commentaries on the long-established and vestigially puritanical civilization of New England. Sandburg's "Chicago" (1914) voices its author's optimistic, populist, urban vision of America. Sandburg believed that Chicago, situated in the heartland, was destined to become the great city of American civilization. His paean to Chicago's inexhaustible energy and industry employs a typically long though wildly fluctuating free-verse line with a breathless rhetorical vigor that derives from Whitman and anticipates Allen Ginsberg. The poem begins by supplying a list of mostly industrial epithets for the city: "Hog Butcher for the World, / Tool Maker," and so forth. Having characterized its public profile in this brief prelude, Sandburg then acknowledges the city's less visible shortcomings: its prostitution, murders, and poverty. Following a typical pattern of classical rhetoric, Sandburg then turns the tables on the city's critics, asserting with true Chicagoan pride that although the city does indeed have its problems, its essence is a kind of terrible and unparalleled vitality, which he attempts to convey with a long list of participles:

> Bareheaded,
> Shoveling,
> Wrecking,
> Planning,
> Building, breaking, rebuilding.

Above all, the city's characteristic activity, as Sandburg depicts it, is "laughing," which he repeats six times. What he attempts to convey is an active, unshaken spirit of meeting the world's challenges with a hard head and ready hands. Chicago's rough vitality represents to him the fulfillment, however imperfect, of American civilization's expansive democratic possibilities.

By contrast, Edwin Arlington Robinson takes an obliquely and somewhat ambiguously critical view of his native region in the sonnet "New England" (1920, rev. 1925). The two parts of the sonnet—the octave (first eight lines) and the sestet (concluding six lines)—are sharply differentiated in Robinson's poem. The octave contrasts traits of New Englanders with a wildly exaggerated account of the characteristics of less frigid and less repressed people elsewhere. The sestet then provides a more direct allegorical portrait of New England's own characteristics. The octave presents the point of view of the New Englanders, suspicious about—but also envious of—the lives of people from less inhibited regions. The hyperbole (or exaggeration) of the New Englanders' views suggests that they lack firsthand knowledge of these people and rather know them through the refracting lens of rumor. Robinson defines New England itself at the outset by referring to the constant north-northeast wind and the children who "learn to walk on frozen toes": in other words, the poem asserts that New England's principal traits are rigidity and coldness. These few data points in the opening two lines allow the reader to see a meaningful contrast between New England's Puritan heritage and the passionate, festive, unrestrained "southern" life described in the following six lines. In the "south," the people "boil" with a "lyric yeast / Of love" and celebrate with such passion that even "demons would appeal for some repose." Robinson's festive images—an overflowing chalice and those who have drunk the least ironically behaving the most wildly—depict an outgoing, hedonistic, uninhibited society that probably exists nowhere except in the minds of the righteous.

In the sestet, Robinson employs allegorical figures to lay bare New England's very "soul." Robinson personifies Passion, Love, Joy, Conscience, and Care in order to illustrate, succinctly, how these "virtues" function in New England. In each case, the poem ironically inverts a reader's expectation of what the virtue will be like, in order to suggest either that regional attitudes toward the virtue are skewed or that too much of even a good thing can be dangerous. In New England, Passion is not embraced but is viewed as something that spoils one's wits. Love is perceived not as an exalted ideal but as a burden, a cross that has to be borne. Joy is so marginalized that she shivers in the corner as she knits. (Robinson, acidly, seems to be suggesting that knitting is the zenith of joyful activity in New England.) The central figure of the allegorical picture of New England's "soul" is none of these; instead, it is Conscience, who "always has the rocking-chair" (i.e., the most prominent position in the house, or the mind). Again, frigidity and repression define the New Englander. Conscience delights in exerting her control, torturing all unrestrained impulses—symbolized here by the cat, a notoriously independent creature. Ironically, however, it is Care who kills the cat, by nurturing it not wisely but too well.

The poem's distorted, exaggerated view of New England scores a number of stinging, satirical points. The fact that Robinson substituted the words "we're told" for "it seems" in line ten when he revised "New England" for book publication, however, complicates one's interpretation of the poem. Some New Englanders were outraged by the poem's depiction of their region, and Robinson allowed himself an "out" with the words "we're told," which suggest that the view the poem presents of New England is not the pronouncement of the author but rather a tissue of stereotypes spoken in a hostile dramatic monologue by a voice Robinson intends not to sympathize with but to mock. The poem, thus, can be seen as double edged, either as a satire of New England or as a satire of those who hold a stereotypical view of New England. Perhaps the poem is ultimately both.

Another satirical sonnet on New England life, "the Cambridge ladies who live in furnished souls" (1923) by E. E. Cummings—who, like Robinson, was a native New Englander—makes similar criticisms, but in a less ambiguous manner. Robinson was born in Head Tide, Maine, whereas Cummings was born in Cambridge, Massachusetts—the very place he takes to task in this unconventional sonnet. Specifically, Cummings targets the comfortable upper-class women of the city. He accuses them of complacency, of gossiping, and of a preference for both the safely enshrined past over the living present and humanity in the abstract over specific persons in their midst (an instance of what Charles Dickens in *Bleak House* termed "telescopic philanthropy"). As in Robinson's poem, knitting appears as a satirical and reductive image of human aspiration. Cummings also wickedly yokes together Christ and Longfellow, implying a rather indiscriminate exaltation of society's heroes. Longfellow represents the "respectable" immediate past, whereas Christ may be seen to represent the revolutionary figure who, safely plastered over by tradition, conventional religious belief, and misleading iconography, no longer seems a revolutionary but comes to be almost thoughtlessly venerated by the establishment. "Christ and Longfellow" is, thus, a snapshot of the womens' safe, conservative values. One could hardly imagine the line reading "Christ and Whitman" or "Christ and Rimbaud," where the second figure would be a revolutionary and unconventional poet at odds with societal norms (and, thus, in many ways, a more apt analog for the historical Christ). The final, surreal image of the moon rattling in the sky "like a fragment of angry candy" evokes the wild strangeness of the universe that, in Cummings's view, far transcends the ordered world of the Cambridge ladies. One thinks of Hamlet's famous retort: "There are more things in heaven and earth, Horatio, / Than are dreamt of in your philosophy." Some readers might find the poem unduly misogynistic, but it can more sympathetically be seen as an assault on the shallow, complacent, self-serving values of the upper classes.

A second famous satirical sonnet by Cummings, " 'next to of course god america i" (1926), casts a wider net, seeking to lampoon the clichéd patriotic and religious sentiments of Americans in general. Cummings ransacks the most famous patriotic American songs, from "The Star-Spangled Banner" to the two entitled "America" (both "America the beautiful . . ." and "My country 'tis of thee . . ."), for phrases that he inserts into an unidentified speaker's monologue in such a way as to make them appear trite and absurd. Heavy enjambment and Cummings's trademark lack of capitalization do much to convey the spirit of irreverence. The satirical sentiments turn more savage as the poem progresses. Cummings wants to trace the connection between jingoism and slaughter—in other words, the way in which the blind patriotic fervor inspired by the traditional songs and the traditional reverence for God and country becomes an instrument the state uses to coerce young men to sacrifice their lives in the name of duty and glory. In this respect, the poem closely resembles Stephen Crane's "Do not weep, maiden, for war is kind" (discussed under "War"). Cummings has the sonnet's principal speaker say, "what could be more beaut- / iful than these heroic happy dead . . . ?" The violent, unnatural enjambment of the word "beautiful" conveys Cummings's irony, for broken apart, the word itself becomes distinctly "unbeautiful" (as Cummings had described the Cambridge ladies in the earlier sonnet). The speaker's monologue concludes with the thirteenth line, and the sonnet ends with a final ironic gesture, as the orator dramatically pauses, like many a speech maker, to drink from a glass of water. Nothing could contrast with the garbled jingoism of the speaker's words more than the purity of water.

Wallace Stevens's "Disillusionment of Ten O'Clock" (1923) appears, on the surface, to be a somewhat enigmatic poem. We first hear of houses filled with white nightgowns; then of various color combinations and accessories to nightgowns not found in these houses; then of dreams people are not having; and finally of an old drunken sailor who dreams of catching tigers "in red weather." Contrasts structure the poem: plain, white nightgowns versus elaborate, colorful nightgowns, and dreams people are not having about animals versus the exotic dream of the sailor. The first term of each pair can be taken as a symbol for drab, unimaginative responses to life, whereas the second term represents the opposite. Reduced to a basic idea, or shorn of its charm, the poem seems to assert that reality—or at least the reality of our culture and culturally mediated experience—is mundane without the poetic imagination to quicken it with color and life. Reality, in other words, is in part what we are able to make of it. In the suburbs, life can be a matter of "keeping up with the Joneses," of having one's imaginative horizons stunted by advertisements, country clubs, taxes, and the passive reception of collective fantasies (which would later be afforded by television). Stevens seems to imply here that commercial standardization can be an apt trope for imaginative impoverishment. Only in the margins of such a world does one find the more vital powers of the imagination being exercised to create a more brilliant version of reality. Perhaps it is only an intoxicated sailor who enjoys visions that soar above the common dreams of conformity and affluence. Such a figure seems to stand for the poet. He might be dismissed as mad, but if so, one can say approvingly, along with Emily Dickinson, "Much madness is divinest sense."

More overtly scathing, Robinson Jeffers's "Shine, Perishing Republic" (1924) qualifies as a jeremiad, or a prophetic denunciation in the spirit of Jeremiah from the Old Testament. The poem, cast in long, flowing free-verse lines, masquerades as a bit of serious advice to the poet's sons. It first takes to task American civilization for its vulgarity and imperialism, noting that protest against such forces is utterly futile, only "a bubble in the molten mass" that will pop and disappear without effect. Jeffers, thus, does not seek to change America by condemning it; instead, he advises his sons (and others with open ears) to make for themselves a life that runs counter to the dominant trends. Jeffers wants to establish a foundation of hope for such resistance. Since it cannot be based on protest, it is instead based on prophecy and the knowledge of civilization's relative brevity. By invoking the cycles of birth and death (lines 3 and 4), the poet establishes a contrast between the transience of society and the continuity of nature. In Jeffers's view, the former is doomed to imminent destruction, whereas the latter provides the example upon which meaningful values can be based.

Two symbolic images—meteors and mountains—develop the contrast. Civilization, like a meteor, flashes brilliantly but rapidly vanishes. (This image is the source of the poem's title.) Mountains, on the other hand, represent the near permanence and great solidity of natural forces. Modern American civilization can be measured in a few centuries, whereas the lives of mountains span hundreds of millions of years. Jeffers bids his children to "keep their distance from the thickening center"; instead of trafficking with human institutions and their attendant corruptions, Jeffers counsels his sons to take to the mountains. The advice can be understood figuratively rather than literally—in other words, stay in contact with nature and keep a distance from the heart of civilization. In the final lines, Jeffers cautions his sons not to love human beings too much. Famous for his "inhumanism," Jeffers preaches a gospel of misanthropy. Salvation lies in tempering one's view of one's fellow beings. Love of humanity is merely a "trap," which has caught many noble spirits—even, the poet asserts, Christ. Jeffers, who embraced an ethical position that included all of nature, wants his sons (and the reader) to love not humanity but the cosmos. Only by stepping outside what Louis J. Halle called the "hive" of civilization will we be able to develop enduring and transcendent values.

Langston Hughes returns us to more overtly political and localized concerns with "Harlem" (1951). Hughes writes of the stifling of African-American culture—what he calls its "dream deferred." Hughes himself had been a key player in the Harlem Renaissance of the 1920s. That shining cultural moment, however, had not yet blossomed into greater things; instead, it had been largely snuffed out by the Great Depression and the lingering oppressiveness of racism. Hughes's poem expresses the frustration of African Americans seeking a richer, more fulfilling life than society affords. The poem poses a question—"What happens to a dream deferred?"—and then provides a series of six "answers," all but the penultimate of which are themselves questions. The first five answers are cast in the form of similes, each with a vivid image to suggest what might be the correct response. The first image of "a raisin in the sun" provided the playwright Lorraine Hansberry with the title of her well-known drama about African-American working-class life in Chicago. It and the other images—a festering sore, rotten meat, a sugary crust, and a sagging load—all suggest a spirit of defeat. The dream might well dry up, fester, rot, crust over, or simply sag—but the poet does not leave it at that. The final line asks if the dream explodes; it provides the poem's initial question with its most vigorous answer, both affirmative and challenging at the same time. Instead of another simile, the line is a metaphor: the dream here has become a bomb. Italics give the line extra force, suggesting that the bomb analogy is the poet's truest, most vital answer. The "dream deferred" will not simply rot or fester; it will galvanize the anger of the oppressed until they claim by force the life they are being denied. The poem promises difficult change and threatens the powers that be with revolutionary rhetoric. In retrospect, the poem's stance may be seen as prophetic, for by 1951, the restless energy that shaped the Civil Rights movement of the later fifties and sixties was already beginning to seethe beneath the veneer of America's complacent civilization. It would soon explode.

Another poet who responded strongly to the undercurrents of post–World War II American culture was Allen Ginsberg, who attempted to assume the venerable mantle of Walt Whitman in such lengthy public and apocalyptic poems as "Howl," "America," and *The Fall of America*. Whitman had sounded the alarm in "To the States" and in prose pieces such as *Democratic Vistas*, but was spared from living in the prosperous, complacent, and acquisitive Eisenhower era. In "A Supermarket in California" (1956), Ginsberg imagines an encounter between himself and the spirit of Whitman as a way of gauging the distance between Whitman's America (or, more accurately, his ideal of America) and Ginsberg's own. Ginsberg pictures himself thinking of Whitman under a full moon and "shopping for images," an ironically capitalist turn of phrase that presages the trip to the supermarket. One can shop for images for free, but in the supermarket, everything has its price (something that Ginsberg and Whitman's spirit will later ignore, as they ransack the food without "passing the cashier"). In the store, Ginsberg sees whole families of consumers, emblematic of the capitalist society that produced them, with Federico García Lorca, the outstanding Spanish poet of the twentieth century, and Whitman in their midst. Both Lorca and Whitman were visionary poets and, like Ginsberg, homosexuals. Poetry and homosexuality stand in the poem in contradistinction to the mainstream values represented by the supermarket itself. Both Lorca and Whitman provided models for Ginsberg's own works, although here Whitman is central, largely by virtue of being American. Ginsberg wonders where the night will take them and if they will dream of a lost America, the one Whitman celebrated, which is now best represented not by "love" but by supermarkets and automobiles. The poem concludes with a question put to Whitman's spirit: "what America did you have" at the time of your death? The question asks the reader to measure the distance between ideals and actuality, represented, respectively, by Whitman's vision of America and the rampant, triumphant materialism of the 1950s.

In contrast with the angry or embittered tones of Cummings, Jeffers, Hughes, and Ginsberg, Howard Nemerov provides a wry and whimsical, though pointed look at modern civilization in his sonnet "A Primer of the Daily Round" (1958). Nemerov takes the reader on a tour of the alphabet, where each letter stands for a person engaged in some activity, inane or otherwise. Nemerov's method yields two major points about modern civilization. The assignment of letters suggests the essential facelessness of the modern world, in which people—or rather "consumers"—are often identified by dehumanizing symbols, like social security numbers, while the constant shifting from one person to the next implies the interconnectedness of a complex technological civilization, wherein mass communication brings one's fellow beings ever closer. The relations between individuals in the poem are often ironic, amusing, and ambiguous. For example, do "A" and "B" occupy the same space, as they perform their ironically contrasted actions (peeling and kneeling)? Is "E," who suffers the hand of "D" on her knee, the wife of "C," who has just phoned "D"? Is "F" in the presence of any other character when he or she coughs? The poem doesn't allow a reader to answer most of these simple narrative questions with any precision. The emphasis falls not on such details but on the simultaneity of contrasting actions—the whole grand comedy of human life, which includes cheating, lying, and sudden death. These things would become poignant if singled out and treated in detail, but Nemerov's detached point of view renders them all absurdly impersonal. The poem's viewpoint almost resembles that of an extraterrestrial observer. Nemerov gets us to see the oddity of human behavior from a new perspective, one that makes us all look trivial, interchangeable, and a bit ridiculous. The poem neatly circles back to the beginning, as "Z" suddenly remembers "A." Life, the poem implicitly asserts, is circular, and the chain of interconnections from person to person could be followed indefinitely.

One of the more significant "public" poems of mid-twentieth-century

America, Robert Lowell's "For the Union Dead" (1960, rev. 1964) takes as its subject the memorial constructed in Boston in 1897 by the accomplished sculptor Augustus Saint-Gaudens (1848–1907) to commemorate Colonel Robert Gould Shaw (1837–1863) and the first all-black Union regiment to fight in the Civil War. Shaw (to whom Lowell was related by marriage) and many other members of the regiment were killed in an attack on Fort Wagner in South Carolina. (The events are depicted in the popular 1989 film *Glory*, starring Denzel Washington.) A Latin inscription on the monument reads "He leaves all behind to serve the Republic"; Lowell modifies this in his own epigraph to the more inclusive "They gave up everything to serve the Republic," which honors all the men in the regiment equally. The memorial stands at the center of Lowell's poem, but flanking it are autobiographical and more recent historical concerns. The poem contrasts personal and public elements as well as the follies of the present and the ideals of the past.

The poem begins with Lowell recalling the old Boston Aquarium, which has since been closed. The poet remembers pressing his nose against the glass of a tank as he watched the fish. Lowell then contrasts this personal recollection with another, more recent one in which he pressed against a fence, watching yellow steam shovels, resembling dinosaurs, at work constructing a new parking garage. These images introduce a contrast between past and present crucial to the poem, but both also record a human tendency to dominate and transform the natural world. The poet notes that his sympathies are with the fish and reptiles, not with the human enterprises that confine and destroy them. Lowell's pacifist stance favors the underdogs.

The garage stands directly across from the Civil War monument. Lowell takes the monument as a fragile but enduring symbol of Boston's past, which the present crowds out more and more. Details are significant here: a seemingly casual reference to the famous psychologist and philosopher William James alludes not only to the fact that James delivered the principal address at the unveiling ceremony of the monument but also to the fact that James's younger brother Wilky, an officer in the Massachusetts 54th, was wounded during the assault on Fort Wagner. In James's day, the monument had been so vivid that the bronze images of the black soldiers seemed able to breathe; but in Lowell's, the monument's precarious hold on existence is indicated by the fact that it has to be propped up by a splint to protect it from the "earthquake" of the garage construction. It belongs to a time before such behemoths as steam shovels rocked the earth. Lowell aligns the monument with the decrepit aquarium by claiming that it is like a fishbone caught in the throat of the city. It is a relic of the past, but a relic that lingers and troubles the conscience. The relief of Shaw himself watches the city with "wrenlike vigilance." The wren may be an alert bird, but it is also a very small one.

Lowell insists upon such a scale, noting that the leanness of Shaw and the soldiers increases with the years. What they represent—courage, authenticity, self-sacrifice—is dwindling away with time. Lowell notes that Shaw's father wanted no greater monument for his son than the ditch into which Confederate soldiers had hurled his body; then, enigmatically and powerfully, he claims that the ditch is now closer. Destruction, in other words, is closer to us. No statues were erected in Boston memorializing World War II; instead, a billboard displays an advertisement for a brand of safe that survived the atomic bomb dropped on Hiroshima.

Mention of Hiroshima illustrates the idea that destruction is closer; Lowell's era, after all, is that of the Cold War, the age of nuclear terror. The contrast between the monument and the advertisement embodies the difference between the heroic nobility and idealism of the past and the commercial wasteland of the present. The advertisement seems to say that any event, no matter how inhuman and atrocious, can be exploited for commercial profit. Lowell then comments on how space is nearer, illustrating the concept with an image of black schoolchildren on the television set. Unlike during the time of the Civil War, the television brings contemporary history into the living room. The schoolchildren are probably those involved in the desegregation of the South and stand as contemporary analogs to the black soldiers who died at Fort Wagner. The pessimistic conclusion notes that the war monument and everything it represents awaits bursting, like a bubble (an image recalling the opening of Jeffers's "Shine, Perishing Republic"). The final stanza returns to the ruined aquarium of the opening and concludes with an ironic image of the "finned cars"—ubiquitous mechanical entities that have replaced the actual fish of the aquarium and remind us, inevitably, of the burgeoning parking garage. They "nose" forward, an ironic transformation of the imagery in the second stanza. Lowell's poem depicts a world in which nature and idealism have been auctioned off by capitalism and in which the example of the past, which might serve as a foil to the present's abuses, is slowly eroding away.

The consumer society excoriated in Lowell's poem becomes the explicit subject of R. S. Gwynn's "Among Philistines" (1986), a humorous yet extremely pointed retelling of the popular biblical story of Samson and Delilah (Judges 16). By transposing the tale into the contemporary world, Gwynn makes the reader acutely aware of the double meaning of "Philistine," which originally designated a traditional foe of the ancient Israelites, but which later was appropriated by the influential Victorian poet and social critic Matthew Arnold to denote persons who are crass, vulgar, and uncultured. By morphing his historical Philistines into modern Philistines, Gwynn turns the familiar story into a vehicle for commenting on the foibles of contemporary society. He elects to dwell only on one episode from the tale: the extrusion of Samson's eyes. He does not recount how Delilah, the archetypal femme fatale, seduced Samson, divulged the secret of his supernatural strength (his unshorn hair), put him to sleep, had his head shaved, and betrayed him to the Philistines; nor does he relate the apocalyptic conclusion, in which Samson pulls down the Philistine temple, killing himself and all his enemies. (The most celebrated poetic version of the story, Milton's *Samson Agonistes*, focuses exclusively on this last part.) The concentrated focus Gwynn maintains on the media circus occasioned by Samson's capture and imminent punishment shifts our interest from the story itself to the civilization in which these events transpire, although along the way, Gwynn does allude to earlier portions of Samson's tale, such as the lion's carcass in which he found honey (Judges 14.8) and the ass's jawbone with which he slaughtered a thousand Philistines (Judges 15.15).

The world of sensationalized evening TV news, lurid films and paperbacks, glossy magazines, ubiquitous advertisements, and shopping malls into which Gwynn transposes the action seems all too familiar. Delilah has become a centerfold starlet, as shallow and materialistic as she is enticing and voluptuous. She complains that she has not been paid enough for betraying Samson, despite the fact that in the biblical version of the story she receives eleven hundred pieces of silver from each Philistine lord. What that sum would be in modern currency, with three thousand or so years of inflation, one can hardly guess; but Gwynn's point about how media stars lose all perspective on financial matters seems only too clear. Delilah becomes the spoiled queen of a world whose norms are greed and exploitation. Samson still, against his will, desires her, even as he loathes everything she represents: she brings to his mind both the rotting carcass of the lion and the honey he found within it. His conflicted feelings are aptly summarized in a nightmare billboard showing Delilah, nude, sucking on the golden shears she had used to rob him of his power. The image combines the titillation of oral sex with the fear of emasculation and the vulgarity of commercialism. The poem ends as Samson's eyes are seared—before he has achieved his vengeance and redemption, but not before the reader comes to wish that Gwynn's narrative were hyperbolical parody instead of an all-too-credible transposition.

ᘒᘉᘜᘕᕽ

"To the States," Walt Whitman
    NAL-1 [4th ed., 1994]
"Chicago," Carl Sandburg

AAL-2; APT-1; ColAP; HAL-2; HoAL-2; MAP; NAL-2; NoAM; NOBA; NoP-4; OxBA; TFi; VGW

"New England," Edwin Arlington Robinson

ATL-2; HAL-2; HoAL-2; NOBA; OxBA

"the Cambridge ladies who live in furnished souls," E. E. Cummings

AAL-2; APT-2; HAL-2; NAL-2; NoAM; NOBA; NoP-4; OxBA

" 'next to of course god america i," E. E. Cummings

AAL-2; APT-2; HAL-2; HoAL-2; LPTT; MAP; NAL-2; NoP-4; TFi; VGW

"Disillusionment of Ten O'Clock," Wallace Stevens

AAL-2; APT-1; ATL-2; MAP; NAL-2; NoAM; OxBA; SoSe-9

"Shine, Perishing Republic," Robinson Jeffers

AAL-2; APT-1; ATL-2; ColAP; HoAL-2; LPTT; MAP; NAL-2; NoAM; NOBA; NoP-4; OxBA; TFi; VGW

"Harlem," Langston Hughes

APT-2 [included in "from *Montage of a Dream Deferred*"]; ATL-2; HCAP; HoAL-2; MAP; NoP-4; SoSe-9 [under title "Dream Deferred"]

"A Supermarket in California," Allen Ginsberg

AAL-2; ATL-2; CoAmPo; CoAP; HAL-2; HCAP; HoAL-2; NAL-2; NoAM; NOBA; TFi; WeW-4

"A Primer of the Daily Round," Howard Nemerov

NoP-4; WeW-4

"For the Union Dead," Robert Lowell

AAL-2; ATL-2; CoAP; ColAP; HAL-2; HCAP; HoAL-2; MAP; NAL-2; NoAM; NOBA; NoP-4; TFi; VCAP; WeW-4

"Among Philistines," R. S. Gwynn

RA

Family Relations

ଔଠ୵ଠ୭

I put on my robe and went downstairs. I was always putting on a
bathrobe and going somewhere to talk seriously to a child.
> Jack "J. A. K." Gladney, in Don DeLillo's *White Noise*

The dark side of family relations has inspired much of the world's
greatest drama, from *The Oresteia* and *Oedipus Tyrannus* to *Hamlet* and
King Lear to *A Streetcar Named Desire* and *Death of a Salesman*. The objectifying power of the stage has made it an acceptable social vehicle for
exploring the tensions and passions that divide families. Lyric poetry,
on the other hand, both intimate and subjective, had rarely been brought
to bear on the volatile theme of family relations, at least before the rise
of the "confessional" mode in mid-twentieth-century American poetry.
Confessional poetry, associated particularly with the work of W. D.
Snodgrass, Robert Lowell, John Berryman, Sylvia Plath, and Anne Sexton, introduced a new autobiographical candor and intensity to American poetry. Poems about sex, divorce, alcoholism, and insanity suddenly
became quite fashionable. A new freedom of subject matter reflected and
contributed to larger shifts in American culture in the late fifties and
sixties. It became possible for mainstream poets—even those only mar-
ginally associated with confessional verse—to write candidly about family life.

Theodore Roethke anticipated certain aspects of the confessional
movement with his seminal volume of 1948, *The Lost Son*. Many of its
poems focus on the greenhouse world in Saginaw, Michigan, where
Roethke had been raised. Roethke's Prussian father, Otto, figures prominently in several of his works (including a late poem simply titled
"Otto"). "My Papa's Waltz" (1948), from *The Lost Son*, succinctly ex-

presses the poet's ambivalent attitude toward his father. The rhythm of the poem nearly approximates the three-quarter time of a waltz; the dance, however, seems more harrowing than frolicsome. The father, drunk and careless, appears as a threatening figure. The descriptions of the uneasy mother and the wreck in the kitchen, along with such words as "battered," "scraped," and "beat," suggest a kind of horseplay that at any moment could erupt into violence. The final image, however, of the father whisking his son off to bed, may be seen as implying an almost arbitrary restoration of domestic order. Counterpoised against the hazards represented by a drunken and despotic father is the intimation of a kinder, gentler figure, the protector and comforter to whose shirt the boy clings. The memorable image of the waltz brings into focus both sides of family life—the threatening and the reassuring.

Sylvia Plath's father was also a Prussian named Otto. He died when Plath was only eight but continued to obsess her throughout her brief life. Her anger toward men, galvanized by the breakup of her marriage to the eminent English poet Ted Hughes, burst forth in a series of strange, terrifying poems written just before she committed suicide. Most notable among these are "Lady Lazarus" and "Daddy" (1962). It would be a mistake, however, to read "Daddy" strictly as an autobiographical poem. For one thing, Otto Plath was a rigid man, but hardly the Nazi tyrant depicted in the poem; in fact, at the time of his death, he despised what the Nazis were doing to Germany. Plath herself conceived of this poem as a dramatic monologue, spoken by a girl whose father actually is a Nazi. In other words, Plath's archetypal imagination amplifies and transforms the memory of Otto. Hardly recognizable, the father becomes a nightmare embodiment of masculine repressiveness, a "Panzer-man," a "devil," and a "vampire." Plath does, however, incorporate some authentic biographical details, such as the father's Polish origin and gangrenous toe. The father figure has made the speaker's life miserable; she likens her experience to living in a black shoe for thirty years (which was Plath's own age at the time the poem was written—but note that she later plays more loosely with chronology when she has the speaker say that her father died when she was ten). The speaker associates the father with the Nazis and herself, rather too easily, with Jews and Gypsies—both victims of the Nazi's genocidal campaigns. The speaker feels frustrated by the fact that she cannot kill her father for the simple reason that he already lies dead. Instead of facing a living foe of flesh and blood, she contends against the impervious specter of her imagination and seeks to get back to—or at—him by committing suicide and then, when that fails, by performing a mock marriage to a grotesque image of the father (lines 58–67). This act sets the stage for a final exorcism. The narrator dismisses the father, figured as a slain vampire surrounded by dancing villagers, with a final dig: "Daddy, daddy, you bastard, I'm through." Indeed, the mentally unstable Plath nearly was.

Robert Hayden's "Those Winter Sundays," published the same year as Plath's poem, presents a refreshingly different viewpoint on a father-child relationship. This explicitly autobiographical poem, an irregular sonnet, concerns the maturation of a son's feelings and understanding. Hayden, born Asa Bundy Sheffey, had been adopted as an infant by foster parents. "Those Winter Sundays" pays tribute to William Hayden, his foster father. In the poem's opening line, "Sundays too my father got up early," the key word is "too," for it implies what the poem later makes explicit: that the father works every day to support his family. Even on Sundays he rises early to warm the house with a fire. The memory of those Sundays compels the speaker into a new appreciation for what, when he was growing up, he took for granted: the sacrifices his foster father made for love. Hayden resists idealizing or sentimentalizing the father; he mentions, in passing, the "chronic angers" that plagued his home, but he emphasizes how maturity has given him a new perspective on it all. The reader can perhaps presume that the speaker, too, has now become a father, quite possibly an underappreciated one as well. Like the house that his father warmed, the speaker's considered recollection warms to his father.

Wealthy families are no more immune to tensions than are working class ones. James Merrill's "The Broken Home" (1966), a sequence of seven irregular sonnets, meditates on the unpleasant side of the poet's privileged upbringing. The first sonnet describes how Merrill caught sight of the people living above him—parents with a child—as he wended home one evening. The sight evoked memories of his own family life and inspired him to write in an autobiographical mode. The six sonnets that follow represent his attempt to ascertain whether he is as "real" as the people he saw in the window. "Authenticity," as Merrill acutely knows, is a trait our culture is prone to impute to the downtrodden and deny to the super-wealthy. Merrill's father, Charles E. Merrill, was a partner in the investment firm Merrill, Lynch, Pierce, Fenner, and Beane and one of the founders of Safeway Stores; he belonged to the tiny top percentage of elite Americans. The legacy and lifestyle of the fabulously wealthy are what Merrill has to account for in ascertaining his own "reality."

The second sonnet focuses on the father and his rather peculiar and exclusive habit of trading in wives. Although the father does not dominate here to the extent of the father figures in the three preceding poems, Charles Merrill does threaten, as the sixth sonnet explains, to haunt the poet like the *commendatore* in Mozart's great opera *Don Giovanni*. (As another high cultural point of reference, the same sonnet also invokes the troubled relations between parents and children in Shakespeare's

King Lear.) Even at seventy, his father was thinking of marrying yet another young woman—"But money was not time." The father, for all his wealth, could not direct his ultimate destiny; he died before he had the chance to remarry again.

The third through fifth stanzas range farther back in time. Merrill first recalls the actions of suffragettes during his parents' youth, which form one chapter in the eternal war between the sexes. By positioning this sonnet between those focusing exclusively on either parent, Merrill strongly intimates the inevitable tension in his parents' marriage. His own father, like the men assailed by the feminists, belongs to the public world of official history, World War I, and Wall Street, whereas sonnet four depicts his mother as a bedridden invalid, hardly distinguishable from a corpse. She seems like an emblem of the private world to which women were confined and against which the feminists were remonstrating. Section five takes place in 1931, after the end of a party, which can be taken both literally, as a social gathering, and figuratively, as the stock market crash of 1929. Merrill juxtaposes the father's offering of facile reassurance with the image of a toy soldier in the young James's room. Neither the words nor the toy, which hints at the coming war, can offer any real measure of security. Merrill invokes the biblical injunction to honor and obey one's parents, only to admit in the sixth sonnet that he has done so "inversely." He has opted for a far more private life than his father, but not an impotent one like that forced on his mother. His poetic imagination still roams the corridors of his broken home, despite the fact that in reality it has become a boarding school. Both the school and Merrill's poetic reverie offer some hope of transforming and redeeming the stifling past. The glimpses Merrill has afforded us into the family life of the rich and the famous—the supposed fulfillment of the "American dream"—do not inspire a reader's envy.

Whereas the poems considered so far are all written from the perspective of a son or daughter absorbed principally in the contemplation of a powerful father, Richard Wilbur's "The Writer" (1976) casts the poet himself in the role of anxious father. The writer of the poem's title, however, is not Wilbur but rather his daughter, who bangs away at a short story on her typewriter. The poet listens as the sounds of the keys rise above the noise made by linden trees against the windows and as his concerns about her future multiply. He expresses these concerns through an extended metaphor that compares life to passage on a ship. He wishes his daughter luck, but is forced to reassess his "easy figure" of the voyage, turning instead to an analogy based on a sudden, unbidden memory of how a starling had been trapped two years ago in the room where his daughter now types. As in Merrill's "The Broken Home," the juxtaposition of past and present structures and gives weight to the poem. Wilbur recalls how the family tried to help the starling by lifting a sash, but even so, the bird flailed about, recklessly harming itself for an hour before it finally escaped. The implication seems clear: even with external assistance, such as a father can provide to a daughter, or a person to a wild bird, life's hardships and follies must finally be borne by the individual. Through the agency of this memory, the father comes into a more complete appreciation of what difficulties may lie ahead for his daughter. He realizes something that he and all of us are prone to forget: that existence is always a matter of life and death. In the end, he can only repeat his wish that her passage be lucky—though more fervently this time.

The father figure, which has obsessed the imaginations of several significant American poets, looms large in all the poems discussed so far, so it is useful, for the purpose of providing some measure of balance, to turn to Julia Alvarez's "Woman's Work" (1985) for a poet's view of her mother. Like Elizabeth Bishop's "One Art" (discussed under "Loss"), the poem is cast in villanelle form, although Alvarez, even more than Bishop, takes liberties with the obligatory repetitions, thereby avoiding the static effect this French form sometimes produces in English. Instead, she creates a dynamic, incremental poetic structure that mirrors the subject matter's concern with the mother's growing influence, as a role model, on the daughter. As with "Those Winter Sundays," this is a poem of belated admiration for a parent. The opening five three-line stanzas concentrate on the mother's selfless diligence and pride in her work, as well as on the resentful attitude of the daughter, who would rather be outside playing with friends than inside helping her mother clean house. The final four-line stanza modifies the story of the relationship by leaping forward in time. The poet rebelled against her mother for a time, but eventually became her mother's child, not in the sense of accepting that housework is "woman's work" but in the sense of assimilating the mother's work ethic and care for craft and detail. The attitude with which the mother had approached housework represents an ideal to which the poet aspires in her own art of "housekeeping paper." The poem documents the changing roles and opportunities of women, even as it traces certain continuities in terms of basic values. Alvarez appropriates her mother's conscientious mind-set, but rejects the idea that woman's work should necessarily be equated with domestic chores.

Li-Young Lee's "The Gift" (1986) offers an unequivocally positive vision of family relations. Lee recalls an incident that occurred when he was seven years old. A metal splinter had pierced his palm, and his father patiently removed it with a blade while diverting Lee's attention from the pain by reciting a story. His father's wise and compassionate action has helped to shape Lee's sense of identity. Paradoxically, it is as if the father had planted something in Lee rather than removed something. Lee then depicts a second, complementary incident—juxtaposing past and present as Merrill and Wilbur had done—in which he carefully removes a splinter from his wife's hand. Clearly, Lee's care derives directly from his father's. The poem speaks strongly of the power of role models and of the potential such virtues as care and compassion have, if properly cultivated, of becoming family traditions. Lee implies an entire philosophy of life and family through the actions of father and son. They remind us how little, really, is required to transcend the unfortunate family situations depicted in many of the other poems discussed in this section. The final image, of the boy kissing his father, shows us, too, that appreciation, unlike in "Those Winter Sundays" or "Woman's Work," need not be deferred.

A more troubled poem, Emily Grosholz's "Eden" (1992) documents both the innocent state of childhood and the anxious state of parenthood. In effect, the poem does for the mother figure what Wilbur's "The Writer" had done for the father figure. The opening stanzas contrast an anthropomorphic animated film about dinosaurs with the reality of a dead squirrel electrocuted by a cable it had gnawed, causing a neighborhood blackout and, thus, the end of the film and the false reassurances it had offered to the poet's child. The film's formulaic narrative patterns may cater to human desires, but they do not correspond in any meaningful way to the actual life-and-death situations of dinosaurs, squirrels, or humans. If the film represents a false vision of the world, the squirrel and the cable represent the irrevocable fact of mortality, which lies beyond the child's comprehension. The child insists on mapping the lesson of the film onto the squirrel's situation: " 'He's sleeping. And his mommy going to come' "; but the parent knows the squirrel is beyond the help of its mother. She likens the child to Adam (which may lead the reader to assume the child is a boy, although no gender is otherwise specified by the poem). Each child, the poem suggests, recapitulates the archetypal figure of innocence, only to live through his or her own fall into the knowledge of the world's harm and death. If the child is Adam, the mother is God, a creator and caretaker, but only seemingly—from the child's limited perspective—omnipotent. In fact, she stands largely powerless before the world's harmful forces, represented earlier by the electric cable and figured in the poem's final stanza by an extension of the mythical Garden of Eden imagery. The serpent, which precipitated the downfall of humanity, and the angel with the flaming sword, which God stationed to prevent Adam and Eve from returning to the garden, represent all the forces of the world that compromise innocence and guarantee the knowledge of good and evil. By associating the mythological figure of the angel with the naturalistic sunset, Grosholz skillfully combines two archetypal images: the one signifying the impossibility of recapturing innocence, the other the inevitability of decline. In effect, the poem defines the limitations of a parent's ability to safeguard a child, for outside the escapist realm of a Disney cartoon, the world's dangerous impositions cannot always be checked.

ᘒᙈᗐᘉ

"My Papa's Waltz," Theodore Roethke

> AAL-2; APT-2; ATL-2; CAPP-6; ColAP; HAL-2; HCAP; HoAL-2; NAL-2; NoAM; NOBA; NoP-4; TFi; VGW; WeW-4

"Daddy," Sylvia Plath

> AAL-2; ATL-2; CAPP-6; CoAP; ColAP; HAL-2; HCAP; HoAL-2; MAP; NAL-2; NoAM; NOBA; NoP-4; TFi; VCAP

"Those Winter Sundays," Robert Hayden

> APT-2; CAPP-6; ColAP; HAL-2; HCAP; HoAL-2; NAL-2; NoAM; NoP-4; SoSe-9; TFi; WeW-4

"The Broken Home," James Merrill

> ATL-2; ColAP; HAL-2; HCAP; HoAL-2; MAP; NAL-2; NoAM; NOBA; NoP-4

"The Writer," Richard Wilbur

> CAPP-6; HAL-2; HCAP; HoAL-2; NoAM; SoSe-9

"The Gift," Li-Young Lee

> CAPP-6; HAL-2; NAL-2

"Woman's Work," Julia Alvarez

> RA

"Eden," Emily Grosholz

> RA

Freedom and Slavery

❦

> The wretchedness of slavery, and the blessedness of freedom, were perpetually before me.
>
> Frederick Douglass, *Narrative of the Life of an American Slave*

The New World has often been depicted by writers, such as Thomas Paine, as a free "asylum" from tyranny and oppression; but, contradictorily, slavery became an institution in the New World from almost the very moment European settlers arrived. The Spanish brought the African slave trade to the New World in 1503, just eleven short years after Columbus's first voyage. (The African slaves, it should be noted, were imported to replace Native American slaves, who suffered high mortality rates from Old World diseases.) A Dutch man-of-war dropped off the first twenty African slaves to the English colonies in North America in 1619, a year before the arrival of the *Mayflower*. By the time the slave trade was outlawed in 1808, nine million Africans had been brought across the Atlantic in bondage, despite the fact that the Declaration of Independence had proclaimed that "all men are created equal" and that "Liberty" ranks among the "unalienable Rights" of humanity.

The flagrant contradiction between the slave trade and the democratic ideals of the United States was not lost on the new country's first significant poet, Philip Freneau. His "On the Emigration to America and Peopling the Western Country" (1785) celebrates both the potential for liberty on the shores of America and the uses to which the natural resources of the new land may be put. (The poem is also briefly discussed in the "Nature" section of this guide.) These two things, liberty and nature, define, for Freneau, the fundamental differences between American and European civilizations. As a protoromantic under the influence of the French philosopher Jean-Jacques Rousseau and the radical libertarian Thomas Paine, Freneau understood liberty as the natural state of humanity before it became corrupted by enslaving institutions. So there is a strong connection between the poem's two themes of nature and freedom, for in Freneau's mind, the one prophecies and helps guarantee the other.

The poem directly treats the theme of freedom in its opening and concluding stanzas. The middle stanzas, the third through the sixth, focus on the utilitarian "redemption" of America's unexploited wilderness. Freneau posits (and then practically discards) an everyman figure named Palemon (after one of the main characters in Chaucer's "Knight's Tale") who leaves crowded Europe for the wild, unspoiled shores of America. The poem then purports to represent what this fictional traveler finds there. The second stanza focuses on the contrast between Europe's "despotic shores" and the "happier soil" of America, free from the tyranny of kings. The final line of the stanza—"No slaves insult him with a crown"—refers to the freedom of the general populace from the institutions of monarchy but temporarily overlooks the African slave trade, not mentioned until the penultimate stanza. Freneau, optimistically and prematurely, wants to equate America with freedom. The eighth stanza declares that "No realm so free, so blessed as this" has ever existed, and goes on to contrast this blissful state of freedom with Europe's enchainment to both kings and priests. (Freneau, a descendant of persecuted Huguenots—the Protestants expelled from France in 1685—had no love for either the monarchy or the Catholic Church.) The following stanza acts as a kind of reality check on Freneau's black and white contrasts between New World and Old. Lines 53 and 54 mention the travesty of African slavery; but in his haste to indict Europe's oppressiveness and to celebrate America's glorious possibilities for freedom, Freneau does not adequately address the issue. The final stanza predicts the end of slavery in America and the establishment of a democratic system happier "Than all the eastern [Old World] sages knew."

Freneau takes a much harder look at slavery in the New World in "To Sir Toby" (1791, rev. 1809). Although the poem, written in heroic couplets, focuses on slavery on a sugar plantation in Jamaica, it implicitly condemns slavery in the United States as well. "To Sir Toby" is based on observations Freneau made while commanding a trading vessel to and from the Caribbean. Freneau pulls no punches here, nor is his criticism practically lost to euphoria, as in "On the Emigration." Freneau likens the plantation to hell and puts the slave owner, along with all tyrants, in his place: "Snakes, scorpions, despots, lizards, centipedes," runs line ten's catalog of malevolent creatures. Toby of the poem's title is simply a generalized figure of the slave owner and Cudjoe, a generalized slave (just as Palemon was a generalized young traveler in "On the Emigration"). Although continuous in form, the poem divides into nine brief sections, each indicated by paragraph indentation. The first two sections introduce and describe the plantation itself, whereas the third focuses on the unjust plight of the slaves. The powerful fourth section presents images that document the cruelties of slavery in a manner anticipating the realism of Robert Hayden's "Middle Passage." One owner displays gallows to strike terror into the hearts of his slaves, another nails a slave by his ears to a windmill, and so forth. Freneau presents a whole catalog of outrageous abuses. In the fifth section, Freneau concentrates on the female slaves, ironically "graced" with their iron collars. Following from this pathetic image, Freneau poses the rhetorical question, "Are such the fruits that spring from vast domains?" Ingeniously, "fruits" here refers not to the yield of crops but of evil. The poem equates power with corruption, and slavery with an agricultural economy. Freneau then explicitly repudiates the notion that wealth gained on such terms is worth possessing. After this climactic sixth section, the seventh quickly notes how the beauties of nature are no compensation for the existence of evil, and the eighth returns to the infernal imagery of the poem's opening. The concluding ninth section introduces an ironic twist on the slave's plight: those that escape from Sir Toby's hell will likely be returned by "brother traitors," or, in other words, by the free blacks who live in the mountains. The poem seeks to show the reader how a slave economy corrupts everyone who comes in contact with it.

Slavery in America continued, however, after Freneau's death in 1832. Three years later the young John Greenleaf Whittier, aspiring poet and champion of humane causes, became an active member of the abolitionist movement. The greatest setback the abolitionist cause suffered was the notorious Fugitive Slave Law passed in the Compromise of 1850. The law mandated the return of slaves who had escaped to northern states and required ordinary citizens to cooperate with federal marshals or else face serious penalties; further, it offered incentives to unscrupulous slave catchers to kidnap free blacks, for the law denied alleged slaves the opportunity of a fair trial. Ralph Waldo Emerson wrote in his journal that "This filthy enactment was made in the nineteenth century, by people who could read and write," and Henry David Thoreau savagely denounced the law in his Fourth of July speech "Slavery in Massachusetts." Whittier turned his own frustration into one of his best-known poems, "Ichabod" (1850). The poem denounces one of the law's champions, the famed senator Daniel Webster, known as the greatest orator of his time. Whittier took his title from 1 Samuel 4.21: "And she named the child Ichabod, saying, The glory is departed from Israel." Whittier felt that Webster's capitulation to the pro-slavery forces in his speech of March 7, 1850, marked another moment in which glory had fled from a nation, and he alludes directly to the biblical passage in his first stanza: "The glory from his gray hairs gone / Forevermore!" Webster, instead of throwing his considerable political clout behind the cause of freedom, furthered the cause of slavery. Whittier, however, advises the reader not to revile Webster but to pity him for having succumbed to the temptation of evil. The poem laments Webster's lost soul and likens him to a fallen angel, a creature whose descent from the brightest promise and unfulfilled potential numbs both passion and scorn with more profound emotions. "Of all we loved and honored," Whittier laments, "naught / Save power remains." The poem raises the stateman's fall to a mythic and universal level, so that Webster becomes the incarnation of betrayal to any valiant cause.

Ironically, the flagrantly unjust Fugitive Slaw Law helped—along with the publication of Harriet Beecher Stowe's melodramatic novel *Uncle Tom's Cabin* (1852)—to galvanize northern sentiments against the institution of slavery. The slave trade had ended in 1808, and President Lincoln had technically freed the slaves with the Emancipation Proclamation of January 1, 1863, but the issue was not definitively decided until the end of the American Civil War in 1865, at which point the states belatedly ratified the Thirteenth Amendment, thereby abolishing slavery in the United States. (In contrast, the British Empire had abolished it in 1833.) Whittier celebrated the bloody war's conclusion and the triumph for abolition in the euphoric poem "Laus Deo" (1865), inspired by the sound of bells ringing on the passage of the constitutional amendment. The Latin title means "Praise be to God." The opening line—"It is done!"—follows directly from this religious sentiment, echoing the final words of Christ on the cross. Whittier maintains this level of elevation throughout the poem, with numerous biblical allusions to Exodus, Job, Isaiah, Psalms, and Luke, all of which serve to remind the reader to what extent abolitionists saw slavery as an unconscionable betrayal not only of democratic principles but also of Christian principles. (Slave owners, for their part, cited biblical passages to justify slavery.) The poem's exclamation points and heavy, insistent rhythm evoke the clamor of the bells and the exultation of those who have waited through an "agony of prayer" for this belated triumph of freedom.

Two decades after the Civil War ended and the slaves were freed, the poet Emma Lazarus wrote an Italian sonnet titled "The New Colossus" (1883) as part of a fund-raising campaign for the pedestal of that most conspicuous symbol of American freedom, the Statue of Liberty. A gift from France for the one hundredth anniversary of American independence, the Statue of Liberty (or, officially, "Liberty Enlightening the World"), designed by the sculptor Frédéric-Auguste Bartholdi (1834–1904), was begun in 1875 and completed in 1884. The 225-ton, 151-foot-high statue arrived in New York the following year in 214 packing cases. Lazarus's sonnet was recited at the dedication of the statue in 1886; later, in 1903, it was engraved on the statue's pedestal. The octave of "The New Colossus" describes the statue, whereas the sestet articulates the "message" of the statue's "silent lips." In her comparison between the new statue and the Colossus of Rhodes (one of the Seven Wonders of the Ancient World), Lazarus highlights differences of attitude, gender, and function. The Statue of Liberty, unlike its predecessor, is not "brazen" or "conquering"; instead, it is welcoming. (The idea that the Colossus of Rhodes actually straddled the harbor entrance, alluded to in the second line, is a medieval legend.) Lazarus's images—such as the torch "whose flame / Is the imprisoned lightning"—suggest both power and gentleness: the lightning, after all, is really frozen sculpture, and the statue's eyes are "mild" yet "command" the harbor. Liberty, as personified by the poet, has no use for gaudy Old World artifacts (despite the fact that it is itself such an artifact). Instead, it asks for the "huddled masses," to give them shelter and freedom after they have passed through the "golden door" of America's coast. The poem obviously expresses an idealized view of American life and opportunities, one that jibes with the symbolism of the statue itself. Lazarus was certainly not blind to the squalid realities of immigrant life, but she was genuinely grateful that America opened its arms to persecuted refugees from abroad.

Slavery in America had ended after the Civil War, but its legacy remained. Millions of black Americans have had to make their way in a world where racial prejudice breeds hatred and limits opportunities, and where the significance of the past cannot simply be eradicated by an act of legislation. White poets, such as Freneau and Whittier, wrote against slavery in a time when—with the notable exception of Phillis Wheatley, who flourished before the War of Independence—there were no black poets to express the sentiments of the oppressed. Paul Laurence Dunbar, the first African-American poet to attain prominence after the Civil War, began to explore just such sentiments, in a figurative manner, in his celebrated poem "Sympathy" (1899), which concerns the frustration of perceiving a better life that one cannot attain. Dunbar explores this idea through the image of a caged bird, with which he sympathizes, for its fate resembles that of black Americans, such as Dunbar's parents, who had lost their freedom. In the first stanza, the bird is depicted as watching the return of spring, including the return of wild birds that serve as reminders of the life the caged bird has been denied. The second stanza focuses on the bird's self-mutilation in its efforts to be free, and the third on the nature of the bird's song, which is not "a carol of joy or glee" but rather a prayer for freedom. Dunbar utilizes a metamorphosing refrain as the first and last lines of each stanza. The verb describing the bird's actions shifts, in keeping with the subject of each stanza, from "feels" to "beats his wings" to "sings." The final variation—"I know why the caged bird sings"—was later used by the contemporary African-American writer Maya Angelou as the title of her autobiography, a testimony to how Dunbar's simple, poignant imagery captures the essence of a people's striving for freedom. Angelou also wrote a "sequel" poem, discussed below.

A vastly more complex poetic effort to come to terms with the legacy of slavery and the impulse toward freedom, Robert Hayden's "Middle Passage" (1962) takes the form of a miniature epic, the genre also of Milton's *Paradise Regained* and T. S. Eliot's *The Waste Land*. The poem owes a great deal to Eliot's technical innovations, such as the use of fragmentation, multiple narrators, abrupt transitions, sustained irony, and literary allusions (in this case, to important imaginative works concerned with the sea: Shakespeare's *The Tempest* in line 19 and Coleridge's "Rime of the Ancient Mariner" in line 34). The poem's title refers to the route slave ships took across the Atlantic from Africa to the New World. The poem defines "middle passage" in lines 6 and 7 as a voyage through death toward a new life on the shores of the New World. Repetition of these lines in the poem's conclusion accentuates their importance. Epic journeys, such as those undertaken by Ulysses, Aeneas, and Dante, often include a descent into the underworld, which presages a kind of rebirth or attainment of greater wisdom by virtue of suffering. The irony of Hayden's use of this epic motif becomes clear when a reader reflects that "rebirth" after the middle passage means the living death of slavery.

Perhaps the poem's most difficult feature is the abrupt shifting between various voices, signaled by stanza breaks and sometimes quotation marks and italics. The challenge for the reader is to determine who is speaking and the speaker's point of view. Of the poem's three unequal sections, the first and third consist of multiple voices, whereas the second is spoken by a single narrator. These voices fall into two basic categories: free-ranging third-person-narrative voices that speak from above or at least outside the poem's events and the first-person voices of whites involved with the slave trade. The first type of voice speaks from the vantage point—and thus with the detachment, irony, and hindsight—of history, whereas the second type speaks in a documentary fashion, trapped in its limited self-understanding and historical moment. The organization of the poem allows for lyrical commentary to be juxtaposed with the voices of the past, voices which more often than not betray their own galling hypocrisy and ethical lapses. Subdividing the voices further, one may discern two different third-person narrative voices. These may be designated as the "scenic" voice (of lines 1–7, 14–16, 94–107, and 172–77) and the intrusive "parodic" voice (of lines 20–21, 25, 47, and 69), which ironically plays off of the title of the Protestant hymn "Jesus, Savior, Pilot Me." First-person narrators relate the rest of the poem. In the first section, we confront an excerpt from a captain's log (lines 8–13), a hypocritical collective prayer of crew members asking for safe passage (lines 22–24); a journal entry by a seaman whose captain (perhaps the one who made the log entry) and crew have been afflicted with ophthalmia, a plague that induces blindness (lines 26–41); and finally a legal voice that recounts atrocities and a disastrous fire aboard the slave vessel *The Bella J* (lines 48–68). A retired slave trader who had been active for twenty years narrates the whole of the briefer second section (lines 70–93). In the final section, a navigator of the *Amistad* speaks out against the slaves who famously rebelled on that vessel in what constitutes the poem's longest continuous portion (lines 120–71). In addition to these various speakers, an enigmatic voice presented in italics comments at intervals (lines 17–19, 42–46, and 108–19; note that its words should not be confused with the properly italicized names of vessels). This voice speaks of the slaves' plight with much greater respect and understanding than do any of the others. Together, these voices give us a fragmentary overview of the slave trade.

The italicized names cataloged by the principal third-person narrator in the first and fourteenth lines are those of slave vessels: Hayden wants, in particular, to take note of the irony implicit in such names as *Jesús* and *Mercy*. The poem documents from first to last the Western world's hypocritical betrayal of the teachings of Christ and of the Christian ideal of mercy. The "Christian" slave traders use conversion as a way of rationalizing their profit-driven actions (see lines 22–24), while at the same time they flagrantly ignore the ethical teachings of Christianity, most conspicuously the Golden Rule. All of the poem's extended narrative sections document the disasters that follow from injustice. Suicide, disease, starvation, rape, and rebellion: these are the fruits of the slave trade. Section two introduces the moral complication that certain African kings (the poem instances a King Anthracite) collaborate in the slave trade. As in Freneau's "To Sir Toby," the blacks themselves are corrupted by the possibility of profit. The extended penultimate section focusing on the *Amistad* rebellion of 1839 introduces the figure of Cinquez, the rebellion's leader, who may be taken as the poem's epic hero. The bigoted, self-righteous navigator who narrates this section tells of how the slaves fell on the crew in the middle of the night with machetes and marlinspikes, killing so many that the decks were slippery with blood. The navigator (who had to be kept alive to pilot the vessel) refers to the slaves as "apes" and to the crew as "true Christians." The navigator helped perpetrate a deception by sailing east during the day and west during the night. Eventually, the ship ended up on the shores of the United States. The navigator, addressing U.S. officials, feels that Cinquez and the others should be tried in Cuba for murder. In fact, former president John Quincy Adams successfully argued before the Supreme Court that the slaves should be freed and returned to Africa. Even here, in what would seem to be an unequivocal triumph of freedom, the poem's moral vision resists a reductive simplicity, for the detestable navigator has a genuine point when he notes the paradox of America defending the Spanish slaves when its own economy depends upon "the labor of your slaves." The poem's concluding accents fall on three things: the "deep immortal human wish" for freedom (first articulated by the voice in italics in line 118), the transfiguring power of Cinquez's heroism and defiance, and the reiterated definition of "middle passage." Through death and suffering, the will to live and to be free are kept alive. "Middle Passage," undoubtedly Hayden's masterpiece, must surely be American poetry's most complex and powerful exploration of the themes of freedom and slavery.

A more recent poem on these themes is Maya Angelou's "Caged Bird" (1983), conceived as a kind of sequel to Paul Laurence Dunbar's classic poem "Sympathy." Angelou, as Dunbar before her, employs resonant bird imagery to express her themes; but whereas Dunbar focused almost exclusively on the caged bird, Angelou develops an alternating contrast between a free bird and a caged bird. The poem's first and fourth stanzas explore the nature of the free bird, which is carefree and in tune with its natural surroundings. The bird's insouciance translates into a grandiose but harmless sense of its place in the scheme of things: it claims the sky for its own and even names it (naming being the act of a free agent). The nature of freedom is thus equated with euphoric self-assertion. The only note of discord in the description is the mention of trade winds in line twenty-four, which might well call to mind the slave trade so brilliantly analyzed in Hayden's "Middle Passage." Thus, the free bird seems to be dimly aware of its counterpart, whose plight occupies stanzas two, three, five, and six (the last of which repeats stanza three, like an extended refrain). Each paired stanza focusing on the caged bird is introduced with the stark conjunction of contrast, "But," to leave no doubt as to the difference between the fates of the two birds. The caged bird is imprisoned not only by its narrow physical cage but also by its own rage over its loss of freedom. As in Dunbar's poem, the bird sings of freedom, but it also stands "on the grave of dreams"—a powerful metaphor that calls to mind the dream deferred that Langston Hughes wrote of in "Harlem" (discussed under "Civilization") as well as the dream that Martin Luther King, Jr. spoke of in his famous "I Have a Dream" speech. Angelou thus selects a word freighted with meaning within the modern history of African-American culture, a word that symbolizes the longing for freedom and equality. The precise relation between Angelou's imagery and American history, however, is left ambiguous. Is the caged bird a figure of the past or the present? What applications does it have for the world of 1983 and beyond? The reader will have to reflect on social conditions and decide for him-or herself.

❧❀☙

"On the Emigration to America and Peopling the Western Country,"
Philip Freneau

    AAL-1; ColAP; HAL-1; NAL-1

"To Sir Toby," Philip Freneau

    AAL-1; ATL-1; HAL-1; HoAL-1; NAL-1; NoP-4

"Ichabod," John Greenleaf Whittier

    AAL-1; APN-1; ATL-1; HAL-1; HoAL-1; NAL-1; NOBA; OxBA

"Laus Deo," John Greenleaf Whittier

    ATL-1; HAL-1

"The New Colossus," Emma Lazarus

    APN-2; NoP-4

"Sympathy," Paul Laurence Dunbar

    APN-2; ATL-2; HAL-2; HoAL-2; MAP; NoP-4

"Middle Passage," Robert Hayden

    APT-2; ColAP; HoAL-2; MAP; NAL-2; VCAP

"Caged Bird," Maya Angelou

    WeW-4

The Individual and
Society

෧෮෴෧

Our fate is to become one, and yet many—This is not prophecy, but
description.
             the anonymous narrator of Ralph Ellison's *Invisible Man*

Literature has dramatized the conflicting claims of society and the individual at least since the time of Sophocles's *Antigone*, which remains
the classic treatment of the theme. In America, where individuals and
expressions of individualism are, at least in theory, highly valued, writers tend to side with the individual against the traditional, conformist,
and legal pressures exerted by society. Thus, a reader's sympathies are
supposed to be with Hester Prynne as she defies Puritan authority in
Nathaniel Hawthorne's *The Scarlet Letter*, with Huck Finn as he lights
out for the frontier to avoid being "sivilized" by his aunt in Mark
Twain's *Adventures of Huckleberry Finn*, and with the nameless narrator
of Ralph Ellison's *Invisible Man* as he retreats into the underground to
define himself against the racism and violence of mid-century America.

In much the same manner as our classic fiction, American poetry has
tended to side with the individual against the norms of society. The
tendency is writ large in the work of perhaps our most eccentrically
individual major poet, Emily Dickinson. Both "I'm Nobody! Who are
you?" (#288, c. 1861) and "Much Madness is divinest Sense" (#435, c.
1862) celebrate the private life of the individual and scorn the values of
society. The first of these poems contrasts being a "Nobody" with being
a "Somebody." Dickinson inverts traditional values that would promote
the latter at the expense of the former. She likens public existence to a
frog croaking "To an admiring Bog!" The poem celebrates the private

and authentic life of the individual, whose values and creative abilities need not be cheapened by publicity, politics, or self-promotion.

"Much Madness," a more incisive and troubling poem, picks up where its predecessor left off. It examines how individuality is not necessarily safe from society's values but can be taken by society for madness—and dealt with accordingly. Certain types of "Madness," the poem asserts, are actually "divinest Sense," whereas much that passes for sense is actually "the starkest Madness." The values of the majority prevail, and you either receive society's stamp of approval by assenting to them or are hauled away and thrown into a lunatic bin—or worse. The poem's reductive but extremely pointed rhetoric comments on both the fine line between genius and madness and the mass foibles societies are apt to entertain. Readers who think of world wars, mutual assured destruction, fascism, racism, religious persecution, and the destruction of the environment can be excused for seeing in Dickinson's poem a prophetic utterance. For her part, Dickinson had before her the historical examples of Socrates, Jesus, Galileo, and other individuals who were condemned by society for their inspired beliefs or discoveries—as well as the long, dismal, war-fraught record of civilization itself.

The tension between individuals and society also figures prominently in the poetry of Edwin Arlington Robinson, although unlike Dickinson, he preferred to explore it in specific case studies rather than through pithy general statements. "Miniver Cheevy" (1910), which Robinson considered a kind of ironic self-portrait, examines the life of a man who feels he has been born too late. Miniver is out of step with a world typified by khaki suits; he longs, instead, for the romantic era of the Middle Ages, when life—supposedly—was filled with heroic potential. This exaltation of the Middle Ages was characteristic of the Victorian literature and art (as exemplified by the work of Tennyson and the Pre-Raphaelites) that immediately preceded Robinson's era. A thoroughgoing modern, Robinson could not turn to the same subject matter without a certain amount of skepticism. He provides us with iconic images of swords and prancing steeds, of Camelot, and of even earlier instances of heroic romance drawn from Greek myth; but irony tinges the portrait with the knowledge of self-delusion when we hear of "the mediaeval grace / Of iron clothing." What is graceful about a suit of iron? Mark Twain had already exploded the idealized fantasies about proverbial "knights in shining armor" in his celebrated novel *A Connecticut Yankee in King Arthur's Court* (1889). For one thing, they were walking lightning rods; for another, a lone bug could wreak havoc on them.

Earlier eras look most attractive to people who know relatively little about what life in them was actually like. Robinson could not simply glorify the—by modern standards—intolerant, brutal, dirty, parasite- and disease-ridden life of the Middle Ages. Instead, his autobiographical protagonist knowingly winks at his own ridiculous longings—and yet still remains unreconciled to the society in which he finds himself. The "commonplace," business-oriented world of modern America does not present itself as a poet's true realm either, even if, hypocritically, he yearns for the very wealth he scorns. Where Miniver really wants to reside is in the ideal world of the imagination, represented by the Middle Ages of lore, not of fact. No amount of futile thought on Miniver's part can resolve the conflict between the real and the ideal, and so he yields to fatalism. The powerful, understated final line of the poem—"And kept on drinking"—discloses Miniver's preferred means of escape, even as it documents what, whether it be the cause or the effect of his alienation, might well be his most serious problem.

A later Robinson portrait, "Bewick Finzer" (1916), examines the life of a man who has not avoided the rat race but become its victim. The poem, narrated by an employee of the bank where Finzer takes his loans, begins by recounting the protagonist's financial history and woes. At one point, Finzer had been a success and had drawn 6 percent interest on his half million dollars (a substantially more considerable fortune in 1916 than today). The poem somewhat obliquely indicates that the dangerous itch of ambition ("the worm of what-was-not") led to Finzer's financial and mental ruin. The poem conveys a powerful sense of the roller coaster of fortune and the marketplace. Although it predates the stock-market collapse of 1929, it perhaps recalls the panic of 1893, which exacted a heavy toll on Robinson's own family inheritance. Having given us a thumbnail sketch of Finzer's history, the poem then depicts Finzer's current state. He appears now hardly to be the same man. The narrator catalogs his outward appearance and describes, with extreme irony, the "cleanliness" of his "indigence" (or poverty) and the "brilliance" of his "despair." Finzer still dreams of getting back into the rat race, but becomes deeply troubled when he notes successful people "who might so easily" have been in his unlucky place. He comes to the bank now not to make deposits but for loans. He has become, in the words of the pungent, penetrating, and memorable conclusion, "Familiar as an old mistake / And futile as regret."

T. S. Eliot's "The Love Song of J. Alfred Prufrock" (1917) depicts the complex tension between a neurotic individual and the high society he finds simultaneously attractive and repulsive. J. Alfred Prufrock, the name of a furniture dealer in Eliot's home city of St. Louis, sounds like an unlikely name to be yoked to a love song, and indeed, his song is hardly conventional or straightforward. Eliot prefaces it with an epigraph drawn from Dante's *Inferno*, in which the damned soul of Guido da Montefeltro addresses Dante, saying he would not speak except that he knows no one returns to the surface world from Hell. The quotation suggests a parallel between Guido and the poem's own speaker, Prufrock, as well as between Guido's listener (Dante) and the reader of "The Love Song." The opening line of the poem invites an unspecified "you" to "go then" to an unspecified destination. The "you" may be understood as the reader of this confiding and depressing poem (although it could also be taken to indicate another figure in the poem or, perhaps, some part of Prufrock's own fractured personality; the anxious Prufrock does not clarify whom, exactly, he means).

The poem as a whole is an exercise in self-revelation cast in the form of a dramatic monologue, in the tradition of Tennyson and Robert Browning. However, the poem's violent transitions and associative alogical structure make it seem more like an interior monologue than a spoken one, a possibility left open by the ambiguous antecedent of "you." The memorable opening lines make clear that the journey Prufrock proposes will be through urban streets on the way toward some social gathering. The refrain "In the room the women come and go / Talking of Michelangelo" first hints at the nature of the gathering. Prufrock seems to be looking ahead to the empty social chatter, replete with name-dropping, of upper-class women he expects to encounter on his "visit." The image further compounds the speaker's mounting anxieties, evident from the refusal to grapple with the "overwhelming question" of line 10 (mentioned again in line 93). The poem's third section, which discusses fog as if it were a cat, does not develop the central social themes and seems almost like a separate composition. Its unusual conceit looks back to the famous simile from lines 2–3 comparing dusk to "a patient etherised upon a table." Both figurative passages indicate that Prufrock possesses a jumbled, miscellaneous, unconventional, and surprisingly creative mind, apt to dwell on languorous imagery. In the fourth section, the poem returns to the social themes implicit at the outset: Prufrock claims there will be sufficient time "To prepare a face to meet the faces that you meet" and also refers to such rituals as "the taking of a toast and tea." The principal emphasis in this section falls upon time itself, as the repetition of the word "time" no fewer than eight times in the space of twelve lines clearly indicates. Three more repetitions in section five follow the return of the brief "Michelangelo" refrain. Prufrock's obsession with time, which exposes his basic indecisiveness, leads directly to the meditation on aging and mortality that dominates the latter portions of the poem.

Details about the social gathering Prufrock anxiously imagines attending start coming more into focus in the fifth section, in which Prufrock speculates on what those who see him will think. The prim, spindly, balding figure he cuts makes him highly self-conscious. These neuroses culminate in a striking image in the seventh section that likens the eyes of the social elite to pins that will spear him to the wall, in the same manner that an entomologist displays an insect. The image conveys both the coolly clinical and judgmental nature of high society as well as the vulnerability and insignificance of Prufrock himself. Although his social fears seem general, what worries him the most are the women who might be at the party, whom he has already alluded to in the "Michelangelo" refrain and whom he conjures up in the ninth section with an image of braceleted arms. Prufrock's feelings of sexual inadequacy and intimidation become clearer when, in line 80, he doubts his ability "to force the moment to its crisis." Various images underscore Prufrock's low self-esteem: he identifies with lonely working-class men; absurdly, he wishes he were a lobster, free of social obligations and able to move rapidly backwards; and he envisions himself in the role of John the Baptist, just after Salome has had his head cut off. The latter image powerfully indicates his fear of attractive women and its unhealthy relation to his even greater fear of death.

Death, figured in line 85 as an "eternal Footman," bars the way to the social gathering. This scarifying vision has a decisive effect on Prufrock's plans, for from this point forward Prufrock speaks only in terms of what "would" have happened had he gone to the gathering. The fear of death allows him to rationalize his anxieties and so avoid any uncomfortable encounters. After a legion of equivocations, Prufrock finally seems to have determined not to make his visit. Nonetheless, his meditation still continues. He eventually acknowledges the opacity of his statements: "It is impossible to say just what I mean!" Instead of saying it precisely ("just"), he does so in a roundabout manner, by recourse to various allusions and comparisons. In line 111, for example, he rejects a comparison with the most famous equivocator in literature—Hamlet. Instead, he resembles "an attendant lord," referring to Rosencrantz or Guildenstern, those famously interchangeable non-entities whom Hamlet arranges to have put to death. Prufrock tells us, in short, that he is not a man of importance (as Hamlet, Prince of Denmark, was) but rather a man doomed to an anonymous, inconsequential death. The poem ends by gathering together the various strands of Prufrock's anxiety-ridden character. An emphasis on aging and mortality returns in line 120, and indecisiveness, taken to an absurd extreme ("Do I dare to eat a peach?"— which perhaps can be interpreted as a sexual image), recurs in line 122. There is something ineffably sad about Prufrock's belief that the mermaids (another image of those attractive, dangerous women who frighten him so much) will not even sing to him. The poem concludes by suggesting that self-consciousness is a dream from which human voices wake us to a social world in which we drown. Prufrock speaks for all alienated individuals whose relation to the rituals, hierarchies, and sexual intrigues of society can only, at best, be fraught with anxious feelings of inadequacy and a desire to refrain from contact. Society, as the epigraph hints, is a kind of hell from which no one escapes.

Claude McKay's sonnet "The Harlem Dancer" (1917) presents a simpler but no less poignant vision of the individual's relation to society, again conceived largely in sexual terms. The poem paints a verbal portrait of a beautiful, exhibitionist singer-dancer (the very opposite, in almost every respect, of poor Prufrock) who performs in front of a crowd of youths and prostitutes. The raucous audience is enthralled by her attractiveness ("even the girls, / Devoured her shape with eager, passionate gaze"); but the narrator detects something more, a hint of struggle: "To me she seemed a proudly-swaying palm / Grown lovelier for passing through a storm." The poem clearly aims at more than simple description; it seeks to make a trenchant comment on the complex, paradoxical, empowering yet degrading nature of exhibitionism. As is typical in the Shakespearean form of the sonnet, which McKay faithfully follows, the "turn" does not occur until the beginning of the thirteenth line. This structural feature places an immense burden on the final two lines to respond to or qualify in some way what has gone before. McKay does an excellent job of modifying the poem's meaning by shifting from how the dancer is seen to what her own gaze reveals. The speaker of the poem seems to see something that none of the enthusiastic listeners and voyeurs detect: the false smile on the dancer's face (the others are looking at her body) and the vacant expression that reveals "her self was not in that strange place." The word "place" here is ambiguous, signifying either the establishment or her body itself. The latter possibility would imply that the performer experiences a disconnection between her sense of self and her own physical presence. Objectified, the dancer withdraws, giving all of her sensuality but nothing of her inner self.

Hilda Doolittle explores a somewhat similar friction between a female individual and society by updating the Greek myth of Helen of Troy. Modernist writers, such as James Joyce, Ezra Pound, and T. S. Eliot, frequently drew upon ancient myths to comment on contemporary realities. Doolittle, who had been engaged to Pound for a time and who remained dedicated to his artistic ideals throughout her career, shared the interest of these writers in revitalizing myths. In "Helen" (1924), she does not draw explicit parallels between Greek myths and the present, as Joyce had done so elaborately in his vastly influential novel *Ulysses* (1922), but she does give the old myth of the Trojan War a feminist slant by focusing on the figure of Helen. Helen was alleged to be the most beautiful woman of the ancient world. Her abduction by Paris, a Trojan prince, touched off the Trojan War, immortalized by Homer in the *Iliad*. What struck Doolittle about the story was how central yet peripheral Helen was to it all. The whole story had been narrated from the male point of view; Helen was simply the victor's prize. Doolittle set out to rewrite the myth from Helen's viewpoint, an enterprise that culminated in her fourteen-hundred-line poem *Helen in Egypt* (1961). The earlier lyric only anticipates the direction of this epic work. It briefly sketches the hatred that Helen arouses in the Greeks, who must fight to win her back. "God's daughter" (i.e., the daughter of Zeus), Helen is held accountable for the war itself. If she had not been so ravishingly beautiful, Paris would not have kidnapped her. The logic here is that of a society that condemns a victim for the crimes perpetrated against her. Helen is like a woman who has been raped and told that her own attractiveness is to blame. The Greeks will only love Helen and her beauty when both have been neutralized by death. The poem charts the ambivalent love-hate relationship between society and an exceptional individual, made all the more complicated by the fact that the individual happens to be a beautiful woman.

Inspired not by Greek mythology but by contemporary film, Hart Crane's "Chaplinesque" (1926) examines the tension between the artist and society. The poem was inspired by Crane's viewing of Charlie Chaplin's *The Kid* (1921). Crane was so taken with the film that he placed Chaplin among the modern poets (hence the initial "We" of the poem) and saw him as an archetypal figure—a Clown, Fool, or Artist—whose devotion to art and feeling stands in contrast to an unimaginative and repressive society principally devoted to utility and order. This conventionally romantic view of the artist as an alienated figure at odds with society's values receives an unconventional development in the poem, for Crane sought to express the antics of the famous actor through his word choices. Crane remains one of the most opaque and difficult of American poets, and even a relatively simple example of his art like "Chaplinesque" does not possess a perspicuous surface. The opening lines indicate that the individual at odds with society must continually compromise between the ideal and the actual. The "consolations" that sustain life and hope come as randomly as the blowing of the wind. Love of the world remains a possibility, one embodied by the symbolic image of a kitten, which recurs in the poem's final line. The "famished" kitten represents all that is good yet helpless in the world, all that must be pitied and protected from "the fury of the street" or "the wilderness" (an urban metaphor rather than a natural image). In opposition to the kitten, Crane introduces the "inevitable thumb" of the policeman who hounds Chaplin and represents society's love of order and conformity and which here becomes a manifestation of death itself. This doom can be delayed but not evaded; society and death will win in the end. The Artist has only a repertoire of well-honed technical maneuvers (such as Chaplin's "fine collapses") and assumed postures (innocence, surprise, obsequiousness) with which to combat and evade these forces.

The Artist's allegiance remains to "the heart," twice mentioned in lines 17 and 18 and, according to Crane, a pun on his own first name. Smirking is one inevitable self-defensive gesture of the unreconciled individual. The ironic stance it implies, however, is not equivalent to a final

surrender to cynicism, for Crane introduces an image in the poem's conclusion that suggests the possibility of transcendence. Moonlight transforms the mundane image of "an empty ash can" into "A grail of
laughter." Here, Crane directly equates the Chaplinesque Artist figure
with Parsifal, the quester after the Holy Grail, whose name, as the composer Richard Wagner pointed out, literally means "holy fool." In this
crucial Grail image, Clown, Fool, Artist, and Quester are all synthesized,
as the possibility of redemption becomes momentarily palpable. Even if
it is ultimately illusory, it shadows forth something—perhaps only an
ideal—that transcends the commonplace, drab reality of the modern city.
It, along with the kitten, is what the individual heart has to counterbal-
ance the impersonal, hostile forces of the world.

Sterling Brown's "Southern Cop" (1936) examines an altogether different social situation. Here, the individual does not stand helpless before
society but rather society, for reasons having to do with race and official
sanctions of power, stands helpless before an individual. The poem examines the relation of an inexperienced, trigger-happy white police officer to the black denizens of Darktown. Ty Kendricks, the officer, has
gunned down an innocent African-American boy who ran out of an
alley. The poem addresses the black community, telling them how they
should respond to this tragic and, as becomes clear, racist incident. Each
stanza begins with an admonishment: "Let us forgive Ty Kendricks" the
poem begins, and subsequent stanzas substitute the verbs "understand,"
"condone," and "pity." The poem grants that Kendricks was nervous,
young, and a rookie, but its smoldering tone clearly indicates that these
are facts, not excuses. Indeed, irony drips from just about every word of
the poem. The poem's embittered speaker notes that the boy must have
been dangerous because he ran, a deadpan way of identifying and implicitly denouncing the twisted, racist logic that governed the officer's
"unfortunate" mistake. Kendricks "has been through enough," the
speaker acidly remarks; he stands "Rabbit-scared" and "alone" (but still
armed and empowered). By ironically focusing on the officer's guilty
plight, the narrator makes us participate all the more acutely in the great,
ineffable pang of loss felt by the women of Darktown.

E. E. Cummings's "anyone lived in a pretty how town" (1940) celebrates the life and death of an individual who, as in Crane's "Chaplinesque," does not keep pace with the values of the society in which he
finds himself. At first glance, the poem can seem merely whimsical, like
something concocted by the Victorian nonsense poet Edward Lear; but
its meaning begins to fall into place when the reader realizes that "anyone" is the name of the poem's protagonist. He lives out of step with
mainstream society, the members of which seem to be engaged in destructive and conformist lifestyles ("they sowed their isn't they reaped
their same"). Anyone, by contrast, marches to a different drummer, sing-

ing and dancing despite the disdain of society at large. Only certain children seem to have insight into anyone's life, which highlights his fundamental innocence, but the children, soon enough, are socialized to accept different values and, presumably, to scorn a nonconformist like anyone. As the growing up of children demonstrates, the poem covers a fair span of time. Throughout, Cummings indicates time's passage with permutations of the seasons and of the series "sun moon stars rain," along with images of leaves and a bird in snow. Eventually, anyone finds a woman named noone who is able to share his life through good times and bad ("she laughed his joy she cried his grief"): they form what Howard J. Campbell, in Kurt Vonnegut's *Mother Night*, calls "a nation of two." Meanwhile, the important men in town ("someones") marry indistinguishable wives ("everyones") and complacently live (or "sleep") the American "dream." The names "noone" and "someone" directly recall Emily Dickinson's "Nobody" and "Somebody" from "I'm Nobody! Who are you?" Cummings's poem can be seen as a dramatic elaboration of that earlier poem's ideas.

The narrator of "anyone lived in a pretty how town" off-handedly reports that anyone died one day and that noone—after kissing his face at the funeral—followed soon after. The "busy folk" of the pretty how town bury them side by side: even in death, they retain their solidarity. Cummings never specifies that they had married—as opposed to the "someones"—which might confirm the suspicion that the poem has distinctly autobiographical overtones. (Cummings lived with a fashion model named Marion Morehouse; they were never married, but he considered her to be his wife; like anyone, he lived at odds with society's rituals and values.) Anyone had at least found happiness in his personal life, which set him in opposition to the conformity and banality of public existence; he dies, having been fulfilled by the graces of love and art. The difference between anyone and the town is perhaps most evident in the fact that anyone and noone "dream their sleep" rather than, as everyone else does, "sleep their dream." The former optimistically suggests the possibility of life after death, as opposed to the dreary death-in-life of social conformity. The couple may turn conventionality on its head, but they have changed nothing in the larger world. The people, ever more numerous, continue to pursue their "dream," while the cycles of the seasons and of life and death continue on.

In "The Drunk in the Furnace" (1960), W. S. Merwin starkly presents a similar dramatic conflict, although in this case, the absolutely peripheral life of the protagonist is enforced by the fact that he never even appears in the poem. Instead, the poem evokes his presence through his effects: "a twist of smoke" and various crashing and bellowing sounds. The drunk, a literary cousin of E. A. Robinson's marginal, alcoholic heroes, stays offstage, as it were, squirreled away in the "black fossil" of the abandoned furnace, while the poem's point of view remains (in physical but not moral terms) with the wary, righteous townspeople. Throughout the poem, Merwin employs diction resourcefully and expressively. The word "staggering," applied to the smoke in line 10, constitutes an interesting example of a deliberately misplaced epithet, calling to mind the unobserved motion of the drunk himself. "Spirits"—another of the poem's key words—puns on liquor and personal energy, in line 15, both of which seem manifest in the drunk's clanging of poker and bottle. The drunk sleeps like "an iron pig," a startling image resulting from an inversion of the "pig iron" that the furnace may once have produced. Religious echoes also enrich the poem: notably, "Resurrection" in line 10 and the congregation's hatred of "trespassers" (ironically summoning to mind The Book of Common Prayer's version of the Lord's Prayer, which calls for the forgiveness of trespassers) in line 24. The respectable townfolk despise the drunk, but their children are drawn to his cacophony like rats to the Pied Piper. They listen "and learn" from this outcast things about life their society would never teach them.

❧❧❧

"I'm Nobody! Who are you?" Emily Dickinson

> APN-2; ATL-2; HAL-1; HAL-2; HoAL-2; NOBA

"Much Madness is Divinest Sense—," Emily Dickinson

> AAL-1; AAL-2; APN-2; ATL-2; HAL-1; HAL-2; HoAL-2; LPTT; NAL-1; NoAM; NOBA; NoP-4; OxBA; SoSe-9; TFi

"Miniver Cheevy," Edwin Arlington Robinson

> AAL-2; APT-1; ATL-2; ColAP; HAL-2; HoAL-2; MAP; NAL-2; NoAM; NOBA; NoP-4; OxBA; SoSe-9; TFi

"Bewick Finzer," Edwin Arlington Robinson

> AAL-2; ATL-2; HAL-2

"The Love Song of J. Alfred Prufrock," T. S. Eliot

> AAL-2; APT-1; ATL-2; ColAP; HAL-2; HoAL-2; MAP; NAL-2; NoAM; NOBA; NoP-4; SoSe-9; TFi; WeW-4

"The Harlem Dancer," Claude McKay

> APT-1; MAP; NAL-2; NoAM

"Helen," Hilda Doolittle

> AAL-2; APT-1; ColAP; HAL-2; MAP; NAL-2; NoAM; NOBA; NoP-4

"Chaplinesque," Hart Crane

AAL-2; APT-2; HAL-2; HoAL-2; MAP; NAL-2; NoAM; NOBA; OxBA; VGW

"Southern Cop," Sterling Brown

MAP; SoSe-9

"anyone lived in a pretty how town," E. E. Cummings

AAL-2; APT-2; ATL-2; ColAP; HAL-2; HoAL-2; MAP; NAL-2; NOBA; NoP-4; TFi; VGW; WeW-4

"The Drunk in the Furnace," W. S. Merwin

AAL-2; ATL-2; CAPP-6; HAL-2; HoAL-2; MAP; NAL-2; NoAM; NoP-4

Innocence and Experience

To be nothing but innocent!

Herman Melville, *Billy Budd*

The myth of the Garden of Eden looms as the archetypal Western story about the fall from innocence into experience. Its vivid iconography—the tree of knowledge (conventionally held to be an apple tree) and the sly, tempting serpent (identified, by typological tradition, with Satan), in particular—has colored many subsequent depictions of these themes. America itself, at least until the middle of the nineteenth century, was frequently viewed as a kind of new Garden of Eden, an unspoiled land where a renewal of innocence and an escape from the burdens of European civilization—and even from sin itself—were possible. Religious movements in the nineteenth century, notably Universalism and Unitarianism, rejected the old Calvinist doctrine of original sin. In literature, as R. W. B. Lewis demonstrated in his classic study *The American Adam* (1955), the archetypal American hero also came to be seen as a kind of Adam, a self-reliant and innocent being, free from the European constraints of history, heredity, and society. Essayists and poets such as Ralph Waldo Emerson, Henry David Thoreau, and Walt Whitman celebrated the possibilities of innocence and renewal in the New World, while fiction writers such as Nathaniel Hawthorne, Herman Melville, and Henry James examined the tragic potentiality of innocence, always on the verge of falling prey to the disfiguring rigors of experience.

Whitman, whom the nature writer John Burroughs described as "the Adamic man reborn" and who referred to himself as a "chanter of Adamic songs," pursued—particularly in his pre–Civil War poetry—the ideal of regenerative innocence more thoroughly than any other American poet. His 1860 poems, titled *Children of Adam*, repudiate traditional Christian views of sex and the body as being shameful and sinful. Instead, Whitman celebrates sex and the body as innocent, natural, and spontaneous. Whitman invokes the primal innocence of Adam before the fall as an appropriate model for the present. In the first poem of *Children of Adam*—"To the Garden the World"—the poet (or his persona) compares the world to the Garden of Eden and implicitly presents himself as Adam, with Eve at his side. In the final poem of the group, "As Adam Early in the Morning," Whitman again likens himself to Adam as he rises in the morning and walks out from his bower. Whitman claims for himself the innocence and originality and what Emerson called "the simple genuine self" of the first man. Whitman seems to say that in the garden of the New World, every American can achieve this kind of freedom and innocence. In the conclusion of the poem, the poet asks the reader to touch him, in a symbolic acceptance of the body, which need not be seen as something shameful or tainted. Whitman wants the body to be re-accepted as something natural and worthy of unashamed admiration. As he makes clear in *Song of Myself*, he considers the body and the soul to be equally sacred. To denigrate either was unacceptable to him.

American attitudes toward innocence underwent a significant change after the Civil War. The emphasis that Emerson and Whitman had placed on Adam before the fall tended to shift to an emphasis on fallen innocence, as one sees in the fiction of Henry James and in Herman Melville's final testament, *Billy Budd*. If we understand American history as a kind of allegory of the human spirit, then the Civil War constitutes the moment at which our civilization fell from innocence into experience. That, at least, is the reading of events Herman Melville provides in his poem "The March into Virginia" (1866). The poem's subtitle, "Ending in the First Manassas (July, 1861)," indicates the subject matter: First Manassas, also known as First Bull Run, was the opening battle of the Civil War. It marked the point at which it was no longer possible to believe that the conflict between the North and the South could be resolved quickly or without mass carnage. Up to that point, American expectations about the war were extremely idealistic. In fact, hundred of picnickers had descended from Washington, D.C., some in carriages or wagons, to watch "the show" at Bull Run; but they were ultimately forced, as the defeated Union soldiers withdrew, to flee the scene in panic. Melville alludes in his poem to this circus in line 19: "No picnic party in the May." From that point forward, the war was no longer naively viewed as a spectator sport. Historian Bruce Catton has called this battle, fought by ill-prepared amateurs, "the great day of awakening for the whole nation."

Melville elaborates this idea of a rude "awakening," though not in terms of the "whole nation" but from the point of view of the uncertain young federal troops. The poet begins by posing a question: If all the obstacles "To every just or larger end" were apparent at the outset, how could one muster "the trust and cheer" to take action? He answers, somewhat obliquely, that the ignorant impulsiveness of youth is a necessary ingredient of the idealism that makes action possible; he implies, in other words, that trust and cheer are the products of both youth and ignorance. Wars, he asserts, "are boyish, and are fought by boys," who are the "champions and enthusiasts of the state." Their passions and vanity, enlisted by governing powers, help determine the fates of nations. In the second verse paragraph, he notes that among the marching figures, none credit precedent or heed warnings from the wise. They go forward with banners and bugles under a blue sky, festively rather than warily. Drunken with the possibilities of glory, they march into the unknown mysteries of battle like sacrifices to Moloch (a heathen god of the Old Testament for whom children were burnt as offerings). The final paragraph grimly notes that those who feel this way will soon either be dead, "enlightened by the vollied glare," or get another chance to be annihilated at Second Manassas, in which the Union Army, in August 1862, was defeated once again. Melville's cheerless poem concerns itself less with a specific battle, or even with war itself, than with a universal pattern of human experience—specifically, how the enthusiastic and obtuse innocence of youth, encouraged and exploited by the state, is transfigured by either death or disillusionment. The profound vein of skepticism about human nature and the world in Melville's poetry is particularly evident also in such poems as "The House-top: A Night Piece," "The Ravaged Villa," and "Fragments of a Lost Gnostic Poem of the 12th Century."

As poems by Robert Frost and E. E. Cummings illustrate, not all contrasts between innocence and experience are as stark as what Melville depicted, with the nation's greatest tragedy fresh in his mind. A complex, multithematic poem, Frost's "Birches" (1916), in which the poem's speaker longs to recapture the lost innocence of his youth, begins with an elaborate description of birches bowed by ice storms. The speaker whimsically imagines that the trees were bent, instead, by a boy who, as we finally learn in line 40, represents a youthful version of himself. He describes the "matter of fact" truth about how the trees were bent by storms in lines 4–20. After this splendidly vivid digression—which far from being merely "matter of fact" is actually charged with highly imaginative figurative language—the emphasis returns to the figure of the imaginary boy who lives "too far from town to learn baseball" and so amuses himself by swinging from the birches. This contrast between the actual (represented by the storms) and the ideal (represented by the boy) sets the stage for further contrasts between innocence and experience and between life and death. The boy gains experience of the trees, learning to climb with care and with a reckless calculation likened to filling a cup above its brim. For all his skill, however, the boy remains fundamentally innocent in a moral sense. The speaker, by contrast, "weary of considerations," has fallen into the complex world of experience and ambiguity, which he finds "too much like a pathless wood" (an image that calls to mind the classic opening scene of Dante's *Inferno*).

The speaker himself dreams of one day regaining the lost youth and innocence symbolized by swinging from the trees. The association of trees and innocence calls to mind the Garden of Eden story, although the speaker stops short of wishing to regain paradise in a literal sense. Cautious of even his own desires and aware that simplification alone does not always provide a sufficient solution, the speaker talks of climbing *"Toward* heaven" in line 56. The italicized emphasis on *"Toward"* makes it clear he does not mean "To." In other words, he wants to move in the direction of the ideal, but he does not actually want to get there. Frost's close friend Edward Thomas, who was killed in World War I, equated death with perfection in his poem "Rain," written the same year "Birches" was published. Here, Frost suggests a similar equation: the very perfection of the ideal threatens the necessary imperfection of life. The speaker wants inspiration, but will not part with the actual in the name of a transcendent ideal. To get there, he would have to perish, which would mean a one-way trip. For this reason, he says he wants no "fate" to "willfully misunderstand" him and "half grant" his wish (i.e., bring about his premature death). The speaker wants to go up and to come back, refreshed and renewed and ready to face the world once more. As he skeptically opines, "Earth's the right place for love: / I don't know where it's likely to go better." Frost symbolizes the middle way between the actual and the ideal through the image of climbing so high in a tree that it can "bear no more" and so dips back to the solid ground, carrying the climber.

A more grim and oblique vision of the contrast between innocence and experience is crystallized in Frost's poem "To Earthward" (1923). Its craggy, largely monosyllabic language conveys a powerful sense of strain, evident from the opening lines with their emphasis on virginal sensitivity: "Love at the lips was touch / As sweet as I could bear." The poem divides symmetrically into four stanzas focusing on the past and four on the present. The first half of the poem concerns the state of innocence and the second, the condition of having fallen into experience. In the first part, Frost emphasizes the speaker's youthful love of sweet things: musk from hidden grapevines, honeysuckle, and the petal of a rose. In the second part, he switches into the present tense. The somewhat confusing syntax of the first line of stanza five might puzzle readers. The "but" here should probably be read in the less familiar sense of "that," as in the phrase "I don't question but you're right." (This reading would seem to be supported by the fact that Frost eliminated the comma his editor had provided at the end of this line. Perhaps Frost simply wanted to avoid repetition, for the word "That" begins the succeeding line.) What we see here is that with age, the sweet things the speaker admired in his youth have become less apt to give him joy. Instead of the superficial delights of sweetness, he has come to crave saltiness and bitterness, the pungency of which adds a necessary element of stark reality. No longer a wide-eyed romantic intoxicated by dreams of abstracted beauty, the speaker is now a man who confronts and accepts the flawed, composite nature of the world. Experience has drawn him away from the innocent pleasures of youth, but it has given him an extra edge of comprehension and, even, sensation. Experience, in other words, as the poem depicts it, is not simply a matter of diminishment but one of painful growth. In the concluding lines, the speaker longs to lie down on the earth, an image perhaps forecasting his inevitable reception by the grave. One might see it as a death wish, a longing to end the strife and struggle of existence through a reunion with the inanimate. If so, this ending can usefully be compared with that of the more famous lyric, "Stopping by Woods on a Snowy Evening" (discussed under "Obligations & Choices"). A rugged, uncompromisingly personal poem, "To Earthward" charts the trajectory from innocence to experience and from youth to death, but its stoicism refuses the temptation to lament the inevitable.

E. E. Cummings attends with spirited insouciance to the theme of maturation in his celebrated poem "in Just—" (1923). The poem's title refers to the beginning of a new season: "in Just—/ spring." Springtime is the season of youth and innocence, to be succeeded by the maturity of summer, the decline of autumn, and the extinction of winter. Cummings paints a picture of spring that captures the very spirit of innocence. His poem does not simply concern innocence and childhood; it embodies these themes. Such portmanteau words as "mud- / luscious" and "puddle-wonderful" convey the essence of youthful perceptions and enthusiasm. (What "proper" adult would find anything "luscious" about mud? And what intrepid child would not?) Cummings also uses spacing to effect, leaving gaps between words, thereby creating a spontaneous impression of kinetic playground games such as "hop-scotch and jump-rope." He also runs together the names of his little protagonists—"eddieandbill" and "bettyandisbel"—suggesting thereby both the inseparability of playmates and the breathless exhilaration of youth. Everything in the poem evokes a world without even a shadow of trouble—except the figure of "the little / lame balloonman." The balloon man may serve as a reminder of youth's transience. He is also "goat-footed," a peculiar detail that cannot be ignored by an interpreter. It can be taken to imply a mythological parallel between the balloon man and Pan—a god of shepherds, nature, and fecundity. The association of Pan with sexual awakenings perhaps forecasts the day when "eddieandbill" might become "eddieandisbel." The poem thus focuses on innocence, but contains within it the seeds of experience.

Theodore Roethke's "The Lost Son" (1948) can, to a certain extent, be thought of as an expansion of Cummings's effort in "in Just—" not simply to write about childhood but to recover its essence and feeling in the words themselves. Thus, the poem's language possesses a decidedly irrational and even nonsensical aspect, reminiscent of Walter de la Mare's haunting "Song of the Mad Prince." Surrealism, obscure symbolism, abrupt transitions, repetition, exhortations, as well as enigmatic questions and riddles are all part of the poem's texture. An attempt to paraphrase "The Lost Son," line by line, might not be possible and would probably miss the point anyway, but its basic themes and structure can still be grasped without too much difficulty. The poem tells an oblique story of how a boy who has run away confronts the darkness of the world and the darkness within himself and then returns home with the wisdom and experience that precede genuine illumination. So while the poem describes a literal action, it does so through a dense tapestry of symbolic and archetypal images that often have more to do with interior states than with exterior reality.

The poem begins in medias res, with the boy already a fugitive and the reasons for his escape left unspecified. In the first section ("Flight"), the boy-narrator finds himself in a cemetery, confronted with the fact of death and uncertain of how to proceed. (It is probably not irrelevant to point out that "Woodlawn" is the actual cemetery where Roethke's own father, Otto, was buried and so has obvious personal significance.) Nature seems merely to mock the protagonist (the leaves stick out their "tongues" at him) or to remind him of his troubles (his lifeless fishing hole is like "an old wound"), and he receives enigmatic responses to the various questions he poses, intimating that regardless of his course of action, no easy answers lie ahead. The section concludes with a lengthy riddle, one possible answer to which might be "muskrat"; in any event, the important thing seems to be the speaker's identification with the furtive, solitary creature he describes.

If the first section initiates the journey and suggests its difficulties, the next two sections take us to the nadir of the boy's experiences. A sense of downward motion is created both by the title of the brief second section ("The Pit") and by its opening question, "Where do the roots go?" The most dense section of the poem is part three (appropriately titled "The Gibber," suggesting gibberish), wherein feeling rejected by both sun and moon (perhaps symbols for his parents), the boy confronts the fact of his mortality. What had been implicit since the opening image of the graveyard now becomes explicit. An allusion in line 84 to the catalog of God's taunts in the book of Job strengthens an archetypal identification between the boy's fearsome father and God himself. It powerfully conveys the boy's sense that the world as a whole is somehow against him. What he has to confront here are the facts of individual isolation ("Only the snow's here") and inevitable mortality ("our doom is already decided"), as well as the economic burdens of independence ("I run to the whistle of money"). Each of these represents the end of innocence and the beginning of maturity.

In section four ("The Return"), the boy comes back to the familiar greenhouse world, the setting for much of Roethke's poetry. Having abandoned this sphere of paternal authority and order to confront the chaos that pervades the natural world and his own inner being, the boy now cries for "Ordnung! ordnung!" (German for "Order! order!"—a reminder that Roethke's family was of German descent) as he ecstatically awaits the fearsome father figure, associated with God, from whom he had fled. That reunion, however, is not depicted directly; instead, in the final section, Roethke offers us a vision of winter's onset. From the restless motion of the other sections, the narrator has now arrived at a contemplative stillness. Action gives way to meditation. As light breaks across a field, the speaker no longer feels shunned or alone. In a moment of religious intensity, the light from the outside has suggested the possibility of a light within. The poem concludes in this static moment of patience and possibility. The narrator has overcome the terrors within himself and can now at least hope for illumination. This pattern of arduous journey leading to transcendent peace will be repeated, in more compressed form but with a less tentative conclusion, in Roethke's celebrated crisis lyric, "In a Dark Time" (discussed under "Skepticism & Belief").

Denise Levertov returns to the primal imagery of the Eden story in developing the theme of innocence and experience in "To the Snake" (1959). That the garden, apple, and serpent imagery had not lost its evocative force had been recently demonstrated by Ralph Ellison's classic novel of innocence and experience, *Invisible Man* (1952), wherein the narrator conceives of his university as a Garden of Eden, glimpses two apples amid a bewildering succession of misadventures, and catches sight of a water moccasin disappearing into a drainpipe after his expulsion. Levertov's poem resembles Ellison's novel in its naturalistic use of traditional symbolism, although Levertov confines herself to just one archetypal image, that of the phallic serpent. The poem recounts the speaker's experience of having hung a green snake around her neck. The speaker dotes on the snake's physical presence, the way it felt and looked and the sounds it made. The speaker swore to her companions that the snake was harmless, but in fact she did not know. All she did know was that she wanted to hold the snake, to come into contact with the experience it represented. The image of the snake "whispering" close to the speaker's ears recalls, inevitably, the serpent's seduction of Eve. Levertov invokes the story of the fall of humanity to suggest the dangers of pursuing experience, such as daring to handle a potentially deadly snake. The poem, however, ultimately revels in the pleasures of experience. It does not posit a sharp divide between innocence and experience, but rather seems to reconcile them into the innocent experience (despite its sexual overtones) of enjoying contact with another creature. The snake may have been deadly, but it does not harm the speaker; instead, it disappears "into the pattern / of grass and shadows." The speaker's gambit has paid off: she has gained a memorable experience without suffering any negative consequences. Perhaps Levertov's principal intention is to demonstrate how life without the risk of experience is an impoverished thing.

Another predacious animal figures as an emblem of experience in Richard Wilbur's "A Barred Owl" (2000). The poem's opening stanza describes how a girl, awakened by a barred owl's cry, is consoled by her parents. The parents, following the traditional mnemonic practice of birders and ornithologists, "translate" the owl's four-note cry ("hoohoo-hoohoo") into a harmless question in English, "Who cooks for you?" (Some actual field guides, as Wilbur must have known, use this very phrase to represent the barred owl's voice.) The second stanza explores the implications of this translation and draws a sharp contrast between the fiction perpetuated by the parents and the reality of the owl's wild existence. The English rendering of the owl's voice "domesticates" the child's fear by associating the terrors of the unknown with the familiar, pleasurable ritual of home cooking. The child's innocent vision is thus reaffirmed, but at the expense of true knowledge of the world. Here is the sheltered innocence that Levertov's poem implicitly critiques and that Dickinson knowingly evokes in "Tell all the Truth but tell it slant—" (discussed under "Truth & Appearance"). In fact, as we well know, the nocturnal bird stealthily roves the forest, looking for prey to kill and eat—not cooked, but raw. Cooking, like the parents' words, becomes in the poem a bulwark of civilization, protecting the child from the harsh realities of the food chain. The protective parents may willfully delay the child's fall into experience, but the poem insists upon the illusory nature of innocence. Innocence seems to exist only as a human ideal, articulated in reassuring narrative structures, but remote from the dog-eat-dog, owl-eat-rodent, human-eat-chicken reality of the world.

❧☙

"As Adam Early in the Morning," Walt Whitman

AAL-1; APN-1; ATL-1; ATL-2; ColAP; HAL-1; HAL-2; MAP; OxBA

"The March into Virginia," Herman Melville

AAL-1; ATL-1; ColAP; HAL-1; NAL-1; NoP-4

"Birches," Robert Frost

AAL-2; APT-1; ATL-2; HAL-2; HoAL-2; LPTT; MAP; NAL-2; NoAM; NoP-4; OxBA; SoSe-9; TFi

"To Earthward," Robert Frost

APT-1; HAL-2; NoAM; NOBA; NoP-4; OxBA

"in Just—," E. E. Cummings

AAL-2; APT-2; ATL-2; HAL-2; HoAL-2; MAP; NAL-2; NoP-4; SoSe-9

"The Lost Son," Theodore Roethke

AAL-2; APT-2; CAPP-6; HAL-2; HCAP; HoAL-2; MAP ("The Flight" section only) NAL-2; NoP-4

"To the Snake," Denise Levertov

ATL-2; NAL-2

"A Barred Owl," Richard Wilbur

Mayflies: New Poems and Translations. Richard Wilbur. Harcourt, Inc.: New York, 2000.

Life and Death

❧

> The cradle rocks above an abyss, and common sense tells us that our existence is but a brief crack of light between two eternities of darkness.
>
> Vladimir Nabokov, *Speak, Memory*

No themes seem more universal than life and death. American poets have grappled with various fundamental aspects of these themes: the transience of life, how to conduct one's life in the face of death's inevitability, the meaning or meaninglessness of life, the difficulty of fathoming one's own mortality, and the possibility of an afterlife. Since every generation must face the facts of life and death, none of these aspects ever become dated, although specific ideas and emphases do evolve over time. The relative triumph of democracy over class privilege has, for instance, made the old idea of death as an equalizer—a favorite notion of aristocratic ages—less compelling as the years have passed, while at the same time poets, for reasons speculated on below, have tended to find the most universal expression of these themes not in the lives, struggles, and deaths of humans bound by civilization but rather in those of the denizens of the natural world.

Philip Freneau issued the nation's first significant poetic statement on the themes of life and death in the form of an apostrophe to a flower. Freneau's "The Wild Honey Suckle" (1786) begins by noting the kinds of death that are unlikely for the flower: it grows in a hidden retreat and is therefore safe from feet that crush and hands that pluck. (Freneau, by the way, seems to be referring not to the familiar vine but to a flowering shrub—*Azalea viscosa*, or swamp honeysuckle.) Freneau conceives of nature as a benevolent entity; he personifies it as a kind of caretaker or gardener that not only planted the honeysuckle far from human settlements but also continues to supply it with shade and water. Even in these idyllic circumstances, however, the honeysuckle's days are numbered. In Freneau's idealizing eyes, early, unspoiled America may be a kind of new Eden, but as he points out, even the flowers of the original Eden decayed after the fall. The poem's philosophical weight, like ballast at the bottom of a hull, resides in the final stanza. For Freneau, the problem the flower brings into focus is that the inevitability of death seems to call into question the value of life. Consolation arises from the thought that life is, as it were, a free lunch. Sunshine and water made the honeysuckle; the honeysuckle itself invested nothing in its life. Thus, the poem's philosophical conclusion: "If nothing once, you nothing lose." Life may be, as Vladimir Nabokov maintained, but a crack between two eternal darknesses, but it is still something—the opportunity of existence. Death in no way mitigates the value of life for Freneau, nor does he feel compelled to look to the promise of an afterlife to redeem life's value. The fact that one has the opportunity to exist at all should be sufficient. Freneau hung a heavy moral on his frail flower, and by doing so, he initiated a type of poem that would be much imitated in subsequent American verse. Other early American poems that move from a concrete symbolic image drawn from nature—usually, as here, a flower—to an abstract conclusion include Freneau's own "On Observing a Large Red-Streak Apple," William Cullen Bryant's "The Yellow Violet" and "To the Fringed Gentian," Ralph Waldo Emerson's "The Rhodora," and Oliver Wendell Holmes's "The Chambered Nautilus."

Among these poems, "To the Fringed Gentian" (1829) also concerns the nature of life and death. Bryant's poem closely follows Freneau's model: the poet apostrophizes the flower; the bulk of the poem is descriptive; and the final stanza draws out an abstract moral. In this case, Bryant selects a late-blooming flower, which comes to symbolize a hopeful manner of greeting one's death. "To the Fringed Gentian" was preceded in Bryant's output by a weightier poem on the themes of life and death: the meditative "Thanatopsis" (1814, rev. 1821), one of the poet's best-known works and a veritable anthology of conventional yet significant ideas about life and death. The original version of the poem (lines 17–73 of the revised version) offers a stoic vision of death's significance. A "still voice" tells us of life's inescapable transience: we shall all, soon enough, become a part again of the inanimate. The only consolation we can find is in the universality of death, the great equalizer that amends the social discrepancies between kings and peasants. Democratically, all are brought low. Bryant then turns his attention to the vast numbers of the dead. The earth he depicts is the sepulchre of humanity, a tomb housing corpses that far outnumber the living. Everywhere one goes, the dead are underfoot. Life is thus but an endless procession toward the grave. The reader can take comfort in the fact that all who survive her or him, whether they mourn or not, will eventually "be gathered by thy side"; it is our common destiny.

The introductory and concluding portions of the poem that Bryant later added soften the stern nature of his original ideas. In the first part, he offers the solaces of nature itself, much as he had in "Inscription for the Entrance to a Wood" (discussed under "Nature"). In the conclusion he enjoins the reader, as a consequence of death's inevitability, to live fully. Both by discussing nature's consolations and by turning to the old theme of *carpe diem* (or seize the day), Bryant partially shifts the poem's focus from death to life. Likewise, the new final image, of the figure who prepares to lie down "to pleasant dreams," perhaps, in an oblique manner, offers something that Bryant had formerly withheld: the hope of an afterlife. "Dreams," in this context, are a common enough metaphor for immortality: one thinks of Hamlet worrying about "what dreams may come / When we have shuffled off this mortal coil." Through his revision, Bryant may have softened the impact of his original verses, but he expanded the range of this sturdy poem of ideas.

One of the most positive (and popular) statements ever issued by an American poet on the themes of life and death, Henry Wadsworth Longfellow's didactic "A Psalm of Life" (1838), subtitled "What the Heart of the Young Man Said to the Psalmist," is intended as an optimistic counterstatement to the pessimistic views of life articulated in portions of the Hebrew Bible—notably in Psalms (e.g., 103 and 104) and Ecclesiastes. Longfellow demands to be free from "mournful numbers" (i.e., verses) that proclaim "Life is but an empty dream." Instead, he wants a more positive philosophy, which he articulates in the poem's most famous and oft-quoted lines: "Life is real! Life is earnest! / And the grave is not its goal." The poet then seeks to mitigate Yahweh's severe admonishment to Adam and Eve in Genesis: "For dust thou art, and unto dust shalt thou return." (Even more proverbial is the related phrase from The Book of Common Prayer: "ashes to ashes, dust to dust.") Longfellow, invoking the doctrine of the soul's immortality, claims that these words were "not spoken of the soul" but only of the body. The poem does not, however, come to rest with the idea of heaven's consolation. It principally concerns this life rather than the next, focusing neither on eternal rewards nor punishments, but on action in the real world. Longfellow paraphrases the great Roman poet Horace to the effect that art is long, but time is short; in other words, there is little time to know or accomplish much in this life, but one must strive to the best of one's abilities. Again with Horace in mind, Longfellow develops, as Bryant had in his revision of "Thanatopsis," what amounts to a *carpe diem* philosophy. He advises the reader to "act in the living Present!" This notion is developed not as a defense of hedonism but within the moral scope of a monotheist ideology ("Heart within, and God o'erhead"). To buttress his notions about how to conduct one's life, Longfellow appeals to the great men of the past, who show us that with sufficient talent and diligence, one can leave behind "Footprints on the sands of time," which may serve as inspiration to the lives of others. The poem concludes by advising the reader to learn both industry and patience.

The taut, disciplined form of the sonnet often brought out the best in Longfellow, and he produced a more incisive poem concerned with life and death with his sonnet "Mezzo Cammin," subtitled "Written at Boppard on the Rhine, August 25, 1842, Just before Leaving for Home" (1842). The poem's title is drawn from the classic first line of Dante's *Inferno*: "Nel mezzo del cammin di nostra vita" [In the middle of our life's journey]. When Longfellow wrote the poem, he was thirty-five, or half the equivalent of his biblical allotment of seventy years—thus, he begins the poem "Half of my life is gone." Just as he would take Milton's sonnet "Methought I Saw" as a kind of model for the poignant sonnet he wrote on the death of his wife—"The Cross of Snow" (discussed under "Loss")—so here he echoes an early Milton sonnet, "How Soon Hath Time," which likewise expresses a poet's dissatisfaction with his achievements up to the present moment. Longfellow laments that he has as yet not fulfilled the promise of his gifts by producing a "tower of song," or presumably an epic poem of the stature of those by Dante and Milton. Although it would not be Longfellow's fate to achieve such splendor, we are acutely aware that Longfellow is setting the bar very high for himself indeed, which is of course admirable if not always completely realistic. After assessing his achievement and documenting his aspirations in the first quatrain, Longfellow identifies the cause of his alleged failure in the second quatrain. It is not "indolence" or "pleasure" or "restless passions" that have held him back, but rather "a care that almost killed," which probably refers to the death of his first wife in 1835. The sonnet's sestet then translates the abstract concern with achievement into the more physical and concrete terms of height by developing a metaphor of life as an ascent up the side of a hill. The past lies beneath the poet, like a city gleaming in the twilight, while the future, with its ultimate promise of death, stands above him, a reminder that we have only one life in which to achieve our goals. At this midpoint of the climb, Longfellow attempts to come to terms with death's inevitability, even as he hopes to strive for greater achievements in life.

Canonical American poems that focus on the proper conduct of life, such as "A Psalm of Life," are less numerous than those concerned with the inevitability of death, as not only "Mezzo Cammin" but also the next several examples serve to demonstrate. Less various than "Thanatopsis" but as stern as that poem's original core, Ralph Waldo Emerson's "Hamatreya" (1847, rev. 1876) mocks the pretensions of men who claim to possess the earth. Emerson adapted his title from "Maitreya," the name of a character in the Vishnu Purana, an ancient Hindu scripture that inspired the poem. Emerson divides "Hamatreya" into two parts, the second of which—titled "Earth-Song"—is a monologue spoken by the earth itself. The poem's first line names the historic settlers of Concord, Massachusetts, Emerson's home. (In the 1876 version, Emerson added a more personal dimension to the poem by changing the first two names, "Minott, Lee" to "Bulkeley, Hunt." Peter Bulkeley was one of the poet's own ancestors.) The land renders to the Concord farmers' toil various yields, which inspire in the farmers proprietary attitudes. But the farmers of that earlier time are all dead now. The earth is not theirs: they can steer the plough, "but cannot steer their feet / Clear of the grave." The owners seek to add ever more to their lands, but death eventually adds them to the land. The earth then asks where the old men are, for it has never seen one—at least not in the sense that it understands "old." The sea, the shores, the valleys, and the stars are old, for their ages may be measured in millions or even billions of years; but men perish, in the earth's patient, long-enduring eyes, with the rapidity of foam in a flood. Soon enough, the men who claim to hold the earth come to be held by it instead. The poem concludes with a chastened, first-person response to the "Earth-Song." The poem calls for a new sense of humility and perspective, one rooted in a full appreciation for how brief the span of mortal life is on a cosmic scale of time.

Freneau, Bryant, and Emerson philosophize about death, but Emily Dickinson seeks to convey the intensity of death itself. Often thought to be the quintessential poet of death, Dickinson is well represented in anthologies by numerous poems on that theme. One of the most famous, "I heard a Fly buzz—when I died—(#465, c. 1862) documents the uncertainty of the moment of death itself. The speaker, who seems to communicate from beyond the grave (or simply by the artifice of poetry), recounts the last moments of her existence. The opening stanzas are pregnant with expectation. A stillness grips the room, like the eye of a hurricane between the storms of life and the anticipated afterlife. Around the dying figure, family and friends, conjured up merely by the synecdoche of "Eyes," wait—as conventional nineteenth-century Calvinists did—for a sign that her soul will be saved. They—and perhaps the speaker as well—expect "the King" (i.e., God) to be witnessed somehow in the room. The speaker has made out her will, and now waits to discover what will happen to the "portion" of her that is not "Assignable." Into this solemn atmosphere a fly, unexpectedly, comes buzzing. It is the speaker's only sign of what awaits her in death. She looks, apparently, to the "Blue" of the sky, an emblem of heaven's promise, but the fly comes between her and the light, distracting her attention at this all-important moment. And then it is too late. The "Windows failed" (i.e., the light and the blue seem to fade as the speaker's consciousness departs) and still there is no sign from God. The speaker "could not see to see," or could not perceive in order to understand. She dies without certainty, and we are left only with the image of the fly. In religious terms, the fly can be associated with the devil, "the lord of the flies," and therefore with damnation rather than salvation. In strictly materialist terms, the fly is a reminder of the body's decay and, thus, the possibility of death's finality. Instead of offering certainty, the poem documents a moment of ambiguity. We are offered no assurances—only the irony of the speaker's efforts to focus on eternity being interrupted by the appearance of the fly.

Another celebrated Dickinson poem about the moment of passing, "Because I could not stop for Death—" (#712, c. 1863) personifies death as a kind of gentleman caller. The speaker of the poem did not have time for him, so he "kindly" stopped for her—a highly ironic description, since she had no choice in the matter. When Death calls, he cannot be refused. The speaker climbs into the carriage with him and the hope-inspiring personification of immortality. Stanzas two through five describe the journey from her home to the graveyard. Death drives slowly, and the speaker herself is in no hurry, for she has "put away" her work and her leisure—again, the description is ironic, for she had no choice in the matter. She sees children engaged in rather fierce play (perhaps a reminder of her own youth), fields of grain (perhaps a symbol of life's continuous cycles), and the setting sun (a common emblem of death). As the night comes on, the speaker feels the dews, "quivering and chill," an omen of her cold interment in the ground. The carriage arrives at the "House," which, as the description clearly indicates, is actually the speaker's grave, her home for eternity. The last section, spoken centuries later, tells of how time is meaningless in eternity, as the narrator presumably waits hopefully for the Resurrection, which may or may not be the reward of her eternal vigil. Readers interested in Dickinson's handling of death as a literary theme should also consult, in particular, "Dust is the only Secret—" (#153), "Safe in their Alabaster Chambers—" (#216), "A Clock stopped—" (#287), "I died for Beauty—but was scarce" (#449), and "Death is the supple Suitor" (#1445), along with the Dickinson poems discussed in this guide under the themes of "Loss" and "Suffering & Joy."

No poet after Dickinson attains the intensity or universality of her best death poems. Nonetheless, significant and persuasive poems documenting particular lives and deaths were produced by such poets as Edgar Lee Masters, Edwin Arlington Robinson, and Robert Frost. "Lucinda Matlock" (1915) by Masters and its companion piece, "Davis Matlock," are portraits of the poet's paternal grandparents, Lucinda and Davis Masters. Both poems appeared in the poet's most famous collection, *Spoon River*

Anthology, in which Masters employed Emily Dickinson's artifice of having narrators speak from beyond the grave. "Lucinda Matlock" is not an expression of woe over the loss of a loved one, but rather a brief meditation on the conduct of life. Lucinda tells us of how she met Davis and how they were married for seventy years. As was common among families in the days before such modern medical innovations as antibiotics and vaccines, the Matlocks had many children, of which only four of twelve survived by the time Lucinda reached sixty. Her life, all ninety-six years of it, was almost entirely spent in work and duty, but she enjoyed its simple pleasures and found it to be wholesome and fulfilling. In short, her life exemplified the conventional ideals set forth in Longfellow's "Psalm of Life." At the end of her monologue, Lucinda has hard words for a younger generation that seems, by comparison with the frugal industry of her own, degenerate and dissipated.

At the opposite end of the spectrum from Lucinda's ideas about living life with stoic discipline lies the possibility of suicide. Undoubtedly, the most famous suicide in American poetry is committed by the enigmatic title character of Edwin Arlington Robinson's "Richard Cory" (1896). The common city folk introduce us to Cory, their social and economic opposite, "a gentleman from sole to crown," "imperially slim," and "richer than a king." Like the storied "robber barons" of the late nineteenth century, such as John D. Rockefeller, Andrew Carnegie, and J. P. Morgan, Cory has amassed a fortune that outshines those of the European despots of yore. This aristocrat of a democratic age walked and "glittered" among his fellow mortals like a demigod, for he represented the very embodiment of the American dream. Robinson's poem, however, is no Horatio Alger story, extolling the gospel of wealth and the infinite financial possibilities available to a man of good character—quite the reverse, in fact. Robinson chooses to examine the underbelly of the American dream, the emptiness and despair at the heart of unbridled materialism. The people think that Cory "was everything / To make us wish that we were in his place"—but this illusion is shattered when "one calm summer night" Cory puts a gun to his head. Because of the poem's point of view, the precise reasons for this suicide remain shrouded in mystery, the significant thing being not why it happened but simply that it did. The narrators may envy Cory and may go at times without meat, but their solidarity, their striving, and their capacity for wonder are, perhaps, worth far more, in human terms, than Cory's fortune. In an oblique way, the poem addresses the things that sustain life and the consequences of their absence.

Robinson dramatizes a double suicide in an even stronger and bleaker poem, "The Mill" (1920). The poem's three stanzas correspond with three separate tableaux. The point of view, this time, hovers over the poem's central figure, the miller's wife, who has followed her usual routine of preparing the fire and the tea for her husband's imminent return from the mill. From all indications, she clearly expects nothing unusual to happen on this particular night. The miller's predictable timetable, however, has been disrupted, and the wife is left to ponder dark thoughts about what that fact might signify. Brooding, she recalls a curious episode that transpired in the morning. He had made a troubling statement before he left—"There are no millers any more." Uttered by a miller, whose very presence was a contradiction, the statement was a paradox. An awkward moment had followed, as he "had lingered at the door," and the wife, apparently, had not known precisely what he meant or how to respond. He left, and the incident appears to have been forgotten—until long after he should have come back. At this point, it suddenly becomes worrisome. This troubled moment begins the compressed narrative.

After the exposition of the first stanza, the second flashes forward. The miller's wife, her impatience and fears having gotten the better of her, has gone to the mill herself. The first thing that greets her there is the "warm / And mealy fragrance of the past," a reminder of a time when the mill was productive and prosperous. Those times, as the miller's comment already made evident, are long past. The full meaning of his words, however, only becomes apparent when the wife happens upon his dead body swinging from a beam. The image says "again what he had meant," only this time its meaning is not paradoxical. If we read the poem literally, the last old-style miller has just killed himself. The final stanza takes us to the weir (or dam) of the mill, where the miller's wife reasons "in the dark" (which refers both to the time of day and to her state of mind). She decides that the "one way of the few there were" (i.e., to kill herself) that will be acceptable is to drown herself in the reflecting water. The conditional tense ("would") creates an ambiguity in the conclusion: the poem may be read as ending either after she has made up her mind to kill herself or after she has already taken the plunge.

The poem compresses a tragic narrative into twenty-four somewhat opaque lines. Why does the miller kill himself? As he tells us, millers no longer exist. The poem can be seen as a parable about the transformation of the American economy in the industrial age. Family-operated mills became anachronisms in the face of the burgeoning factory system. Robinson universalizes the miller's plight by withholding his name. His identity was wholly bound up with his occupation. Likewise, the "miller's wife" is never identified as anything more than that. Even though Robinson wrote the poem in a year when women took an immense stride toward equality by claiming the vote, the poem concerns an earlier time, when such a woman as the miller's wife would have been fully dependent on her husband's income. While others may have been celebrating the triumphs of industry and society, Robinson, characteristically, focused his attention on the toll that the new economy exacted from those who were unable to adapt to its demands. As in "Mr. Flood's Party" (discussed under "Time & Change"), and many other poems his interest fastened on forgotten lives that slip through the cracks while most other eyes are directed elsewhere.

Death and forgetfulness also figure in Robert Frost's grim poem, " 'Out, Out—' " (1916). The title—taken from one of the greatest passages in English poetry, Macbeth's magnificent soliloquy (*Macbeth* 5.5.17–28)—alludes to the fleeting nature of existence. Life, according to Macbeth, is as abrupt as a brief candle and as meaningless as a tale told by an idiot: these ideas supply the context for our consideration of the tragedy that unfolds on a Vermont farm. The poem begins by shifting its focus from the sound of a boy's buzz saw, which snarls like a wildcat and rattles like a rattlesnake, to five mountain ranges under a sunset (an appropriate image of decline). The wider context afforded by the mountains seems to emphasize the relative triviality of the poem's human drama. The world, in all its splendor and enormity, remains utterly indifferent to what may happen to any individual. Almost cinematically, the poem "cuts" back from the sunset to the saw again, still vehement at the end of a workday. The day, however, as the poem's speaker notes, does not end soon enough. As the boy is about to retire for supper, the saw strikes out like a pit viper at the boy's hand. The narrator, however, retreats from this initial personification into ambiguity: the boy, he rationally decides, "must have given the hand." Either way, the boy's hand has been lost. Pathetically, after an uncanny laugh indicating shock and surprise, the boy holds up the hand "to keep / The life from spilling," but it is too late. Even the doctor cannot save him. What perhaps shocks more than the accident and the sudden death is the family's reaction: "they, since they / Were not the one dead, turned to their affairs." The poem ends abruptly at this point. We are left to decide for ourselves whether the family's stoicism represents a healthy response to death or mere callous indifference. Or perhaps protracted mourning is simply a luxury that a hard-working rural family cannot afford. The poem's purpose seems less to judge the family's reaction than to provoke the reader to think about how the living should respond to death.

On its surface, Wallace Stevens's "The Emperor of Ice-Cream" (1923) appears to be one of the most peculiar and enigmatic of anthologized American poems; nonetheless, thematically, it is closely related to " 'Out, Out—.' " The poem juxtaposes two somewhat bizarre scenes, presented in the form of imperative statements by the narrator. The speaker first bids his listener (or listeners) to summon a roller of cigars and to allow certain "wenches" and boys to do as they please. The imagery of the first stanza suggests something of the voluptuousness of existence: the cigar roller is "muscular"; he is to whip "concupiscent [lustful] curds"; wenches "dawdle"; the boys will bring flowers rolled in newspaper. The second stanza stands in antithetical relation to the first. Instead of the many vibrant figures of the first stanza, we confront the corpse of a single woman. The woman's feet, said to be "horny" (i.e., callused), "show how cold she is, and dumb" (i.e., silent). The listener apparently receives two instructions: to cover the corpse with a sheet, which the woman herself had embroidered, and to turn on the lamp, which will starkly illuminate the corpse. The two scenes can be thought of as taking place in adjacent rooms of the same house, a hypothesis that the boy's flowers—quite possibly a tribute to the dead—tempt one to entertain. Together, the scenes show us life going on in all its animation right beside the presence of death. The conclusion Stevens draws from this juxtaposition ends both stanzas and gives the poem its title: "The only emperor is the emperor of ice cream." The line suggests that the only viable ruling principle of life is what ice cream represents (enjoyment, sustenance). On its second appearance, after the presentation of the corpse, it may also suggest something about the transience of life, for the ice cream will inevitably melt. The implication seems clear: one must seize the moment and live life to its fullest, before it vanishes. Stevens almost jokingly—and obliquely—presents a powerful and rather hedonistic idea: that life's proper object is enjoyment, not death. Death may be inevitable, but it should not cast a pall on the vitality of the living moment. The living, as in Frost's much sterner poem, must get on with their lives.

Another poem that subtly contrasts life and death, John Crowe Ransom's "Piazza Piece" (1925) inventively uses the two-part sonnet form as a pair of dramatic monologues spoken by an old gentleman and an attractive young woman he apparently hopes to seduce. The poem seems to present a comedy of mismatched expectations; but close inspection reveals a darker meaning. In fact, courtship, as in Dickinson's "Because I could not stop for Death—," functions here as a metaphor for mortality. The key lines that suggest an allegorical reading are 5 and 6. The old gentleman first calls attention to the roses dying on the woman's trellis. One could construe his words as a *carpe diem* plea in the manner of such seventeenth-century seduction poems as Andrew Marvell's "To His Coy Mistress," but something more troubling emerges when in the next line he invokes "the spectral singing of the moon." The two images of mortality, combined with the woman's dim apprehension of his words, imply that the old man is in fact a personification of death, inexorably stalking this rather idealistic maiden. When he says he "must have" her, sexual possession has become a trope for the grim reaper's harvesting. For her part, the woman is not contemplating time's wingéd chariot, but pining for a "truelove" whom time, apparently, will never afford her the luxury of meeting. She willfully ignores the possibility of death until the moment when he uncannily seems to emerge from her trellis. We leave her as she makes an empty threat of screaming and desperately, futilely reiterates her identity, as if somehow the force of her words could help her cling to it at the very instant it is about to slip away. Ransom's commentary on unpreparedness for death's inevitability includes the darkly humorous touch that Death himself appears in a "dustcoat," as if to protect himself from his own work of returning what came from dust back to dust again.

Life and death are by no means the exclusive province of the human world, as poets whose imaginations have not been confined by the boundaries of civilization—such as Robinson Jeffers, William Carlos Williams, and Mary Oliver—remind us. In the drama of their poetry, the lives and deaths of animals assume an importance equal to those of humans. In an overcivilized and overpopulated world, in which human birth and death transpire mostly in sanitized hospitals, the lives of animals, in fact, present themselves to the poetic imagination as purer and more elemental exemplifications of these universal themes. At the same time, evolutionary theory has taught poets to regard animals as next of kin, thus making their lives and deaths more poignant.

Jeffers, who advocated a philosophical position he dubbed "inhumanism," describes the life and death of a hawk in what is perhaps his most powerful lyric, "Hurt Hawks" (1928). Jeffers does not specify how the hawk was injured, only that its wing has been reduced to a "broken pillar." The hawk waits for death, as it slowly starves under an oak bush. The carrion creatures come each day to torment the hawk, but are still afraid to approach too closely. Only at night does the hawk escape from its incapacity by dreaming of its former freedom. This association with dreams serves as a prelude to an association between the hawk and supernatural power. The hawk, claims the poet, stands closer to God than "communal people." Jeffers rejects the schema of orthodox religion for a more primal conception of God as one who still communes with the earth's wildness.

The poem's second section opens with Jeffers's confession that he would rather—"except the penalties"—kill a man than a hawk. The hawk's "unable misery," however, compels him to take action. Jeffers had kept the hawk alive for six weeks by feeding it, but as the hawk prefers death to an aimless existence, the poet shoots the bird at twilight. The final images of the poem contrast the hawk in death and life. "Unsheathed from reality," in Jeffers's powerful metaphoric phrase, it has become only a bundle of soft feathers. Alive, its merest rising had inspired terror in even the larger birds, such as the night herons by the "flooded river" (an image that, by way of allusion to Noah's story, would seem to buttress the first section's claim about God's wildness). Jeffers evokes the hawk's terrible vitality in life most palpably through the vigorous enjambment of lines 25–26. The emphatic initial stress on "Soared" expresses the poem's central purpose: to impress upon readers a sense of the hawk's majestic wildness.

Jeffers's "Vulture" (1954) looks not to the vulture's death but to the poet's own. Jeffers recounts how he lay down near the ocean and his prone form attracted the attention of a vulture, who inspected him as possible carrion. Jeffers plays along until the huge bird hovers so close he can see its red head (which indicates it is a turkey vulture rather than a black vulture; these are the only two vulture species in North America). Then he speaks, and the bird flies off, in search of nourishment elsewhere. Jeffers, rather unexpectedly, "solemnly" regrets having disappointed the vulture. Being devoured by the bird, becoming a part of its wings and eyes, seems to him a "sublime end"—or, as he strikingly puts it, "an enskyment." This idea of perpetuating one's own being in the life of a different species may stem, in part, from Walt Whitman, who in the conclusion of his *Song of Myself* bequeaths himself to the dirt to grow anew as grass. Jeffers creates a variation on this idea of organic immortality, one directly recalling the practice of certain Buddhist monks and Parsees, whose remains have traditionally been left for carrion birds to consume. For both Jeffers and Whitman, immortality is material rather than spiritual. What indisputably survives our death is not an immortal "spirit," separate from the body, but rather the organic atoms of the body, recycled among living things, as Aldo Leopold memorably depicts in his imaginative essay "Odyssey" from *A Sand County Almanac*. Whitman, Jeffers, and Leopold all celebrate the ecological balances that promise a productive, if perhaps unsettling, immortality to us all.

Immortality is also very much at issue in J. V. Cunningham's "The Phoenix" (1947). Instead of taking for his subject an actual bird, like a hawk or a vulture, Cunningham ponders the legendary Arabian bird that destroys itself every five hundred years and then rises back to life from its ashes. The phoenix has traditionally been viewed as a triumphant symbol of resurrection, as in the Old English "Phoenix" and Shakespeare's "The Phoenix and Turtle"; but in Cunningham's poem, its elusive, mythical nature calls into question the tantalizing possibility of survival after death. If the bird is a myth, so might be what it represents. The poem's first stanza depicts the attributes of the mythical bird. More than ash survives its destruction, and nowhere is there a pyre so hot that it can permanently destroy the bird. But a hint of the poem's ultimately skeptical position obtrudes as Cunningham focuses next on the paradoxical aspects of the legend: the infinite regression that is the phoenix's life, the varying consistency of the phoenix's fire, and, in a clever play on words, the fact that the bird's burying is also a bearing. A shift from legend to personal experience comes with the twice-repeated clause "I have not found you" in stanza two, which suggests that the immortality the bird represents cannot be discerned in the world of the senses. Instead, the poet finds only mutability, symbolized by frosty breath, blowing snow, and a graveyard: all frigid images that suggest the finality of death. The phoenix and all the potentiality it represents hover over the scene, "singing there without sound"—another paradox suggesting that the desire for immortality is a phantom of the mind rather than a fact of existence. The poem leaves us not with the fiery embers of immortality but with the "crystal embers" of the snow, which seem to cancel the promise of the legend. In Cunningham's severe vision, immortality, however desirable and psychologically comforting a concept, appears to be illusory, a triumph of hope over reason and evidence.

We return to an actual bird in William Carlos Williams's spritely poem "The Sparrow" (1955), which, in contrast to Jeffers's bird poems, presents a bird's life and death with only tangential reference to any sort of human presence. Williams communicates the familiar house sparrow's vitality with the zigzagging of his lines and the exuberance of his language. As in his better-known poems about a wet wheelbarrow and plundered plums, the poet remains true to his democratic temperament by selecting for his subject not a conventionally "poetic" bird, like a hawk or a thrush, but one generally taken for granted and often considered a nuisance. By keenly observing its characteristics and habits, Williams shows the reader that the sparrow is a far more lively and interesting character than most would think. The poem, composed of brief vignettes, focuses on various aspects of the bird's life: the way it deals with lice, how men flee before its multitudinous flocks, its image, its lovemaking, and how a female sparrow once caught a male far above the city streets. The episodes range widely from generalities true of all house sparrows to singular episodes, bits of natural history viewed by the poet. Williams, thus, conveys something of the life of the species and something of the life of particular individuals (and note that the poem's title also refers both to the species and to a specific individual). The final vignette focuses on the death of the particular sparrow Williams had been observing at his window. He finds its flattened body, which, in the poet's mind, endures as an emblem of the bird's practical and energetic—and therefore, for Williams, thoroughly poetic—existence. The poem challenges the notion that such an existence is not worthy or remarkable.

Examples of significant twentieth-century American poems on the lives and deaths of animals could be multiplied further: one might think, particularly, of Louise Bogan's "The Dragonfly," Richard Eberhart's "For a Lamb" and "The Groundhog," Stanley Kunitz's "The Wellfleet Whale" (discussed under "Loss"), Robert Penn Warren's "Red-Tail Hawk and Pyre of Youth," Elizabeth Bishop's "The Armadillo" (discussed under "Nature"), and Richard Wilbur's "The Death of a Toad." But modern poets did not, of course, cease to write about human lives and deaths. "We Real Cool" (1960) by Gwendolyn Brooks takes a brief, hard look at life and death in urban America. The lives of the seven pool players who collectively narrate the poem represent a triumph of style over substance. The stylized "coolness" of the players is mirrored by the poem's unusual composition, in terms of both point of view and enjambment. The "We" that hangs at the end of each line (except, notably, the last) forces the reader to hesitate unnaturally and to emphasize both subject and verb. The pregnant pause brings out the loaded significance of each repetition of "We" and of each new line. (As an exercise, it can be useful to read the poem as if the pronouns were placed at the beginning of each line. One readily sees how much is lost in terms of tone and emphasis.) The players, as they present themselves, are dropouts, nighthawks, immoralists, and boozers. Their imminent deaths are a direct product of the destructive lifestyle they exalt. Brooks's poem allows them to damn themselves: their words sharply satirize a nihilistic youth culture in desperate need of higher goals and sustaining values.

Another contemporary poem concerned with human life and death, James Dickey's audacious "Falling" (1967) imaginatively re-creates the situation described in its epigraph, taken from a *New York Times* news story. A stewardess had been sucked by decompression through the emergency door of a plane and plummeted thousands of feet to her death in a Kansas field. Dickey saw in the event a stark reminder of human frailty but also discerned a mythical potential. The poem's opening seven lines paint the picture of an airplane speeding around the states in the night. Details about a passenger demanding coffee, trays, and a blanket almost lull the reader into a comfortable sense of the ordinary, but mention of "the vast beast-whistle of space" intimates a latent metaphysical malevolence in the scene. As the stewardess tries to pin the blanket over an unsealed door, the door suddenly blows open, and she is sucked into space. For the next 135½ lines, Dickey describes in great detail, mimicking the length of the fall itself, her terrifying descent through space. Only the desperate improbability of landing in deep water (lines 69–74) offers any hope at all. Throughout the depiction of the stewardess's fall, Dickey focuses on the superhuman perspective she is granted and on her sexuality, with particular attention to such things as position, legs, stockings, skirt, and lipstick. These two emphases presage a mythic transformation of her character, signified by the thrice-repeated word "goddess" (lines 94, 155, and 161), for as she sheds her clothing in midair, even as the fields of the farms draw inexorably closer, she becomes a kind of goddess of love, desired by all the adolescent boys and widowed farmers below. Her impact on the ground, registered by the capitalized word "THIS," violently ends her brief tenure as superhuman goddess. (Ironically, she has landed near a water tank.) The remainder of the poem describes the discovery of her remains on the ground, as her clothes rain down over the farms. As if hypnotized, the farmers are drawn toward her once-lovely corpse. With harvests imminent, she has retained a vestige of her goddesshood after all: no longer Aphrodite, she has become Demeter. The terrible sacrifice of her death stands as the necessary cyclical complement to the burgeoning life of the crops. A grim, perhaps even misogynistic poem in certain respects, "Falling" ultimately represents an appropriation of brute fact for the purpose of mythmaking.

Mary Oliver's "The Black Snake" (1979) brings into focus some important universal ideas about life and death by charting the deadly intersection of the natural world and civilization. Like Richard Wilbur's "The Death of a Toad" (1950), it concerns a wild creature inadvertently destroyed by a human mechanism—in this case, a black snake run over by a truck. Oliver focuses, initially, on the suddenness of death, conveyed in part by the placement and italicized emphasis of the word "death" itself. She also focuses on the physical appearance of the dead snake, which she likens both to an old bicycle tire and to a braided whip. The philosophical heart of the poem is the meditation on death in the last three stanzas. Reason tells us that death is certain and often sudden and unexpected, yet the irrational vitality of our own bodies seems to tell us a different story: that we, alone, are exempt from oblivion. Personal mortality, hard to fathom, disposes us to underestimate the relative fragility of our bodies. Instead, we easily succumb—especially in youth— to an utterly false assurance of invincibility. It was this very confidence, Oliver asserts, that sent the snake "coiling and flowing forward" all through the spring—and right into the road.

❦

"The Wild Honey Suckle," Philip Freneau
    AAL-1; ATL-1; ColAP; HAL-1; HoAL-1; NAL-1; NOBA; OxBA

"Thanatopsis," William Cullen Bryant
    AAL-1; APN-1; ATL-1; ColAP; HAL-1; HoAL-1; NAL-1; NOBA; OxBA; TFi

"A Psalm of Life," Henry Wadsworth Longfellow
    AAL-1; APN-1; ATL-1; HAL-1; HoAL-1; NAL-1

"Mezzo Cammin," Henry Wadsworth Longfellow
    AAL-1; APN-1; ColAP; HoAL-1

"Hamatreya," Ralph Waldo Emerson

AAL-1; APN-1; ATL-1; HAL-1; HoAL-1; LPTT; NAL-1; NOBA; OxBA

"I heard a Fly buzz—when I died—," Emily Dickinson

AAL-1; AAL-2; APN-2; ATL-2; ColAP; HAL-1; HAL-2; HoAL-2; MAP; NAL-1; NoAM; NOBA; NoP-4; SoSe-9; TFi; WeW-4

"Because I could not stop for Death—," Emily Dickinson

AAL-1; AAL-2; APN-2; ATL-2; ColAP; HAL-1; HAL-2; HoAL-2; LPTT; MAP; NAL-1; NoAM; NOBA; NoP-4; OxBA; SoSe-9; TFi; WeW-4

"Lucinda Matlock," Edgar Lee Masters

ATL-2; HoAL-2; MAP; NAL-2; NoAM; NOBA; OxBA

"Richard Cory," Edwin Arlington Robinson

AAL-2; APN-2; ATL-2; ColAP; HAL-2; HoAL-2; LPTT; MAP; NAL-2; NOBA; NoP-4; OxBA; SoSe-9; TFi

"The Mill," Edwin Arlington Robinson

APT-1; ATL-2; HAL-2; HoAL-2; MAP; NAL-2; NoAM; NoP-4; SoSe-9; WeW-4

" 'Out, Out–,' " Robert Frost

APT-1; ColAP; HoAL-2; NAL-2; OxBA; SoSe-9; VGW; WeW-4

"The Emperor of Ice-Cream," Wallace Stevens

AAL-2; APT-1; ATL-2; HCAP; HoAL-2; MAP; NAL-2; NOBA; NoP-4; OxBA; TFi

"Piazza Piece," John Crowe Ransom

AAL-2; APT-1; ColAP; HAL-2; HoAL-2; NAL-2; NoAM; NOBA; NoP-4; OxBA; TFi

"Hurt Hawks," Robinson Jeffers

AAL-2; APT-1; ColAP; HAL-2; HoAL-2; MAP; NAL-2; NoAM; NOBA; NoP-4; OxBA; TFi

"Vulture," Robinson Jeffers

APT-1; MAP; NAL-2; NoAM; NOBA

"The Phoenix," J. V. Cunningham

NoAM [1st ed., 1973]

"The Sparrow," William Carlos Williams

ATL-2; VGW

"We Real Cool," Gwendolyn Brooks

AAL-2; ATL-2; CAPP-6; HoAL-2; MAP; NAL-2; NoP-4; SoSe-9; TFi; WeW-4

"Falling," James Dickey
    MAP; NAL-2; NoAM
"The Black Snake," Mary Oliver
    NAL-2

LOSS

ख़्र्ज

The losses I encountered at the Bear River Migratory Bird Refuge as
Great Salt Lake was rising helped me to face the losses within my
family. When most people had given up on the Refuge, saying the
birds were gone, I was drawn further into its essence. In the same
way that when someone is dying many retreat, I chose to stay.

Terry Tempest Williams, *Refuge*

No event precipitates more powerful emotions than the loss of something dear to us. Time and change promise the inevitability of loss, but
rational apprehension of this fact rarely spares us emotional pain when
we are confronted by the actuality of loss. We think we know of what
Hamlet calls "the thousand natural shocks / That flesh is heir to," but
the death of a friend or a loved one often cruelly exposes the gap between that which we claim to understand and that with which we are
prepared to deal. Does knowing that approximately one hundred billion
humans have already lived and died on this planet, or that an average
of 164,300 people die each day prepare us to face the mortality of those
we love? Much of the world's finest poetry has been written in response
to loss, out of a desire to offer tribute to the departed, to protest against
fate, or to produce some "immortal" thing as compensation for the disappearance of something mortal. The elegiac impulse is as strong in
American poetry as in any national poetry.

Edgar Allan Poe, in his essay "The Philosophy of Composition,"
claimed that the death of a beautiful woman was "the most poetical topic
in the world." This belief led directly to the composition of his two most
famous poems, "The Raven" (1845) and "Annabel Lee" (1849), as well
as to such lesser works as "Lenore," "The Sleeper," "To One in Paradise,"

and "Ulalume: A Ballad." Both "The Raven" and "Annabel Lee" are dramatic monologues spoken by the bereaved and somewhat deranged lover of a beautiful woman. Both poems vividly dramatize the dark side of the psychology of loss. In "The Raven," the studious but somnolent protagonist, seeking solace from the death of his beloved Lenore, is disturbed by ceaseless rapping at his chamber door. When he finally rouses himself to greet the unknown visitor, he finds only darkness. For a moment his fanciful mind entertains "dreams no mortal ever dared to dream before." What those "dreams" are becomes clear when he whispers into the darkness, "Lenore!" The speaker hopes, however irrationally, for his lover's return from beyond the grave (a scenario Poe had already depicted in the famous tale "Ligeia"). After the speaker returns to his chamber, the rapping resumes, but this time at the window. When the protagonist flings open the shutter, in flies the "stately" raven.

The raven, as apparently trained by some former master, mechanically repeats the word "Nevermore" in response to all statements, a fact that the speaker exploits for purposes of self-torture. A masochistic verbal dance ensues, as the speaker deliberately implores the unthinking bird to answer "Nevermore" to queries for which most sane persons would desperately hope to receive positive answers. The climax arrives in the sixteenth stanza, as the speaker, goaded by some personal imp of the perverse, asks if, in the afterlife, he will again clasp that "rare and radiant maiden," Lenore. He, of course, receives a negative answer, which seems to shatter his fraying nerves. After the speaker fails to drive the demoniac bird from his premises, the monologue rather uncannily shifts to the present tense for the final stanza, presumably to heighten the immediacy of the speaker's woe. The poem comes to rest on the word "nevermore," now appropriated by the disconsolate lover himself. We leave him in the bird's shadow, a fitting image suggesting that despair has eclipsed his hopes for a reunion with Lenore in this world and the next. The poem, however, is not a philosophical statement on the possibilities of the afterlife but rather a psychological dramatization of what Poe, in "The Philosophy of Composition," calls "the luxury of sorrow." Loss, the poem shows us, can engender not only legitimate grief but also self-indulgent despair. Like so many of Poe's narrators, the speaker typifies a specific kind of human pathology.

If "The Raven" suggests that death is stronger than love, "Annabel Lee," the last poem Poe ever wrote, does the reverse—although in a peculiarly disturbing manner. The poem's speaker believes that his childhood lover, the beautiful Annabel Lee, was taken from him by envious supernatural powers. The scenario—probably inspired by the death of Poe's wife, Virginia, his cousin whom he married when she was just thirteen—is a familiar one from mythology. Tempt the powers-that-be by asserting or demonstrating the superiority of some mortal attribute (in this case love), and they will exact revenge. For instance, according to one Greek myth, Marsyas, the satyr, challenged the musical skill of Apollo, lost the competition, and was summarily flayed alive. There are many such stories, and all of them seem to assert the ineluctable nature of mortal limitation. In "Annabel Lee," the speaker refuses to accept the decree of fate, which had taken the form of a chilling wind. One should note that we only have the speaker's word that this fatal wind was something other than a natural occurrence; the speaker's rhetoric—"Yes!—that was the reason (as all men know, / In this kingdom by the sea)"—smacks of grandiose rationalizing. Nonetheless, the lover's willful defiance inspires an unnatural pattern of behavior: each night, he lies at Annabel's side, inside her sepulchre. The reader is left with a rather troubling ambiguity: is love truly stronger than death, as the speaker claims, or is the speaker simply a deranged and deluded necrophiliac? Again, Poe confronts us with a desperate narrator whose brains may be more than slightly addled.

In "Telling the Bees" (1858), John Greenleaf Whittier conveys the acuity of loss by employing, as Poe had done, a first-person narrator, although there is no hint that the speaker suffers from an abnormal psychological profile. Whittier is no less interested than Poe in the toll of loss on the individual lover, but he achieves, through restraint and indirection, a more poignant effect. The poem lovingly describes the farm on which Whittier grew up, but the narrative itself is fictional and rooted in local custom and legend. In the opening stanza, a "gap in the old wall" introduces the theme of missing things, but not until the third stanza, with its image of the unweeded garden, are we given even a subtle sign that something ominous may have transpired. Any initial fears, however, appear to be placated by stanzas four and five, which emphasize continuity: "the same rose blows, and the same sun glows, / And the same brook sings of a year ago." But as we will see, the transient life of an individual cannot be gauged by this natural backdrop, with its illusions of permanence.

Starting with stanza six, the speaker recalls the events of one year earlier, as he returned home from a month's absence. As sundown forebodingly settled over Fernside farm, the narrator, as in stanzas four and five, had noted how unchanged the place seemed. But there was one significant exception then: the beehives, first glimpsed in stanza three, were each being draped with a shred of black by the small chore-girl. Suddenly, the narrator found that "the summer sun / Had the chill of snow"—for he knew how to interpret this ritual. In old rural New England, dressing the hives in mourning was a customary way of "informing" the bees of a death in the family; it was also a superstitious way of preventing them from deserting their hives for a new home. The narrator had made the unwarranted assumption that it must have been his lover's blind grandfather who had died—but then he had spied the old man on the doorway sill. The speaker had no time for further defensive hypotheses, as the chore-girl's song curtly informed him that it was his beloved Mary who had died. Whittier's decision to end the poem abruptly at this point emphasizes the shock of realization and the finality of death. We know now why the somber narrator characterizes the year that has passed since as "Heavy and slow."

Poe and Whittier present loss at the remove of a dramatic monologue, in which it is understood that the events portrayed are fictional and that the speaker is not the poet himself. Walt Whitman's grand elegy "When Lilacs Last in the Dooryard Bloom'd" (1866), on the other hand, presents the poet speaking in his own voice and responding to an actual event— the assassination of President Abraham Lincoln on April 14, 1865. Whitman had already prepared a volume of poems about the Civil War— *Drum-Taps*—but decided to delay its publication after the tragic and untimely assassination. Eventually he added four poems to the volume— three short ones, "O Captain! My Captain!" "Hush'd Be the Camps Today," and "This Dust Was Once the Man," and one long one, "When Lilacs Last in the Dooryard Bloom'd"—grouped together under the title *Memories of President Lincoln*. "O Captain! My Captain!" instantly became—and has remained—Whitman's best-known work, much to the poet's chagrin ("I'm almost sorry I ever wrote the poem," Whitman once said); but it is the far greater "When Lilacs Last in the Dooryard Bloom'd" that stands alongside Milton's "Lycidas" and Shelley's "Adonais" as one of the great elegiac poems in the language.

The elegy, which never mentions Lincoln by name, is as much about the struggle to translate grief into poetry as it is about the death that occasioned it. Three symbolic images structure the poem's sixteen sections: the lilacs, a great star in the west (i.e., the planet Venus), and a hermit thrush, who sings in a secluded swamp. Whitman focuses on the lilacs and the star in the first three sections, delaying the introduction of the thrush until section four. The lilacs, as flowers conventionally do, represent the continuity of life and the tribute of the living to the dead. The star, "fallen" and hidden by a "black murk," is an image clearly associated with Lincoln's death. The full significance of the thrush, however, does not become clear until later in the poem. In sections five through seven, Whitman describes Lincoln's coffin traveling through the land and his own initial response to the death, which is to place on the coffin a sprig from the lilac bush. As the poet acknowledges, we place flowers on coffins and graves to cover over death with life. But is this an adequate response to death? Is it not a sign of fear and of our inability to accept the inevitable? The poem goes on to sketch answers to these troubling questions.

In section nine, the thrush arrests Whitman's attention again, but again, the poet resists approaching it and prefers instead to linger in order to contemplate the star for a while longer. Symbolically, Whitman represents a psychological struggle in his own mind. His attachment to the individual star (i.e., Lincoln) prevents him from rising above the conventional, mournful response to death—represented by his use of the lilacs—to a higher, more universal conception of death—represented by the thrush's song. The struggle to formulate an adequate response to death continues in sections ten through thirteen. In section fourteen, Whitman resists the thrush's song only until he completes a panoramic inventory of the land that leads him to contemplate a symbolic "cloud ... a long black trail." Finally, he arrives at "the sacred knowledge of death" itself. At that crucial moment, he is prepared to turn his attention away from the star, to descend into the swamp (where life continually decays and is reborn in new forms), and to meet the thrush's song on its own terms. The italicized concluding portion of section fourteen represents the thrush's "carol of death," which celebrates death as a *"Dark mother"* and *"strong deliveress."* Death appears no longer as something to be covered over and hidden away, but as the central, inescapable fact of life that—because it is necessary and inevitable—should be celebrated rather than feared.

Section fifteen presents a vision of battle corpses, expanding the consideration of death from Lincoln's alone to that of the 600,000 men who perished in the war. The living continue to suffer, but the dead are at rest. Whitman seems to be implying the need for a healthier attitude toward death, one that would help to put the horrors of war and the nation's aching, demoralizing sense of loss into perspective. In the final section, Whitman completes the symbolic trajectory of the poem by formally taking leave of his opening images, the lilac and the star; yet they remain with him as "retrievements from the night," transformed by being "twined" together in his memory with the thrush's song. The thrush's song has allowed Whitman, like some Eastern mystic, to transcend his merely personal grief and to see death in a more universal light. The attitude the poem ultimately takes toward loss seems practically inhuman—or perhaps superhuman—but only because it challenges and transcends deeply ingrained Western attitudes toward death.

Emily Dickinson—one of American literature's major poets of loss—never wrote an elegy on the scale of "Lilacs," and so her complex treatment of the theme of loss has to be ascertained by looking at a number of shorter lyrics. In "I never lost as much but twice" (#49, c. 1858), she describes, in her characteristically pithy manner, the impact of the death of loved ones on herself, the compensation of having new generations to love, and the inevitable loss of them as well. The poet is reduced to "a beggar / Before the door of God!" who waits for "Angels" to reimburse her store (by "descending" and bringing new souls for her to love).

Here, God is not only the traditional "Father" but also, in a pair of startling metaphors, a "Burglar" (who steals away loved ones) and a "Banker" (who keeps the accounts of life and death): he gives with one hand and takes away with the other. Another equally brief and incisive poem, "The Bustle in a House" (#1078, c. 1866) describes the aftermath of the death of a family relation. This "Bustle," the most solemn of human activities, involves "Sweeping up the Heart / And putting Love away" until the hoped-for reunion in "Eternity."

A more substantial and particularized poem about loss, "The last Night that She lived" (#1100, c. 1866), inspired by the death of Laura Dickey, the daughter of Dickinson's neighbors, examines how death "Made Nature different" to those who waited upon and cared for the dying person. The perceptions of the mourners are altered, so that "Things overlooked before" appear "Italicized." Suddenly, the mourners, waiting in silence for the inevitable, feel guilty for the continuity of their own lives in the face of the dying one's irrevocable extinction. Dickinson registers the moment of death itself with a striking simile: "lightly as a Reed / Bent to the Water," the young woman expires. The survivors are left to tend the corpse and to live on in "awful leisure" after completing what the earlier poem had called the "Bustle." The poem ends on this note, raising questions about the power of belief to cope in the face of death's reality.

A brief poem whose date of composition is unknown, "My life closed twice before its close" (#1732) is similar, in some respects, to "I never lost as much but twice" in its language, although it focuses on the author's own death as well as the painful deaths of loved ones. Its brilliant concluding lines serve as a powerful, shrewd, and skeptical summation of Dickinson's treatment of the theme of loss: "Parting is all we know of heaven, / And all we need of hell."

Yet another Dickinson poem, "The Frost of Death was on the Pane—" (#1136, c. 1869) records a struggle against death and its aftermath. The speaker, a friend or relation of a dying woman, or "Flower," records the metaphorical threat presented by the "Frost of Death," which issues a hostile challenge to the Flower's loved ones: " 'Secure your Flower,' said he." Halfway through this highly compressed first stanza, the metaphors shift rather violently, and the loved ones are represented as sailors fighting against a mortal leak in their vessel. They invoke all the regenerative agencies that nature could offer a flower: water ("Sea"), earth ("Mountain"), sunlight ("Sun"), but the Frost inexorably approaches. When they attempt to interpose themselves, Death, metamorphosing into yet another form, eludes them like a snake, an image that evokes the serpent from the Garden of Eden, whose actions, according to the standard interpretation of Genesis, introduced mortality into the world. The Flower dies, perhaps in agony, "all her helpless beauty bent," and the living are left to chafe in their futile frustration. They pursue Death, like some hunted wild creature, back to his "Ravine" and even to his "Den," but they have no hope of catching him. Instead, they turn back, cursing the blatant injustice of both life and death. Their sense of loss expands from a personal to a cosmic level. In its conclusion, the poem swells, like an organ adagio, with ineffable sorrow. The loved ones have discovered something larger than a sea or a continent: their own inconsolable woe.

Henry Wadsworth Longfellow's "The Cross of Snow" (1879, pub. 1886) gives such direct utterance to personal grief that the poet elected not to publish the sonnet in his lifetime. Ironically, given Longfellow's extreme popularity in his day, the poem has come to be one of his most highly regarded works. It commemorates Longfellow's second wife, Frances Appleton, who, despite the poet's valiant efforts to save her, perished in a fire in 1861. The poem was written on the eighteenth anniversary of her death, at which time Longfellow's muffled grief must have been ready to spill out in long-contemplated words. Longfellow draws upon two main sources of inspiration, which make a somewhat unlikely pair: the poetry of Milton and an image from the American West. The sonnet's octave distantly recalls Milton's masterful sonnet "Methought I Saw," another poem of tribute to a deceased wife. Longfellow, who composed his poem in the very room where his wife had died, depicts himself as an insomniac gazing at the portrait of his departed wife. Like Milton, he recalls the purity of his wife's soul, which "through martyrdom of fire was led / To its repose." In the sestet, however, he strikes away from Milton's example and appropriates, for personal use, an image that had come to stand, in the popular imagination, for the divine sanction of westward expansion: a cross of snow, formed by deep ravines, discovered on the side of a mountain in Colorado. In Longfellow's poem, the unmelting cross of snow represents the chill of grief that afflicts the poet's heart even after eighteen years. Implicitly, the poem asserts that the only release from such intense grief is death; but, unlike Milton's sonnet, it offers no explicitly hopeful intimation of an otherworldly reunion. Loss is simply a wound that never heals. The poet confronts this prospect without the psychological evasions that Poe's narrators evince and without the philosophical transcendence of Whitman.

One of Herman Melville's finest poems is the uncharacteristically delicate and restrained "Monody" (1891), usually thought to be a lament for Melville's old friend and fellow writer Nathaniel Hawthorne, who had died in 1864. The title "Monody," one should note, refers to a genre of poetry—a dirge, or a lament spoken by a single voice. The first stanza recounts the frustration Melville still feels at having been faultlessly estranged from his friend at the time of his death. Hawthorne and Melville had been close in the early 1850s, and Melville's wild letters to Hawthorne in 1851 rank among the great documents of American literature. The two authors, however, were not destined to be so close again: they met infrequently in later years and not at all in the last eight years of Hawthorne's life. The only solace from the loss of his friend that Melville can find is in the composition of his poem. He closes the first stanza by reminding us, explicitly, of how writing poetry can be a therapeutic act. The second stanza, imagistic in character, substantially contrasts with the first. Melville employs a series of winter images, conventionally associated with mortality, to portray death as a smothering presence. His friend's "hermit-mound" stands surrounded by "wintry hills" and draped with snow drifts; a lone "snow-bird flits / Beneath the fir-trees' crape"; and the grapevine is glazed with ice. The last image provides subtle yet important clues about the identity of the lost friend. Melville had portrayed Hawthorne as a character named Vine in his epic poem *Clarel* (1876); this final image seems to be an allusion to that earlier work. The unusual personification of the frozen grape as "shy" also points to Hawthorne's famously reclusive character. Melville achieves a poignant effect by placing the full burden of grief on so inconsequent yet apt an image.

Sometimes profound feelings of loss will not erase more ambivalent feelings one may harbor toward a loved one. Edwin Arlington Robinson's "For a Dead Lady" (1910) describes the poet's reaction to the death of his mother, Mary Robinson; but the lyric's poignancy is paradoxically increased rather than diminished by the fact that the poem does not idealize her. Robinson's mixed feelings, in fact, help create a more vivid portrait of this lively but flawed and all-too-human woman. Robinson symbolizes the two sides of her character in the opening four lines by contrasting the light that overflowed her eyes and the darkness that haunted them. The first stanza concludes by acknowledging the inadequacy of language to capture her complex, "many-shaded" essence, and the poem returns several times in near-disbelief to the simple, terrible fact of her oblivion. The second stanza, however, introduces a mingled note of resentment that suggests a certain hardness in her character. In perhaps the poem's most memorable line—which well illustrates how Robinson uses alliteration throughout for extra emphasis on key words— we are told of "The laugh that love could not forgive." Apparently, the mother was not above ridiculing her son, who perhaps loved her more than she him—although the limits of even his love are here defined. Corroborating this notion of a certain coldness in her character is the description of her breast as a place "where roses could not live." Even in life, something deathly clung to her. The final stanza makes explicit two facets of her person already hinted at: her beauty and her social accomplishment. The world saw her loveliness and social grace, but not the private self that was capable of both mild cruelty and, as line 20 indicates, maternal vigilance. In the poem's concluding lines, we find no epiphany or reconciliation. Instead, the poem confronts the bare fact of time's "vicious . . . reaping." A great deal of force is accumulated in the word "vicious" and in the polysyllabic word "inexorable" of the preceding line. With these words, ambivalence and portraiture give way to a stark lament for the human condition. Robinson is not blinded by love to the defects of his mother's character, but upon considering what her passing means to him, he rises to a universal contemplation of mortality.

In contrast with the situation in Robinson's poem, Robert Frost's "Home Burial" (1914)—surely one of the most powerfully dramatic of all American poems—explores the difficulties a married couple have in coping with the loss of their son. The poem takes its departure from the death of Frost's own three-year-old son, Elliott, and the effect it had on his marriage, though it would be a mistake to read it as strict autobiography, for Frost has quite deliberately altered characters and events to distance the poem from his own life. Additionally, the narrative point of view, as in certain Hemingway stories, functions throughout the poem principally like a camera eye: it describes scenery and records dialogue and action, but almost never directly reveals the thoughts or feelings of the characters. The reader views the characters as if they were actors on a stage, and indeed, the poem could be considered a kind of one-act closet drama. The objective presentation, however much it distances us from Frost's own life, heightens the dramatic tension, for it makes the words and actions of the characters seem charged with explosively unpredictable possibilities.

At the beginning of the poem, the unnamed husband at the bottom of the stairs catches his wife, Amy, staring out the window at the top of the stairs. Spatial arrangements in the poem are significant, for by line 34 the two characters have switched positions, and Amy stands by the door. Her threat, throughout the poem, is to walk through that door, as she has done in the past ("Amy! Don't go to someone else this time," the husband implores in line 41). The husband's threat, on the other hand, is one of barely repressed physical violence, as subtly indicated by the aggressive verbs that characterize his actions ("Advancing," "Mounting") and by the fact that he sits with his chin fixed between closed fists (line 43). The poem depicts one incident in an ongoing cycle of threats and misunderstandings that have engulfed the relationship since the death of the child. Both characters tend to underestimate and misjudge the other, starting with Amy's assumption that her husband will not see what she was looking at through the window at the top of the stairs. She is wrong: it takes him a moment, but he sees that what has absorbed her attention is the "little graveyard where my people are!" The window frames the entirety of the graveyard, which includes the dead child's mound. The husband notes that the graveyard is about the same size as a bedroom, a comparison that pointedly calls to mind life's trajectory, from conception to interment. As in Whittier's "Telling the Bees," the poem's title refers to a rural New England custom—in this case, burying family members on home property. The title, though, clearly has a double meaning, for both characters are buried alive in their marriage.

After the husband's initial discovery of what commanded his wife's attention, the poem focuses on the bereaved parents' effort to overcome silence and miscommunication. This effort takes the form of two extended monologues, which ultimately only serve to spin a web of further misunderstandings. During the monologues, the reader's sympathies are yanked back and forth between the tortured protagonists. Neither is wholly sympathetic or wholly despicable; both are flawed and miserable and all-too-human. The husband begins by acknowledging that his words invariably give offense—a savvy rhetorical gesture but a futile one, for, ironically, he will quickly offend again. He pleads with Amy to let him into her grief, but then makes the mistake of judging her grief to be too intense and too inconsolable. This prompts her denunciation of his alleged insensitivity and leads to the heart of the poem, for it is her monologue that clarifies what has happened and precisely how the problem between the two of them originated.

She blames him, first, for having dug the child's grave himself. From this clue, a reader can guess that home burial was probably not a practice in her family. She might have hailed from the city and, therefore, might feel ill at ease or even alienated by such rural practices as home burial. In any event, the burial clearly marked a traumatic moment in her life, for its every detail seems engraved in her mind. She recalls the way the gravel leapt in the air as he dug—"like that, like that"—and the way he tracked the fresh earth into the kitchen. It is also at this point that the full significance of the poem's opening lines becomes clear: fascinated with loathing, she had watched him from the same window she was staring through when he confronted her at the beginning of the poem. Repetition, compelled by unsettled memories and emotion, structures their unhappy lives. What gnaws at her is an overwhelming sense of alienation at the prospect of the boy's father having become his gravedigger. "I didn't know you," Amy says. She still does not, and he does not possess the verbal resources to make her understand his own sense of loss.

Instead, she blames him, above all, for callous indifference. The most telling lines of the poem are her verbatim repetition of his words when he came in from digging the grave:

> I can repeat the very words you were saying:
> "Three foggy mornings and one rainy day

Will rot the best birch fence a man can build."
Think of it, talk like that at such a time!
What had how long it takes a birch to rot
To do with what was in the darkened parlor?

What was in the darkened parlor was, of course, the body of the boy, waiting to be interred. The husband's comment, superficially heartless, actually obliquely (but probably unintentionally) reflects on the situation at hand. If the reader generalizes his comment, it becomes apparent that what he is saying is that no human investment of time or effort can preserve a valued thing from the force of change and dissolution. The birch fence, in other words, stands metonymically for the dead child. Frost represents the psychology of the situation very subtly here, for it is only the perceptive reader—not the obtuse husband, much less his enraged wife—who will comprehend this touching yet unwitting act of sublimation. Only the reader understands what the statement actually represents: the sorrow of a man who has too thoroughly assimilated a masculine code of stoicism. His grief is hidden even from himself, yet cannot be fully repressed.

The perceptive reader will probably be tempted to side, instinctively, with the beleaguered husband, but only for the moment. His emotional cache diminishes before our eyes, as he boorishly fails to comprehend his wife's determined statement to keep living in the fullness of her inconsolable grief. Too hastily, he responds, "There, you have said it all and you feel better." It is clear to the reader, however, that she does not feel better and will not, for the foreseeable future. Her grief needs space to mature, but he will not grant this space. The offense given by this alarming condescension is quickly compounded by his worries that a passing stranger will witness their private quarrel. Amy, who had just eloquently spoken of the impassable breach between how loss affects insiders and outsiders, lashes out at this concern with something so shallow as social respectability: "*You*—oh, you think the talk is all." The poem ends abruptly, without resolution, with Amy threatening to leave and her husband threatening to bring her back by force. Frost's interests, clearly, are not in the narrative's plot but in the polarized psychological responses to loss that divide and ceaselessly wound his protagonists.

Loss is usually associated with the terminal points in nature's cycles, such as sunset and winter (as in Melville's "Monody"), so the choice of season adds an unexpected and poignant contrast to expressions of grief in William Carlos Williams's "The Widow's Lament in Springtime" (1921). Williams was certainly not the first to exploit this incongruity; see, for instance, Dickinson's "I dreaded that First Robin, so" (discussed under "Nature") as well as Renaissance antecedents dating back at least to the Earl of Surrey's "The Soote Season." Williams does, however, achieve a genuine mood of pathos that in no way seems conventional. His poem explores the theme of loss by reviving the dramatic monologue form favored by Poe and Whittier. The speaker has recently lost her husband of thirty-five years. Williams imagined the poem being spoken by his mother, Elena; his father, William George, had died of cancer in 1918. In the past, the mother had reveled in the splendors of spring, the new grass as well as the blossoming plum and cherry trees; but this year's season of renewal fails to console her sense of loss. The fecundity of spring, in fact, can only stand in stark contrast to the unalterable loss of her lifelong partner. Life returns, but not the one life dearest to her. Her changed attitude toward the spring exemplifies Emerson's dictum that "Nature always wears the colors of the spirit." The mother's son (Williams himself) has told her of white flowering trees in the distant meadows—presumably in order to revive her flagging spirits. If his intention was to arouse her interest in going there, he has succeeded, but probably not precisely for the reason he would have wished, for her mind fixates not on the beauty of the flowers but on the cool release from the burdens of suffering that the marsh might afford. The world's beauty is no consolation for the loss of her husband. Only death will free her from her overwhelming sense of loss.

Profound and moving poems on loss are not always inspired by the deaths of those the poet deeply loved or admired, as Milton's "Lycidas" has long demonstrated. Both John Crowe Ransom's "Bells for John Whiteside's Daughter" (1924) and Theodore Roethke's "Elegy for Jane" (1953) share the fact that the poet did not intimately know his subject. In the case of Ransom's poem, the situation is even more unusual: Ransom had been watching a neighbor's daughter at play and only imagined what it would be like if she were to die. The poem is not a true elegy, but rather an imaginative confrontation with unexpected death. It is structured by the tension between the "speed" in the little girl's living body and her "study," or motionless reverie, in death. The girl's former liveliness is depicted through the "wars" she waged against the "sleepy and proud" geese by the pond. Many of the poem's effects depend upon highly self-conscious lexical choices: not only the unfamiliar meaning of "study" and the hyperbole of "war," but the anachronism of "bruited" and the sheer unexpectedness of "astonishes," "tricking," "sternly," "vexed," and the final unsettling alliterative pair, "primly propped," which calls to mind more a doll than a dead child. The poem does not plumb the depths of mourning but evokes something more immediate: our sheer inability to believe in the mortality of the very young.

Roethke's poem also contrasts the vigor of its subject when alive with the imperturbable reverie ("sleep") of death. In this case, however, the death was not imaginary. As the poem's subtitle indicates, Jane had been a former student of Roethke, who taught poetry at Lafayette, Penn State,

Bennington, and the University of Washington. Jane died as she lived, outdoors. As in Ransom's poem, the natural world provides an inevitable context for conveying the subject's liveliness, although Roethke makes more sustained and various use of natural imagery. Ransom's girl had lorded over the natural world, whereas Roethke's Jane was herself a part of nature. Roethke compares Jane to a fish (pickerel), to several bird species (wren, sparrow, and pigeon), and to a fern; he also claims that when she sang, the shade, leaves, and even mold sang with her. In dejection, she is still associated with straw and water. The conclusion of the poem emphasizes the impotence of the poet to do anything but speak his words of love (and, just to clarify matters, Roethke assures the reader that he was neither Jane's father nor her lover). The sense of loss at the end is underscored by one of Roethke's favorite devices, progressively shorter lines.

Like "When Lilacs Last in the Dooryard Bloom'd," Frank O'Hara's "The Day Lady Died" (1959) is an elegy to a public figure who is never mentioned in the poem by name. Unlike Whitman's poem—so oratorical and elevated in manner—O'Hara's characteristically cultivates an unadorned, matter-of-fact, distinctly unpoetic style. Its strategy is to re-create the mundane context of everyday life that a sense of loss can suddenly and unexpectedly invade. Most of the poem has actually nothing to do with its subject, but rather recounts the trivial details of the poet's Friday afternoon in New York City. He gets a shoeshine, thinks about going to dinner that evening, eats lunch, reads some foreign poetry, goes to the bank, buys a copy of Verlaine's poems for an artist friend, stops at the liquor store and then at the tobacco shop. In addition to cigarettes, he purchases a copy of the *New York Post*, which features a front page obituary and picture of "her." Throughout the poem, O'Hara has made numerous more-or-less obscure references to everyone from Jean Genet (the controversial French writer) to Miss Linda Stillwagon (the poet's fastidious bank teller). O'Hara assumes an "insider" audience that can command the bulk of his various allusions. The crucial reference to "her" is explained by the poem's title: the jazz singer Billie Holiday (1915–1959) was given the nickname "Lady Day" by her sometimes collaborator, the renowned tenor saxophonist Lester Young (whom Holiday in turn dubbed "Prez"). Holiday had led a troubled life: she had been a prostitute in her youth, drank heavily, smoked fifty cigarettes a day, was addicted to heroin, and served several prison sentences. She also had a small voice that barely spanned one and a half octaves, but despite hardships and technical limitations, she is usually regarded, along with Ella Fitzgerald, as one of the two greatest female singers in the history of jazz. Holiday had an inimitable vocal style that conveyed profound emotion, and she broke new ground for popular music with her performance of "Strange Fruit," a song about lynching. The tone of O'Hara's elegy changes dramatically as he realizes New York has just lost one of its luminaries. The poet recalls hearing Holiday at the Five Spot as "she whispered a song along the keyboard" to her accompanist while the entire audience held its breath. This final image contrasts with the banality of what has gone before (although O'Hara, in character, does depict himself leaning against the club's restroom door as he listens). It also pays an extraordinary tribute to the power of Holiday's art, which from that moment on will be confined to recordings.

As highly wrought as O'Hara's poem is loosely improvised, Elizabeth Bishop's "One Art" (1976) concerns the loss of many things: objects, time, places, a loved one; ultimately, it is about the nature of loss itself. The poem is cast in the complex form of a villanelle, which, among other things, means that the speaker's opening assertion—"The art of losing isn't hard to master"—will be repeated three times. Bishop's brilliance in composing this poem is that she has made the repetitions psychologically significant: they come to sound like a desperate attempt on the speaker's part to convince herself that what she says is true, even as the losses she mentions escalate in personal importance and obviously undermine her assertions. She first mentions losing keys, then an hour, then a family heirloom (her mother's watch), then houses, cities, rivers, continents. The reader sees that she means "lost" in several different senses—"wasted" and "parted with" as well as the more conventional "cannot find." Loss itself is repetitious and justifies the repetitive form of the villanelle. In the final stanza of the poem, the speaker's tone becomes intimate as she mentions losing "you"—in other words, a loved one. This "lost" person represents the culmination of the speaker's woes. In the final repetition of the opening line, the slight modification of the words ("losing isn't hard" becomes "losing's not too hard") indicates the emotional strain of supporting her thesis when it has touched on something so dear. She has to insert that "too" as a kind of concession. The strain also becomes evident in the final line, as the speaker (or rather, writer) of the poem forces out the final repetition of "disaster" after the parenthetical interjection "(*Write* it!)"—as if only sheer force of will completes the poem. The reader comes to see the gap between what the poem asserts and what it really means. A masterful performance on Bishop's part, "One Art" exemplifies much that is essential about the poignancy and psychology of traumatic loss.

Finding ways, however unintentionally and unexpectedly, of vanquishing one's overwhelming sense of loss is the theme of A. R. Ammons's "Easter Morning" (1981). Ammons had celebrated change in his signature poem "Corsons Inlet" (discussed under "Time & Change"), but here, sixteen years later, he confronts the human toll exacted by change. Ammons often writes in the first person, and in this poem, his engagingly self-deprecating persona appears at its most exposed and vulnerable. As Longfellow and others did before him, he is writing about an actual loss in his own life: that of his younger brother, who died, the poem tells us, in a mishap by the side of a road while he was still very young. The loss forces Ammons onto a route through his life he did not expect; he is haunted by the life he might have led had his brother lived. The poem that commemorates his loss is that of an aging man. When Ammons returns to his home country in rural North Carolina, he visits the place where his parents, uncles, teachers, and other acquaintances are all assembled: the graveyard. But it is his brother's grave that arrests his attention above all others. He returns to it obsessively, less in tribute to the dead than out of an imaginative need to see their lives "by"—as he puts it in a brilliant phrase—"the light of a different necessity." The grave, however, will not "heal." And so he is doomed to stand before it and to fail to protect or to redeem, time and again.

The final section of the poem initiates a tentative movement beyond this sense of impotence toward some kind of meaningful acceptance of the unchanging past and the ever-changing present. Still at the graveyard, Ammons sees two majestic birds, probably bald eagles, "oaring" their great wings through the still air of an ideal Easter morning. The trailing bird veers "a little to the / left" (an enjambment that forces the reader's eye to move in the same direction as the bird). This act of breaking away distantly recalls the death of the younger brother, who also trailed behind, at least in age. The first bird eventually circles back, breaking from its established route, and then the two, reunited, disappear over the treetops. Ammons is left to contemplate the nature of patterns, routes, and returns. The connection between the observation of birds and the understanding of human realities recalls Richard Wilbur's "The Writer" (discussed under "Family Relations"). Ammons's poem leaves us with a transcendent blaze of sunlight that intimates the infinite possibilities of renewal. Ammons does not "solve" the problem of loss, but he points toward a mature acceptance and understanding that take the reader beyond the impasse of dejection.

The poems covered to this point all principally concern the loss of human companions: lovers, spouses, siblings, children, friends, public figures. Our sympathies tend to diminish in concentric circles. We care most about our family members, then our friends, then our acquaintances, then citizens of our country, and so on. As the distance increases, our feelings typically become more detached. We are crushed at the death of someone close to us, but barely bat an eye when we read that hundreds or even thousands of people in other countries have died in some disaster. If we do not seem to care deeply about what happens to people of other nations, can we care much at all about what happens to other species? Pets, of course, are a special case, adopted members of the family, and there have been several notable elegiac poems for dogs in particular in American literature, such as William Carlos Williams's "Death," Yvor Winters's "Elegy on a Young Airedale Bitch Lost Two Years Since in the Salt-Marsh," and John Updike's "Dog's Death." Stanley Kunitz's "The Wellfleet Whale" (1983), on the other hand, expresses a different order of sympathy, one that reaches beyond the circle of the human family and its domestic appendages. Kunitz has written an elegy to a creature he saw only once, a sixty-three-foot finback whale that came aground on Cape Cod.

The poem is a feast of carefully observed imagery, which Kunitz employs to evoke the whale's physical majesty. Kunitz has divided the poem into five sections, the first of which concerns the whale's complex vocalizations. The second and third describe how the people of Wellfleet thrill to the whale's presence, but at dawn find the massive creature stranded on the rocky shore. Section four, which can usefully be compared with Barry Lopez's contemporaneous essay "A Presentation of Whales," is a kind of sociological study of human reactions to the dying leviathan. An assortment of people and dogs are drawn to the whale's mighty presence. Most are simply curious, but someone carves his initials into the whale's side, and others make off with "souvenirs" of peeled skin. Despite such abuse, the whale lingers for a full day, meeting its end with an opened eye at the following dawn. Section five apostrophizes the departed whale and attempts to make sense of the entire episode. Kunitz imagines the whale's life, as it ranged north from Trinidad to Greenland and back again. Beached, the whale is like "a god in exile," suddenly as vulnerable as any mortal. The poem stems from an extraordinary act of imaginative sympathy. It enlarges our perception and our sense of pain, and promises that even nonhuman losses will not go unlamented.

❦

"The Raven," Edgar Allan Poe

    AAL-1; APN-1; ATL-1; ColAP; HAL-1; HoAL-1; NAL-1; NOBA; NoP-4; OxBA; TFi

"Annabel Lee," Edgar Allan Poe

    AAL-1; APN-1; ATL-1; ColAP; HAL-1; HoAL-1; NAL-1; NOBA; NoP-4; OxBA; TFi

"Telling the Bees," John Greenleaf Whittier

    AAL-1; APN-1; ATL-1; ColAP; HAL-1; HoAL-1; NOBA; NoP-4

"When Lilacs Last in the Dooryard Bloom'd," Walt Whitman

AAL-1; APN-1; ATL-1; ATL-2; ColAP; HAL-1; HAL-2; HoAL-1; HoAL-2; LPTT; NAL-1; NOBA; NoP-4; OxBA; TFi

"I never lost as much but twice," Emily Dickinson

AAL-1; AAL-2; ATL-2; NAL-1; NoAM; NOBA; NoP-4

"The Bustle in a House," Emily Dickinson

AAL-1; AAL-2; ATL-2; HAL-1; HAL-2; HoAL-2; NAL-1; NoP-4; OxBA

"The last Night that She lived," Emily Dickinson

ATL-2; ColAP; HAL-1; HAL-2; HoAL-2; OxBA

"My life closed twice before its close," Emily Dickinson

AAL-1; AAL-2; APN-2; ATL-2; ColAP; HAL-1; HAL-2; HoAL-2; NAL-1; NoAM; NOBA; OxBA; TFi

"The Frost of Death was on the Pane—," Emily Dickinson

HoAL-2

"The Cross of Snow," Henry Wadsworth Longfellow

AAL-1; APN-1; ATL-1; ColAP; HAL-1; HoAL-1; NOBA; NoP-4; OxBA

"Monody," Herman Melville

APN-2; ATL-1; HAL-1; HoAL-1; NoP-4

"For a Dead Lady," Edwin Arlington Robinson

AAL-2; APT-1; HAL-2; HoAL-2; NoAM; NOBA; OxBA; TFi

"Home Burial," Robert Frost

AAL-2; APT-1; ATL-2; ColAP; HAL-2; HoAL-2; MAP; SoSe-9

"The Widow's Lament in Springtime," William Carlos Williams

APT-1; MAP; NoAM; NOBA; SoSe-9

"Bells for John Whiteside's Daughter," John Crowe Ransom

AAL-2; APT-1; ATL-2; ColAP; HAL-2; HoAL-2; MAP; NoAM; NOBA; NoP-4; OxBA; SoSe-9; TFi; VGW; WeW-4

"Elegy for Jane," Theodore Roethke

APT-2; ATL-2; CAPP-6; CoAmPo; ColAP; HAL-2; HCAP; NoP-4; TFi; WeW-4

"The Day Lady Died," Frank O'Hara

ATL-2; CAPP-6; HAL-2; HCAP; HoAL-2; MAP; NAL-2; NoAM; NOBA; NoP-4; VCAP

"One Art," Elizabeth Bishop

APT-2; ATL-2; CAPP-6; DiPo; HAL-2; HoAL-2; MAP; NAL-2; NoAM; NoP-4; SoSe-9; VCAP; WeW-4

"Easter Morning," A. R. Ammons
    ATL-2; HAL-2; HCAP; NAL-2; NoAM
"The Wellfleet Whale," Stanley Kunitz
    CAPP-6; DiPo; MAP; NoAM

Love and Sex

❧

Love is the answer—but while you're waiting for the answer, sex raises some pretty good questions.

                                        attributed to Woody Allen

Walt Whitman introduced a new frankness of subject matter into American poetry. Even today, the sexual candor of some of his poems can surprise, shock, and even outrage certain readers. From the onanism of *Song of Myself*, to the poems celebrating heterosexual love entitled *Children of Adam*, to the homoeroticism explicit in *Calamus* and implicit in some of the Civil War poems and elsewhere, to such cosmic love poems that seem to embrace all of humanity as "Crossing Brooklyn Ferry" and "The Sleepers," Whitman defied all the prudish, puritanical conventions of early American culture. Even Emerson, who claimed that limitation was the only sin, advised him to tone down the sexual content of his work—but Whitman refused. Whereas a conservative strain of Western thought has always treated the body and sex with suspicion, Whitman unabashedly celebrates both. "From Pent-Up Aching Rivers" (1860, rev. 1881), included in the *Children of Adam* section of *Leaves of Grass*, illustrates the forthrightness with which Whitman approached these "taboo" subjects, "singing the phallus, / Singing the song of procreation" (lines 4–5). The transparent metaphor of the title refers to repressed sexual energy that Whitman's tumbling, turbulent poem seeks, symbolically, to release. Throughout the poem, Whitman associates sexual love with nature, which for him, as a modern and a romantic, is something more fundamental than laws, religions, and mores, all of which are seen as human constructs that attempt to channel and control natural impulses. These ideas become clear in the first parenthetical aside addressed to a

101

hypothetical lover (lines 27–30): "you and I escape from the rest and go utterly off, free and lawless, / Two hawks in the air, two fishes swimming in the sea not more lawless than we." Whitman also celebrates the attractiveness of bodies, the "utter abandonment" of lovemaking, and the selflessness of love. Physical and spiritual love fuse in the poem; prudery and shame evaporate. Whitman concludes this forthright poem by celebrating the "act divine" and the "stalwart loins" that make it possible.

If "From Pent-Up Aching Rivers" praises the "female form," as Whitman does elsewhere as well, it remains true that Whitman is better known for his homoerotic poetry. "In Paths Untrodden" (1860, rev. 1867), the opening poem of the *Calamus* section of *Leaves of Grass*, speaks out on behalf of homosexual love. The "paths untrodden" of the opening line refer both to the love itself and to the poetry that celebrates it. Both defy "all the standards hitherto publish'd," which the poet has for "too long" allowed to nourish his repressed soul. Whitman speaks out against these standards, clearing the way for a more open and unashamed view of what he calls "manly attachment" and "athletic love." As with his general view of sexuality in "From Pent-Up Aching Rivers," Whitman uses natural impulses as his standard. Whatever silences and judges such impulses, forcing them into the "margins" and maintaining "conformity," should be resisted. Speaking out, as in this poem, is the first step toward challenging society's prejudices. The poem guardedly clears new ground for poetry, but ends—as exuberantly as "From Pent-Up Aching Rivers"—with a pledge to "tell the secret of my nights and days" and with a celebration of "the need of comrades."

Emily Dickinson, despite her popular reputation as a death-obsessed solitary, was along with Whitman, one of the first vital and significant American love poets, even though she never read Whitman, whom she had been told was "disgraceful." Dickinson might seem ill-suited to such a role; but her biographers have, on the basis of both letters and poems, increasingly become convinced that she loved several men, although the precise nature of these relationships remains clouded in obscurity. The intrigues of the past may have vanished from our ken, but the poems remain. "Wild Nights—Wild Nights!" (#249, c. 1861) is perhaps the most overtly erotic of all Dickinson's poems. Its ecstatic nature is underscored by the preponderance of accented syllables in the opening stanza, with the double stress of "Wild Nights" repeated no fewer than three times in the space of fourteen words. The "Wild Nights" themselves may be taken to signify both stormy weather and sexual passion. The first and third stanzas express the speaker's longing for her lover ("Were I with thee"), whereas the second details her feeling of contentment when she is united with the lover ("a Heart in port"). Nautical imagery pervades the poem, from the storms indicated by both "Wild Nights" and "the

Winds" to such terms as "port," "Compass," "Chart," "Rowing," "Sea," and "moor." Water images have conventionally served, for obvious reasons, as symbols of both love and sex, as we have already seen in Whitman's "From Pent-Up Aching Rivers." Dickinson elaborates such imagery with remarkable dexterity within the confines of her extremely brief poem. A witty allusion to the metaphysical poet John Donne may be lurking in the lines "Done with the Compass—/ Done with the Chart!" "Done" may be playing off of "Donne," since the seventeenth-century English poet, with whom Dickinson shares certain notable characteristics, wrote poems that prominently feature the images of a compass ("A Valediction Forbidding Mourning") and a chart ("Hymn to God My God, in My Sickness"). As both Donne poems express love, secular and divine, and as Donne remains famous for his own erotic poems, the allusions are apt and enrich Dickinson's composition. On a literal level, the lines indicate that the instruments of navigation are useless to "a Heart in port." The final stanza with its image of "Rowing in Eden" suggests the innocence of love, which brings the lovers back to a kind of prelapsarian state of worldly bliss. Eden is equated with the sea (of love) on which the two would be reunited. The final lines offer an unmistakably erotic image of fulfillment: "Might I but moor—Tonight— / In Thee!"

An even more complex Dickinson love poem, the thoroughly figurative "My Life had stood—a Loaded Gun—" (#754, c. 1863) makes highly inventive use of imagery relating to guns and hunting. The speaker describes herself in the first stanza as "a Loaded Gun" standing "In Corners"—in other words, as a creature full of untapped potential. Then one day her "Owner"—the natural "owner" of her heart—"identified" her and carried her away. What we have here is a highly unorthodox way of telling a familiar story, one not far removed from fairy tales involving such figures as Cinderella and Prince Charming. The rest of the poem elaborates the tale in terms of the chosen symbolic imagery. The hunter (i.e., the male lover) and the gun (i.e., the speaker) rove the world hunting. The mountains "reply" to the speaker (line 8) in the sense that they give back the echo of her discharges. Throughout the poem there is a curious mixture of pastoral beauty and latent violence, the latter indicated both by the gun imagery and by the peculiar image of the sun as "a Vesuvian face," or a face that resembles the volcano Vesuvius, which destroyed Pompeii. These mingled images of beauty and violence represent the two poles of an existence defined by both love and death. The fourth stanza focuses on domestic love, whereas the fifth and sixth concern different aspects of death. The undying gun is deadly as long as its master lives, which leads to an unresolved paradox in the final stanza. The gun hopes its master will outlive it, but knows it can never die. The idea is clever and poignant and applies in the case of an actual gun, but the virtuosity of the imagery has brought us to a point where it is difficult to map these metaphors back onto an actual relationship between male and female lovers, both of whom are mortal.

After Whitman and Dickinson broke down the genteel restrictions governing polite literature in the nineteenth century, love and sex became much more common themes in twentieth-century American poetry. One particularly notable development was the revival of the sonnet as a vehicle for love poetry. Although love had been the great and practically exclusive theme of the form in its first centuries of use—notably in the hands of such Renaissance masters as Dante, Petrarch, Sidney, and Shakespeare—in later centuries the sonnet had come to be used for a variety of themes, including religion, politics, and nature. Modern American poets, most notably Edna St. Vincent Millay, reclaimed love as an important theme of the sonnet. An early example of the tendency to use the sonnet once again as a love poem is Ezra Pound's "A Virginal" (1912), a dramatic monologue in which the speaker pines for a former lover.

The title, which refers to a sixteenth-century keyboard instrument resembling a harpsichord, bears a somewhat enigmatic relationship to the rest of the poem. Several possibilities as to how the title functions may be considered, none of which excludes the others: it may be a clue as to the poem's historical setting; it may yield a metaphorical image that relates lovers to a musician and an instrument; it may be seen to pun off such words as "virgin" and "virginity"; and it may be an indication that the poem is like a song that would be accompanied by such an instrument.

Regardless of precisely how the title is interpreted, the poem clearly presents a situation in which a disappointed male lover rejects the advances of another woman. "No, no! Go from me," the speaker begins (and later repeats at the beginning of the sestet, or second part of the sonnet), addressing a potential lover who is described as a "lesser brightness" by comparison with the former lover who still haunts his imagination. The lover has left him only "lately"—how or why is never specified. She may have found another lover or she may have died or she may simply have grown weary of him. Regardless, she has left him still very much in the thrall of her charms. Paradoxically, her "Slight" arms have bound him tightly and left him mesmerized by her memory. The magical nature of the woman—a conception that derives directly from the femmes fatales of the Pre-Raphaelite poets and painters who influenced Pound's early work—is associated with renewal and the return of spring in the poem's conclusion. Her "sleight hand" (a transformation of the "Slight . . . arms" mentioned earlier, cleverly metamorphosing slenderness into craftiness) has staunched the "wound" of winter; implicitly, however, the speaker is left with his own wound—

his life without her is a perpetual winter. He prefers to live in his languorous, bewitching, but ultimately barren memories rather than to move forward and engage the present, represented by the lover he is in the act of rejecting.

Edwin Arlington Robinson's great, opaque poem "Eros Turannos" (1913) presents a narrative of love and entrapment that resembles, in some respects, a compressed version of the relationship between Isabel Archer and Gilbert Osmond in the masterful novel *The Portrait of a Lady* by Henry James, a writer who deeply influenced Robinson. As in *The Portrait of a Lady*, the point of view principally focuses on the thoughts and perceptions of the woman, who, along with her lover, is unnamed in the poem. The woman fears her lover and wonders "What fated her to choose him," with his duplicitous yet charming manner that is conveyed in the image of "his engaging mask." She has many "reasons to refuse him"—a potential refusal indicating both a courtship and a marriage proposal. Nonetheless, as much as she may dread him, she dreads the prospect of losing him and living her life alone even more. The poem equates the loneliness of old age with drowning. One must recall that it was written at a time when women faced the choice of either marrying or bearing the social stigma of being a spinster. Perhaps the poem's heroine feels that the man, despite his various defects, represents her last chance to escape spinsterhood. The poem's Greek title means "Love, the Tyrant," the appropriateness of which becomes more fully apparent in the second stanza. The woman's insight ("sagacity") has become "blurred" over the duration of their acquaintance; she no longer possesses the "power to sound him," or to see through that "engaging mask." Her love has blinded her to the fact that he is, as she realized perfectly well when she first met him, a betrayer (or "Judas"). She seems to console herself with the idea that marrying him will exact only the cost of her pride; the narrative voice, however, implies that the price will be much higher.

In the last two lines of the second stanza, the point of view shifts to the man and stays with him through the first four lines of the next stanza. Like Gilbert Osmond in *The Portrait of a Lady*, he is a creature of caution, patience, and tradition. He seems to be satisfied that if he plays the game properly, she will not give him up. He is also allured by a stretch of ocean-front property—the site on which he perhaps plans to build their home. In the second half of the third stanza, the point of view shifts back to the woman, whose doubts about the veracity of the man's statements fade, just as he hoped. And so she marries—or, as the narrator ironically puts it, "secures"—him. Autumn ("The falling leaf") symbolizes the fallen, diminished state of her married life. She becomes a recluse, a prisoner in her own home "where passion lived and died." Meanwhile, the town and harborside "vibrate" with gossip about her unhappy married life. The reader might well wonder if the implication here is that the man, who had still been "look[ing] around" while he awaited her answer, is unfaithful to her.

The final two stanzas shift the point of view yet again, this time to the meddlesome townspeople. Because they almost never see her, they have to piece the story of her existence together from meager scraps of information. Mystery, as is often the case, breeds speculation. The townspeople, however, are not successful in penetrating the "kindly veil" that obscures the woman's domestic life. No one, the poem implies, can truly understand the intimate relations of others, even though that fact will not prevent the proliferation of idle gossip. The townspeople disavow that they are causing any harm by talking about the woman, although the reader need not take this claim at face value. The woman's reputation, no doubt, has suffered greatly from all the gossip. Somewhat enigmatically, the townspeople refer twice to a "god," which can be interpreted as referring to fate, to tradition, or to the man. The strongest reading would connect the god to the title, "Eros"—for Eros was the Greek god of love. Such a reading makes the unexpected metaphor seem far less arbitrary. A further ambiguity attends the word "they," which may be read either as the man and the woman or as all people who have been deeply affected by the god of love. In the second interpretation, the woman becomes a concrete example of a general trend: she represents all those whom love has trapped in unhealthy relationships. The final images function like a coda and suggestively convey the blind desperation of her plight. Breaking waves and the barren tree in lines 45–46 refer back to images from lines 17, 25, and 27. In their final appearance, these images symbolize the harsh fate that the god of love has meted out to her. The final shattering image of the "stairway to the sea" recalls the desperate imagery of line 7. She had feared that losing the man's love would usher her toward a loneliness like drowning; ironically, having "secured" his treacherous love also proves to be like drowning. The poem presents genuine difficulties to the interpreter, but its rich imagery, implications, and thematic content reward careful study.

Edna St. Vincent Millay, noted in her time for frank treatments of love and sex, wrote a large number of sonnets on these themes, including such anthology pieces as "What lips my lips have kissed, and where, and why" (1923), "Love is not all: it is not meat nor drink" (1931), and "I too beneath your moon, almighty Sex" (1939). Somewhat less well-known but equally striking is "Oh, sleep forever in the Latmian cave" (1931), which originally appeared as the final sonnet in the sequence *Fatal Interview*. The poem retells the Greek myth of the shepherd Endymion, with whom the goddess of the moon (identified in different versions of the myth as Diana or Selene) fell in love. The basic outline of the story is as follows: Diana sees Endymion naked on top of Mt. Latmos and desires to be near him, but as the goddess of chastity, she does not want to compromise her virginity. So, she puts him to sleep in a cave, in order to kiss him without being detected. Zeus grants the youth immortality, so that Diana can visit his unconscious form forever. The great English romantic poet John Keats wrote an allegorical poem of 4,050 lines on this myth, titled "Endymion," which alters the name of the goddess to Cynthia. Millay goes to the opposite extreme, compressing the tale into the fourteen lines of the sonnet. Although the poem's syntax is, in places, difficult to parse (perhaps an indication of the strain of extreme compression), the imagery and tale seem reasonably clear. The poem apostrophizes the insensible Endymion, sketching in its octave a striking picture of the hectic Moon shining above his sleeping form. The sestet alludes both to past events and to future possibilities. In Millay's revision of the myth, which provides a striking instance of the poet's frank treatment of sexuality, the relationship between Endymion and the Moon was not strictly chaste before he was cast into slumber. Bereft of her lover, she now wanders through the sky, paradoxically driven mad by the fact that she cannot die for love. Millay plays off the traditional association between the moon and madness (or "lunacy") and seems to suggest that only by being able to die for love is one made fully human. Millay's femme fatale heroine lacks that painfully humanizing mortal capacity that Shakespeare so eloquently describes in Sonnet 73: "To love that well which thou must leave ere long."

Robert Frost's "The Silken Tent" (1942), yet another modern love sonnet, consists of a single sentence that compares a woman to a silken tent billowing in a summer breeze. The image is developed in loving detail, with indications of location ("a field"), time ("midday"), weather condition ("sunny"), and season ("summer") contributing to the cheerful pastoral flavor of the poem's opening. The image of the tent's central pole pointing "to heavenward" calls to mind other Frost poems with similar images, such as "After Apple-Picking" and "Birches" (discussed, respectively, under "Thought & Perception" and "Innocence & Experience"). As in these earlier poems, "The Silken Tent" contrasts the actual with the ideal. A passage from "Birches" helps to clarify the point Frost builds to in this later work: "Earth's the right place for love." Heavenward represents an ideal, also symbolized by the way the tent—and thus the woman—seems to freely float; but the key word here is "seems." As the poem continues, it reveals that the ropes first mentioned in line 3— which function here as metaphors for love—bind the woman to earth. Complete freedom, in other words, is an illusory ideal. Love buoys the soul, but also necessitates responsibilities that limit absolute freedom. Mortal existence always involves compromises and imperfections, an idea that Frost symbolizes by the one rope that goes "slightly taut," making the woman aware of her "bondage." That word in the final line, even though modified by "slightest," hits home with real force, as its creepy connotations seem remote from the carefree mood of the poem's opening. Frost, ever the poet of tough-minded realities, gives us a picture of love at once undeniably tender yet inescapably earthbound.

Adrienne Rich depicts the vicissitudes of an imperfect relationship from a woman's viewpoint in "Living in Sin" (1955). The title refers to the conventional, conservative notion that for an unmarried couple to live together is sinful. Rich's principal concern here is not to challenge superficial assumptions about relationships but to question the traditional assignment of gender roles and duties. The poem contrasts the idealism of love with the mundane chores of quotidian life. The poem's female protagonist has fallen into a relationship with a bohemian artist, apparently a pianist. She keeps his studio clean, while he wanders "out for cigarettes" after having accomplished comically little in the morning in terms of practice. The studio itself appears in two different guises, both as a chic artist's flat, complete with pears, a piano, a Persian shawl, and a cat, and as an unkempt dwelling with scraps of cheese and empty bottles lying around to attract roaches ("a pair of beetle-eyes"). The woman was clearly attracted by the studio's fashionable aspect, but her daily life consists of dealing with the grime and the dust and the unmade bed. Night is associated with idealism and love in lines 23–24, whereas day is associated with chores and cabin fever. These oppositions help to explain the prominence of the milkman, mentioned in line 9 and then (if only figuratively) again in the final line. The milkman arrives each day at five o'clock in the morning; his presence signals the end of night's charms and the beginning of another tedious day. The poem indicates that although night revives her love, the days are taking their toll, so that one day, perhaps, she will quit her lover to seek a new life. The lover himself is not directly criticized in the poem; he appears not to be an intentionally bad or abusive man in any way, but he is lazy and too willing to allow his partner to play the role of housekeeper. The poem expresses dissatisfaction with womens' roles in or out of wedlock. Being unmarried simply means that finding a new and potentially more fulfilling life will be that much easier for the woman.

Theodore Roethke's "I Knew a Woman" (1958), a pure and sensuous hymn of praise to love and to the beauty of the female form, strikes a rare balance that gives full license to the viewpoint of the enraptured male without reductively objectifying the admired female. Instead, the poem insists upon the integrity and complexity of both the woman's personality and her physical presence. Roethke casts the woman in the role of teacher and the poem's speaker in the role of meek and willing follower. He also focuses, throughout, on the intricacy and multiplicity of her physical movements (see especially lines 3–4, 18, 21, and 28), deftly portraying the dynamism of a voluptuous body: "when she moved, she moved more ways than one." The poem contains many puns, some of which are bawdy ("mowing" in line 14) and some learned ("Turn, and Counter-Turn, and Stand" of line 9 are traditional Greek stanzas, tying back into the image of the poets growing up learning ancient Greek in line 6). The poem's stance of worshipful adoration culminates in the idea of finding personal redemption through love, conceived in both physical and spiritual terms. The poet lives to know both eternity and the ways of his lover. The two come together in the image of him measuring time by how her body sways. She is the rhythm of his life, which makes his time meaningful and therefore redeems his existence. As Roethke writes in another poem, "A Walk in Late Summer": "My moments linger— that's eternity." In "I Knew a Woman," the intensity of the woman's physical presence and of the speaker's love for her allow the speaker to find eternity in the moments they share together.

As austere as "I Knew a Woman" is exuberant, J. V. Cunningham's "The Aged Lover Discourses in the Flat Style" (1960) considers the paradox that sexual union can be a solitary activity. Like the earlier poems discussed by Pound, Millay, and Frost, it is a sonnet, cast in the strict Italian form, and thus plays against the conventions of a well-established tradition. The speaker, of indeterminate sex, delineates his or her present condition in the octave: unattractive, clumsy, and solitary, the speaker has become ironically reconciled to an imposed state of abstinence. Sex without love is, for the speaker, merely a ridiculous embrace, fundamentally solipsistic in character. As the sestet describes, each partner may be so preoccupied with his or her desire that the other one barely seems to exist, except as a mechanism of satisfaction. The dehumanizing nature of this arrangement is made explicit by the simile describing sexual union as being "Like gears in motion." The lovers are simultaneously together and alone, only dimly aware of the needful humanity of the other. The ethical responsibility to overcome self-absorption and to recognize and respect the unique, complex individuality of others is a recurrent theme in Cunningham's underrated work.

Timothy Steele, a poet who has found inspiration in Cunningham's meticulously crafted work, gives us an image of a healthy sexual relationship within the context of a loving marriage in "An Aubade" (1986). An "aubade," or "dawn serenade," is a medieval French genre of poetry that had been favored by the troubadours. Steele delivers quite literally on the promise of his title: the poem pictures the morning ritual of a modern, well-adjusted couple. The poem's speaker wakes to an awareness of his wife's presence that is both visual (the earrings) and aural (her showering and singing). The pillow and sheets retain further reminders of her recent proximity and of their lovemaking. Feeling contented as he inventories some suggestive images revealed by the dawn's early light, the speaker comes to feel he can forgive "Pleasure for being brief and fugitive." As traditional aubades often lament the return of day because it signifies the end of sexual bliss (as in, for example, John Donne's "The Sun Rising"), Steele offers here a significant revision of the genre. Before arising, however, the speaker takes voyeuristic pleasure in watching his wife towel-dry her shapely legs and breasts—making it clear that he has not renounced pleasure per se but only grudgingly admitted its inescapably fleeting nature, even within the context of a stable sexual relationship. The civilized adoration the male speaker evinces for his female partner recalls, if in more muted tones, that of Roethke's speaker in "I Knew a Woman."

"A Story about the Body" (1989) by Robert Hass, the one prose poem discussed in this guide, concerns yet another relationship, that of a young male composer and a much older female Japanese painter at an artist colony. The poem examines the consequences of frankness and of rejection and contrasts appearances with realities. The composer comes to think that he is in love with the painter, for he loves her work, her movements, and the way she responds to his questions. But the love of outer things is not necessarily the love of inner things. One night the painter quite candidly states that she believes he would like to sleep with her; but she does not want him to do so without first understanding that she has suffered from breast cancer and has had a double mastectomy, or in other words—as she has to explain to the obtuse composer—she has had both breasts removed. The composer's feelings for her, which are pointedly likened to music, suddenly evaporate, and his sexual ardor instantaneously cools. His resolve to look her in the eyes when he rejects her seems a rather dubious effort to maintain his dignity and integrity. The relationship ends there, but the painter leaves the composer a "message" in the form of a small blue bowl apparently filled with rose petals. Underneath the petals, however, are dead bees that the painter has probably swept up from the corners of her studio. Roses are a common symbol of love, whereas the bees may be associated with pollination and therefore with sexuality; the fact that they are dead reflects on the failed sexual relationship between the artists. The painter, from the wisdom of her experience, seems to be instructing the young man about the relationship of surfaces and interiors, about how external beauty (clothing, manners) can conceal ugliness and disfiguration (her chest, his attitude), and about the difference between infatuation and love. Her seemingly transparent gesture asks him to reflect on these matters, although the poem does not record his reactions. Instead, it gives the reader a new way of thinking about the ideas embodied in the cliché that one should not judge a book by its cover. The poem brings into focus the problematic relationship between the physical and "spiritual" aspects of love central to several other poems discussed in this section.

❦

"From Pent-Up Aching Rivers," Walt Whitman

    AAL-1; APN-1; HoAL-2; NAL-1; NOBA

"In Paths Untrodden," Walt Whitman

    AAL-1; APN-1; HoAL-2; NOBA; OxBA

"Wild Nights—Wild Nights!" Emily Dickinson

    AAL-1; AAL-2; APN-2; HoAL-2; NAL-1; NoAM; NOBA; NoP-4; OxBA

"My Life had stood—a Loaded Gun—," Emily Dickinson

    AAL-1; AAL-2; APN-2; HAL-1; HAL-2; HoAL-2; MAP; NAL-1; NoP-4; WeW-4

"Eros Turannos," Edwin Arlington Robinson

    AAL-2; APT-1; ATL-2; HAL-2; HoAL-2; NAL-2; NoAM; NOBA; NoP-4; OxBA; TFi

"A Virginal," Ezra Pound

    ATL-2; ColAP; HoAL-2; NAL-2; NOBA; OxBA

"Oh, sleep forever in the Latmian cave," Edna St. Vincent Millay

    NoAM

"The Silken Tent," Robert Frost

    AAL-2; APT-1; ColAP; HAL-2; NOBA; NoP-4

"Living in Sin," Adrienne Rich

    AAL-2; ATL-2; HAL-2; HoAL-2; NoP-4; SoSe-9

"I Knew a Woman," Theodore Roethke

    AAL-2; APT-2; ATL-2; CAPP-6; HoAL-2; MAP; NAL-2; NoAM; NOBA; NoP-4; SoSe-9; TFi; VCAP

"The Aged Lover Discourses in the Flat Style," J. V. Cunningham

    NoAM (1st ed., 1973)

"An Aubade," Timothy Steele

    RA; WeW-4

"A Story about the Body," Robert Hass

    CAPP-6; MAP

Memory

❦

How often have I lain beneath rain on a strange roof, thinking of home.

Darl Bundren in William Faulkner's *As I Lay Dying*

According to Greek mythology, Mnemosyne—goddess of memory—was the mother of the Muses; the Greeks, in other words, related all the arts back to the power of memory. Certainly memory often serves as one of the strongest inspirations of artistic creation. The recollection of an arduous journey, an old love, a dead friend, an encounter with a wild animal, a war or other public occurrence—all these and more can ferment in an artist's mind, demanding expression. Poetry, so often animated by an impulse to eulogize or commemorate, has a particularly close connection to memory. In fact, memory is the very stuff from which many, perhaps even most, poems are carved by the imagination—so it is not surprising to find that a number of renowned poems are meditations on the nature of memory itself. Most poems that take memory for their theme cut in two directions simultaneously: by connecting the present (the time of the poem's composition) with some recollected past, they, with varying emphases, at once mourn what has been and is no more and celebrate the power of memory itself to recover and to console.

Ralph Waldo Emerson's "Concord Hymn" (1837, rev. 1876), was, as the subtitle—"Sung at the completion of the Battle Monument, July 4, 1837"—suggests, actually sung at the unveiling of a monument commemorating the battles of Lexington and Concord. Emerson himself could not attend the celebration, but his friend Henry David Thoreau was there and joined in the singing of the hymn. Unusual among Emerson's better-known works for its overtly public character, it more resembles Oliver Wendell Holmes's "Old Ironsides" or John Greenleaf Whittier's "Ichabod," than a typical Emerson meditation. It also possesses a greater formal polish than most of Emerson's lyrics. The opening stanza recalls the "embattled farmers" who first took arms against the British in what would prove to be the first round of the American War of Independence. Emerson's own grandfather, who had lived in the famous "Old Manse" beside the Concord North Bridge, had witnessed the first outbreak of fighting on April 19, 1775, between redcoats and minutemen. It was left to Emerson himself to immortalize that event, and his "Hymn" will always be remembered, even by those who have never heard of Emerson, if only for its fourth line: "And fired the shot heard round the world." Throughout, however, the "Concord Hymn" is a marvel of compression and of felicitous sound and metrical patterns (e.g., "Down the dark stream which seaward creeps"). After the first stanza's imposing evocation of the event being commemorated, the second notes how the generations on both sides of the conflict—in addition to the original North Bridge itself—have been washed away by the tides of time. The third stanza invokes the power of collective memory to redeem the courageous actions that led to the founding of the United States: both the monument and the poem will serve the cause of fixing the important sacrifices in the minds of future generations. In the poem's conclusion, Emerson addresses a "Spirit," which may variously be interpreted as the spirit of freedom or courage or America, or perhaps as Emerson's Over-Soul. Regardless, the poet asks it to bid time and nature not to ravage the newly unveiled monument (as they have already ravaged the men themselves and the bridge). The hymn, which memorializes both the monument and the events that inspired it, may well be the most aesthetically satisfying occasional poem in the annals of American literature.

Far more personal in character is Frederick Goddard Tuckerman's most celebrated sonnet, "An upper chamber in a darkened house" (1860). Subdued, introverted, enigmatic, and innovative in form—as are most of this underrated poet's works—the sonnet weighs the burden of painful memories. Haunted by a departed, phantasmal presence, the narrator drifts through his house, seemingly a prisoner, and spies upon the signs of autumn—that season of diminishment so seductively conducive to elegiac musings. The figure that the speaker meditates upon is not specified, beyond being male. One is therefore free to imagine a friend or brother who died while young, or alternately an earlier and irretrievably lost incarnation of the speaker himself. Whoever he was precisely, the figure was afflicted by "Terror and anguish," and even the memory of him is so painful to the speaker that he can neither stop thinking of him nor bear to dwell too closely upon him. A psychological compromise is roughed out: the speaker will "dimly dream" of the departed figure, as he inventories clouds, insects, and grass. The effort to fasten his attention on material objects, however, fails, as the "lifted sash" vividly evokes the departed presence once again. From the more neutral realm of perception, the speaker is inexorably drawn once more into the painful inward world of recollection. Tuckerman finds no way for his speaker out of this sorrow and so leaves the reader with a final image, a symbolic gathering in of the poem's theme of the inevasible memories occasioned by loss: the tiny, white petals of the mountain ash shattered against the black shingles of the roof.

A far more expansive personal reminiscence, John Greenleaf Whittier's signature poem, "Snow-Bound: A Winter Idyl" (1866), recalls a sedentary interlude from the poet's lost youth. "To the memory of the household it describes this poem is dedicated by the author" Whittier added in a prefatory note for the 1892 edition of the poem. "Snow-Bound" is a vivid evocation of a vanished past, of family, friends, hearth, and blizzard, structured by central dichotomies: inside and outside, fire and snow, past and present, immortality and death. The lengthy (759-line) poem can be broken down into several discrete parts. First, Whittier gives us a vivid description of the storm, its coming, its duration, the "universe of sky and snow" it leaves behind, and the night after, as the north wind roared "In baffled rage at pane and door" and "The great throat of the chimney laughed" (lines 1–178). A transitional passage (lines 179–211), signaled by the apostrophe to "Time and Change," follows, which compares the poet's gray hair at the time the poem is written to that of his father during the time the poem describes. Of the "inmates" of the old house, we learn that only the poet and his brother are still alive. Whittier then, in the lengthiest section of the poem (lines 212–628), recalls how the family passed the time when they were snowbound, with stories, puzzles, riddles, and poetry reading. He conjures up memories associated with his father, mother, uncle, aunt, and sisters, as well as with George Haskell, the visiting schoolmaster, and Harriet Livermore, the "not unfeared, half-welcome guest," part "vixen" and part "devotee," who is compared to Kate from Shakespeare's *The Taming of the Shrew* and to St. Catherine of Siena.

The next morning teamsters arrive, and the doctor of divinity calls on the mother to help a sick Quaker woman. This passage also includes a brief observation about how Christian charity unites the doctrinaire Calvinists with the inwardly illumined Quakers, such as the Whittier family (lines 629–73). The family passes the week reading books and pamphlets, including the Almanac, an unspecified but "harmless" novel, and a volume of poetry by the Quaker poet Thomas Ellwood, which Whittier gently derides (lines 674–707). Finally, the snow melts, and the door of the household swings wide once more (lines 708–14). The poem concludes with a meditation on the passage of time ("The restless sands' incessant fall") and the consolation of memory (lines 715–59). It stands as a tribute to the memory of common people and common things caught in an exceptional and elemental moment. Whittier's snowbound household becomes a symbolic framework for considering not only the poet's own youth but also the youths of his elders and the ultimate philosophical questions inescapably raised by the sorrows of time and age. Along the way, as part of the sketch of George Haskell, it also celebrates the end of the Civil War and of slavery, a reminder of Whittier's keen commitment to the abolitionist cause. Although Whittier expresses profound grief at the passing of his loved ones, he finds consolation in the possibilities of memory (the clasping "Angel of the backward look") and the afterlife.

Another intensely private poem about memory, Trumbull Stickney's "Mnemosyne" (1902) recalls the minor key tonality of Tuckerman's verse. Stickney's title acknowledges the mythic source of poetic inspiration, even as it indicates the poem's thematic concerns. These have to do, specifically, with the discrepancy between a place as it is remembered and the place as it exists in the present, particularly after a long period of hardship and decline. "Mnemosyne," a poem of contrasts and of lost ideals, makes the discrepancy between past and present felt structurally through the separation of the one-line refrain, which describes the present, from the three-line reminiscences of the past. The poem's speaker recollects the pastoral scenery and companionship of bygone days: hills, swallows, time spent with his sister and children. Starting with line 14, the three-line stanzas shift into the present tense and for the first time are not separated by an intervening refrain. We learn that the pastoral world of the speaker's youth has now been demolished by cattle and storms (and perhaps the logging industry). The tortured landscape seems to mirror the speaker's inner misery. Stickney also evokes the dreary present through the varying adjectives of the refrain: "cold," "empty," "lonely," and "dark." Only in the first and last repetitions does Stickney deviate from his adjectival pattern, substituting a noun ("autumn") and a verb ("rains") that vividly symbolize decline and sorrow. Memory of the past is the speaker's only consolation for what he has lost; it is both a joy and a torment.

Memory functions not as consolation but purely as sorrow in Countee Cullen's "Incident" (1925). This brief poem makes a notable statement about the psychological trauma suffered by those subjected to racism. Cullen recalls a trip to Baltimore when he was but eight years old. He depicts himself as full of joy, until his fateful encounter with a "Baltimorean" roughly his own age. Cullen smiled at the boy, but the boy stuck out his tongue and called him "Nigger." Cullen remained in Baltimore for seven months, but as he says in the conclusion of the poem, "Of all the things that happened there / That's all that I remember." Not being treated as an individual but instead being rejected and insulted just because of the color of his skin casts a pall over the boy's experience. The intensity of the moment blots out a thousand other perceptions because it changes his sense of identity and his consciousness of self in the eyes of others. Probably for the first time he understands his portion in a racist society. The tragedy of this psychological disfigurement, this mutilation of one's precious memory, is the poem's principal concern; but the reader should also reflect on the fact that it is another child who hurls the insulting term. That white boy, too immature to really know better, is also a tragic presence in the poem, for his young mind has already been corrupted by racial hatreds that he neither originated nor understands. He acted simply as the vessel through which the prejudice and hatred of his culture flowed. The poem shows us how racism afflicts and distorts both blacks and whites; it also shows us how memory is distorted by the thoughtless, hurtful behavior of others.

Rita Dove's "Dusting" (1986) forms part of a book-length sequence titled *Thomas and Beulah*; yet taken by itself, without the context furnished by the other poems in the sequence, it retains its haunting resonance. The sequence, based on the lives of Dove's grandparents, tells the story of an African-American couple who marry, have four daughters, and struggle to make a living during the Great Depression and World War II. "Dusting" simply documents a luminous moment of recollection, as Beulah recalls a boy she had known in her youth. Important to a full understanding of the poem is the significance of Beulah's name, which means "married one" and which is used in the Bible to refer to the Promised Land. If the reader recalls that the Israelites had to wander for forty years through the wilderness before reaching the Promised Land, then Dove's use of the word "wilderness" in the poem's first line suddenly seems to be freighted with extra meaning. As she toils in a solarium, polishing wood, Beulah attempts to recall the name of a boy she had kissed at a fair. In a rather modest way, the memory is its own kind of Promised Land, and we watch as Beulah struggles to get there.

Beulah remembers that the boy had worked in a rifle booth and that she obtained from him, as a gift or a prize, a clear bowl containing a single fish. She thinks for a moment that his name might have been Michael, but then decides that it must be something similar, but rarer and more fine. As she tries to bring the name into focus, images from her past crowd into her mind. She remembers coming home from the dance at the fair. It must have been in winter, for the water in the fishbowl had frozen solid. She thawed the ice, and the fish swam free—an image that presages the release of the forgotten name. Dove's description of the ice as a "locket" also suggests that the bowl had a distinctly romantic significance for Beulah.

Beulah's attempt to recall the name is really an attempt to get back in touch with pleasurable feelings from her youth, before the hard times that have shadowed the intervening years. As her mind roves forward, she contemplates the significance of her own name, which came to mean "Promise" and then later "Desert-in-Peace" (presumably both variants of Promised Land). The thought of those last words—"Desert-in-Peace"—triggers the memory of the name she has been searching for: Maurice. She stumbles on the name associatively, through the accidental agency of rhyme. A subtle study of psychological processes, the poem ends in a tiny yet affecting triumph of time regained through memory.

Another poem about a positive memory, Mary Oliver's "Picking Blueberries, Austerlitz, New York, 1957" (1992) recalls how the poet, then a teenager, awoke when a female deer carelessly stumbled against her. For a moment, before the deer "went floating off toward the trees," the poet and the deer regarded each other with amazement. For thirty years, that fortuitous moment has been a source of astonishment and renewal for the poet. It stands as an example of what the great English romantic poet William Wordsworth dubbed a "spot of time," or a moment that acquires in the memory a transcendent and regenerative vividness. Oliver's Wordsworthian reminiscence concludes on a wistful note, blending aesthetic appreciation with longing and concern, as the poet wonders what became of the doe she encountered so many years ago.

The wistful aspect of memory also plays a significant role in Dana Gioia's brilliant poem "Summer Storm" (1995). The poem's opening six stanzas describe a few seemingly trivial events at a wedding party. The poet recalls as he stood watching a rainstorm against a patio wall, beside a woman he has just met. An unexpected intimacy develops, as she takes his arm and they converse in whispers. But it ends as suddenly as it began: as the storm recedes, the woman is called back into the party. The two speak again only to say goodnight. In the seventh stanza, the significance of the event is recast by the fact that we are now informed they took place twenty years ago. Presumably, the poet has never again seen the woman, but he has also never forgotten her. A storm in the poem's present time is what has brought back this memory; but memory here is not a matter of either passive recollection or Wordsworthian redemption. It functions, rather, as a focal point for the poet's imagination to envision other possible outcomes. The reader becomes aware of the full significance of the wedding party only with the line in the eighth stanza: "Strangers we might have married." The poet had been a friend of the bride, the woman an acquaintance of the groom; they were friends of friends, unacquainted yet perhaps attracted to and even compatible with one another. The wedding that actually occurred calls to mind one that did not. What if their lives had become more deeply enmeshed? What would the poet's life have been like? Who would he have become? Life suddenly appears like a garden of forking paths, but as in Frost's famous poem, the ramification of paths from one's initial choice precludes returning to the road not taken. The memory of what *is* thus becomes a constant reminder of life's diminished potentiality. The poem's conclusion, however, reminds us that if other possible lives, besides the one we have actually chosen or been stuck with, seem alluring, it is only because we are drawn to the possibility of difference. Who's to say that a different life would necessarily be a better one?

∽∾∾∿∽

"Concord Hymn," Ralph Waldo Emerson
   AAL-1; APN-1; ATL-1; ColAP; HAL-1; HoAL-1; LPTT; NOBA; NoP-4; OxBA; TFi

"An upper chamber in a darkened house," Frederick Goddard Tuckerman
      APN-2; HAL-1; HoAL-1; NOBA; NoP-4

"Snow-Bound," John Greenleaf Whittier
      AAL-1; APN-1; ATL-1; ColAP; HAL-1; HoAL-1; NAL-1; NOBA; OxBA; TFi

"Mnemosyne," Trumbull Stickney
      APN-2; NOBA; OxBA

"Incident," Countee Cullen
      AAL-2; APT-2; ATL-2; HoAL-2; MAP; NAL-2; NoAM; NoP-4; SoSe-9; VGW

"Dusting," Rita Dove
      ATL-2; HAL-2; HCAP; NAL-2; NoP4

"Picking Blackberries, Austerlitz, New York, 1957," Mary Oliver
      NAL-2

"Summer Storm," Dana Gioia
      RA

Nature

꘎

And as the moon rose higher the inessential houses began to melt
away until gradually I became aware of the old island that flowered
once for Dutch sailor's eyes—a fresh, green breast of the new world.
Its vanished trees, the trees that had made way for Gatsby's house,
had once pandered in whispers to the last and greatest of all human
dreams; for a transitory enchanted moment man must have held his
breath in the presence of this continent, compelled into an aesthetic
contemplation he neither understood nor desired, face to face for the
last time in history with something commensurate to his capacity for
wonder.

F. Scott Fitzgerald, *The Great Gatsby*

Ralph Waldo Emerson defined "nature" in terms still useful today. In a
philosophical sense, Emerson wrote, nature is all matter (as opposed to
spirit); in a common sense, it is matter not altered by human activity. A
leaf would seem to be part of nature in both senses, whereas a chair or
an automobile would be part of it in the first sense but not in the second.
In the modern world, however, the leaf may be eaten by acid rain and
coated with pesticides. The distinction Emerson draws has come, increasingly, to be one of relative degrees rather than of absolute kinds. Few
things in the world have not been altered by human activity, and with
each passing year, there is less of nature—on this planet at least—in
Emerson's common sense.

The history of the United States is largely a record of how nature in
this common sense has been converted into human commodities (or
what Emerson called "Art," in the broadest sense). The Puritans viewed
the virgin land as, in the words of their chronicler, William Bradford, "a

121

hideous and desolate wilderness," full of dangerous creatures and infernal savages. Their early assault on the land was, as they viewed it, both the work of God and a matter of self-preservation. Once settlers established a foothold, however, they began to view the land not so much as an enemy but as something to be exploited for economic gain. The settlers soon came to be amazed at the abundance of nature in America: tracts of virgin forest and wildlife populations seemed inexhaustible in their plenitude. These early settlers were encouraged to act as though infinite riches were spread before them. But the wilderness was not inexhaustible. By 1831, beavers had nearly vanished east of the Mississippi. By 1844, the great auk had become the first creature actually driven to extinction by the new settlers. In the meantime, the massive deciduous forests of the east were broken and numerous species that depended on them disappeared from the region. Henry David Thoreau confided to his journal on March 23, 1856,

that the nobler animals have been exterminated here—the cougar, panther, lynx, wolverine, wolf, bear, moose, deer, the beaver, the turkey, etc., etc.—I cannot but feel as if I live in a tamed, and, as it were, emasculated country. . . . I take infinite pains to know all the phenomena of the spring, for instance, thinking that I have here the entire poem, and then, to my chagrin, I hear that it is but an imperfect copy that I possess and have read, that my ancestors have torn out many of the first leaves and grandest passages, and mutilated it in many places.

Thoreau's work, more than that of any other major American writer, represents a turning point in perception. Thoreau saw, clearly, that the cant of progress concealed both a shortsighted anthropocentric, or human centered, set of values and a terrible diminishment of nature, with aesthetic, ethical, and ultimately economic consequences. By the end of the nineteenth century, European settlers had, in the span of a few hundred years, undone ecosystems that had evolved over millions of years. Ironically, at the same time, new advances in human understanding, particularly in the fields of geology and biology, equipped humans to understand the enormity of what was being done; but few were listening, and the destruction continued, as it still continues.

American poetry has—as much as American industry—depended upon nature as a resource, but with the important difference that poems do not transform or exhaust natural objects. Natural images and symbols abound in our poetry; but relatively few of the poems that employ them are principally concerned with nature itself as a theme. The more typical procedure has been to use a natural image as an illustration of something else, as Philip Freneau does in "The Wild Honey Suckle" and "On Observing a Large Red-Streak Apple." The history of American poetry that does address itself directly to nature largely follows that of the culture at large, as sketched above. In other words, the early poetry celebrates the plenitude of nature, whereas the later poetry laments the destruction of nature and also seeks to foster awareness of the problem. Freneau provides an example of the early reaction in the poem "On the Emigration to America and Peopling the Western Country" (discussed more completely under "Freedom & Slavery"). He writes of forests that have "bloomed but to decay" and of rivers that "idly through the forests rove"—the implications being that forests not cut for timber and rivers not adorned with barges serve no purpose in the world. Freneau promises a new order—decreed by the heavens no less—in which all of nature shall achieve fulfillment by serving the ends of commerce. Freneau, in other words, was an eloquent spokesman for anthropocentrism, early American style. Knowing that he had access neither to the clarity of hindsight nor the larger perspectives afforded by modern geology and biology, we can understand how his naive optimism was a product of his historical moment. The tenor of American poetry would shift fairly radically in the space of a single generation.

William Cullen Bryant stands as the first American poet who valued nature for itself rather than for what humans could make of it. Bryant's position was informed by European romanticism much more than by scientific inquiry, but in many ways these two intellectual traditions—despite superficial complaints against science aired by Keats and Poe and other romantic poets—tended to converge (as they did in a highly productive manner in the writing of Thoreau). Bryant's "Inscription for the Entrance to a Wood" (1817) provides almost a précis of romantic notions about woodlands. The woods, as Bryant portrays them, are not the infernal region imagined by the Puritans but a place that offers respite from the unpleasantness of the world. One's thoughts and feelings tend to harmonize with the calm of the natural world, and even original sin itself (what Bryant refers to as the "primal curse") seems to have no particular authority when one communes with "the unsinning earth." To visit the woods is to be relieved of care and to be spiritually renewed; it is to escape from the guilt and misery of civilization. The woods exist as part of the divine plan; they are the refuge of innocence. All of these ideas derive from the great English romantic poet William Wordsworth, whose "Lines Composed a Few Miles above Tintern Abbey" and *The Prelude* articulate the powerful romantic vision of nature as consolation. In the second part of the poem, Bryant provides a succession of natural images that put flesh on the bones of the poet's ideas. Birds, squirrels, insects (which "dance" rather than sting or transmit disease), green trees, the sun in a blue sky, wildflowers, mossy rocks, a brook: all of these images leave us with an impression of self-sufficiency, far removed from the calculus of Freneau's economic imperatives. Bryant seems to love the woods both for their promise of consolation and for their own sake.

Bryant's "To Cole, the Painter, Departing for Europe" (1829, rev. 1832) effectively exploits the sonnet's binary form by following the simple dichotomy of Washington Irving's famous sketch "The Author's Account of Himself," which established a precedent for identifying Europe with civilization and America with wild nature. Bryant exhorts Thomas Cole, the English-born painter of American landscapes and founder of the Hudson River school of painting, to keep the "earlier, wilder image" of America bright in his mind as he surveys a Europe where he will find "everywhere the trace of men." The poem catalogs some of the glories of America's untrammeled nature and counterpoints them against the cultural riches of European civilization. It offers no explicit prophecies, but the image of European civilization shrinking only "from the fierce Alpine air" does suggest something about humanity's propensity for filling all available space. The poem's primary purpose, however, is simply to contrast (with a definite patriotic bias) the different inspirations America and Europe make available to the creative imagination. What Bryant chiefly offers in his nature poetry is an education of the reader's sensibility and taste with respect to wild nature. He attempts to set in place the kind of values that point toward a conservation ethic, just as his poetry certainly points the way toward such visionary masterpieces of American prose as Emerson's *Nature* and Thoreau's *Walden*.

Not all American poets, however, have shared the romantic and transcendental vision of nature as a benevolent force. In the later nineteenth century, the temporarily suppressed puritan suspicion of nature breaks out in a new form in the work of Emily Dickinson and Herman Melville. Neither writer was by any means an orthodox believer, yet both shared an intellectual debt to Calvinism's pessimistic views of human depravity and the malevolence of wild nature. As such, both writers are like an undertow moving in the opposite direction to the poetic mainstream, with its steady progression from romantic appreciation to environmental consciousness. Although Dickinson did write poems in an overtly romantic and transcendental mode that celebrate nature's beauty, her strongest and most startling nature poems view their subject more skeptically. Both "A Bird came down the Walk—" (#328, c. 1862) and "I dreaded that first Robin, so," (#348, c. 1862) depict human alienation from nature. Unlike Melville, who relies upon the spectacular imagery of the sea, Dickinson employs, in a quite literal sense, garden-variety scenes to illustrate her points. In the first poem, the speaker witnesses an unidentified bird (quite probably, as in the companion piece, a robin) bite an angleworm in half and swallow it raw. The language of the poem conveys an unexpected intensity of violence for such a seemingly ordinary and trivial event. The reader must reflect on whether this violence indicates something amiss with the most familiar arrangements of nature, such as those that grace suburban lawns. The second stanza conveys a more normal sense of order and balance, as the bird drinks dew from a blade of grass and then courteously hops aside to let a beetle pass; but the third stanza reestablishes the mood of the opening. The bird's sense of fear, with its eyes "like frightened Beads," reminds us that what dominates its consciousness is the sense that predators could do to it what it has done to the worm. The poet attempts to approach the hopelessly neurotic creature, but is rebuffed. Dickinson depicts the scene with striking verbs: the bird "unrolled his feathers / And rowed him softer home." The violence inherent in nature breeds mistrust between species. Humans, in particular, stand isolated from their fellow creatures. For the bird, approach can only be prelude to attack. Nature here, as Tennyson memorably put it, is "red in tooth and claw."

The second poem reverses the equation: the poet dreads the robin's approach. The speaker of the poem has apparently suffered some unspecified yet apparently grievous pain, as she identifies herself with the mother of Christ at the crucifixion. Whatever this terrible woe was, it has ill prepared the speaker for the return of spring. If what sorrows her is the death of a loved one, then the reawakening of life all around her must be all the more painful. Unable to participate in the season's colorful moods, the speaker suffers as a figurative orchestra of life (Dickinson employs such unexpected tropes as "Pianos" and "Drums" to describe the animals) impinges on her anguished solitude. What disturbs her most is the "unthinking" inevitability of spring's pageant: "not a creature failed— / No Blossom stayed away," the speaker complains. Instead of a romantically conceived harmony between the season of rebirth and the aspirations of the human spirit, such as Thoreau vividly depicts in *Walden*, Dickinson confronts us with a memorable portrait of discord, one with pre-romantic antecedents dating back at least to the Earl of Surrey's sonnet "The Soote Season." Dickinson, in other words, produced a startling and unconventional poem by reviving and revivifying an earlier convention.

Melville shared Dickinson's distrust of nature's elusive beauty and alleged beneficence. The ostensible subject of his awkward but powerful poem "The Maldive Shark" (1888) is the partnership between pilot fish and a deadly, ravenous shark off the Maldive Islands of the Indian Ocean. The pilot fish serve as "Eyes and brains" to the "lethargic and dull" shark, steering it to prey. Although the poem appears fairly matter-of-fact in its presentation, the experienced reader of Melville will recognize in this symbiotic relationship another symbol for the metaphysical proposition described in chapter 114 of *Moby Dick* as "the tiger heart that pants beneath [the ocean's skin]." Melville, in other words, sees in the shark and its helpers a hint of a general design of darkness to appall, much as Frost would later in the unlikely conjunction of an albino spider, a moth, and a flower (see "Design," discussed under

"Skepticism & Belief"). Against the tenets of such deists as Philip Freneau, who saw in nature's designs the hand of a benevolent creator, Melville raises the possibility that arrangements in nature may indicate a pervasive malevolence in the universe. After all, this Maldive shark could be one of those that participates in "The Shark Massacre" (chapter 66 of *Moby Dick*), an event that elicits from the harpooner Queequeg the observation that "de god wat made shark must be one dam Ingin." If the Maldive shark is Melville's symbol for the true nature of nature itself, then Melville's conception of nature is far removed indeed from the regenerative pastoralism of Wordsworth, Bryant, and Emerson.

After Dickinson and Melville, poets tended to return to a more romantic conception of nature, although they were inevitably influenced both by the revelations of modern science and by the growing environmental crisis. The twentieth-century American poet who has most effectively exploited the simplicity and resonance of natural imagery must be Robert Frost. Like his predecessors, Frost often employs natural objects as symbols: nature is often the subject of his poetry without being its theme. Certain poems, however, such as "The Wood-Pile" and "The Most of It," directly concern themselves with humanity's relation to some aspect of nature. "The Wood-Pile" (1914), a quiet masterpiece, divides neatly into three sections: a man walks through a wooded swamp "far from home"; he inadvertently pursues a small bird with a white tail feather; the bird disappears from sight behind a wood pile abandoned many seasons ago by some unknown person. Frost employs this rather slight narrative scaffolding to support the full weight of one of his perennial themes: the tendency of nature to break down humanly imposed order. A subtheme in such classic poems as "Mending Wall" and "Home Burial," it assumes center stage here. Of the poem's three parts, the title directs our attention to the last—the speaker's description of and musings about the woodpile itself, which finally marks a spot in the otherwise undifferentiated expanse of "tall slim trees." What strikes the speaker is the way nature is reclaiming the wood pile. The dead wood of the pile is gray, the bark warps off, clematis (a vine) wraps around it, and the stake that propped it up is being forced aside by the growth of the tree that holds the pile on the other side. All of these are images of nature's glacial but inexorable tendency to change. The woodpile will not be burned in "a useful fireplace" but will meet its end at a slower pace, "With the slow smokeless burning of decay" (a line that must rank among the strongest to close any American poem). Like the stone wall of "Mending Wall" and the birch fence of "Home Burial," the woodpile serves as a reminder that all human creations are impermanent arrangements. The speaker imagines that the person who cut the wood must live by "turning to fresh tasks," an idea that might prove a source of inspiration for both the speaker and the reader. Nonetheless, if the wood pile represents the fruit of those tasks, what it signifies is the ultimate futility of human endeavors. The poem's final word is "decay." The human desire for order and permanence is fundamentally at odds with the nature of the world itself, which slowly but inexorably flows into new forms. Decay follows order—a symbolic progression in Frost's work, indicating humanity's profound alienation from nature.

"The Most of It" (1942) presents an even bleaker portrait of human alienation from the natural world. The poem employs an almost allegorical narrative to depict the gap between human desire and natural reality. An unidentified man exists in a state of solitude comparable to that of Adam before the creation of Eve. His overriding desire is to elicit some response from the natural world around him, beyond "the mocking echo of his own" voice from a cliff across the lake. He wants "counter-love, original response"—and one day seems to get it. The "embodiment" of nature's response is a mysterious figure that crashes down the slope of the cliff and boldly swims across the lake. But it is not another person; instead, it turns out to be a great buck that stumbles over the rocks and forces its way through the underbrush, without even acknowledging the man at all. The buck's indifference represents nature's true attitude toward humanity. The poem implies what the narrator of Stephen Crane's classic story "The Open Boat" (1897) directly states: nature is not "cruel . . . nor beneficent, nor treacherous, nor wise," but "indifferent, flatly indifferent." The poem, thus, in its conception of nature, rejects the extremes of romantic beneficence and Calvinist malevolence and adopts instead the value-neutral, empirical viewpoint of modern science.

Wallace Stevens' wry, unsettling "Anecdote of the Jar" (1923) studies, if rather obliquely, another aspect of the relationship of humanity to nature. Here, humanity has not been decentralized, as in "The Most of It," but, through its power to transform nature, has assumed a central position represented by the jar itself. The peculiar tonality of the poem, which includes such an unusual word choice as "of a *port* in air" (emphasis mine), is underscored by the studied comic incompetence of the form. After the conventional rhyming of the initial quatrain, the poem seems to abandon rhyme altogether, only to get stuck for three lines running on the sound "air." It then concludes with an identical rhyme to the now fairly distant opening line. Certainly, one does not hear such a rhyme but only discovers it through critical examination. Likewise, the iambic tetrameter rhythm breaks down at various points—most notably in line 3, where the word "slovenly" is placed, metrically, so as to enact the very idea of slovenliness. Much in the poem seems ajar. Such witty caprices may appear like ends in themselves, but the poem can be seen also as making a serious comment on the ecological history of America. The speaker claims to have placed a jar in Tennessee. The act seems trivial only if we fail to see it in terms of synecdoche: the jar is part of a greater whole; what Stevens, rather playfully, seems to be talking about is not a single jar but rather the conquest of the American wilderness. Tennessee, a state lying mostly just to the west of the Appalachians, might, legitimately, conjure up for the reader the early era of westward expansion, while the effect the jar has on its surroundings suggests the whole long saga of "taming" the wilderness. An alien presence ("Like nothing else" in the landscape, because it is man-made), the jar transforms the wilderness, robbing it of its essential quality, wildness; and what the jar represents—namely, civilization—takes "dominion everywhere." Stevens's anecdote actually tells, from a seemingly rather detached and neutral perspective, a much-truncated history of the European conquest of American nature.

A poet who could not cultivate such detachment and who, like Frost, had been deeply influenced by the perspectives of modern science is Robinson Jeffers. No early twentieth-century American poet comes close to rivaling Jeffers as an advocate of nature or as a spokesman for an anti-anthropocentric viewpoint. His "November Surf" (1929) depicts great waves scouring cliffs that have been soiled with human artifacts. This image figures the basic relationship between humanity and the rest of nature. If it calls to mind the similar vision of Stevens's "Anecdote of the Jar," the poet's stance toward the relationship is very different. Human civilization, for Jeffers, exists like a garbage heap strewn over something much more pure and long-lasting. One day, the poem asserts, a greater wave will scrub the earth's surface clean. The wave stands for any future event that will redress the imbalance of modern humanity's polluting and destructive presence. Jeffers imagines a time in which the cities have shrunk, the people are fewer, and other animals are more numerous again. He acknowledges that humanity is in "someways one of the nobler animals," but still maintains that it needs to regain "The dignity of room, the value of rareness." Jeffers's commentary is, as usual, far from subtle; but in retrospect, from the vantage of a world afflicted by global warming and the presence of over six billion humans, it appears prophetic. "Carmel Point" (1951) can be read as a sequel to "November Surf" and as a more advanced diagnosis of the human problem. Jeffers compares Carmel as he first beheld it to what is has become. Then, it was all flowers and "clean cliffs," with only a few farms to testify to a human presence. "Now," the poem continues, "the spoiler [human civilization] has come"; nature, however, remains indifferent to this presence, which, by its own standards of geological time, is merely a "tide" that will ebb before long. Jeffers concludes the poem with a plea for a sensibility based on wider views of time, the world, and our origins— what conservationist Aldo Leopold called "Thinking Like a Mountain."

Jeffers's poetry, along with such classics of environmental nonfiction as Henry Beston's *The Outermost House* (1928), Leopold's *A Sound County Almanac* (1949), Loren Eiseley's *The Immense Journey* (1957), and Rachel Carson's *Silent Spring* (1962), helped to popularize radical new ideas about the place of humans in the world and our ethical responsibilities to the rest of nature. They set the stage for the environmental movement, which began in earnest in the 1960s. Some mainstream American poetry from this time forward reflects the major concerns of that movement.

Perhaps the greatest of these concerns is the possibility of the complete destruction of the natural world in a nuclear holocaust. Richard Wilbur's "Advice to a Prophet" (1961) addresses a scientist—a prominent public figure somewhat like the late Carl Sagan—who stands as the prophet of an age in which nuclear winter is a possibility. The poem offers advice on how to best approach the difficult subject of complete annihilation. Wilbur employs the end-of-the-world scenario as a way of discussing not so much global conflict itself as the relationship between humans and the natural world. Stanzas two and three advise the scientist on what not to talk about: the weapons themselves and the extinction of humanity. The poem claims, first, that the weapons' power and range are too great to inspire either understanding or a useful emotional response, and, second, that humanity is incapable of imagining the universe without itself. Instead of employing these arguments, Wilbur advises the "prophet" to "Speak of the world's own change." The poet believes that although we cannot imagine nature without ourselves, we can imagine ourselves without nature. Wilbur reminds the reader of the Emersonian idea that nature is the ultimate source of our language and imagery and, thus, of our self-understanding. As a poet, Wilbur is acutely aware of how the subtle process of deriving concepts from natural objects works and continues to work in living poems. "Advice to a Prophet" provides numerous examples of the relationship between understanding and natural imagery, such as the way the rose stands for love (line 29). The relationship is summarized in the brilliant final image of the oak tree as "annals" (or written accounts): the tree is the source of such writing in two very different ways, both as the raw material of paper and, perhaps more importantly, as the inspiration of conscious reflection. What should we be without nature? is the poem's central question. Who would we be without it, and how would we understand ourselves? These questions provide one rationale not only for averting nuclear war but also for preserving nature in a more general way.

Although perhaps not an environmental poem per se, Elizabeth Bishop's "The Armadillo" (1965) does register the impact of human activities on the natural world. The poem is set in Brazil, where Bishop lived from 1951–1974. Bishop writes of the fire balloons that beautifully— but also illegally and irresponsibly—rise into the night sky on the Feast of St. John (June 24) and, sometimes, come crashing down in flames. The second half of the poem focuses on the damage wrought against the region's animals in images so sharply observed as to become inscribed in the reader's mind. Consider the baby rabbit: "a handful of intangible ash / with fixed, ignited eyes." The final, italicized stanza is a commentary on the poem and an indictment of its emphasis on beauty at the expense of responsibility. Bishop realizes that she has aestheticized destruction and so attempts to make amends in the last three lines, which form a cry of protest. The *"weak mailed fist"* represents the armadillo, protected by its armor from most dangers but not from fire. Its "panic" ironically calls to mind the etymology of the word, which derives from the nature god Pan. Here however, humans threaten nature rather than the other way around. The mailed fist also seemingly points the reader back to Mars, god of war, for whom the planet is named that presides— along with its feminine opposite Venus—over the fiery proceedings. Like the balloons fading against the backdrop of stars and planets, the poem itself moves between beauty (Venus) and destruction (Mars). The martial reference in the final stanza is further underscored by an allusion to the concluding line of Matthew Arnold's famous poem "Dover Beach": "Where ignorant armies clash by night." In Bishop's poem, the ignorance is that of the wild creature threatened and driven from its home by it knows not what. Bishop finds herself caught between conflicting impulses that structure the poem—one disinterestedly aesthetic, the other humanely compassionate. The final accent falls on the latter. The poem's wider historical implications seem clear from the dedication to Robert Lowell, a conscientious objector during World War II due to his opposition to the random terror bombing of civilians. The destruction of innocent animals functions as a trope for the destruction of innocent human beings.

W. S. Merwin's apocalyptic "For a Coming Extinction" (1967), an apostrophe to the gray whale species, more directly engages contemporary environmental concerns. The poem's deep irony results from Merwin's knowledge that the whales cannot understand him and that he can do nothing to help them. An even more bitter layer of irony emerges from Merwin's presentation of human pretensions. The intended effect of the poem is to puncture anthropocentric assumptions based on our myths of superiority, which Merwin deftly punctures in a line from another poem ("The River of Bees") from the same collection (*Lice*): "Men think they are better than grass." Several linguistic parallels in "For a Coming Extinction" with Genesis remind us of the source, or at least justification, of some of these anthropocentric positions. Merwin alludes at one point to Genesis 1, in which God creates whales on the fifth day and humans on the sixth. The reference calls to mind the whole Western baggage of belief in separate creation and in humanity's divinely sanctioned mission to conquer and subdue the earth. At another point, Merwin invokes the myth of Eden by presenting the image of a "black garden," inhabited not by God's original creations but by the various creatures humans have nearly or completely destroyed. All of the extinct and endangered species are presented as—with scathing irony—sacrificial witnesses to *our* importance. The "great god" of the poem, however, is "The End," toward whom humans follow the gray whale. Our destruction of the whale is seen as only a prelude to self-destruction; such is the logic of short-sighted and voracious greed. Merwin's poem cuts to the heart of contemporary humanity's unfortunate relationship with the other species of this planet and the planet itself. According to the conservative estimates of the great biologist Edward O. Wilson, humans are, at present, driving no fewer than 27,000 species to extinction each year, most concentrated in the world's rain forests and coral reefs. Many of humanity's other major environmental problems, ranging from pollution and global warming to overpopulation and bio-invasions, contribute to what may well be our most ethically appalling contemporary predicament. The sixth great extinction in earth's history is upon us, but with the difference that one species, rather than some extraterrestrial object such as a comet or meteor, is the culprit. Merwin's poem stands as an early attempt to assess the damage and prophecy the end result.

Wendell Berry's "The Peace of Wild Things" (1968) brings the American poetic response to nature full circle. Berry articulates, in more contemporary terms, the romantic idea that nature provides a respite from the burdens of civilization. His poem, in other words, updates the sentiments of Bryant's "Inscription for the Entrance to a Wood." Whereas Bryant had struggled against a Calvinist notion of original sin, Berry struggles against a modern psychological notion of the burdens of consciousness. The opening lines of the poem focus on the poet's knowledge of life's precariousness, both for himself and for his children. Berry's response to these feelings of fear and despair is to go out into the regenerative natural world. The poet feels his consciousness come in tune with such "wild things" as a wood drake and a great heron, "who do not tax their lives with forethought / of grief." Nonhuman animals, in other words, live fully in the present, without constant worrisome speculation about what the future may bring. They do not dwell, self-consciously, on the notion of their own mortality, and so, in some sense, live more fully and freely than humans tend to do. Through sympathy with these animals, Berry comes to an almost Zen-like awareness of the present moment, of the calm water and the stars that are the prominent features of his immediate environment. The poet finds both grace and freedom in this almost pantheistic experience, but he also recognizes that he will inevitably fall back into self-consciousness. Communion with nature is presented, in other words, as necessarily transitory, but also cleansing and revitalizing. The poet, a reader may feel sure, will again, at some point and probably at many points, be afflicted by fears and doubts, but nature—as long as it continues to survive in Emerson's "common sense"—will be there as an object of contemplation to mitigate the burdens of consciousness and to restore a necessary sense of perspective and sanity.

Charles Martin's "Metaphor of Grass in California" (1985) draws a cunning parallel between the history of grass and the history of humans in America. Taking up the very relevant topic of bio-invasions, which has become an increasingly grave problem in the modern world of global commerce, Martin traces the history of indigenous European grasses brought to America in the hooves of Spanish cattle. These grasses, like the European settlers, conquered their American counterparts. Significantly, the grasses are identified with Troy and, thus, with the entire history of military engagements in the West. In depicting the conquest of the grasses itself, Martin cleverly puns on the word "blade," which denotes both a single leaf of grass and a sword. In the next line, Martin similarly puns on "field," meaning both "field of grass" and "battlefield." Perhaps deliberately alluding back to a somewhat similar poem—Stevens's "Anecdote of the Jar," which also depicts the European conquest of the American wilderness—Martin employs the word "dominion" to describe the new order established by the invaders. The American grasses are driven out of their native ranges and survive only in proximity to the mineral serpentine, which is repellent to the foreign grasses. If the pun on "blade" had made the comparison between grasses and men strongly implicit, the final stanza makes it wholly explicit, by likening the vanquished vegetation to men from a fallen city who think of the grass that will grow from and conceal the corpses of the dead. "Men think they are better than grass," Merwin had written; but Martin, like two poets before him—Sandburg in "Grass" (discussed under "War") and Whitman in *Song of Myself* (discussed under "The Self"), reminds us that grass can be made from the corpses of men. The metaphor's equation is, at that point, complete. The poem's final line merely suggests that the only important difference between grass and men, on a cosmic scale, is that the grasses die without cries of anguish or protest.

❧❀❧

"Inscription for the Entrance to a Wood," William Cullen Bryant
 AAL-1; APN-1; ATL-1; HAL-1; HoAL-1; OxBA
"To Cole, the Painter, Departing for Europe" (aka "To an American Painter Departing for Europe"), William Cullen Bryant
 AAL-1; APN-1; ATL-1; ColAP; HAL-1; HoAL-1

"A Bird came down the Walk—," Emily Dickinson

> AAL-1; AAL-2; APN-1; ColAP; HoAL-2; NAL-1; NoAM; NOBA; NoP-4; OxBA; TFi

"I dreaded that first Robin, so," Emily Dickinson

> APN-1; NAL-1

"The Maldive Shark," Herman Melville

> AAL-1; APN-2; ATL-1; ColAP; HAL-1; HoAL-1; NOBA; NoP-4; OxBA

"The Wood-Pile," Robert Frost

> APT-1; ATL-2; ColAP; HAL-2; MAP; NoP-4

"The Most of It," Robert Frost

> APT-1; HAL-2; HoAL-2; NAL-2; NoP-4; WeW-4

"Anecdote of the Jar," Wallace Stevens

> AAL-2; ATL-2; ColAP; HAL-2; HCAP; HoAL-2; MAP; NAL-2; NoAM; NOBA; NoP-4; OxBA; TFi

"November Surf," Robinson Jeffers

> MAP; NAL-2; OxBA

"Carmel Point," Robinson Jeffers

> APT-1; NAL-2; NoAM; NoP-4

"Advice to a Prophet," Richard Wilbur

> AAL-2; CAPP-6; MAP; NoP-4; VCAP

"The Armadillo," Elizabeth Bishop

> AAL-2; APT-2; ATL-2; CAPP-6; ColAP; HAL-2; HCAP; HoAL-2; MAP; NAL-2; NoAM; NOBA; NoP-4; VCAP

"For a Coming Extinction," W. S. Merwin

> HAL-2; HCAP; HoAL-2; MAP; NAL-2; VCAP

"The Peace of Wild Things," Wendell Berry

> VGW

"Metaphor of Grass in California," Charles Martin

> RA

Obligations and Choices

๛

"I always want to know the things one shouldn't do."
"So as to do them?" asked her aunt.
"So as to choose," said Isabel.

Isabel Archer and Mrs. Touchett,
in Henry James's *The Portrait of a Lady*

In the conclusion of *The Portrait of a Lady*, Isabel Archer confronts a difficult, no-win decision. Should she return to Rome, where her cruel husband will surely make her life a living hell, or should she, in violation of her marriage vow and the promise she has made to her step-daughter, remain in England, where she will be hounded by an indefatigable American suitor? One great power of literature is its ability to dramatize the full complexity of situations that cannot easily be reduced to simple statements of principle. Unlike the philosophy of ethics, literature concretely presents the nuances, emotions, and complications that, at times, make practical choices in the world extremely problematic. From a dramatic perspective, situations that involve complex or ambiguous choices are the most interesting, for they cut straight to the conflicted essence of human existence. Life, our finest writers remind us, is imperfect and often tragic.

On the other hand, even in the seemingly worst circumstances, it can often be comic as well, as John Greenleaf Whittier's "Abraham Davenport" (1866), a moral fable about the necessity of fulfilling one's obligations, reminds us. The situation of this narrative poem is ambiguous, but the eponymous hero's response to it is not. The comedy of the poem results from the juxtaposition of uncertain and ominous circumstances with simpleminded clarity. According to Whittier's note, the poem dramatizes an event on the "famous Dark Day" of May 19, 1780. Whittier depicts a meeting of the Connecticut legislature on a day in which "A horror of great darkness" filled the air and seemed to portend nothing less than an apocalyptic catastrophe on the order of "The Twilight of the Gods" or the Second Coming. Whittier attends not only to the superstitious reactions of the New England citizenry but also to such foreboding naturalistic details as the silence of the birds and the flitting of bats. While the state's lawgivers cower in terror, Abraham Davenport, the composed and wise representative from Stamford, demands that candles be brought into the old State House. Resolutely ("Albeit with husky voice and shaking hands"), he fulfills his legal obligation to his community. That what he reads is an "act to amend an act to regulate / The shad and alewive fisheries" is the crowning touch of the anecdote. The juxtaposition of doomsday with the insignificant piece of legislation creates an effect that is, unexpectedly, both ironic and awe-inspiring. Davenport's determination to attend to trivial matters, in the face of seemingly imminent cosmic destruction, paradoxically enhances his stature. No matter how mundane the business, Davenport has maintained he will not be a "faithless servant frightened from my task." He emerges as a moral exemplar, a man who accepts and yet simultaneously transcends his own limitations, thereby inspiring awe in his colleagues. Whittier does not hesitate to explicate the poem's moral in its final line: "simple duty hath no place for fear."

Of all American poets, Robert Frost is outstanding in his treatment of the themes of obligation and choice. In one of the best-known of all American poems—"The Road Not Taken" (1916)—Frost employs universal imagery to represent, symbolically, the nature and consequences of choice. "Two roads diverged in a yellow wood," the speaker tells us and laments that he cannot travel both. He stares down one road as far as he can see for a time, then takes the other. Coyly and ambiguously, the narrator first tells us that the second path is preferable because it "wanted wear," then retracts the statement: both paths are really just about equal. So the speaker's choice isn't necessarily a matter of taking "the one less traveled by," as he willfully and contrarily asserts in the final stanza. The poem is often read as endorsing unpopular or unorthodox decisions in life (like Frost's to become a poet), but it may in fact really be dramatizing the willful self-aggrandizing tendencies of the speaker. The last stanza, in which he imagines himself rationalizing the decision many years into the future, may be taken merely as a wistful boast. It seems to offer a moral, but a dubious one in light of what we learn about the paths in the second stanza and the third ("both that morning equally lay / In leaves no step had trodden black"). The poem would perhaps be more perfect, though less psychologically complex, if the poet had cut the final stanza. Its famous—and rather smug—conclusion tempts readers into overly simplistic interpretations of the poem. Thematically, the heart of "The Road Not Taken" is the speaker's comprehension, in the conclusion of the third stanza, that his choice will lead, irrevocably, to still other paths that will take him ever further away from the one he did not select. Choices in life ramify like paths through a wood: when we have made a decision as to how to proceed, it will often lead to new choices that we would not have confronted had we selected otherwise. We will never know what decisions we would have confronted and even who we would have been had we made a different initial choice. The brilliance of Frost's poem inheres in the apparent simplicity and suggestiveness of its symbolic representation of these truths.

In another of his most famous poems, "Stopping by Woods on a Snowy Evening" (1923), Frost represents a conflict between desire and obligation. The speaker, out on a snowy evening on some unspecified errand, finds himself beside picturesque woods, owned by a man from the village. Furtively, the traveler stops to watch the secluded woods "fill up with snow," a decision that he imagines his practical-minded horse cannot fathom. The speaker has a different regard for the woods than either their owner or the horse: his aesthetic appreciation dictates his actions rather than profit or necessity. The poem, however, presents a complicated view of aesthetics. The woods are not only "lovely" but also "dark and deep." The latter adjectives, along with the fact that it is the "darkest evening of the year" (presumably the winter solstice), hint that the poem contains a darker undercurrent of meaning. This possibility seems to be reinforced by the implications of the word "sleep" in the final lines. The beautiful imagery of snow falling through woods may be seen as a temptation not only to linger but to capitulate, to abandon the difficult obligations of life for the pursuit of serenity and beauty, which the poem implicitly equates with a decadent and even morbid tendency. The "easy wind" and the flakes that are "downy" (a term that usually refers to something made from feathers, as a pillow) almost lull the speaker, but he seems to be brought out of his contemplative mood by the horse's insistent harness bells. They recall the speaker to his duties, to the fact that he has "promises to keep," presumably in the village. The solitude and beauty of the woods has offered him a pleasant respite, but to linger further would be to shirk the necessary though perhaps unpleasant obligations of communal life. At a certain point, the poem suggests, aesthetic contemplation can become self-indulgent and even self-destructive. Instead of traveling on the many miles the speaker has to go before he sleeps, he could simply lie down in the woods and end all cares peacefully; but the traveler chooses to forge ahead, with the knowledge that sleep must be deferred until obligation has been fulfilled.

The repetition of the final lines has perplexed many readers and occasioned much commentary. Frost himself offered little help in the matter, for he once claimed, quite disingenuously, that he simply could not think of another rhyme for "sweep." (Of course, there are many other rhymes, as Frost knew perfectly well. Frost's public statements about his poetry were sometimes cagey and calculated to mislead.) Formally, the repetition neatly closes out the poem's interlocking rhyme scheme (AABA BBCB CCDC DDDD). Thematically, it suggests either extreme weariness on the speaker's part or a symbolic meaning of "sleep"—or both. In psychological terms, the repetition of "And miles to go before I sleep" may be seen as the speaker reluctantly confronting the prospect of what lies ahead. He pores over the words the way someone might keep repeating "I can't believe it—I just can't believe it" in response to unhappy news. In symbolic terms, the repetition may indicate that the lines have two meanings, one literal and one figurative. A common figurative use of "sleep"—as in Hamlet's "To be or not to be" soliloquy—is as a metonymy for death. In that case, the speaker might be understood as first saying, "I have a long way to go before I rest this evening" and then "I have a long time left ahead of me before I can take my final rest." Frost was a master of simplicity; he could convey rich implications through the most elementary words and images.

The imagery and situations of at least two later Frost poems derive, in part, from "Stopping by Woods on a Snowy Evening": "Desert Places" (discussed under "The Self") and "Come In" (1942). The latter poem is not set in a winter landscape (the presence of the singing thrush indicates as much), but it does involve a solitary figure peering into dark woods and making a decision. The poem transpires at dusk, by which time the woods have been sufficiently darkened that a bird cannot maneuver through them. The thrush, however, can still sing from the branch where it has settled. From the "pillared dark" of trees, its voice sounds in the speaker's ears almost like a summons to the woods. The darkness here is explicitly linked with the psychological darkness of lamentation. The bird's "invitation," in other words, is a temptation to yield to negative, pessimistic emotions. The speaker hesitates (as is indicated by the word "But," which precedes his "no"), then decisively says "I was out for stars." Stargazing here represents a positive, engaged, curious attitude toward the world. A person who goes out looking at stars is obviously in a different frame of mind than one who sulks in the dark. One should note that the speaker resists anthropomorphizing the thrush: its song is "Almost" like an invitation, and in the end, the speaker acknowledges that he has not *really* been asked to come into the woods at all. Thrushes do not issue invitations, and the speaker is forced to acknowledge that any meaning he finds in the bird's song has been put there by his own imagination. Like the speaker of "Stopping by Woods on a Snowy Evening," the narrator of "Come In" leaves the woods and what it represents for something else—in this case not a duty, but a positive approach to life.

Yvor Winters's "Sir Gawaine and the Green Knight" (1941) turns, as Whittier's "Abraham Davenport" had, to legendary material in order to dramatize the poet's thematic concerns—although in this case, Winters reaches back well before the European discovery of America to a tale derived from the great anonymous Middle English poem of the same title. Winters shifts the point of view to the hero himself and condenses the action of his 2,530-line source into nine quatrains that distill the story's themes of choice and obligation. The poem begins in medias res, after Sir Bertilak de Hautdesert, aka the Green Knight, has crashed King Arthur's New Year's feast and issued the challenge of a beheading contest. Thus, the poem's first image is of the Knight's "reptilian green" neck. Sir Gawaine, in order to preserve the court's reputation, has just accepted the challenge. Winters's first three stanzas describe the Green Knight's alien physical appearance, the first phase of the beheading contest, the intruder's miraculous survival, and Gawaine's realization that now he must, in one year's time, receive a similar blow in the Green Knight's own land, albeit with slimmer odds of surviving. Having willingly accepted the Green Knight's challenge, Gawaine is bound by honor to accept the unpleasant consequences of his failure. Instead of embarking on a quest for a damsel in distress or a magic dingus, Gawaine sets out in order to lose his own head. Winters compresses Gawaine's journey and the better part of a year into half a line. The remainder of the next four stanzas documents Gawaine's stay at the foreign keep, where he is tempted by the Green Knight's seductive lady, who clings and wraps around him like a vine.

Gawaine, however, keeps his trust, or obligation, to his host: although he loves the lady and is dazzled by her charms, he retains his chastity. (Winters omits the episode of the magic girdle, crucial to both the outcome and meaning of the original poem.) The reward for his conscientiousness and sincerity is life. The Green Knight lets him go "with what I knew." In the final stanza, Gawaine, dignity and identity in tact, returns from the wild, disorderly, organic world of the Green Knight to that of ordinary men, represented by an imposition of man-made order on the natural world—a road. The poem can be read as symbolically portraying a struggle for moral clarity and self-definition against the irrational forces that would subvert them, which in Winters's mind seem to be associated with nature and sex. Essentially, it portrays an adherence to Apollonian virtues in the face of a Dionysian world. Gawaine chooses to accept a daunting challenge and further elects to accept the terrifying consequences of his initial failure. Tested, his resolve remains firm. Having met his obligations without fatally faltering, he returns to the world a wiser man.

"A Note Left in Jimmy Leonard's Shack" (1959) by James Wright dramatizes a difficult ethical dilemma thrust onto the shoulders not of a great hero but of an ordinary young boy. The poem takes the form of a note—which embodies and provisionally resolves the dilemma—left by an unnamed boy for Jimmy, a violent drunkard, to find. Minnegan, Jimmy's brother, has been found by a dry river's watermark in ground made muddy by the rain. The boy has been dispatched by a kid named Beany to inform Jimmy of the news. The poor boy is terrified at the prospect of waking Jimmy while he still might be drunk; further, he is afraid that Jimmy will blame him for the brother's misfortune and do something violent, like throw a rock at him. Clearly, the boy knows a good deal about the man he is supposed to reach. The boy also knows he's going to be in trouble at home for coming out to Jimmy's shack, but he's willing to risk his parents' wrath for Minnegan's sake. He hopes that Jimmy will come to take care of Minnegan before the police arrive, but his method of informing Jimmy hardly guarantees this result.

The boy decides to write the message as a note to resolve his obligation to inform Jimmy and, simultaneously, to prevent the messenger from being held immediately accountable for the message. The note, which might not be found until it is too late, represents an unsatisfactory but psychologically realistic and perfectly understandable compromise between duty and fear. The boy's own frustrations over this compromise can be seen as prompting the candid insult in the final stanza. The conclusion also reveals that Minnegan isn't, as the opening stanza had seemed to imply, necessarily dead yet. The image of Minnegan rolled around "in the roots and garbage like a fish" vividly evokes the reader's sympathy for the old man, which is also, as the poem's final line clearly indicates, shared by the boy himself. Wright's poem dramatizes the result of unfair obligations thrust onto the shoulders of someone not fit or adequately prepared to deal with them.

William Stafford's "Traveling through the dark" (1960) resembles Frost's poems in its dramatic presentation of choice as well as in its first-person narration, natural imagery, understated tone, and depiction of solitary action. The narrator, out driving one night on a narrow road beside a canyon, happens across a deer that has recently been killed in an accident. Whoever hit the deer did not bother to remove it from the road. The speaker feels the obligation to do so himself, since he knows the deer could cause another accident. The decision to roll the deer into the canyon (something that the speaker has clearly done before) is unexpectedly complicated by the discovery that the doe is pregnant with a still-living fawn. The speaker, caught in an ethical bind, hesitates. He knows that to roll the doe will be to kill the unborn fawn, but he also knows he does not have any clear way of delivering the fawn. The car in this poem functions in a manner similar to the horse in "Stopping by

Woods on a Snowy Evening," as a spur to action. Symbolically, the forward aim of the car's lights and the steady purring of its engine may be understood as reminders to the speaker of the straight, steady, unwavering path he has to follow, despite his sentiments. The surrounding wilderness seems to listen, waiting for his decision—a personification that reveals the gravity of the situation in the speaker's mind. He thinks hard a moment further, what he calls "my only swerving"—a phrase that echoes the "swerve" of line 4. The implication is that by swerving away from his ethical duty, he could cause other drivers to swerve to their deaths. His first duty remains to the drivers on the Wilson River road. The realization steels his resolve, and he pushes the pregnant doe into the river. Stafford ends the poem abruptly, without apologizing for or diminishing the effect of the speaker's difficult decision.

❦

"Abraham Davenport," John Greenleaf Whittier

ATL-1; NoP-4

"The Road Not Taken," Robert Frost

AAL-2; APT-1; ATL-2; HAL-2; HoAL-2; MAP; NAL-2; NoAM; NoP-4; OxBA; SoSe-9; TFi

"Stopping by Woods on a Snowy Evening," Robert Frost

AAL-2; APT-1; ATL-2; ColAP; HAL-2; HoAL-2; LPTT; MAP; NAL-2; NoAM; NOBA; NoP-4; OxBA; SoSe-9; TFi

"Come In," Robert Frost

APT-1; ATL-2; NOBA; NoP-4

"Sir Gawaine and the Green Knight," Yvor Winters

NoAM; VGW

"A Note Left in Jimmy Leonard's Shack," James Wright

ATL-2; HAL-2; HCAP; HoAL-2; NoP-4

"Traveling through the dark," William Stafford

CAPP-6; CoAmPo; CoAP; ColAP; HAL-2; HoAL-2; MAP; NoAM; SoSe-9; WeW-4

Poetry

꧁꧂

He would be a poet who could impress the winds and streams into his service, to speak for him; who nailed words to their primitive senses, as farmers drive down stakes in the spring, which the frost has heaved; who derived his words as often as he used them—transplanted them to his page with earth adhering to their roots; whose words were so true and fresh and natural that they would appear to expand like the buds at the approach of spring, though they lay half smothered between two musty leaves in a library.

Henry David Thoreau "Walking"

In American literature, poems about poetry are apt to assert the necessity of both originality and a connection between the poet and nature. This tendency reflects several facts about American life. First, American poetry matured during the romantic period of literature; second, America itself was a relatively wild country at the time, in which virgin nature existed in all its glory and ruggedness as it did not in Europe; and third, American poetry has tended to reflect both the dynamism and the freedom ideally associated with the character of life in America. In order to achieve their goals, American poets, by and large, have adopted and defended an organic theory of poetry, which states that form should be determined by meaning. The typical American poet sees form not as something analogous to a vessel, which would be filled up with the content of a poem, but rather as a plant or animal grown from the original idea, image, impression, or experience that led the poet to write. Many American poets, starting with Emerson and Whitman, have equated organicism—which they derived from the English poet and theorist Samuel Taylor Coleridge and his German precursors—with free verse; by so doing, they have attempted to create a distinctively American poetic tradition, relatively free from the formal accentual-syllabic tradition of English poetry. Certainly, however, not all American poets have accepted that American poetry must be organic in nature or free in form. Why, they have asked, is a free-verse poet like Whitman more essentially American than more formal poets like Dickinson and Frost?

Regardless of its precise nature, a distinctively American cultural and poetic tradition was hardly founded the moment the United States became independent from British rule. The first and most formidable barrier American poetry faced was that of language. American poetry is written in English, which makes it, seemingly, a natural adjunct to English literature and English poetic techniques, which evolved with the language. Early American poets had to grapple with the stigma of being lesser cousins to a great tradition and in addition, had to demonstrate what precisely was American about their work. Philip Freneau, the first American poet deeply interested in the idea of an American literary tradition distinct from that of the British, discovered that founding a new tradition was not an easy task. He often wrote about distinctively American subjects, such as virgin nature, the slave trade, and Native Americans, but he did so in a style deeply indebted to British neoclassicists. What eluded him even more than originality of form were respect and financial rewards. Freneau found early America to be a practical-minded and business-oriented environment with little patience or use for the work of a poet. One purpose of his "To a New England Poet" (1823), one of the earliest American poems about poetry, is to vent his frustrations over the situation of the American poet who has neither a viable tradition to mine nor a captive audience to reach. In the poem, Freneau's frustrations seethe beneath the veil of caustic irony.

The basic problem that "To a New England Poet" identifies is the lack of cultural traditions in America. Though becoming politically independent, it remained culturally dependent on England and, to a lesser extent, continental Europe. Freneau takes the career of Washington Irving, a younger and far more successful writer than Freneau himself, as a case study in the problem of dependency. The terms of Irving's success strike Freneau as emblematic: Irving attained prestige by writing about, drawing ideas from, and being accepted first in Europe. These facts lie behind all of Freneau's "advice." The hypothetical poet addressed by the poem is first apprised of the economic situation in America: knowing Latin and Greek (which Freneau, as a good neoclassicist, assumes are essential skills for the poet) will not distinguish one from the "meanest drudges." The paradoxical difficulty of the American poet's situation is diagnosed in stanzas two and three: democracy and commerce, the twin foundations of the American civilization that Freneau wants so badly to celebrate, actually work against the poet's favor. Equality undermines the poet's privileged stature, while commerce brings the impractical poet only scorn. Irving's defection to the British court provides a solution, but a distinctly problematic and unpatriotic one. Success and monetary rewards may be won abroad, but at the price of one's ideals. Freneau's bitterness over this catch-22 situation manifests itself in the sardonic opening of the final stanza: "Dear bard, I pray you, take the hint, / In England what you write and print, / Republished here in shop, or stall, / Will perfectly enchant us all." The deepest irony Freneau explores is the idea that political independence should foster so little cultural initiative. American tastes at that time, both timid and derivative, merely echoed those of the British. According to Freneau, the former oppressor even dictated the terms of success in the case of America's own talent. Unable to find an adequate solution to the dilemma, Freneau lapsed into ironic cynicism. He foreshadows Emerson and Whitman in his desire to found a vital national literature, but the times were distinctly unfavorable to his ambitions.

Two generations later, Ralph Waldo Emerson would clear the path that Freneau had only indicated. Emerson's "Merlin" (1847), along with his essay "The Poet" of three years earlier, attempted to point the way toward a distinctively American brand of poetry. Unlike Freneau, Emerson felt that American poetry—in order to free itself from England's influence—would require new forms to express its subjects. The "Merlin" of his poem is an idealized poet-figure whose work depends not on pleasing sounds that keep their distance from coarse reality but rather on "Artful thunder" that chimes with all the rudeness and variety of nature and civilization. Emerson, in other words, rejects the publicly sanctioned strain of American poetry represented through the nineteenth century by such "fireside" poets as Henry Wadsworth Longfellow, John Greenleaf Whittier, Oliver Wendell Holmes, and James Russell Lowell, all of whom adhered to English formal models as well as to the niceties of poetic decorum and conventional subject matter (which, of course, English poets themselves, from Chaucer to Browning, often did not). The "bard" envisioned in Emerson's poem "shall not his brain encumber / With the coil of rhythm and number," but shall instead "mount to paradise / By the stairway of surprise." Emerson privileges content over form; for him, the true poet is one who challenges conventions and articulates new thoughts, thereby expanding our horizons by liberating us from our own failures of perception (which is why, in the essay "The Poet," Emerson refers to poets as "liberating gods"). The key is "surprise," or originality, not mastery of traditional forms. Emerson does not subscribe to the neoclassical theory that poets should dress up conventional thoughts in beautiful language. Like the English romantics—particularly Percy Bysshe Shelley—he envisions an exalted role for the poet as a seer and an unacknowledged legislator. The true poet must alter the world ("The rhyme of the poet / Modulates the king's affairs") and resolve into wholeness the illusion of opposites. At the same time, the poet has to open up new subject matter, as Emerson indicates in his essay "The Poet." An American poet must be able to make poetic use of such cultural raw materials as "Banks and tariffs, the newspaper and caucus, methodism and unitarianism . . . the northern trade, the southern planting, the western clearing, Oregon, and Texas." The poet has to persuade us to see the poetry in such things. Few poets can rise to such imaginative and idealized heights, but Emerson undoubtedly paved the way for a new, freer style of American poetry that would be most fully realized not in his own work but in that of Walt Whitman and his successors.

Whitman's "Out of the Cradle Endlessly Rocking" (1859, rev. 1881) could be considered under several thematic rubrics, notably "Life & Death," "Loss," and "Nature"; fundamentally, however, the poem is Whitman's mythic account of how he became a poet. It thus reveals what his idea of the poet is. The many fructifying influences on his younger self that ultimately made him a poet are indicated in the highly complex opening paragraph—a single sentence, twenty-two lines and 203 words in length, consisting mainly of prepositional phrases. Parsing this sentence, one discovers that the subject and verb are actually very simple: "I . . . sing." This is what the poem is about: how Whitman came to "sing" (or write poetry). For him, learning to "sing" related directly to the experience of seeing two mockingbirds, champion singers among the avian clans, on Long Island in the month of May. The poem is notable both for its faithful use of natural details ("four light-green eggs spotted with brown") and for its imaginative "translation" of the mockingbird's song in the poem's italicized sections. Each of these sections begins with a thrice-repeated phrase—fitting, for an actual mockingbird usually repeats its musical phrases three times. (Whitman had learned his bird lore from one of his disciples, the great American naturalist John Burroughs.)

The narrative of "Out of the Cradle Endlessly Rocking" concerns the fate of the mockingbirds. One day the female mockingbird disappears, never to return, despite the exhortations and lamentations of her mate. What remains is a "trio" of figures: the male mockingbird, the young Whitman, and "the fierce old mother" (the sea). The poet-to-be hears the "aria" of the mockingbird (a term that might remind us how Italian opera directly influenced Whitman's conception of poetry) and wonders whether it is actually addressed to its mate or to him. Regardless, he feels himself transformed: "Now in a moment I know what I am for, I awake . . . A thousand warbling echoes have started to life within me, never to die." But the song of the bird is soon replaced by the sound of the waves, which repeat a chant of their own: "Death, death, death, death, death." This word, "stronger and more delicious than any" (line

14), fuses in his soul with the song of the mockingbird to inspire his poetry: "My own songs awaked from that hour," he says. Whitman portrays an Adamic return to poetry's primal sources—the inspiration of nature and the terrible knowledge of death. The poet that Whitman depicts (and strives to be) is not pedantic or bookish in the least. He reassumes his most basic functions: to name things and to preserve their memory. Of course, this "return" to origins is mythic, in that Whitman cannot truly remake poetry from its source without laboring to some extent under the long shadow of the history of poetry and language; but he has nonetheless created an inspiring and liberating myth of poetry regaining its vitality by drawing upon its aboriginal sources.

Emily Dickinson's conception of the poet owes, as Whitman's does, a profound debt to Emerson, even if she does not embrace the organic theory of form. Like Emerson and Whitman, she insists upon the poet's originality of inspiration and direct intercourse with nature. "This was a Poet—It is That" (#448, c. 1862) is her most comprehensive poem on the theme of poetry. The poet, she says, "Distills amazing sense / From ordinary Meanings," such as the familiar flowers "That perished by the Door— / We wonder it was not Ourselves / Arrested it—before—." In other words, the poet is one who finds words to express an aspect of ordinary reality that the rest of us pass mutely over. This is Emerson's "stairway of surprise" all over again. Dickinson herself ascends this stairway with an unexpected and ironic twist, by claiming that the perceptive poet "Entitles Us . . . To ceaseless Poverty." All poetic creation robs the potential of others to express—at least in an original manner—the same idea, even as it enables others (including the majority who would never have stumbled on the expression for themselves) to share the idea. Poetry is a double-edged sword that gives even as it takes away, and the stakes could not be higher. The poet's reward for such genuine insight is immortality ("a Fortune— / Exterior—to Time—").

After Whitman and Dickinson, American poetry enters, for a brief time, into a twilight phase, in which poets were far less confident about the direction and significance of their work. The anxieties some poets entertained are well expressed in both Edwin Arlington Robinson's sonnet "Oh for a poet—for a beacon bright" (1897) and Edgar Lee Master's "Petit, the Poet" (1915). Both poets acutely felt how far their own work fell short of the expansiveness of Whitman's. It seemed to them that poets had lost their vital connection to nature and had become too preoccupied with form—in other words, that poets had sacrificed what were often conceived as the most distinctly American characteristics of their work. Thus, Robinson, in a gesture fraught with self-mockery, disparages "these little sonnet-men" in his own sonnet. He looks for a new bard to "rift" the age's "changeless glimmer of dead gray" and to reassert the inspiring power of the Muses. The poets of the day seem, instead, to "fashion" their poems "in a shrewd mechanic way." In the materialistic Gilded Age of the late nineteenth century, Robinson suggests, even the poets have been infected by the spirit of industry. The poem ends with a series of questions, the final one of which asks whether any eternal poet will arise in this day and age. Like Dickinson's poems on poetry, the final accent falls on immortality; the difference, however, is that Robinson doubts that he or his contemporaries can achieve such a lofty goal. As his later sonnet "Many Are Called" clearly implies, few are chosen.

That Robinson's standard of comparison for modern poetry is Whitman's vast accomplishments becomes clearer if we juxtapose "Oh for a poet—for a beacon bright" with his poem "Walt Whitman," which begins "The master-songs are ended"—ended, that is, by Whitman's death. Edgar Lee Masters seemed to have shared such a feeling, for in "Petit, the Poet," he contrasts the "Faint iambics" that "tick, tick, tick" along in the verse of his contemporaries with the work of truly great poets, such as Homer and Whitman (ignoring, however, that Homer wrote in dactylic hexameters). The poem develops a contrast between the attenuated, fashionably Gallic, and thoroughly decadent formalism of the day ("Triolets, villanelles, rondels, roundeaus, / Ballades by the score with the same old thought") and an inclusive, original poetry that embraces the whole range of human experience as well as the variety of the natural world. Like Robinson's, Master's poem ends tentatively with a question rather than an assertion: "what little iambics / While Homer and Whitman roared in the pines?" Robinson blames the character of the age, whereas Masters blames the poets themselves for a sterile, dilettantish fascination with form at the expense of content; but what both poets offer is a diagnosis of the problem rather than a solution.

One "solution" would come with the modernist revitalization of the poetic tradition in the 1920s, at which time America witnessed an unprecedented proliferation of poetic talent and innovation. Foremost among the poets of the new movement was Ezra Pound, whose "A Pact" (1916) also looks back to Whitman, but with a more critical eye than either Robinson or Masters. Whitman had obviously become a formidable and legendary figure in American poetry by the turn of the century. He represented all that was truly dynamic and distinctive about American poetry—its inclusive, democratic instinct, its freedom from the authority of form and tradition, and its vital connection to the natural world. But for Pound, Whitman was both a blessing and a curse. As the essay "What I Feel about Walt Whitman" makes even clearer, Pound saw Whitman as a genius, but a very crude one. Shrewdly and not a little egotistically, he writes in the essay: "I honour him for he prophesied me." "A Pact" documents Pound's attempt to come to terms with his spiritual predecessor. Pound grants that Whitman "broke the new wood" of the American poetic tradition, just as the pioneers literally broke the wood of the new world's forests, but he asserts that "Now is a time for carving"—in other words, a time for artistry to lend shape to Whitman's vigorous but relatively formless pioneering work. Unlike Robinson and Masters, Pound is not daunted by Whitman's example; rather he sees himself as one who can build on it and even improve it—which is precisely what he attempted in his esoteric *Cantos*, a lifelong poetic project that is the nearest twentieth-century equivalent to Whitman's *Leaves of Grass*.

In contrast to the celebrations of poetry formulated by most of the poets considered in this section, Marianne Moore's "Poetry" (1921) offers a skeptical view of her subject, at least initially: "I, too, dislike it," her poem famously begins. In her final revision of the poem in 1967, Moore reduced "Poetry" to its first three lines. Anthologists, however, have usually preferred the earlier version, which is twenty-nine lines long. The short version redeems poetry by finding in it a "place for the genuine." The longer version elaborates what, precisely, Moore means by "the genuine." An unlikely list of animals, persons, and objects (lines 15–25) demonstrates that Moore, like Emerson and Whitman before her, feels that all of reality is a fit subject for poetic expression—even the "business documents and school books" to which Tolstoy, as Moore's footnote indicates, had taken exception. Poetry must result from the active work of imagination operating on any object or surface that reality presents. The "half poets" are those whose work is derivative and, thus, does not result from a direct and original impression of life. Moore's famous formula for successful poetry—"imaginary gardens with real toads in them"— illustrates the fusion of artistic imagination with the "raw material" of reality. Moore's defense of "the genuine" is a kind of apologia for the hard surface of her own poetry and a polemic against conventional, "agreeable" poetry; but it also perpetuates the main line of American thought about poetry from Emerson's "Merlin" to her own time. Poetry, once again, must be original and must have a vital connection with the natural world, even if nature has been reshaped by human hands into that epitome of the pastoral ideal—the garden.

Along with Whitman's free verse, the great influences on the new poetry were French symbolism, which tended also to employ *vers libre* (free verse), and the Japanese haiku, which places special emphasis on the objective presentation of imagery. One of the most influential movements of modern American poetry, imagism—associated with the early work of Pound and cohorts such as Richard Aldington, Hilda Doolittle, F. S. Flint, and T. E. Hulme as well as later with Amy Lowell and William Carlos Williams—drew inspiration from the haiku and asserted the primacy of the poetic image. Archibald MacLeish's "Ars Poetica" (1926), a manifesto of modern poetry, emphasizes the same type of "objective" imagery and ably summarizes the basic tenets of imagism. Through a series of similes, MacLeish obliquely indicates the type of poetry he would like to see—poetry that is, paradoxically, "mute / As a globed fruit" and "wordless / As the flight of birds" (images that, one should note, reassert the old organic theory of poetry). MacLeish, in other words, does not want poetry to comment on things; instead, he wants it to present things directly and concretely. The distinction is familiar from fiction; just as in a good modern short story, such as those written by Chekhov and Hemingway, poetry should concern itself with *showing* rather than *telling*. If poetry performs that task well, it will be "equal to: / Not true." In other words, it will embody the world's mystery rather than attempt to explain it. MacLeish then gives examples of how images can stand for abstractions: "An empty doorway and a maple leaf" for grief, "leaning grasses and two lights above the sea" for love. The conclusion contains the poem's most famous and oft-quoted lines—"A poem should not mean / But be"—which crystallize the imagist agenda.

William Carlos Williams came as close as anyone to realizing the new ideal of imagism, especially in such poems as "The Great Figure" and "The Red Wheelbarrow." In other poems, notably "The Wind Increases" (1934) and "A Sort of a Song" (1944), Williams comments on the kind of poetry he wanted to create. "The Wind Increases" is a spatial poem; in other words, it uses the arrangement of words on the page as an expressive device. The poem is about the blowing of the wind, and the irregular indentations cause the words to appear "windblown." The poem is also about the nature of the poet ("if any exists"). Adhering to the organic analogy favored by the romantics, Williams compares the poet's words to plants blown by the wind. Poetry must be anchored in the ground, but it must also register "the form / of motion," the way a plant blown in the wind does. Such a form will obviously be both complex and relatively free, but it will not be ephemeral if the wind cannot blow it away. True poetry, in other words, is both spontaneous and enduring: it reconciles these opposites. Williams's ideas, though novel in form, hark back to Emerson and Melville's "Art" (discussed under "Art & Beauty"); the poem also seems very close in spirit to the punning quotation by Thoreau that serves as the epigraph for this section. In "A Sort of a Song," Williams introduces the famous parenthetical aside "No ideas / but in things," which reformulates the principal theme of MacLeish's "Ars Poetica." Williams exhorts the poet to compose and to invent and also likens poetry itself to both a snake waiting to strike and a flower that splits rocks. As in "The Wind Increases," he places the emphasis on the startling originality and the unexpected tenacity of the true poet's words, as well as on the connection between poetry and nature.

J. V. Cunningham formulated a salty counterstatement against the mainstream of American poetry with "For My Contemporaries" (1942). Specifically, Cunningham dissents from the majority's adherence to an organic, free-verse conception of poetry. Instead, he aligns himself with Robert Frost's (in)famous statement that writing free verse is like playing tennis without a net. Cunningham, who rejected the romantic tradition of self-expression and took instead the more austere Latin and Renaissance poets as his models, preferred to refer to his work as "verse," in contradistinction to "poetry." Verse, by which he meant rigorously metered and rhymed composition, was, he insisted, a public from with objective standards of excellence, whereas poetry, by which he mainly meant free verse, had become a mostly private or coterie affair, with subjective and largely arbitrary, quasi-religious qualitative standards. Undoubtedly, many American poets and critics, starting with Emerson and Whitman, have been overly eager to find in free verse some ideological significance as well as a peculiarly indefinable "American" quality, all the while forgetting that English poets such as Christopher Smart, William Blake, and Martin Farquhar Tupper had employed it before Whitman, that French *vers libre* had inspired the modernist movement, and that many of the nation's best and most distinctively American poets—from Bryant and Longfellow to Melville and Dickinson to Robinson and Frost—had written in meter.

"For My Contemporaries" documents how Cunningham, in good conscience, gave up "poetry" for "verse." The short lines of the poem contrast with the long lines, swollen, as Cunningham puts it, with "spiritual noise"—which one immediately associates with Whitman and his many modern heirs. The poem insists upon the difficulty and integrity of good craftsmanship and asks the indulgence of those prone to undervalue or even to despise the traditional virtues of verse. The stinging final stanza aligns good sense and skill with verse and seems, also, to align poetry with madness. (Similar sentiments can be found in several short poems on poetry by Cunningham's sympathetic colleague and acquaintance Yvor Winters, including "To a Young Writer," "On Teaching the Young," and "Time and the Garden.") Cunningham's severe, denotative style precludes natural imagery and implicitly criticizes organic form. "For My Contemporaries" is a somewhat cranky but undeniably individualistic statement of resistance against the dominant modes of American poetry. It is usefully provocative in the way that all intelligently formulated dissenting statements are, and has no doubt served as an inspiration to the "new formalist" movement of the past several decades, associated with the work of such outstanding poet-critics as Timothy Steele and Dana Gioia.

Louis Simpson's "American Poetry" (1963), on the other hand, resembles Moore's "Poetry" in its call for omnivorous poems that can "digest" anything existing in the world, even "uranium." Simpson, like Moore and unlike Cunningham, thus stands in the main line of American thought about poetry, extending back to Emerson and Whitman. None of the principal theorists of American poetry has wanted to limit the subject matter of poetry to conventionally "poetic" topics. Everything in the world, as Emerson had implied in his essay "The Poet," must be seen as suitable raw material for the poetic imagination to exercise itself upon. Simpson objectifies American poetry through the figure of a shark, which, when cut open, may be found to contain surprising objects (Simpson instances a shoe, which may stand for any of a number of supposedly "unpoetic" things one might find in an authentically American poem). He develops the figure further in the concluding two lines: the "shark" must be able to swim tirelessly through "the desert" of American culture, and it must, under such dehumanizing conditions, also manage to find or retain a voice that is "almost human." The connection with nature in this poem is tenuous at best—"moons" and "the desert" hardly conjure up a pastoral ideal—but this may be part of the point. Huge swaths of modern America conspicuously lack any vestige of nature, but poetry, still as adaptable and heterogeneous as Emerson had prophesied, must forge ahead and find new sources of inspiration; it must, paradoxically, make the unpoetic poetic.

None of the poems considered so far have tackled the most basic and difficult question of all: What is poetry? Howard Nemerov's "Because You Asked about the Line between Poetry and Prose" (1980) sets out to do just that, though somewhat indirectly. In this terse, imagistic poem, Nemerov coyly indicates the shades of grey that separate poetry from prose. He does so by means of a metaphorical illustration: the moment at which a freezing drizzle turns into snow. The precise instant of this change eludes scrutiny, but the change itself is nonetheless unmistakable. Nemerov, in other words, refuses to draw a hard and fast line between poetry and prose. The line is blurry, yet distinct—what A. R. Ammons in "Corsons Inlet" calls "sharpness spread out." Nemerov indicates, through his brilliantly described example, that the precise line between many related things is difficult to draw with precision. Where does "middle age" end and "old age" begin? We would probably have a hard time saying, yet we still think we can recognize a middle-aged person or an old person when we see one. A concrete example can, in some cases, be worth many abstract arguments. Much poetry is predicated on this notion, and here, Nemerov has not just written about poetry but given us a good example of what poetry is.

Dana Gioia explores yet another aspect of poetry in "The Next Poem" (1991), a pointed exposition of hope with which all practicing poets will sympathize. Gioia describes the Platonic ideal of a poem to which he (and many other poets of a formalist bent) aspires each time he sets pen to paper (or, perhaps, taps at the keyboard). The poem he envisions will have an unforgettable opening line, will make expert and organic use of stanzaic form, will employ subtle rhymes, will combine common speech with the vital surprise of good music, will avoid fragmentation and obscurity, and will contain an implicit yet unmistakable significance. "How much better it seems now," he laments, than it will after it has actually been finished. Gioia contrasts the dream of perfection with the rigorous compromises and dissatisfactions of actual performance. Many poets strive to write "the perfect poem," knowing all the while how elusive it remains. Yet the dream itself, Gioia implies, is what inspires some of the best writing, for without an ideal of perfection there can be no straining after greatness. The poem, which in many respects exemplifies the enviable virtues it details, concludes with a striking analogy: the poet is like a fisherman, waiting for the next fish to bite and hoping it will, finally, be "the big one."

e⌒⌄⌒o

"To a New England Poet," Philip Freneau
>AAL-1; HAL-1; NAL-1

"Merlin," Ralph Waldo Emerson
>APN-1; ATL-1; HAL-1; HoAL-1; NOBA; OxBA

"Out of the Cradle Endlessly Rocking," Walt Whitman
>AAL-1; APN-1; ATL-1; ATL-2; ColAP; HAL-1; HAL-2; HoAL-2; LPTT; MAP; NAL-1; NOBA; NoP-4; OxBA; WeW-4

"This was a Poet—It is That," Emily Dickinson
>AAL-1; AAL-2; APN-2; HAL-1; HAL-2; HoAL-2; NAL-1; NOBA

"Oh for a poet—for a beacon bright," Edwin Arlington Robinson
>APN-2; OxBA

"Petit, the Poet," Edgar Lee Masters
>ATL-2; ColAP; MAP; NoAM; NOBA; OxBA

"A Pact," Ezra Pound
>AAL-2; APT-1; ATL-2; ColAP; HAL-2; HoAL-2; MAP; NAL-2; NoAM; NOBA; OxBA

"Poetry," Marianne Moore
>AAL-2; APT-1; ATL-2; ColAP; HAL-2; HCAP; HoAL-2; LPTT; MAP; NAL-2; NoAM; NOBA; NoP-4; OxBA; TFi

"Ars Poetica," Archibald MacLeish
>APT-1; ATL-2; ColAP; HoAL-2; LPTT; MAP; NOBA; NoP-4; OxBA; SoSe-9; TFi; WeW-4

"The Wind Increases," William Carlos Williams
>   NAL-2

"A Sort of a Song," William Carlos Williams
>   APT-1; ATL-2; NAL-2; NoP-4

"For My Contemporaries," J. V. Cunningham
>   APT-2; CoAP; VCAP

"American Poetry," Louis Simpson
>   CAPP-6; HAL-2; NoAM; NOBA

"Because You Asked about the Line between Poetry and Prose," Howard Nemerov
>   VCAP; WeW-4

"The Next Poem," Dana Gioia
>   DiPo; NoP-4

The Self

There is no need to traverse the earth and sky to find a wondrous object full of contrasts of infinite greatness and littleness, of deep gloom and amazing brightness, capable at the same time of arousing piety, wonder, scorn, and terror. I have only to contemplate myself; man comes from nothing, passes through time, and disappears forever in the bosom of God. He is seen but a moment wandering on the verge of two abysses, and then is lost.

Alexis de Tocqueville, *Democracy in America*
(translated by George Lawrence)

Some of the most innovative and vital poetry in America, starting with the publication of Walt Whitman's *Leaves of Grass* (1855), took an inward turn and began scrutinizing the self. Whitman's idea that the self could serve as an adequate theme of poetry was confirmed—independently— by Emily Dickinson, whose hermitical habits made her own being an ideal subject for her work. It was almost as if modern American poetry took its cue directly from the conclusion of Henry David Thoreau's *Walden*, published just one year before *Leaves of Grass*: "be a Columbus to whole new continents and worlds within you," Thoreau advised, arguing that "it is easier to sail many thousand miles through cold and storm and cannibals, in a government ship, with five hundred men and boys to assist one, than it is to explore the private sea, the Atlantic and Pacific Ocean of one's being alone." Fourteen years earlier, Alexis de Tocqueville had predicted that without the ideals and mythologies of the past to draw upon, modern, democratic poetry would inevitably have to turn to nature and, increasingly, to the self for its subject matter. Tocqueville did not mention in his discussion the great English romantic poet William Wordsworth, often taken to be the father of modern poetry in English; but it was Wordsworth, more than any other poet in English, who confirmed and inspired these trends. His focus on the self had been evident as early as his first collection, *Lyrical Ballads* (with Samuel Taylor Coleridge, 1798), and had come to fruition in the long autobiographical poem *The Prelude*, finally published in 1850.

Walt Whitman followed the advice of Thoreau, the prophecy of Tocqueville, and the example of Wordsworth—with a vengeance—in his *Song of Myself* (1855, rev. 1881). As the poem consists of 1,345 lines, it cannot be discussed here in adequate detail, but some of the main ideas it presents about the self can be indicated. The central ambiguity of the poem is the status of the narrator, the poem's insistent "I." This figure can usefully be understood both as a personal representation of Whitman himself and as a kind of mythical creation, a representative man, whose characteristics embody American and, at times, universal experience. Whitman has often been castigated as an egotist for such lines as those of the famous opening: "I celebrate myself, and sing myself, / And what I assume you shall assume." Whitman himself openly acknowledges his egotism, but at the same time he is also devoted to egalitarianism and the common ground of human experience: "For every atom belonging to me as good belongs to you." Whitman's contemporaries were shocked by the poem's flagrant disregard for poetic decorum—not only the apparent self-aggrandizement but the sprawling free verse, the poet's self-representation as a loafer and a sounder of "barbaric yawp," and, of course, the sexual frankness of various passages.

Whitman is the most expansive of American poets. His goal in *Song of Myself*, as he states at the outset, is to channel nature directly, without diminishment: "I permit to speak at every hazard, / Nature without check with original energy." Sometimes Whitman's efforts to encompass the outward world manifest themselves as epic catalogs, in which the poet seems to take Adamic delight simply in naming things, as in sections eight and fifteen. The conclusion of section fifteen explicitly states the theme of subject and object merging: "these tend inward to me, and I tend outward to them, / And such as it is to be of these more or less I am, / And of these one and all I weave the song of myself." The self grows from its engagement with the inexhaustible variety of the world; this is a central idea of the poem. At the same time, an inner, inviolable self (the "Me myself") remains separate and distinct from the influence of external things. The paradox of the self is that it is simultaneously engaged with and withdrawn from the world.

Throughout *Song of Myself*, Whitman makes explicit statements about his personal characteristics and inclinations: "I resist any thing better than my own diversity" (line 350); "I wear my hat as I please indoors or out" (line 397); "I am the poet of the Body and I am the poet of the Soul" (line 422). The most directly autobiographical section is twenty-four, which begins: "Walt Whitman, a kosmos, of Manhattan the son / Turbulent, fleshy, sensual, eating, drinking and breeding, / No sentimentalist, no stander above men and women or apart from them, / No more modest than immodest." This self-portrait presents the poet both in transcendental terms, as a self-contained spiritual universe ("a kosmos"), and as someone who enjoys and celebrates the "primitive" animal side of human existence. In this section, Whitman also presents himself as a channeler of "dumb voices," such as those of "prisoners and slaves." He presents "forbidden voices, / Voices of sexes and lusts, voices veil'd and I remove the veil, / Voices indecent by me clarified and transfigur'd." Passages such as section twenty-eight, which concerns masturbation, do indeed tear the veil off taboo subjects. Whitman deals with the self, in all its physicality, with unexampled candor. He does not discriminate against any part of the body: "Welcome is every organ and attribute of me ... / Not an inch nor a particle of an inch is vile." Further, he maintains that the body "must not abase itself" to the soul. Both equally compose the self, which in Whitman's view is a divine entity. In section forty-one, for instance, he looks to all the mythologies and religions of the world as potential sources of inspiration—but insists that the self must ultimately transcend them all.

For many readers, the four concluding sections contain some of the poem's outstanding passages. Whitman has already explored the physical and spiritual life of the self and its relationship to what Emerson called the "NOT ME." At the end of the poem, quite naturally, he considers the extinction of the self. He has already claimed that "to die is different from what any one supposed, and luckier" (line 130), and "I know I am deathless" (line 406); the conclusion of the poem develops these ideas. Whitman's nonchalance in the face of death is heartening: "And as to you Death, and you bitter hug of mortality, it is idle to try to alarm me." Through the image of roses springing up from a corpse, the poet illustrates the idea that life is built on death, that all lives are made from many deaths. To celebrate life, then, is to celebrate death and the natural cycles of mortality. The self is made up of many selves and many voices; therefore, Whitman can utter the famous lines: "Do I contradict myself / Very well then I contradict myself / (I am large, I contain multitudes)." The self is not a stable entity but ever enlarging, ever grasping, ever conflicted, ever changing. Death is simply the final, inevitable change of the self, as the self is then absorbed back into the world to become the raw material of other selves. Whitman does not embrace the doctrine of the soul's immortality, but he does celebrate the material immortality of the body. Even though the body decays, its constituent atoms are indestructible and may serve as the organic basis of other lives. Thus, at the end, Whitman bequeaths himself to the dirt, to grow again as grass. His self lives on both through its atoms and through its words. Hence, we can find a double meaning in the title *Leaves of Grass*, which can be seen as referring not only to actual spears of grass but also to the leaves of Whitman's book describing the grass.

Emily Dickinson, concise as Whitman is expansive, explored what Loren Eiseley called "the inner galaxy" in nearly all of her best-known poems. Many poems discussed elsewhere in the guide (e.g., "I'm Nobody! Who are you?" under "The Individual & Society") could have been considered here. "I dwell in Possibility—" (#657, c. 1862) provides a representative example of Dickinson's treatment of the isolated self (or Whitman's "Me myself"). The free, imaginative self dwells in "Possibility," a "fairer House" than its opposite, "Prose" (representing the unimaginative life), for it offers more openings upon and visions of ("Windows" and "Doors") reality. In the infinite possibilities of imaginative play (rather than the mere literality of prose), the self can arrive at its true fulfillment. The realm of the imagination, in other words, is for Dickinson the true home of the self. The second stanza indicates how solitude and nature minister to the self and its imaginative exuberance. The third begins by allowing for the fruitful interaction of the self with select "Visitors," who like nature, are another source of inspiration external to the self and indispensable to its growth. (A more solipsistic reading might suggest that the visitors are merely the poet's own thoughts.) The final image, of the self spreading out its "narrow Hands/ To gather Paradise—," suggests that the sovereign realm of the self is a kind of paradise, wherein the primitive art of "gathering" becomes a gratifying occupation. The narrow hands of the self may seem inadequate for the task, especially when compared to the vastness of paradise and possibility; but the opportunity to strive, to exercise the senses and the imagination is, for Dickinson, the highest bliss afforded by our existence. The self may be finite, but as Browning's Andrea del Sarto famously notes, its reach should exceed its grasp.

In contrast with the celebrations of the self in Whitman and Dickinson, Robert Frost writes about the terrors of the self in "Desert Places" (1934). Like such earlier Frost poems as "The Wood-Pile" and "Stopping by Woods on a Snowy Evening," the poem positions a solitary speaker in a snowy landscape. In some respects, "Desert Places" seems like a more explicit rewriting of "Stopping by Woods on a Snowy Evening," although the later poem suffers by comparison in terms of both its looser form and its relative lack of subtlety. The poem contains no literal "desert places" but three metaphorical ones, the first and most obvious of which is the snowy landscape described in the first three stanzas. The description emphasizes barrenness, loneliness, and finally nothingness: "A blanker whiteness of benighted snow / With no expression, nothing to express." The final stanza introduces two further desert places. It begins, jarringly, with a pronoun ("They") for which there is no logical antecedent. The second desert place—the vacuum of outer space—suggests that the "They" who discuss it are probably scientists, specifically astronomers and physicists. The speaker is unmoved by their disclosures about the vastness and emptiness of space because he feels such emptiness within himself. The outer world of snow and space becomes but a distant reflection of the speaker's own desert places. The idea is an intriguing one, but the speaker comes across as perhaps overly self-involved and smugly cynical. Nonetheless, he is a representative spokesman for a modern world that has lost traditional faith but found nothing to replace it that would keep the self from lapsing into nihilism.

Delmore Schwartz's "The Heavy Bear Who Goes with Me" (1938) seems to take its point of departure from William Butler Yeats's memorable phrase about being "fastened to a dying animal" from the astonishing poem "Sailing to Byzantium." Schwartz, like Yeats before him, explores the Cartesian duality of mind and body and the problems of a being that is aware of itself as both consciousness and material substance. Schwartz focuses on his feeling of estrangement from his own body, which he figures as the "bear" of the poem's title and—in Emerson's terms—identifies with the realm of the "NOT ME." The body is "In love with candy, anger, and sleep," and its drives and needs and clumsiness are a constant source of embarrassment and irritation to Schwartz's more spiritually conceived inner self. Schwartz's feelings of being separate from his own body manifest themselves in the use of the third-person pronoun for the body and the first-person pronoun for the inner self. The "quivering meat" of the "inescapable" animal, harking back to Yeats's line, serves as a reminder of the self's mortality, its absolute dependence on the inexorably decaying flesh. Exploring various facets of his animal existence, Schwartz turns in the middle of his syntactically complicated third stanza to a consideration of love. He contrasts two ways his feelings for the woman he loves ("the very dear") manifest themselves. The "bear" (or "him") longs for physical contact, whereas the inner self (or "I") would like some sort of platonic relationship, unmediated by mere gross physicality. Schwartz puns on the word "bare," as he develops a final contrast between the world of words and feelings, which characterizes the inner self, and the world of appetites (for both food and sex), which characterizes the physical self. The tension between the two parts of the self cannot be surmounted: a clumsy duality, in Schwartz's poem, is the very condition of the self.

Self-identity is a particularly important theme in African-American literature. Historically, black writers have often found that they have had to struggle to define themselves against the stereotypes and expectations of society. In *The Souls of Black Folk* (1903), W. E. B. Du Bois discusses the problem of "double-consciousness," of constantly being forced into an awareness of one's identity as both an American and a black. Identity has rarely been a simple issue for African Americans, and that is the subject Langston Hughes tackles in his "Theme for English B" (1951). The poem should be regarded not as an autobiographical confession but as a dramatic monologue, for the narrator is only twenty-two, less than half Hughes's age at the time the poem was written. In response to an English teacher's instructions to write an authentic page that will *"come out of you,"* the young man wonders, first, if it will be that simple. He then ticks off some of the basic facts that define our identities in the eyes of society: age, race, birthplace, schools attended, and present home. The school he now attends stands "above Harlem," where he finds himself "the only coloured student" in the class. Obviously, these facts provide ample opportunity for the development of "double-consciousness" and make the boy's precise identity somewhat slippery, even in his own eyes. "Me—who?" he asks. He knows both Harlem and the rest of New York. He listens to both Bessie Smith and Johann Sebastian Bach. His world is divided between territories and cultural appreciations clearly labeled "black" and "white." He feels these divisions, yet does not allow them to dampen his enthusiasms.

In the end, he decides that doubleness of identity—being yourself and a part of something very different—is what being American is all about. This reciprocity seems fundamental: he is part of his instructor, just as the instructor is part of him. White and black interpenetrate, yet remain distinct. The sometimes strained and self-conscious relations between races is, the writer recognizes, a basic fact of American life and must be both accepted and transcended through learning. The main difference that the writer defines between himself and his white teacher is that the latter is "somewhat more free," not least in terms of the stigmas of identity. The poem does not attempt to sketch a solution to this problem; instead, it focuses on the inescapable realities of the writer's present moment. Hughes only implicitly appeals to the sympathetic reader to will some positive change that would alter the imbalances between black and white identitites.

Perhaps no contemporary American poet has more relentlessly focused on the self than W. D. Snodgrass, who, along with Robert Lowell, is usually credited as being the co-founder of the "confessional" school of poetry. "April Inventory" (1959) gauges the poet-professor's growing awareness of his self's fading prime against the campus trees and the ever-youthful waves of attractive female students who fill his classes each year. In this sense, the poem reverses the basic situation of "Theme for English B," for here it is the professor, not the student, who grapples with the problem of identity. The poem's emphasis on the season calls to mind the celebrated opening line of T. S. Eliot's *The Waste Land*: "April is the cruelest month. . . ." For Snodgrass, it is at least a season of diminishment. As the blossoms snow down, so does his remaining hair. Throughout the poem, Snodgrass compares himself and the female students to opposed aspects of the trees. Whereas he aligns himself with the falling blossoms, he aligns the young women with the ever-renewing vitality of the trees: they "Bloom gradually out of reach." The trees (and the poet) "turn bare" while the women "turn wives," the verbal parallelism enforcing the uneasy experience of all professors, as they watch themselves grow older while their students remain perpetually young. But the poem's overall tone is more resigned than bitter. The poet tends to view himself self-deprecatingly, with a bemused detachment. He mocks his own incompetence, his failure to achieve his goals or to pull himself together, and his slow, inevitable physical degeneration, symbolized not only by baldness but also by spectacles and fillings. The poet almost seems to see himself as a version of the protagonist of Eliot's "The Love Song of J. Alfred Prufrock" (discussed under "The Individual & Society"): aging, ineffectual, anxious about his relations with the opposite sex. Nevertheless, Snodgrass does not ultimately subscribe to Eliot's pessimism. Stanzas six and seven demonstrate that the speaker remains capable of positive actions and of positively influencing the lives of those around him, and the final stanza speaks optimistically of a sustaining gentleness and beauty in the world. The poem, ultimately, defends the dignity of the self against the ravages of time.

Another key work of the confessional movement, Robert Lowell's "Skunk Hour" (1959) might not seem, on first reading, to have as clear a theme or center as "April Inventory"; but upon careful reconsideration, one might find that Lowell's sick self resides at the center of the poem, both structurally and thematically. The poem, dedicated to Elizabeth Bishop and modeled, in part, on the poem she had dedicated to him, "The Armadillo" (discussed under "Nature"), moves, as Bishop's does, from human activity toward an image of a single animal—the primary difference being that Lowell interposes himself between these two sections as something more than merely an observer (as the "we" from "The Armadillo" functions). This crucial readjustment of emphasis tilts the meaning of the poem toward the self. It encourages us to read the descriptions of landscape, colorful characters, and skunks as emblematic in some way of the poet's inner state of mind. The poem divides into three fairly discrete sections. The first describes several eccentric denizens of Castine, Maine, where Lowell had a summer house. We hear of a hermit heiress in her dotage, who buys up the ugly surrounding properties in order to let them fall into dilapidation and who longs for "the hierarchic privacy" of the preceding century; of a spiffy millionaire who summers there and recently sold his sailboat to lobstermen; and of a decorator who finds his work unremunerative. These brief sketches represent light, somewhat humorous social satire, but also suggest a world oddly out of sorts, wherein people engage in peculiar actions and contradictory long-ings. The heiress lives in a "Spartan cottage"; her servant is the highest ranking official in the town; the homosexual decorator wants to marry; even Blue Hill is stained red by the autumn leaves. A sense of uneasiness and disorder is also reflected in the six-line stanzas themselves, with their shifting line lengths and irregular rhyme schemes.

The vague, hovering sense of uneasiness becomes concentrated in the poem's second and central section in the figure of the poet himself. One dark night—which Lowell said was meant to refer to St. John of the Cross's "Dark Night of the Soul"—he climbs the "skull" of Blue Hill, where lovers frolic in their cars. The image of the lovers' cars and the sound of the radio playing the popular song "Careless Love" contrast meaningfully with the "skull" image and the graveyard. Lowell con-fronts yet remains isolated from two extremes of human experience: love and death. The poet abruptly admits, "My mind's not right," and soon adds that he feels as if his hand were at his spirit's throat, which sobs in every blood cell in his body (an image of the self as both spirit and matter that points back to Delmore Schwartz's "The Heavy Bear Who Goes with Me"). Lowell identifies himself at this point with Satan, by alluding to a famous passage from *Paradise Lost*: "Which way I fly is Hell; myself am Hell" (4.75). The reference underscores Lowell's sense of being a fallen creature in a fallen world; Satan's isolation from God in hell becomes an analog for the poet's existential despair. Almost par-adoxically, Lowell affirms his isolation: people are in fact near, but the private transactions in the darkened cars make them extremely remote.

In his lonely, disturbed frame of mind, the poet unexpectedly con-fronts a skunk with its litter of kittens. The movement from the grand satanic allusion to the skunks that have overrun Main Street might seem like a comic incongruity, but this song of the sick self consistently broods in a minor key. The poem inverts the situation of "The Armadillo": there, animals were driven from their homes by human activity; here, animals invade deserted human territory. Nonetheless, the moonlight-reflecting eyes of the skunks pay homage to the "fixed, ignited" eyes of Bishop's rabbit. The hungry, nocturnal creatures, another instance of the world's mysterious, chaotic aspect, afflict the poet's soul, which seemingly longs for certainty and order. Lowell finds neither, and the poem ends in im-potence, as he is unable even to scare away the vividly evoked mother skunk. The failure of the poet to assert his will, to master exterior reality, mirrors the poet's inner uncertainties. The self inhabits a world it never made and can never fully control or even understand. The spiritual mal-aise described in the poem results from the alienation of the "Me myself" from the "NOT ME." As Lowell does not attempt to describe or even indicate a movement toward acceptance, reconciliation, or redemption, the poem leaves us only with a portrait of incongruity and despair.

Elizabeth Bishop's "In the Waiting Room" (1976) documents the uncomfortable dawning awareness of the self, an early symptom of maturation. Another confessional poem, it recalls an incident from 1918, when the poet would have been just shy of her seventh birthday. She has accompanied her aunt to the dentist's office and now finds herself in a painfully self-conscious waiting-room situation. The room, along with an issue of *National Geographic* that she browses as she waits, triggers an unsettling epiphany: the girl suddenly realizes what it means to be an individual, not unlike the people whose pictures she sees in the magazine and who surround her in the waiting room. She breaks through, in other words, into an awareness of self. Although she is old enough—as she is careful to point out—to read, she had not been old enough to know herself in any meaningful sense until the conjunction of circumstances in the waiting room forced that knowledge upon her.

The pictures in the issue of *National Geographic* are perfectly realistic, yet at the same time suggestive, even symbolic. The girl focuses on five images: a volcano, a pair of famous explorers, babies with pointed heads, a corpse strung up by cannibals, and naked black women. The volcano seems to represent the latent (and potentially dangerous) power of transformation, foreshadowing the girl's own eruption into self-awareness; the explorers of the outside world mirror the girl's exploration of her own interiority; the babies and the corpse suggest the entire trajectory of each and every individual life from birth to death; and the naked black women, with their "horrifying" breasts, traumatically bring the girl into an awareness of her own inevitable female maturation and sexuality. Despite these uncomfortable revelations about the world, the girl is too shy to set the magazine down; she seems to imagine that all eyes are fixed on her activities—a sign of exaggerated self-consciousness. When she has finally finished, she looks at the cover and hears a cry of pain. The prepositional phrase "from inside" (line 36) is ambiguous, since it is not clear whether the cry has come from her aunt within the dentist's office or whether the cry has simply come from within the girl herself. The fact that she does not know herself is significant, for the cry marks her epiphany: she understands that she is "an *I*" yet also "one of *them*." She is an individual but also part of humanity, represented by her aunt, by the others in the waiting room, and most exotically by the figures in the magazine. Part of the point is that she is forced into an awareness of kinship with others who seem quite different from herself and into some understanding of her place within the larger history and culture of the world.

The physical correlative to her dawning sense of self is a feeling of vertigo. She clings to a simple fact—her age—and dares not look up at the people around her, so frighteningly similar to her own self. The moment seems prolonged by huge black waves of sheer anxiety, but finally it passes. The poem concludes with a return to its opening stability, with an assertion of facts: place, time, weather conditions. Bishop also reminds us that World War I was still raging at the time, thereby providing a context against which the turmoil in a single breast can be placed in perspective. What the girl has experienced is both momentous and trivial. Subjectively, it is one of the key moments of an entire life. Objectively—as the pictures and mention of the war enforce—a single life is both a common and a precarious thing. The girl becomes aware of the one (her own self) and of its troubled relationship to the vastness of the many.

❦

"Song of Myself," Walt Whitman

AAL-1; APN-1, ATL-1; ATL-2; ColAP (selections only); HAL-1; HAL-2; HoAL-2; NAL-1; NoAM (selections only); NOBA; NoP-4 (selections only); OxBA

"I dwell in Possibility—," Emily Dickinson

AAL-1; AAL-2; APN-2; HAL-1; HAL-2; HoAL-2; MAP; NoAM; NOBA; OxBA

"Desert Places," Robert Frost

AAL-2; APT-1; ATL-2; HAL-2; HoAL-2; LPTT; MAP; NAL-2; NoAM; NOBA; OxBA; SoSe-9

"The Heavy Bear Who Goes with Me," Delmore Schwartz

APT-2; ColAP; NoAM; NOBA

"Theme for English B," Langston Hughes

APT-2 (included in "from *Montage of a Dream Deferred*"); ColAP; HAL-2; HCAP; HoAL-2; NoAM; NOBA; NoP-4

"April Inventory," W. D. Snodgrass

ATL-2; CAPP-6; CoAP; ColAP; NoAM; NoP-4; VCAP

"Skunk Hour," Robert Lowell

AAL-2; ATL-2; CAPP-6; CoAmPo; CoAP; ColAP; HAL-2; HCAP; HoAL-2; MAP; NAL-2; NoAM; NOBA; NoP-4; TFi; VCAP; WeW-4

"In the Waiting Room," Elizabeth Bishop

AAL-2; ATP-2; ATL-2; CAPP-6; ColAP; HAL-2; HoAL-2; MAP; NAL-2; NoAM; NOBA; NoP-4; VCAP

Skepticism and Belief

❦

> My own mind is my own church.
>
> Thomas Paine, *The Age of Reason*

American poetry was born into an age of diverse beliefs. The Reformation had fractured Christendom, and the Protestant movement, lacking the central authority of Rome, continued to shatter into a bewildering assortment of sects. In addition, by the Revolutionary War era, the Enlightenment had exerted its rational influence on the beliefs of intellectuals on both sides of the Atlantic. The old Puritan doctrines of predestination, original sin, damnation, and divine providence tended to give way in enlightened areas of the new country under the triple pressures of optimistic egalitarianism, modern biblical scholarship, and the logic of Sir Isaac Newton's "world machine." Increasingly, natural theology superseded traditional beliefs. God's wisdom was not seen as manifest in providential interventions but rather in the works of the creation and the natural laws that govern the universe. The creation, it was asserted, implies the existence of a creator, a divine "watchmaker," who designed the universe and set it in motion, but did not tamper with it thereafter. This new naturalistic religion, a child of Enlightenment rationality, came to be known as deism. First formulated by Edward Herbert (elder brother of the English metaphysical poet George Herbert), it affirmed God's existence, but embraced the findings of science and simultaneously rejected both dogma and superstition. It looked back to Aristotle's idea of a Prime Mover and forward to Einstein's famous claim that "God does not play dice with the universe."

Philip Freneau, the first significant poet of the United States, became an outspoken champion of natural religion. His intellectual mentors included Thomas Paine, the author of *The Age of Reason* (1794), a controversial critique of scripture from a rationalist perspective, and Thomas Jefferson, whose deistic leanings can clearly be discerned in the phrase from the Declaration of Independence "the Laws of Nature and of Nature's God"—hardly a Puritan formulation. Paine and Jefferson (along with Benjamin Franklin) were among the most prominent deists in early America. Freneau penned a tribute poem to the former ("On Mr. Paine's Rights of Man") and was appointed translating clerk in the State Department by the latter. Three of Freneau's poems, "On the Uniformity and Perfection of Nature," "On the Universality and Other Attributes of the God of Nature," and "On the Religion of Nature" (all 1815) distill the concept of natural religion he derived from his intellectual forebears.

As the three poems have relatively little individuality and overlap to some extent, their substance may be considered collectively. The main ideas Freneau presents are these: nature is the evidence of God's existence; it is rational and obeys fixed laws; it does not stoop to suit the whims of men (who are simply "the insects of an hour"); it is a "vast machine" created by a "great first cause" that was "all-sufficient, all-supreme"; the laws of nature are homogeneous throughout space; nature provides all things, including religion; natural religion excludes sophistry and damnation; and natural religion will, in its spread, triumph over superstition and persecution. Some of these rational and optimistic ideas, such as the homogeneity of natural laws, are basic tenets of science. Some, such as that God does not interfere in the daily affairs of people, directly challenge popular Christian beliefs that descend from Puritanism. (For purposes of comparison, contrast Freneau's ideas with those of the Puritan poet Anne Bradstreet, as expressed in such an explicitly providential poem as "Here Follows Some Verses upon the Burning of Our House.") Other of Freneau's ideas are clearly dubious, as when he echoes Alexander Pope's "Essay on Man" in the conclusion of "On the Uniformity and Perfection of Nature": "No imperfection can be found / In all that is, above, around— / All, nature made, in reason's sight / Is order all, and *all is right*." Freneau has allowed theory to take precedence over experience. The world in which we live obviously contains a host of imperfections that cannot so easily be explained away. Freneau also, at times, seems to cross the boundary between deism (which postulates a creator separate from nature) and pantheism (in which God and nature are one). Such ambiguities characterize an age of transition, in which religious ideas are undergoing rapid metamorphoses.

William Cullen Bryant's celebrated "To a Waterfowl" (1815, the same year as the three Freneau poems considered above) illustrates the same point. The poem records the flight of a waterfowl as it disappears in the dusk. True to generalizing neoclassical principles, Bryant does not specify what kind of "waterfowl" the poem immortalizes, although the line

"And scream with thy fellows" might bring to mind a Canada goose. The religious aspect of the poem is introduced in the fourth stanza: "There is a Power whose care / Teaches thy way," the poet asserts. Bryant does not profess allegiance to any specific creed and does not even mention "God" explicitly, but he does affirm the role of divine guidance in the affairs of all creatures: the waterfowl, with its unerring instinct, becomes a symbol for the Creator's design. The waterfowl's purposive movements inscribe a lesson on the poet's heart: he comes to feel that this "Power" will also guide his steps "aright." The poem's viewpoint seems to fall somewhere between the providential conception of Puritanism and the naturalistic conception of deism. Its conclusion is strikingly similar to that of Freneau's "On the Universality and Other Attributes of the God of Nature": "O'er all he made he still presides, / For them in life, or death provides." The question is whether such provisions are part of the fixed, original plan of the creator (as Freneau and the deists would have it) or are—as the word "still" might encourage us to conclude—divine interventions that ignore the consistency of natural laws (in the Puritan tradition of belief). Bryant himself was raised a Calvinist, passed through a deist phase, and later became a leader in the Unitarian movement, so it is not surprising that his poem seems sufficiently ambiguous to be interpreted either way. In all likelihood, the poem's great popularity owes something to its doctrinal vagueness. Readers can find in it an echo of whatever they believe.

Among the burgeoning offshoots from older forms of Protestantism, Unitarianism has a special prominence as a stepping-stone for one of America's major literary movements. Unitarianism derived in part from deism and attempted to demystify faith by explicitly denying the doctrine of the Trinity (thus the prefix "Uni-" for one indivisible God, much like that of Judaism or Islam). Unitarians looked to Christ as an exemplary figure but not as a divinity and saw God as a benevolent being rather than the angry Old Testament figure of Puritan sermons. Ralph Waldo Emerson began his career as a Unitarian minister, but found that even this liberal faith constrained him. He resigned his position after he could no longer administer the sacrament in good faith. Emerson went on to formulate a quasi-religious philosophy that has come to be known by a term not of his own choosing: transcendentalism. The transcendentalist movement synthesized its ideas from diverse sources: Neoplatonism, oriental scriptures, Christian mystics such as Swedenborg, German idealists such as Kant, and English romantics such as Coleridge and Carlyle. Transcendentalism retains the traditional dualistic distinction between matter and spirit (which "transcends" matter). It affirms that matter is known through "understanding" and that spirit is known through a higher mental faculty rather misleadingly dubbed "reasoning." Each of us, it further maintains, is but a rivulet ultimately connected to the vast ocean of the "Oversoul." Extrapolating from these premises, transcendentalism emphasizes the importance of nature, progress, individualism, personal growth, and finding the divine in the commonplace.

Emerson's Harvard lecture "The Divinity School Address" (1838), which criticizes the desiccated state of the church and its cult of Jesus, is a major document in American religious history. Even though its points were merely applications of principles developed in Emerson's earlier work, the establishment was sufficiently scandalized to banish Emerson, unofficially, from his alma mater for thirty years. Both his defection from Unitarianism and the "divinity school" scandal lie behind the most overt religious statement among his poems, "The Problem" (1840). The poem, however, is not the strong denunciation of the conservative establishment that we might expect. Instead, it poses a question about the poet himself. The poet admits he likes the trappings of religion but would not himself be a clergyman. The question is why. The poem answers the question in a roundabout manner. First, it provides examples of what the poet considers genuine religious expression. Emerson's rather miscellaneous list includes Phidias's statue of Jove, the pronouncements of the Delphic oracle, various litanies and canticles, and St. Peter's cathedral. Most of these are viewed in a wholly positive light, although the Bible itself is considered somewhat more ambiguously as both a product of nature (or natural faith) and a burden to posterity. To understand Emerson's view of the Bible, we must remember that he felt that inspiration was holy and that the mistake of traditional and institutionalized religions inheres in transferring holiness from inspiration itself to its record in particular texts, which are then set up as infallible and unchallangeable. Thus, the word and its laws displace the potential for further revelations and establish a stifling dogmatism.

Emerson's various images of human religious expression are then complemented by natural objects—a woodbird's nest, a fish's shell, a pine tree—all images of growth by accretion. The works of humanity are presented as similar "growths" or modifications of nature: the Parthenon, the pyramids, and English abbeys all take their place beside forests and mountains as examples of the achievements of progressive forces. The human refashioning of nature—which Emerson considered to be "art" in its broadest sense—does not fall outside the bounds of nature but is part of it, in the same way that a bird's nest or a beaver's dam is. In the final verse paragraph, the poem's underlying organic analogy becomes explicit: "These temples grew as grows the grass." The same inspiring spirit that lies behind the forms of nature lies behind the forms of human artifacts, so that both a pine tree and a pyramid are genuine tributes to the order of the "vast soul" (or Oversoul), whose physical manifestation, according to Emerson's metaphysics, is the universe itself. Thus, Emerson sides with the universal inspiration of culture and nature against the narrower tradition of "The Book" that "before me lies." Emerson affirms at the end that despite the various authorities of the church, he "would not the good bishop be." There is no going back for the lapsed Unitarian. The "problem" that prevents him from doing so is that of rigidifying traditions. The true nature of religion, as Emerson conceives it, is to flow constantly into new forms and revelations. Emerson, in short, wants a religion that is dynamic and alive to the character of the present moment—a religion that is poetry rather than tradition.

Similar sentiments inform Oliver Wendell Holmes's "The Chambered Nautilus" (1858), which resembles such symbol-making poems as Freneau's "The Wild Honey Suckle" (discussed under "Nature") and Bryant's "The Yellow Violet." Here, the central image is not the proverbial flower but "the ship of pearl"—a nautilus shell. The poem, however, still moves conventionally from description to symbolism. Integral to the description and the meaning of the poem is the history of the creature that has inhabited the shell and subsequently, as is its nature, moved on to larger shells. The poem's theological implications arise from the actions of growth and relocation. The final two stanzas draw out this significance in a way that clearly rebukes static theological concepts. What the shell comes to represent is the husk of outworn tradition, cast off for "more stately mansions" and a "new temple, nobler than the last." The law of progress demands incremental changes and, metaphorically, larger shells that carry one closer and closer to nature and the truth. The smaller "shells" of the past (such as Calvinism) must not be allowed to confine the growth of the human spirit. Holmes's emphasis on incremental changes seems auspicious when one recalls that Darwin's *On the Origin of Species* was published the following year. "The Chambered Nautilus" is decidedly a theological poem for a scientific and progressive age.

The nineteenth-century poet who most profoundly and extensively explored the tension between the old beliefs and the new skepticism was Emily Dickinson. The uncertainty of the age is reflected in the various attitudes expressed in her work, which range through moods of flippancy, withering skepticism, and smug assurance (as in "I never saw a moor," #1052). The early quatrain " 'Faith' is a fine invention" (#185, c. 1860) displays the ironic, impish, and knowing skepticism that has kept Dickinson's poetry perpetually fresh. In the opening line, the considered word "invention" accomplishes half of the poem's work. The quotation marks around "Faith," in conjunction with the italicized "*microscope,*" suggest the gap between religious credulity and scientific investigation. Only the latter is "prudent / In an Emergency," for without such tools as the microscope to enhance and extend human observation, phenomena like disease can only be regarded superstitiously. "Faith" alone cannot deliver the world from the ravages of plague.

Dickinson celebrates her rejection of institutionalized religion in "Some keep the Sabbath going to Church—" (#324, c. 1860). Dickinson prefers to stay at home Sunday mornings, "With a Bobolink for a Chorister— / And an Orchard, for a Dome—." Instead of clerical garb and tolling bells, she prefers her own poetry (figured in the second quatrain both as "Wings" and singing). The poem thus illustrates the transcendental turn away from institutionalized religion toward more individualistic and unmediated forms of worship. Without the guiding hand of the church, Dickinson communes directly with God through his masterpiece, nature. Thus, she stands in the direct line of Protestant radicalism extending from deism and transcendentalism. She further tenders the heretical suggestion of an earthly paradise: "So instead of getting to Heaven at last— / I'm going, all along." We are very close here to a purely naturalistic religion that rejects orthodox Christian metaphysical concepts, such as heaven and hell, altogether. In several ways, her poem anticipates Wallace Stevens's "Sunday Morning" (discussed below).

Dickinson, however, never wholly abandoned her faith; instead, she merely allowed doubt to range freely throughout her troubled work. A poem such as "I know that He exists" (#338, c. 1862) presents something akin to a dialogue between her will to believe and her uncompromising intellectual skepticism. The poem addresses the existential problem of God's silence: "He has hid his rare life / From our gross eyes," she writes. This metaphysical game of hide and seek is figured, positively at first, as leading toward a kind of "fond Ambush" that will "make Bliss / Earn her own surprise!" But Dickinson is too rational not to entertain doubts about such an arrangement. Might the game, without corroborating evidence, merely be an expression of human hopes, rather than of the truth? One can claim to commune with an invisible, intangible monkey—but one must finally ask if there is a difference between such a monkey and no monkey at all. Dickinson applies this same logic to the problem of God's silence in the last two stanzas. What if God does not exist? What if death is final? Then, would not faith be a rather cruel joke? "Would not the jest— / Have crawled too far!" With a simple shift of pronouns, we can apply what Hawthorne said of Melville to Dickinson: "She can neither believe, nor be comfortable in her unbelief; and she is too honest and courageous not to try to do one or the other."

The skeptical progression of American poetry culminates in the work of another poet deeply indebted to Emerson—Wallace Stevens. His "Sunday Morning" (1915) attempts to resolve the previous century's impasse between belief and skepticism by advocating a purely naturalistic and atheistic religion. Stevens's poem rejects metaphysical dualism in favor of a materialism that still provides sustenance for the poetic imagination. The opening of the poem situates the reader in a world of physical presences: a peignoir (or nightgown), coffee, oranges, a cockatoo.

These presences "dissipate / The holy hush of ancient sacrifice." The central figure of this little skeptical drama is a woman, home from church on a Sunday morning, who contemplates how she can find "In any balm or beauty of the earth, / Things to be cherished like the thought of heaven?" Various possible answers are sketched in sections two, three, and four of the poem, but they leave the woman still feeling "The need of some imperishable bliss." The poem's narrative voice then sketches a riposte to the woman's metaphysical inclination, beginning with the twice-repeated assertion that "Death is the mother of beauty." The woman, despite her desires, "strews the leaves / Of sure obliteration on our paths." From this idea of change as the essence of reality follows an almost parodic vision of paradise as a place where nothing ever happens. "Does ripe fruit never fall?" Section seven develops a countervision to that of a static paradise in its representation of a group of pagan men worshiping the sun. These men "know well the heavenly fellowship / Of men that perish"—in other words, they have come to terms with the impossibility of "imperishable bliss." They symbolize the natural religion the poem has been groping toward. The breathtaking final section sketches a naturalistic vision of deer, quail, berries, and pigeons that "make / Ambiguous undulations as they sink, / Downward to darkness, on extended wings." The final image brings together physical presences (alluding back to the cockatoo's wings) with the reality of death (figured in the death of the day). We are left with the visionary beauty of transience—this world, the poem asserts, is enough, is in fact all. As Thoreau succinctly puts it in *Walden*: "Talk of heaven! ye disgrace earth."

Stevens did eventually, on his deathbed, convert to Roman Catholicism. Whatever solace the religious will take from that fact, it has little bearing on the ideas Stevens expressed in 1915. At that time, he could be seen as representing one pole of Western religious thought, that of atheistic materialism, as descended from such Greek philosophers as Democritus. The other pole of Western belief, that of traditional Christianity, increasingly came to be represented by a very different American poet, T. S. Eliot. The question of Eliot's nationality remains a vexed issue. Born in St. Louis, but for most of his adult life a British subject, Eliot is the only figure represented in both the American and English *Norton Anthologies of Literature*. In his religious convictions, Eliot stands far removed from the radical Protestantism and post-Protestantism of most of his American peers. It is as if in order to try to recapture something like an authentic, traditional religious spirit in poetry, he had to distance himself both from the mainstream of American poetry and from America's anti-intellectual mainstream religious traditions. Eliot represents the intellectual as believer, akin more to the great French Catholic apologists than to American Protestant revivalists. Sadly, after the demise of Jonathan Edwards, the intellectual spirit tended to disappear from American religion's more public manifestations. Eliot, like various continental theologians, rediscovered it in war-ravaged Europe.

Eliot's entire career can easily be read, in retrospect, as a groping movement toward faith. Such a reading can oversimplify a reader's reaction to earlier poems of anguished anxiety, such as "The Love Song of J. Alfred Prufrock," "Gerontion," and *The Waste Land*. But after the unmitigated bleakness of "The Hollow Men" (1925), Eliot, under the influence of his study of Dante, turned increasingly toward a faith first given expression in "Journey of the Magi" (1927). The bleakness of "The Hollow Men" still hovers over this retelling of the Nativity story, but faith is asserted at the end. The opening lines of the poem, placed in quotation marks, paraphrase a 1622 sermon delivered by Lancelot Andrewes, one of the translators of the King James Bible. Eliot's principal change is to cast the words in first-person rather than third. The first verse paragraph then extrapolates from the paraphrase, building up a more complete picture of the obstacles that the magi faced on their journey. The second paragraph records the inauspicious arrival at Bethlehem. Some of the details appear to be symbolic, such as the "three trees on the low sky," which call to mind not only the three "wisemen" but also the trinity. The scene of the presentation of the gifts, however, is absent. Eliot lends the poem an air of distance and mystery by eliding the center of the story and by not depicting the figures of Mary, Joseph, and the infant Jesus. Instead, the concluding paragraph informs us that many years have elapsed since the speaker undertook his journey. What he has lived with ever since is a feeling of uneasiness and isolation, living among "an alien people clutching their gods." No longer a pagan among pagans, the speaker can only look forward to the delivery of his own death, which according to his newly ordered beliefs will be an escape from the heathens and an entry into the kingdom of heaven.

Eliot's religious ideas were developed further in "Ash Wednesday" (1930) and *Four Quartets* (1943), works whose length and complexity preclude consideration here. Back in America, Robert Frost, Richard Wilbur, and Theodore Roethke were formulating their own metaphysical visions. Frost, whose poetry tends to be fiercely skeptical, takes an ironic look backward at deism in his sonnet "Design" (1922). The sonnet's octave paints, through a series of vivid similes, a simple yet disturbing picture of an albino spider that has caught an albino moth atop an albino heal-all. Whiteness here signifies "death and blight" rather than innocence and purity. The sestet then poses a series of questions about this unholy trinity. Frost asks us to reflect on whether the scene is merely a random but highly improbable coincidence or a revelation of some metaphysical truth about the nature of reality. If the latter is the case, then the reality disclosed by the scene hardly resembles the benevolent universe envisioned by Freneau and the other deists. That universe had been destroyed by nineteenth-century biology, which taught one to look at the world not as a harmonious set of divinely ordered relationships but as an ongoing, bloody struggle for survival. How could one reconcile divine benevolence with the activities of the ichneumon wasps, which paralyze their prey in order to implant larvae that eat their way out from their unwilling and still living hosts? Frost does not answer his own difficult questions definitively, but notably does not even introduce benevolence as an option. The universe he observes is either random or malevolent. Design is that of "darkness to appall"—"If design govern in a thing so small."

Richard Wilbur confronts related ambiguities in a much more cheerful manner in his signature poem "Love Calls Us to the Things of This World" (1956), the unusual title of which is drawn from St. Augustine. The poem begins abruptly, with its speaker suddenly called to wakefulness by the sound of laundry pulleys outside his window. The dimly aware "soul" of the speaker seems disembodied for a moment. This effect is likened to a "false dawn," a first hint that the poem will be partially concerned with misleading perceptions. Still groggy, the speaker mistakes the billowing laundry outside his window for an array of angels. The contrast between the speaker's "disembodied" state and the "incarnation" of the angels in the laundry represents the traditional Western dualistic view of the separation of the mind and body and of spirit and matter. A hint that this dualism is in some ways untenable appears in line 16, as the wind dies down and no one seems to be inhabiting the laundry. Perhaps spirit is merely an illusion created by physical forces, such as the wind. Is consciousness another such force? The soul's first response to its sudden descent from the spiritual to the material is to cry out for a world in which angels do actually dance, embodied as laundry, to glorify the heavens. The rising sun, an emblem of the real world (as opposed to the "false dawn" of the opening), draws the soul back "in bitter love" to the fact of the real world over and against the ideal and imaginary one represented by the "angels." The "soul" must learn to love, as the title insists, the things of "this" world, not some hypothetical "next" world. In the final stanza, the speaker's "soul" accepts the impure world represented by the vice of thieves and the sexuality of lovers. The final image of the nuns summarizes the poem's themes. The heaviness of the nuns and their floating habits (or religious costumes) represent the opposing principles of materiality and spirituality. Only with faith, such as the nuns possess, can the two be kept in balance. The poem leaves open this possibility of balance, but the speaker seems decisively to opt for a spirituality not abstracted from reality. After all, even the floating habits are more like laundry than like angels.

The difficulty of reconciling the principles conventionally associated with "body" and "soul" is depicted in Theodore Roethke's "In a Dark

Time" (1960), a poem of crisis and redemption. The poem begins with a paradox: "In a dark time, the eye begins to see." The "dark time" indicates not merely an ordinary evening but "the dark night of the soul." Roethke implies that only through a spiritual crisis do we come to have adequate vision. He meets his shadow (or soul) as the day symbolically darkens and defines his position on the open ground against that of creatures of the water (the heron), the air (the wren), the highlands, and the underground. In the second stanza, he associates his crisis with madness; but madness here is "nobility of soul / At odds with circumstance." The conception reminds one of Dickinson's "Much madness is divinest sense" (discussed under "The Individual & Society"). The segue to the vision of twilight—"The day's on fire!"—is abrupt enough to simulate the associative processes of madness itself. From this point forward, the crisis takes the form of a journey, almost like that of a classical hero's descent into the underworld. Roethke finds himself in an ambiguous landscape, in which distinguishing a cave from a path is difficult; one might lead to a dead end, the other to new territory and new possibilities.

Surreal imagery haunts the journey: the night flows with birds, and the daylight comes again at midnight. Roethke presses forward, toward the extinction of his self. Even as the self dissipates, he becomes aware of a spiritual dimension to reality, as all "natural shapes" blaze with an "unnatural light." His own light, the third stanza paradoxically asserts, is dark. Again he feels a kind of acute Cartesian dualism, so that his soul and body seem separate entities. A specifically Christian allusion appears in the antepenultimate line, when Roethke refers to himself as a "fallen man." The "fall" here, however, does not seem to be so much a result of original sin as of fear. In overcoming that fear, Roethke reunites body and soul, with the added presence of God. In such manner, Roethke feels he has successfully related himself to something larger: "one is One," where the capitalized "One" represents the union of self and God. The final image of "the tearing wind" opens itself to two distinct (but not necessarily contradictory) readings. Is the wind stripping away the vestiges of uncertainty, or is it that the blowing rain, in contradistinction to the "tearless night" of the preceding stanza, resembles tears of benediction?

At the opposite end of the spectrum from Roethke's inwardly focused mystical journey stands Howard Nemerov's "Boom!" (1960), a biting and hilarious public satire on the complacent platitudes of modern religious rhetoric. The poem takes for its epigraph a newspaper clipping concerning comments made by President Eisenhower's pastor, Rev. Edward L. R. Elson, to the effect that the fruits of material progress have provided the means for achieving a new level of spiritual values. Nemerov finds the statement unconscionably superficial and wrongheaded, for he well knows that the highest spiritual values of the past were derived from the experience of adversity, suffering, and self-sacrifice—not from luxury. One cannot serve both God and Mammon. The modern tendency to conflate spirituality and materialism, Christianity and capitalism, is represented by the "cruciform" planes that everyone can believe in. Nemerov acknowledges that the churches are full, but so is every place else: beaches, filling stations, and so forth. The phenomenon has resulted from overpopulation: the baby boom, rather than a spiritual boom, accounts for the apparent abundance of believers. The first eighteen lines breathlessly survey contemporary American spiritual practices—the tone, repetitions, and syntax conveying the poem's attitude as much as the particular words. The second part of the poem, lines 19–26, sarcastically but pointedly juxtaposes the modern scene with several great spiritual figures of the past: Job, Father Damien, St. Francis, and Dante. The modern disappointment of having it rain during a paid vacation is counterpoised against the sacrifice of Father Damien, a nineteenth-century priest who selflessly worked with lepers in Hawaii for twelve years until he, too, contracted the horrible disease and died. Nemerov again weighs past and present in line 24, by yoking Nagasaki together with ancient Athens and Karnak. The implication seems to be that modern American technology has not only produced unexampled comfort but also casually annihilated 36,000 Japanese civilians. Who will atone for such a sin, in a world of cheerful platitudes? With line 27 we return again to the self-inflated trivialities of the present, in which "every modern convenience runneth over." Conspicuous consumption rather than a serious commitment to morality or reflection or virtue or self-sacrifice define, for Nemerov, contemporary America. A Buick and a Chris Craft boat, a superliner and disposable diapers, hotels and Miss Universe: these things symbolize the values and aspirations of a society clearly committed to materialism but only able to pay lip service to spiritual matters. Nemerov suggests that society at large knows nothing of the kind of hard-won spiritual quest depicted in Roethke's "In a Dark Time"; in place of genuine striving stand hypocrisy and self-delusion.

Andrew Hudgins offers a survey of contemporary beliefs concerning death and the possibility of an afterlife in "The Hereafter" (1988), thereby returning our attention to the plurality of American beliefs. Hudgins divides the people he knows into several distinct groups of believers. First, there are those who approach death with trepidation and desperate hopes of redemption. Then there are the True Believers, certain down to the most mundane details and specific activities of what the afterlife will be like for them. The antithesis of this group are the materialists, who feel that their immortality will only subsist in the transformation of their atoms into new forms, such as trees and birds. Hudgins alludes in this discussion to two notable American poets who advocated the materialist position. The phrase "live oaks" puts one in mind of Whitman's famous poem "I Saw in Louisiana a Live-Oak Growing," while the whole notion of flesh being incorporated into plant tissue recalls the conclusion of *Song of Myself* (discussed under "The Self"). Then, the neighbor's colloquial reference to "buzzards" that will give wings to the dead alludes directly to Robinson Jeffers's "Vulture" (discussed under "Life & Death"). Having covered these three major positions, Hudgins then turns his attention to the more exotic notions entertained by his brother and by an acquaintance who believes in reincarnation. The poet does not commit himself to any of these alternatives but glories in the ambiguity of the possibilities, which to his mind enrich both life and death. The poem concludes with a surprising comparison between the state of uncertainty and a swig of moonshine ("busthead"). The drink, in which the poet tastes both a hint of corn and a dead mockingbird, represents a transformation like that of life to death in two ways: it was made from the essence of something else (namely, the corn) and its inebriating quality transforms the drinker's state of mind. The barely discernible corn taste, like some hint of a previous life, reminds the poet of walking through fields where wind both stung and caressed him. This final, ambiguous image enforces the poem's point about the uncertainty of life and death. Belief and skepticism end in a kind of stalemate. The only certainty is that, despite dogmas and entrenched beliefs, no one knows for sure what it's all about.

ෙ᪲ᨎᖰᩎ᦯

"On the Religion of Nature," Philip Freneau

AAL-1; HoAL-1; NAL-1

"On the Uniformity and Perfection of Nature," Philip Freneau

HAL-1; HoAL-1

"On the Universality and Other Attributes of the God of Nature," Philip Freneau

AAL-1; ATL-1; HoAL-1

"To a Waterfowl," William Cullen Bryant

AAL-1; APN-1; ATL-1; ColAP; HAL-1; HoAL-1; LPTT; NAL-1; NOBA; NoP-4; OxBA; SoSe-9; TFi

"The Problem," Ralph Waldo Emerson

AAL-1; APN-1; ATL-1; HAL-1; HoAL-1; NOBA; OxBA

"The Chambered Nautilus," Oliver Wendell Holmes

AAL-1; APN-1; ATL-1; ColAP; HAL-1; HoAL-1; NOBA; NoP-4; TFi

" 'Faith' is a fine invention," Emily Dickinson

> AAL-1; AAL-2; APN-2; HAL-1; HAL-2; HoAL-2; NAL-1; NOBA; NoP-4; OxBA

"Some keep the Sabbath going to Church—," Emily Dickinson

> AAL-1; AAL-2; HAL-1; HAL-2; HoAL-2; NAL-1

"I know that He exists," Emily Dickinson

> AAL-1; AAL-2; APN-2; HAL-1; HAL-2; HoAL-2

"Sunday Morning," Wallace Stevens

> AAL-2; APT-1; ATL-2; HAL-2; HCAP; HoAL-2; MAP; NAL-2; NoAM; NOBA; NoP-4; OxBA; SoSe-9; TFi; WeW-4

"Journey of the Magi," T. S. Eliot

> AAL-2; HoAL-2; MAP; NAL-2; NoP-4; TFi

"Design," Robert Frost

> AAL-2; APT-1, ATL-2; ColAP; HAL-2; HoAL-2; MAP; NAL-2; NoAM; NOBA; NoP-4; SoSe-9; TFi

"Love Calls Us to the Things of This World," Richard Wilbur

> CAPP-6; ColAP; HAL-2; MAP; NAL-2; NoAM; NoP-4; TFi; VCAP; VGW

"In a Dark Time," Theodore Roethke

> AAL-2; APT-2; ATL-2; CAPP-6; HoAL-2; NAL-2; NoAM; NOBA; NoP-4; TFi; VCAP

"Boom!" Howard Nemerov

> LPTT

"The Hereafter," Andrew Hudgins

> RA

Suffering and Joy

❧

> While I was downstairs before, on my way here, listening to that woman sing, it struck me all of a sudden how much suffering she must have had to go through—to sing like that.
>
> Sonny in James Baldwin's "Sonny's Blues"

The extremes of suffering and joy, both real and imagined, have inspired some of poetry's most eloquent and memorable passages. On the one hand, one might think of Macduff responding to news that his wife and children have been massacred: "All my pretty ones? / Did you say all? O hell-kite! All?" (*Macbeth* 6.3.216–7). On the other hand, one might recall how the sonneteer, when he thinks of his loved one, compares himself "to the lark at break of day arising," which "From sullen earth, sings hymns at heaven's gate" ("Sonnet 29"). Examples from Shakespeare's work alone could be multiplied indefinitely. If on balance, suffering—understood as both physical pain and mental anguish—has produced the greater share of superlative passages in our poetry, it may simply be because giving authentic, persuasive verbal expression to joy, without lapsing into saccharine platitudes, may be the more difficult feat. If American poetry does not possess a verbal genius on the order of Shakespeare to beg the voice and utterance of both woe and bliss, it can at least show a clutch of memorable poems that address the extremes of human emotion.

Perhaps the best-loved of all American poems is Clement Moore's "A Visit from St. Nicholas" (1822), not merely a poem about joy but one that has brought joy to generations of delighted American readers and listeners. Who can resist the magic of its opening, anapestic rhythm? " 'Twas the night before Christmas, when all through the house / Not a creature was stirring, not even a mouse." Throughout the poem, Moore successfully integrates realistic detail into his fanciful narrative, as we see from his memorable description of moonlight just before the "jolly old elf" himself arrives: "The moon on the breast of the new-fallen snow / Gave the lustre of mid-day to objects below." Throughout the poem, Moore manages innumerable felicities of description and rhythm, as in this notable mock-epic simile: "As dry leaves that before the wild hurricane fly, / When they meet with an obstacle, mount to the sky." Here, the word "mount" enacts what it describes, as alliteration with "meet" along with the line's caesura (or pause after the word "obstacle") and the metrical stress pattern all conspire to lend it a majestic emphasis. Such effects are delightful in and of themselves, but joy, as the poem's theme, only takes center stage with the appearance of St. Nicholas himself. In Moore's famous description—which has fixed an image of "Santa Claus" in the minds of many Americans—St. Nick appears as the very embodiment (or archetype) of joyfulness, a Falstaffian presence shaking with laughter and dispensing good cheer. The narrator—significantly not a child but an adult whose testimony lends special credence to the myth of the jolly intruder—laughs as he eyes him "in spite of" himself, thus recapturing some measure of his own carefree youthfulness. St. Nicholas has the final say, and his proverbial words have resonated in our culture ever since: "*Happy Christmas to all, and to all a good night.*" Moore's is not a profound poem, but it is perhaps something even rarer: a purely delightful fantasy, an exercise in nostalgia that captures to perfection the innocence and joyfulness and sheer magic that many can happily recall from the Christmas seasons of their youth.

Taking us to the opposite end of the spectrum, Emily Dickinson presents a tersely reductive yet unsettlingly pointed view of life in "The Heart asks Pleasure—first—" (#536, c. 1862). Dickinson places the word "suffering" at the center of her poem and the idea of suffering at the center of human experience. In just eight lines, the poem provides an overview of the typical human life. Dickinson defines five distinct psychological stages of existence: first, innocent and naive expectation of pleasure in life; second, desire for exemption from pain; third, reliance on some way of alleviating pain; fourth, a preference for unconscious over conscious existence; and last, a longing for the "privilege to die." Life, in other words, is principally a matter of pain and dissolution, and our expectations, conditioned by experience, are adjusted downward at each step along the way. Dickinson's pessimism extends to whatever higher power may govern life. In this poem, that power is not named as a "Father," nor with any word bearing a potentially positive connotation, but rather as an "Inquisitor," which implies, further, that life consists principally of a series of trials and tortures. Dickinson's poem achieves its effect by boiling existence down to essentials and presenting a wholly one-sided view of life.

In contrast, alleviating the suffering of others is the theme of Walt Whitman's "The Wound-Dresser" (1865, rev. 1881). If Dickinson gives us a dispiriting and reductive overview of human suffering, Whitman offers hope by dramatizing what a fellow mortal can do to compensate for life's sea of troubles. Whitman, who had already been accustomed to providing cheer to prisoners, adopted with relish the role of nurse during the Civil War. "The Wound-Dresser," written in the typical documentary mode of his war poetry, offers an enduring image of Whitman among the injured and dying soldiers, providing solace and assistance as best he can. Whitman characterizes himself as an "old man," although at the time of the war he was only in his mid-forties. His trademark Old Testament beard made him appear much older, so the characterization may be taken either as a bit of mythic self-fashioning or simply as a matter of contrast, relative to the young soldiers. After providing an initial glimpse of himself and the soldiers, Whitman renounces the jingoistic call to arms he had proclaimed in an earlier poem, "Beat! Beat! Drums!" Having witnessed the carnage of war firsthand, he is less eager to fan the flames of patriotic fervor. Instead, he offers an equitable sympathy: "was one side so brave? the other was equally brave." Men have been tested and not found wanting; now it is time for healing.

The "world of gain and appearance and mirth" may go on despite the grave catastrophe that has engulfed the nation's young men, but Whitman, who has no obligations to do so, turns all his considerable energies to assisting those wounded in the line of duty. He pictures himself "Bearing the bandages, water and sponge," going "Straight and swift to my wounded"—the possessive pronoun being, perhaps, an indication both of self-aggrandizement and of his urgent, productive sense of obligation. Whitman, following his usual impulse to comprehensively catalog his subject matter, freights the poem with realistic details: tents, cots, pails, bloody rags, bloody stumps, gangrenous limbs. Yet these realistic details are tempered by more abstract considerations, such as Christ-like self-sacrifice and the merciful beauty of death (the latter a theme explored in greater depth in two of his grandest lyrics, "Out of the Cradle Endlessly Rocking" and "When Lilacs Last in the Dooryard Bloom'd," discussed, respectively, under "Poetry" and "Loss").

The poem's final sections leave us with affecting and memorable images of Whitman the nurse, an image he has successfully projected to near mythic status within our culture. Section three ends by picturing Whitman as impassive without, yet burning with the flame of anger and compassion within: efficiency and passion are, thus, productively united in his being. What greater virtues could one ask for in a nurse? At the conclusion of the poem, we get parenthetical glimpses of Whitman's neck, about which the "loving arms" of many soldiers have rested, and his "bearded lips," which have received "Many a soldier's kiss." Scholars have often supposed that a homoerotic attachment to the young soldiers, whether consciously recognized by Whitman or not, was one motivation for his hospital work, and these images provide persuasive support for that view. Clearly, though, it was not his only motivation: genuine concern, paternalism, patriotism, and a desire for friendly companionship were certainly others. Regardless, Whitman served his country selflessly and thereafter created American poetry's most enduring image of one person easing the suffering of others.

Transcending suffering by transforming it into song is the aesthetic strategy of African-American blues. The blues is a traditional form that descends from slave songs and was popularized in the early twentieth century by such figures as W. C. Handy, Bessie Smith, Blind Lemon Jefferson, Leadbelly, and Robert Johnson. The noted African-American poet Langston Hughes examines the relationship between suffering and African American music in two poems that may be considered side-by-side, "The Weary Blues" (1925) and "Trumpet Player" (1947). The first focuses on a blues pianist, the second on a jazz trumpeter. "Weary Blues" was an actual blues song written in 1915 by Artie Matthews, with lyrics by Mort Greene and George Cates; it was recorded by, among others, Louis Armstrong's Hot Sevens. Hughes's title refers to this famous song, but the lyrics of the poem are Hughes's own invention and are considerably darker than those of the original. "The Weary Blues" presents the African-American artist as creating something sublime in a squalid context. The piano may be "poor" and the stool "rickety," but both piano and man moan with syncopated music, drawn straight from the soul, throughout the entire night. There can be no doubt about the authenticity of this music or the way it represents and speaks to the misfortunes of African Americans.

"Trumpet Player" largely reprises the themes of the earlier poem, but adds to them a harsher view of political and social realities. Behind the jazz trumpeter's eyes and bittersweet music lies "the smoldering memory / Of slave ships." The poem's most pointed metaphor occurs in the penultimate stanza, wherein we are told that the music "slips / Its hypodermic needle / To his soul—." Reference to the relationship between music and the soul reminds one of "The Weary Blues," but the image of the hypodermic needle evokes the drug culture associated with jazz around the time of the poem's composition. Many significant jazz artists of the forties and fifties were heroin addicts. Some, like Miles Davis and John Coltrane, eventually beat their habit; but others, like Charlie Parker and Bill Evans, were destroyed by it; and others still, like Dexter Gordon and Billie Holiday, were incarcerated for it. Drugs and jazz were both means of transcending the harsh realities of urban African-American life.

Both promised access to a world beyond cares, beyond squalor and oppression. Hughes symbolizes the limited, diminished world of the trumpet player by showing how his moonlight is reduced to a spotlight and his sea to a glass of liquor. Despite the fact that its imagery is more foreboding than that of "The Weary Blues," "Trumpet Player" ends on a positive note, by emphasizing how the musician transforms trouble into "a golden note"—an image recalling the "golden in the sunset" from Hughes's signature poem, "The Negro Speaks of Rivers" (discussed under "Tradition & Heritage"). Like Sonny, the jazz pianist in James Baldwin's classic story "Sonny's Blues," both the blues pianist and the trumpet player have clearly suffered to play the way they do. Suffering gives their playing emotional force and authenticity, even as it is transformed from something personal and negative to something public and positive.

Randall Jarrell's "90 North" (1942) also examines the personal pain of existence. The poem contrasts a youthful, romantic view of life with a seasoned, existential one. Jarrell presents the first view in the opening two stanzas, as a dream of the narrator's childhood in which the narrator becomes an older version of himself ("with my black beard"), and his bed transmogrifies into a ship that sails to an exotic, adventurous destination, the North Pole (which had only first been reached by Robert E. Peary in 1909, just five years before Jarrell was born). The dream unfolds on a "childish" night, the misplaced epithet strongly hinting at the naivete of the fantasy. The dreamer imagines the moment of his death, and then the poem abruptly shifts, in the third stanza, into the present tense. The speaker, no longer expressing the romantic sentiments of his youth (this time he, as did Jarrell himself, "really" sports a black beard), reflects on the final meaninglessness of all endeavors. Once one gets to the Pole, what is there to do? "Why, go back." Having reached the apex of the world, he finds that every step is southward, suggesting the inevitable anticlimax that follows achievement. He has set out to discover something, and he has—only it is not what he had expected. What he has found is chaos, or the "whirlpool"—in other words, the meaningless at the heart of existence. In the face of such nothingness, all knowledge is "worthless as ignorance." This dark, unconsoling poem ends by stripping away the illusions that provide comfort and keep such meaninglessness at bay. People experience the pain that "comes from the darkness," but they call it wisdom. The poem's terse, final sentence—"It is pain"—negates all gestures toward transcendence; it denies that suffering grants even wisdom. Suffering is simply suffering: to call it something else is an evasion, a lie. Thus, the poem concludes on the word "pain." "90 North" offers as bleak a view of existence as Dickinson's "The Heart asks Pleasure—first—"; both poems expose the dreams of youth as futile, idealized delusions, and both place suffering at the center of human existence.

The last three poems discussed in this section all concern joy rather than suffering. If none is quite so innocent or untroubled as Moore's vision of Christmas, all at least realistically depict the possibility of joy-fulness in life. Theodore Roethke's "Child on Top of a Greenhouse" (1948), for instance, is a brief evocation of a transcendent moment, pre-sumably based on an experience from the poet's own childhood years spent in the greenhouse world of Saginaw, Michigan. Many of Roethke's poems recall the greenhouses his family owned, but no other in so un-equivocally positive a manner as here. On a beautiful day, the child who speaks the poem stands atop a greenhouse and becomes fully alive to the sensations of the world around him. Specifically, the boy's tactile and visual senses are engaged. He feels the wind billowing out his britches and the glass and putty beneath his feet. The latter momentarily distracts him, as he looks down into the greenhouse to see growing chrysanthe-mums "staring up like accusers"; but the flash of sunlight off the glass redirects his attention outward to the work of the wind, evident from the fast-moving clouds and the tossing elms, which remind him of horses. Any negative feelings associated with the interior of the green-house are utterly effaced by the boy's sense that the entire scene has come alive in the wind and that every tree is offering its lively praise to the sheer exuberant beauty of the world. The boy's identity seems to disappear momentarily: he, too, is part of the "everyone, everyone" rap-turously pointing upward. Roethke portrays here a nourishing, regen-erative "spot of time," as described by the English poet William Wordsworth in his book-length autobiographical poem *The Prelude*. "Such moments," Wordsworth writes, "Are scattered everywhere, taking their date / From our first childhood" (12.223–25). For poets such as Wordsworth and Roethke, these moments of transcendent joy help re-new and sustain one's existence; they come only rarely but are never forgotten.

Roethke was a talented and inspiring teacher of poetry writing, and the most celebrated of his pupils, James Wright, wrote a somewhat sim-ilar poem about a special moment of heightened joy and awareness. As with "Child on Top of a Greenhouse," "A Blessing" (1963) depicts a seemingly simple scene suddenly charged with such extraordinary eu-phoric energy that it seems to become, as the title suggests, beatific, holy. The poet and his friend step off a highway in Minnesota into a pasture where two Indian ponies graze. Wright's description brings the energy of the scene to life: twilight "bounds," and the ponies, barely able to contain their joy, "bow shyly as wet swans." They, we are told, love each other, but also clearly love the presence of the two visitors. The slender female pony approaches the poet; in a moment of joy that verges on the erotic, he becomes aware that the pony's ear is as delicate as the skin of a girl. Having already crossed the boundary of the barbed-wire fence, the poet feels as if he could cross another: the boundary of physicality or embodiment itself. He feels as if his life force might suddenly step out of his body and blossom from sheer joy. The word "blossom," clearly related by virtue of its sound to "Blessing," becomes the focal point of the entire poem, the trope that gathers the emotion of the moment into a single pregnant image.

For yet another antidote to the pessimistic visions of Dickinson and Jarrell, one might turn to Richard Wilbur's "Hamlen Brook" (1987). One can infer that the speaker of the poem, has traveled by foot a fair ways, for he is both sweaty and thirsty. As he bends down to take a drink from a clear stream, he startles a trout. The entire middle portion of the poem (lines 8–19) describes, in a single syntactically complex sentence, the trout and its eventual disappearance, all in extraordinary detail, placing before the reader the very fullness of the world. Wilbur, much like Elizabeth Bishop in her poem "The Fish" (discussed under "Thought & Perception"), meticulously renders the textured surface of reality, which can easily be taken for granted and go all but unperceived. The extraordinary images, which will reward a reader's careful concentration, lead toward a question formulated with Wilbur's characteristic wordplay, "How shall I drink all this?" The word "drink" here is a pun, for the speaker initially intended to drink the water of the stream, but is now referring, metaphorically, to "drinking" in the scenery. The final stanza extends this metaphor in a way that makes a significant point about the nature of joy itself. Joy here arises from the perception of the unexpected and remarkably complex beauty of the fish and the scenery. The "trick" of joy is, again metaphorically, to satisfy one's thirst, but also to leave one with an ache that cannot be satisfied. The mind cannot fully grasp the complexity it admires—nor can the moment be indefinitely protracted. The mind's awareness of these limitations leads to a kind of bittersweet melancholy, even in the midst of joy. In fact, it is joy itself that paradoxically makes one aware of a longing to transcend limitation. So, in a peculiar way, joy and suffering meet at the point of desire.

ଚେଠ୦

"A Visit from St. Nicholas," Clement Moore
    APN-1
"The Heart asks Pleasure—first—," Emily Dickinson
    AAL-1; AAL-2; APN-2; HAL-1; HAL-2; NAL-1; NOBA; NoP-4; OxBA

"The Wound-Dresser," Walt Whitman

> AAL-1; APN-1; ATL-1; ATL-2; ColAP; HAL-1; HAL-2; HoAL-1; HoAL-2; NAL-1; NOBA

"The Weary Blues," Langston Hughes

> ATL-2; ColAP; HAL-2; HoAL-2; MAP; NAL-2; NoAM; NOBA; NoP-4

"Trumpet Player," Langston Hughes

> ATL-2; HoAL-2

"90 North," Randall Jarrell

> CAPP-6; CoAP; NAL-2; NoAM; NOBA; VCAP

"Child on Top of a Greenhouse," Theodore Roethke

> HoAL-2; NoP-4; VGW

"A Blessing," James Wright

> AAL-2; CAPP-6; CoAmPo; MAP; NAL-2; NoAM; NOBA; NoP-4; VCAP

"Hamlen Brook," Richard Wilbur

> CAPP-6; VCAP; WeW-4

Thought and Perception

❧

> How much happier the wide-awake indolents, the monarchs among men, the rich monstrous brains deriving intense enjoyment and rapturous pangs from the balustrade of a terrace at nightfall, from the lights and the lake below, from the distant mountain shapes melting into the dark apricot of the afterglow, from the black conifers outlined against the pale ink of the zenith, and from the garnet and green flounces of the water along the silent, sad, forbidden shoreline.
>
> Charles Kinbote in Vladimir Nabokov's *Pale Fire*

Good poets typically posses both a heightened sensitivity to internal thought processes and to external stimuli, or to what Robert Frost called inner and outer weather. Poets depend upon fresh thoughts and fresh perceptions—these become the raw material of their work. Poetry itself is largely a matter of attending carefully to these two types of weather and then of fitting the right words to them. Successful poetry, in other words, usually issues from a mind well stocked with ideas and first-hand sensory impressions. Too heavy a reliance on conventional imagery drawn from the great storehouse of past poetry will not be sufficient. By the same token, the ability to perceive the world carefully is, by itself, no guarantee that one will be able to write good poetry; the poet's internal resources of thought and verbal invention must also rise to the occasion. In the prose passage from Nabokov quoted above, one instinctively feels that the writer has deeply perceived the sunset scene his narrator describes so vividly—but if many writers recycled such descriptions as "the dark apricot of the afterglow" or "the pale ink of the zenith," they would quickly lose their imaginative force. Poetry is the work of knowing; it results from the mind's active engagement with the world.

Walt Whitman's "When I Heard the Learn'd Astronomer" (1865) demonstrates how the poet's concerns differ from those of the scientist. In the modern world—and all American poetry belongs to the modern world—thought and perception have been disciplined by the exact demonstrations of empirical science. Poets, despite some grumbling from Wordsworth, Keats, and Poe, have had to become more self-conscious about the imaginative liberties of earlier ages, even as the scientific worldview itself has opened new vistas for thought about the immensity of time and space and for perception through the agencies of the telescope and the microscope. On the surface, Whitman's poem seems simple enough. The poet attends a lecture by a noted astronomer. He watches as the astronomer produces columns of figures, charts, and diagrams, but he becomes unaccountably "tired and sick." He leaves the lecture hall and "in the mystical moist night-air" looks up occasionally "in perfect silence at the stars."

The poem is more than an anti-intellectual rejection of empirical knowledge; it contrasts two ways of knowing the world. The poet does not claim or imply that the astronomer with all his careful computations is wrong, only that the knowledge he offers is incomplete. The star charts, the figures, and the rest are models of the world, not the world itself. They are *knowledge of*, not *experience with*. The poet's realm, as defined by Whitman's poem, is the latter. When Whitman looks up at the stars, he feels the "mystical" wholeness of being—something that cannot be reduced to a chart. He perceives the night directly through his senses, not through the filter of some abstracted paradigm. He involves us not with a model of thought but with the specific thoughts he, an individual, has at a specific moment in time.

Unlike Poe in his "Sonnet—To Science," Whitman is neither lamenting the rise of science nor arguing that it has had a negative impact on poetry. In *Song of Myself*, in fact, Whitman wrote: "Hurrah for positive science! long live exact demonstration!" Instead, the poem contrasts one way of understanding with another, and we are left to see for ourselves that this second way (personal experience) is the way of poetry. Sensory perception alone, of course, can lead us into all sorts of errors. If we trust merely what we see, we will conclude that the sun goes around the earth, and so on; but, conversely, when we have understood that the earth, despite appearances, is rapidly revolving around the sun, we still find that our perceptions have not changed. (And, thus, we still talk of "sunrises" and "sunsets.") Information can condition how we interpret our perception of the world; but can we live exclusively in a world of abstracted knowledge? Of course not; human experience, based on direct sensory perception of the world, remains the fundamental condition of our existence. We ignore this condition only at our own peril and impoverishment.

Two poems that illustrate Emily Dickinson's handling of the themes of thought and perception are "I felt a Funeral, in my Brain" (#280, c. 1861) and "The Brain—is wider than the Sky—" (#632, c. 1862). The first of these must qualify as one of the more enigmatic of Dickinson's widely anthologized poems. Part of the difficulty (but also the fun) inheres in the elaborate funeral metaphor, which dominates the poem's first three stanzas. First there is a funeral procession, then a service, then a casket being carried away—presumably to be interred—while a bell begins to ring. Note that everything is felt and heard but not seen: the speaker is not in a position to see this "funeral," for it is not a literal event, but rather a metaphor for a change in the speaker's state of consciousness. Precisely what the speaker is enduring can be debated. Is she falling into unconsciousness, or dying, or merely experiencing the "death" of some cherished idea or belief system? Regardless, the experience proves to be both terrifying and liberating, as "a Plank in Reason" breaks and the speaker drops into new, unimagined worlds before the poem abruptly cuts off, either because the speaker has died or because she has passed into the realm of the ineffable.

"I felt a Funeral, in my Brain" deals strictly with the hidden events of the mind's interior, or the mind's relation to its own states of being. "The Brain—is wider than the Sky—" is a poem about a different relationship, that of the mind to the exterior world. Dickinson—in a poem much less ambiguous than the preceding one—states her grand conception of the mind's powers. The brain (by which she means not the physical object but the mind) is not merely wider than the sky but "deeper than the sea"; indeed, it is "the weight of God." In Dickinson's poem, the mind appears as an infinite container that can hold the world with a power barely distinguishable from omniscience. To perceive is to exceed (although it is interesting to contrast Dickinson's confident viewpoint with the more cautiously ironic one in the third of Wallace Stevens's "Six Significant Landscapes": in that poem, which seems consciously to refer to Dickinson's, perception is at first privileged above what it perceives; but the poet then notes how ants crawl in and out of his shadow—an image reminding both poet and reader of the finite limitations of human beings).

On its surface, Robert Frost's "After Apple-Picking" (1914) appears to be a simple poem about an exhausted apple picker. A careful reading of the poem, however, will clearly indicate that it has symbolic overtones and troubling depths. For instance, in line 2, the picker's ladder is said to be not simply pointing up but pointing "Toward heaven" (a key phrase repeated in the poem "Birches," discussed under "Innocence & Experience"). The term "heaven" is not a neutral description of the sky; it immediately connotes something about belief, ideals, life and death, and the hope of eternal rewards. The rest of the poem develops these concepts. For instance, in lines 30–36, the poet discusses the difference between apples that are dropped in the course of work and those that are not. The passage functions on a literal, naturalistic level, but at another level, it contrasts perfection (associated back with "heaven") with imperfection (the apples that have "struck the earth" and will end up on "the cider-apple heap"). These contrasts between perfection and imperfection and between heaven and earth relate directly to the apple picker's own weariness and subtly indicated sense of mortality. At the end of the poem, he wonders what kind of sleep it is that is "coming on"—ordinary sleep as a natural result of working too hard, or something more, something associated with winter in line 7 and with the woodchuck's hibernation in lines 40–41? Fairly obviously, the ideas of "winter sleep" and a "Long sleep" suggest the possibility of death—as does the twice-repeated word "sleep" in the conclusion of "Stopping by Woods on a Snowy Evening" (discussed under Obligations & Choices).

"After Apple-Picking," however, concerns not principally the theme of death but rather that of perception. It remains ambiguous in the poem whether the picker actually stands close to death or is merely so exhausted that his thoughts magnify his weariness in this ultimate fashion. The centrality of perception in the poem is clear from the remarkable imagery of lines 9–13, in which the picker recalls skimming a sheet of ice (metaphorically described as a "pane of glass") from a trough and being startled at how distorted the frosted grass appeared when he looked through it. That sense of distortion haunts the whole poem. It aptly characterizes the weary frame of mind of the speaker, who has, as lines 4–5 and 30–31 clearly indicate, worked both diligently and carefully. The sensory distortion continues in the hallucinatory dream the picker describes in lines 18–20: "Magnified apples appear and disappear," he begins. The sudden shift to the present tense makes the dream-like perceptions that much more vivid. The speaker's other senses are also engaged: he feels the pressure of the ladder against his instep arch and hears the "rumbling sound" of apple loads being deposited in the cellar bin. A deceptively simple and thematically rich poem, "After Apple-Picking" records the distortion of thoughts and perceptions that result from exhaustion. What makes the poem so powerful is that the distortion intimates the deepest mysteries of human existence.

No American poet has made the themes of thought and perception more central to his work than has Wallace Stevens. Nearly all of his poems engage these themes at some level. His particular interest is in the relationship of the mind to the exterior world (the same relationship explored in "The Brain—is wider than the Sky—"). A representative group of three poems—"The Snow Man," "The Idea of Order at Key West," and "A Postcard from the Volcano"—demonstrates some of the complex and ingenious ways Stevens developed this theme. Although less difficult than Stevens's later works, these are not simple poems, and no honest discussion of them will make them appear to be more simple than they are. Superficially, "The Snow Man" (1923) resembles certain poems by Robert Frost, in which a lone figure confronts a winter land-scape. But this poem addresses the relationship of mind to reality in a more abstract, philosophical manner than any poem by Frost. "The Snow Man" consists of a single sentence, arranged into tercets. Both the form and the crisp, memorable imagery can divert one's attention from the poem's complicated syntax. The first line, "One must have a mind of winter," appears somewhat less formidable after we have parsed the poem-sentence. "One must have a mind of winter" to see these wintry scenes and "not to think / Of any misery" in the sounds of the land—that's what it boils down to, at least up to the first relative clause. In other words, a "mind of winter" is defined by the poem as the ability to behold certain winter scenes and not to anthropomorphize (or impute human characteristics to) certain sounds. The "mind of winter" sees the winter landscape for what it is: inhuman, alien, absolutely distinct from the mind's symbols for it. Such a mind knows there is no emotion in the sound of the wind; the only emotion is in the perceiver's response to such phenomena. These responses, the speaker clearly recognizes, can be conditioned by our culture. We may conventionally associate misery with the "howling" winter wind; but that is because we have learned to do so. When we do such things, we are not, in all likelihood, experienc-ing the wind directly but experiencing it in a way that is mediated by our cultural and linguistic traditions; in a sense, we are employing the figures of speech of anonymous, long-dead poets. We betray that we do not have a "mind of winter" but rather a "mind of culture."

In their early phases, most cultures have an animistic tendency to per-sonify the world. Rivers, trees, the wind, sun, and moon: all things with motion are thought to have spirits. Only empirical observation, which discovers the mechanism of insentient motion, frees us from the illusion that spirits and gods animate the world. The mind seems to have a ten-dency to look out and, instead of seeing the world for what it is, to find a reflection of itself. It is the myth of Narcissus, as Ishmael recognizes in the opening chapter of *Moby-Dick*. The "misery" of the wind in "The Snow Man" is a last echo of this tendency to foist the mind upon the world—what John Ruskin, Victorian critic of art and society, called "the pathetic fallacy."

Stevens's poem distinguishes what is from what the mind imputes and imports. The "listener" of the poem—apparently a separate figure from the speaker and perhaps an actual snow man, which would make an appropriate symbol for a mind free from the pitfalls of consciousness—undergoes, through this discipline of stripping human association away from the world, a triple epiphany of "nothings." If the listener, by possessing "a mind of winter," has come to be "nothing himself," in the sense that he no longer imposes his own mental schemata on the scene, then the scene itself contains "Nothing that is not there" (because the listener is adding nothing—not even words) as well as a "nothing that is"—in other words, an alien order of reality. It is alien because it is antithetical to the conscious meanings the mind so readily desires to impose upon it; but a tree, of course, is not "a tree": a thing is not a symbol. Between the symbolic understanding of the mind and the meaningless reality of the physical world lies a gulf, full of illusions for the unwary.

In his essay "The Noble Rider and the Sound of Words," Stevens writes that "what makes the poet the potent figure that he is, or was, or ought to be, is that he creates the world to which we turn incessantly and without knowing it and that he gives to life the supreme fictions without which we are unable to conceive of it." This exalted view of the poet as a creator of our mental horizons continues a line of thinking that goes back to Emerson and the English romantics. As Percy Bysshe Shelley famously said, "poets are the unacknowledged legislators of the world." Stevens, as did his predecessors, views the fundamental work of poetry as being the creation of our sense of reality. "The Idea of Order at Key West" (1936) steps beyond the contrasts of drab reality and poetic potential Stevens had explored in "Disillusionment of Ten O'Clock" (discussed under "Civilization") to the actual creation of imaginative, poetic order. Such creation eventuates from making something of what one perceives and thereby enabling others to see in a new way. Stevens himself gives us a striking example of this kind of creation in line 16, when he refers to "The ever-hooded, tragic-gestured sea." Having read that line, can one ever look again at the sea as before? The figure in this poem who represents poetic creation, however, is not Stevens himself but a woman who walks on the shore. "She sang beyond the genius of the sea." Is there a lovelier opening line in American poetry? Certainly, few possess more complex or sonorous sound patterns.

As in several other crucial Stevens poems, such as "The Snow Man" and "Sunday Morning" (discussed under "Skepticism & Belief"), the central figure of the poem is being observed. In this case, there are two other figures—the narrator and a man named Ramon Fernandez. The two see the woman singing by the sea. In her singing, the woman is a "maker" (the original Greek meaning of the word "poet"), creating meaning out of the "meaningless plungings of water and wind." The world we have access to is a world of our perceptions, which we interpret with such language as we can muster. The woman seems to be one of those who has the potential to expand our understanding of the world by articulating new ways of perceiving it; if so, she is a true poet, in Stevens's terms. The last two paragraphs provide an image that complements that of the woman singing: the lights of the seaside town portion out the darkness and the sea in much the same way that her song had. The lights are Stevens's apt symbol for humanly imposed order. This "Blessed rage for order" is, as "The Noble Rider and the Sound of Words" makes clear, the true poet's vocation and passion. The poet must enlarge our perceptions by creating "ghostlier demarcations, keener sounds."

"The Idea of Order at Key West" meditates on the relationship between imaginative perception and our sense of the world. "A Postcard from the Volcano" (1936) examines the same theme, but in a historical manner. It considers how the perceptions of the past have modified the reality of the present. This time, the narrators ("we") are a voice from the past, a voice that, as in several Dickinson poems, seems to speak from beyond the grave. The speakers, representatives of an earlier generation, assert that the dead have left more than their bones; they have left behind feelings, thoughts, and perceptions that secretly help to shape the way the living know the world. The sky "Cries out a literate despair"—the key word here being "literate," for as with the "misery" of the wind in "The Snow Man," the despair of this line is not an inherent property of air but has resulted from the personifying tendencies, transmitted by language and culture, of the dead. A second example helps to clarify the process: what the speakers said of the mansion "became / A part of what it is." Reality, for Stevens, is not a given but something shaped by thought and language. Collectively, human beings construct a sense of reality through language, just as bees build hives. The perceptions of the past haunt our imaginations; these secret visitations are the true relics of our predecessors, in a far more vital way than such physical remnants as the bones and even the mansion. The theme of the poem seems to derive from a passage from Emerson's essay "Self-Reliance": "perception is not whimsical, but fatal. If I see a trait, my children will see it after me, and in course of time, all mankind,—although it may chance that no one has seen it before me. For my perception of it is as much a fact as the sun." (Is it merely a coincidence that the final word of Stevens's poem is also "sun"?)

Stevens's poems, highly intellectual in nature, cogitate philosophically on the complexities and interconnections of objects, perceptions, language, and poetry. A very different type of poem also concerned with perception consists primarily of description. Instead of offering ideas about perceptions, these poems attempt to offer the perceptions themselves, in as direct a manner as possible. This kind of poem is thus about perception in a much more implicit manner. Marianne Moore and Elizabeth Bishop, poets admired for their discriminating and meticulous powers of observation, wrote poems of this variety. Each also wrote a poem entitled "The Fish," but with this difference: in Moore's poem the title is plural, whereas in Bishop's it is singular. Both poems offer a carefully delineated record of perceptions. Moore's "The Fish" (1921, rev. 1935) offers the pleasure of a closely observed scene that has been translated into superbly evocative English. The diction certainly arrests one's attention. The fish do not swim through the region of the sea Moore describes, but rather "wade," which indicates precisely the far more labored locomotion necessary in such proximity to a sea cliff and its surrounding turbulence. The fish themselves, however, are only part of this aquatic scene. After six words (if we include the title, which, as was fashionable for poems of this period, runs into the text), the poem turns its attention to "crow-blue mussel-shells." This description provides an excellent example of Moore's discriminating powers of perception, for a more casual observer would have been apt to conclude that both crows and mussels are simply black. The simile that follows offers another kind of vivid, eye-opening description: one of the mussels opens and shuts itself "like / an / injured fan." What reader—once reminded that Moore does not mean an electric fan—cannot take pleasure in such an unexpected yet appropriate comparison? The rest of the poem follows this strategy of imaginative description and comparison until a whole section of the sea, at war with the "defiant edifice" of a cliff, has been set before us, in a way we almost certainly could not have seen for ourselves. The cliff itself might be taken for a symbol of endurance, but the symbolic value of the image remains almost entirely implicit. Like much of the best of Moore's poetry, "The Fish" offers, first and foremost, a cornucopia of sensory delights.

A very different poem, despite its identical title, Elizabeth Bishop's "The Fish" (1946) can be divided into three unequal sections. The largest of these, the second (lines 7–64), provides a keenly observed description of a single fish. Bishop's poem, both longer and more concentrated than that of Moore (Bishop's friend and mentor), employs a number of figures of speech that function as startlingly effective visual clarifications. A very definite pattern of imagery emerges in the poem, for Bishop compares the relatively unfamiliar aspects of the fish with common domestic items: wallpaper, rags, feathers, tinfoil. One can also observe a pattern of flower imagery: roses, rosettes, a peony. Bishop's alert descriptions serve to familiarize this strange denizen of the deep that she has hauled into her little rented boat. The fish, probably based on a parrot fish that Bishop described in a letter to Moore on January 14, 1939, is said not to have fought at all, a fact that assumes greater importance when Bishop later describes the hooks in its jaw, indicating it had indeed fought valiantly against fishermen in the past, presumably when it possessed greater youthful vitality. The careful observations seem to lead directly to the poem's denouement, for in taking such careful notice of the fish, Bishop can hardly help from coming to respect and even to sympathize with it. Bishop may have succeeded where previous fishermen had failed, but her true victory arrives at the moment she throws the fish back where it belongs. Perhaps what the poem ultimately asserts is that when we perceive the world clearly, it has the power to change us.

Robert Creeley's "I Know a Man" (1957) combines the themes of thought and perception in a rather different and somewhat comic manner. This brief, heavily enjambed, and very concise ("sd," "yr") poem can be passed over as something of a lark; but beneath its casual exterior lurks some real substance. The speaker is driving; he is talking to his friend, John ("which was not his / name"). He first expresses some existential angst: "the darkness sur- / rounds us," he says. (Note that the neat enjambment of the word "surrounds" enacts the idea expressed by the word.) With no solution to this metaphysical dilemma in sight, he proposes that the friends pitch in and buy "a goddamn big car." The desire to own this big car suggests that the car he is driving is probably not big, which no doubt further underscores the friend's alarm in the final stanza, when he has to remind the narrator to keep his eyes on the road. The poem not only presents a complete dramatic situation but also contrasts two philosophies of life, each aligned with one of the two themes under consideration here—thought and perception. The speaker appears to be something of an idealist, with vague fears and big dreams. He is so wrapped up in his thoughts that he apparently comes close to having an accident. The friend, on the other hand, seems to be practical, down-to-earth, observant. His perceptions "save" the two of them. By contrasting the two characters, the poem makes a sardonic comment on how idealistic preoccupation can blind us to practical necessity. Dreams are indispensable, but so is cautious alertness.

James Wright's "Lying in a Hammock at William Duffy's Farm in Pine Island, Minnesota" (1961) documents how an unexpected thought may arise from perceptions. The poem describes a reasonably pleasant natural scene that contains a sleeping butterfly, cowbells, horse droppings, and a "chicken hawk." What startles here is the unexpected shift in the final line from description to assertion: "I have wasted my life." This abrupt ending reminds one of the quite similar conclusion to a sonnet by the German poet Rainer Maria Rilke entitled "Archaic Torso of Apollo," which must have served as Wright's model. In Rilke's poem, a description of a decapitated statue concludes with the words "Du musst dein Leben ändern" (You must change your life). In both poems, we are left wondering how we arrived at the conclusion. In the case of Wright's poem, a rereading may focus our attention on details that previously seemed innocuous or unobtrusive. Is the ending suggested to the poet by the juxtaposition of the "empty house" behind him and the hawk that is "looking for home"? Or is it the coming of night that brings on the poet's thought of having wasted his life? If the latter, the poem can fruitfully be compared to Emerson's "Days" (discussed under "Time &

Change"). The precise connection between thought and perception may seem elusive, but the sheer order of the poem leads us to believe that the one must arise from the other.

A. R. Ammons's "Gravelly Run" (1965) and Howard Nemerov's "The Blue Swallows" (1967) may usefully be compared as skeptical statements about the mind's ability to contain or order the reality it perceives. In this sense, both poems descend from Stevens's "The Snow Man" and are further rejoinders to the transcendent view of the mind's powers presented in Dickinson's "The Brain—is wider than the Sky—." The speaker of "Gravelly Run" resigns himself to the mind's failure to contain the complexity of external reality, or what he identifies as the triumph of natural objects, such as stones and trees. His is a world filled only with "unwelcoming forms." The idea of constructing some religion of nature tempts the speaker briefly (lines 17–20), but transcendental illusions are quickly banished; ultimately, the speaker asserts—as did Stevens before him, reality is an alien order. Gods, personifications, and philosophies of design (such as that of Hegel) are revealed as nothing but constructs of the mind. Cold-eyed, empirical observation fails to discover them in the world. The speaker ultimately stresses the unmeaning, nonlinguistic nature of inanimate reality, which represents the opposite of the mind, with its perpetual quest for symbolic pattern and meaning. The poem concludes with a tough admonition from the speaker to himself to shoulder his troubles and move along. In other words, the only way out of the impasse brought on by the pale cast of thought is in taking action. The world itself can offer no meaningful assuagement.

Nemerov's poem also confronts both the temptation to anthropomorphize nature and the hard truth of the world's otherness. As the poet stands on a bridge, poised rather unusually above seven blue swallows, the birds fly below in patterns of such intricacy that the mind cannot begin to comprehend their motions. Perception, as in Ammons's poem, is unequal to the complexities of reality. For a moment, however, Nemerov allows himself to weave a fanciful analogy: the tails of the birds, he halfheartedly proposes, are like the nibs of pens, writing secret messages in the sky. The moment corresponds with Ammons's desire to found some religion of nature. Both efforts express each poet's longing for assurance that the world is both hospitable and meaningful; but both poets are ultimately compelled by skepticism and knowledge to rise above this desire into a less comfortable but more rigorously accurate view of reality. Nemerov might attribute the invisible "writing" of the swallows to God or nature, but he accepts the logic of Occam's razor, that the simplest solution—that there is no meaning in the world, only in the mind—is the correct one. The collective mind of humanity, he asserts, is only beginning to see the real world rather than its own fanciful creations. Again, it is language, with its tricks of analogy and personification, that is the barrier between accurate perception and reality. Nemerov's poem moves toward as stern a conclusion as Ammons's, but then swerves toward a final consolation similar to that of "The Idea of Order at Key West." The artistic mind creates our sense of reality: that is the only redemption Nemerov's skeptical poem offers.

Robert Hass's "Meditation at Lagunitas" (1979) attempts to find a way out of the philosophical quandary that leads to a complete distrust of language. Loss, the poem proclaims, has been at the center of our thought all along. Hass provides two examples: first, the idea that the division of the world into discrete parts is a falling off from some primal unity; and second, the idea that an impassable gulf exists between words and what they signify. (The first is an old idea, the second a modern one that recalls quite directly the skeptical positions staked out by Stevens, Ammons, and Nemerov.) Hass then refers to a conversation he had with a friend who had taken the skeptical view of language; as a result of it, the poet came to understand that a certain way of looking at words dissolves their significance. Against this possibility, he positions certain vivid memories of a woman he once knew. Lovemaking restores, however temporarily, a sense of unity, although longing (an appropriate word, he reminds us, since "desire is full / of endless distances") always returns. The point, however, seems to be that loss is not an absolute condition; it can be overcome, at least in the moment, by acts of love, memory, and articulation. In making his case, Hass even goes so far as to assert the "numinous" property of words. But the final argument of the poem depends not on opposing the withering rationality of his friend and predecessors with mysticism, but on the heft of the simple word "blackberry." By invoking it three times at the poem's conclusion, Hass makes us feel the physicality of the word and the way it scrapes against reality. Against the rationality of the skeptics, the poem quietly reasserts the power words have, in however qualified a manner, to evoke and correspond with reality. In doing so, it attempts to redeem the processes of perception, thought, and memory in their relationship to what we take to be reality.

♻

"When I Heard the Learn'd Astronomer," Walt Whitman

> AAL-1; ATL-1; ATL-2; ColAP; HAL-1; HAL-2; HoAL-2; LPTT; NAL-1; NoP-4; OxBA; SoSe-9; WeW-4

"I felt a Funeral, in my Brain," Emily Dickinson

> AAL-1; AAL-2; APN-2; ColAP; HAL-1; HAL-2; HoAL-2; MAP; NAL-1; NOBA; NoP-4; OxBA; SoSe-9; TFi

"The Brain—is wider than the Sky—," Emily Dickinson

> AAL-1; AAL-2; APN-2; HAL-1; HAL-2; HoAL-2; NAL-1; NoAM; OxBA

"After Apple-Picking," Robert Frost

> AAL-2; APT-1; ATL-2; HoAL-2; MAP; NAL-2; NoAM; NOBA; OxBA; SoSe-9; TFi

"The Snow Man," Wallace Stevens

> AAL-2; APT-1; ATL-2; ColAP; HAL-2; HCAP; HoAL-2; MAP; NAL-2; NoAM; NoP-4; SoSe-9; WeW-4

"The Idea of Order at Key West," Wallace Stevens

> AAL-2; APT-1; ATL-2; ColAP; HAL-2; HCAP; HoAL-2; MAP; NAL-2; NoAM; NOBA; NoP-4; OxBA; TFi

"A Postcard from the Volcano," Wallace Stevens

> APT-1; ATL-2; HAL-2; HCAP; HoAL-2; MAP; NAL-2; NoAM; WeW-4

"The Fish," Marianne Moore

> AAL-2; APT-1; ColAP; HAL-2; HoAL-2; MAP; NoAM; NoP-4; OxBA

"The Fish," Elizabeth Bishop

> AAL-2; APT-2; ATL-2; HAL-2; HoAL-2; MAP; NAL-2; NoAM; NOBA; NoP-4; TFi; WeW-4

"I Know a Man," Robert Creeley

> CAPP-6; CoAmPo; NOBA; NoP-4; VCAP

"Lying in a Hammock at William Duffy's Farm in Pine Island, Minnesota," James Wright

> CAPP-6; CoAmPo; ColAP; HCAP; HoAL-2; MAP; NOBA; VCAP

"Gravelly Run," A. R. Ammons

> AAL-2; CoAP; HoAL-2; MAP; NoAM; VCAP

"The Blue Swallows," Howard Nemerov

> NoP-4

"Meditation at Lagunitas," Robert Hass

> CAPP-6; ColAP; NoP-4; VCAP; WeW-4

Time and Change

೧⌒∧⌒೧

> To the attentive eye, each moment of the year has its own beauty,
> and in the same field, it beholds, every hour, a picture which was
> never seen before, and which shall never be seen again.
>
> Ralph Waldo Emerson, *Nature*

Few themes are closer to the heart of American poetry than those of time
and change. In the work of some representative American poets, such as
Robert Frost, Robinson Jeffers, and A. R. Ammons, such themes seem to
haunt virtually every line. Poems have long addressed themselves to the
problems of mutability and loss (a closely related theme)—in fact, such
phenomena are the virtual wellsprings of poetry. The way American
poets have handled these themes, however, says something important
not only about the protean nature of our world but also about America
itself and the character of modern thought. As a tale such as Washington
Irving's "Rip van Winkle" strongly implies, American civilization,
throughout its history, has been irremediably dynamic and prone to
change quite dramatically, even within a single generation. The pace of
American westward expansion and technological development has challenged and practically defied the powers of an individual imagination.
In 1782, for instance, J. Hector St. Jean de Crèvecoeur predicted, in his
famous *Letters from an American Farmer*, that "Many ages will not see the
shores of our great lakes replenished with inland nations, nor the unknown bounds of North America entirely peopled. Who can tell how far
it extends?" The answer to his question was supplied a generation later
by Lewis and Clark, and by 1890, the United States Census Bureau had
declared the frontier to be closed. In little more than a hundred years
American civilization had accomplished what Crèvecoeur predicted

would take "many ages." No nation in the history of the world, it is safe to assert, has grown and changed more rapidly and unpredictably, in such a short time, than America.

William Cullen Bryant's great poem "The Prairies" (1832) appeared at a time when the transformation of the American continent no longer seemed like a distant prospect, as it had to Crèvecoeur, but still well before it was an accomplished fact. The poem, a meditation on changes past and changes to come, resulted from a visit Bryant made to his brothers, who lived on the prairies of Illinois. Bryant had never seen the prairies before, and one thing he takes pains to demonstrate to the reader is that they are deceptive. In recording his reactions to these "gardens of the Desert," Bryant initially presents them as "motionless." He quickly corrects himself, however, when he perceives that every part of the lovely natural scene he witnesses—from the clouds above, to the surface below, to a prairie-hawk suspended in-between—moves. The hawk remains fixed in the sky, hovering but not motionless, for its wings constantly flap; in a sense, this image, with its deceptive, almost paradoxical motionless motion, is the perfect representative of both the landscape and Bryant's themes. This poem is ultimately about large-scale changes that are not immediately apparent to the eye but must instead be inferred from careful attention to the landscape. The first portion of the poem (lines 1–34) records the adjustment of Bryant's vision so that he can see change in an environment that superficially appears unchanging.

Bryant initially asserts that "Man hath no part in all this glorious work," but in the second part, this, like the initial appearance of motionlessness, turns out to be a false impression. Nature, or nature's God, may have constructed the prairies, but humans have altered them and will continue to do so. Bryant's attention turns to the "mighty mounds" on the prairies—the most obvious sign of human-made change—which he mistakenly believed were constructed by a civilization predating that of the Native Americans. We must understand that Bryant's sense of history was a product of his times and could not benefit from the research of modern anthropologists and archeologists. Whereas today a superbly informative museum stands near the Cahokia mounds, in Bryant's time the history and construction of the mounds were a mystery. Although Bryant's history is faulty, it does not impair his presentation of the theme of change. He depicts, in a vividly imagined scene, the siege of the mounds by the Native Americans and the assimilation of a surviving mound builder into the conqueror's society. The point here is how one civilization takes the place of another.

"Thus change the forms of being," Bryant begins the third section of the poem, in the clearest explication of his central theme. Perhaps the belief that the Native Americans had driven out an earlier civilization can be taken as a mitigation, or even a justification, of the conquest of "the old conquerors" by the new; but the real point of the poem is not manifest destiny but change in an abstract and universal sense. In the third section of the poem (lines 86–102), Bryant begins to record the impact of westward expansion on the prairies. This record takes an unusual form: the expansion is apparent only from certain absences. The presence of the mounds in section two contrasts with three crucial absences in section three: those of the Native Americans, the beavers, and the bison. Bryant indicates the cause for this change when he notes that the beaver now builds by waters whose surfaces "ne'er gave back / The white man's face" and that the bison now roam beyond the smoke of hunter's camps. The hungry, merciless, money-driven expansion of the United States has altered the prairies. What the prairies once were is apparent only from the mounds and from the footprints of departed bison.

Section three shows us that although the frame of the picture—the clouds and surfaces of the prairie introduced in section one—remain unchanged, the figures within the picture have changed dramatically. Section four (lines 103–23) looks ahead to future change, which will involve even portions of the frame itself. First, Bryant inventories the creatures that remain. Change, these images of lingering species remind us, is often gradual and partial. But change is also constant and inevitable. The bees that Bryant sees introduce a new note; they are described as "more adventurous" colonists than the white men. The bees came across the Atlantic with the settlers, whose progress they have since outstripped; they are further indications of how drastically, and irrevocably the environment of the prairies has been altered. In the humming of the bees, Bryant rightly hears the sound of "that advancing multitude / Which soon shall fill these deserts." Here is where the frame itself will change, for instead of flowers to adorn the prairie's surface, there will be "the rustling of the heavy grain." The poem ends with Bryant's vision of the future swept away by a breeze; the poet, drawn out of his reverie and back to his senses, stands alone in the prairies as they were in 1832, enjoying his solitude but aware of how transient it is. Thus, at the poem's end, we are returned to a paradoxical sense of motionless motion, for it is only the imagination—not the eye—that can apprehend the large-scale changes wrought by time.

Bryant's poem registers change on the scale of civilizations and landscapes, but some American poets have preferred to focus the theme more narrowly on the life of an individual—another's or their own. Often, such poems record, almost subliminally, larger changes in American culture. One such poem, contemporaneous with "The Prairies," is "The Last Leaf" (1831) by Oliver Wendell Holmes. The poem's central metaphor—the last leaf itself, introduced in the final stanza—reminds the reader of Freneau's similar image of the clinging apple in "On Observing a Large

Red-Streak Apple." "The Last Leaf" begins with the poet perceiving an old man, said to be modeled on Thomas Melville, the grandfather of Herman Melville. The appearance of this old man, tottering on his cane and cut down by "the pruning-knife of Time," sets in motion the poet's recollections of what he has heard about the man's life and reputation. Stanzas four and five, which discuss the man's lost loves and the recollections of the poet's long-dead grandmother, are the poem's most poignant. They seem to be building toward a profound meditation on the nature of change, loss, and mortality, but the final two stanzas pull away from such a task. The poet can muster nothing more than a view of the old man as an unfashionable figure of fun—something the poet expects to become himself if he lives to a comparable age. The attention to change in fashion ("the old three-cornered hat, / And the breeches") does at least remind us of the rapid generational changes in American culture; but this expansion of meaning hardly compensates for the poem's seemingly callous (or perhaps even cowardly) failure to address the personal significance of old age and alienation.

Henry Wadsworth Longfellow's "My Lost Youth" (1855) examines the effects of time and change on the self. The poem provides an excellent example of the light, skillful verse that made Longfellow an icon of his day. For its evocation of the past, it relies not on a sudden, sharp image but on an accumulation of detail and a famous refrain ("A boy's will is the wind's will, / And the thoughts of youth are long, long thoughts"—the source, by the way, for the title of Robert Frost's first volume of poetry, A Boy's Will). Longfellow devotes the first seven stanzas of the poem to describing Portland, Maine—his native town—as he recalls it from his childhood. Along the way, the town's history, most particularly a sea engagement, blends with the poet's sense of his personal past, thereby creating a vital connection between the poet and his community. In the final three stanzas, the poet suffers nostalgic pangs, as he depicts himself looking at an utterly changed town—much as Holmes had depicted the old man of "The Last Leaf" and with the same implication about the pace of American cultural change. But, here, even if the "forms" of the town are different, the streets remain "well-known." The lost time still exists in the poet's memory and becomes accessible as he views the symbolically "fresh and fair" woods that still seem to repeat the old refrain. The poem anticipates an idea that would become quite significant in the next century: how memory and art ("the strange and beautiful song") can redeem lost time.

A more concise poem addressing the same relationship of time and change to the self, Ralph Waldo Emerson's "Days" (1857) adopts the strategy of personifying the passage of time. In Emerson's depiction, Days come equipped with gifts—food, power, natural beauty. At first the poem seems to be more of an allegorical narrative than a personal statement; only in its second half does it take a subjective turn and introduce the first-person pronoun. At this point, the poet depicts himself watching the procession and forgetting his "morning wishes": he has become an observer rather a participant in the pageant of the day. Time, in other words, is passing him by. He has taken from the day only "a few herbs and apples," whereas it could offer "kingdoms, stars." Only at the end does he glimpse the scorn, directed at himself, concealed beneath Day's headband. The glimpse startles both poet and reader into a stern recognition—for the glimpse is the echo of our own conscience, telling us to make the most of our limited time in this life. We comprehend—but perhaps "too late"—the things we might have accomplished had we not been so complacent and listless. *Carpe diem* (seize the day), the poem whispers—an admonishment of many poems dating back to Horace, the Latin poet who coined the famous phrase.

A somewhat neglected gem on this theme, Frederick Goddard Tuckerman's sonnet "And Change, with hurried hand, has swept these scenes" (1860) comments, in a subtle, restrained fashion, on the rapidity of change in modern America. The poem charts the intersection between change at the level of a civilization and change in terms of its significance to the sensibility and imagination of the individual. Dense with resonant imagery, the poem's delicate, perfectly managed argument cannot easily be paraphrased without doing it disservice. Tuckerman employs a variant form of the English sonnet, the four parts of which (three quatrains and a couplet) he utilizes to great effect. The first quatrain depicts a region of New England where woods have been cleared to make the world safe for civilization. Strikingly, he notes how "fire has drunk the swamps of evergreens!" The second quatrain commences with what seems like a premature conventional turn ("Yet"), as the poet strives to recapture, in his imagination, a former time when the woods still stood and shaded the Quonecktacut River and housed wild doves and deer. Such had been the state of things only, as the third quatrain reveals, a single generation ago. Thus, the change in the scene has a profound personal significance, since it corresponds with the poet's own lifespan. At a purely personal level, the landscape mirrors the changes Tuckerman senses in his own being. Now, houses (quietly evoked by synecdoche) stand in place of the woods. The sonnet's actual turn comes with the judiciously selected images introduced in the final two lines, which bring the poem's central contrast between civilization and unspoiled nature into sharp focus. Tuckerman writes from the former "forest-heart," where in his youth a wolf-bait "blackening" on a bush presaged the complete destruction of the wilderness. The juxtaposition of the poisonous bait and the life-giving spring, in the poem's final line, measures the worlds of men and nature. Perhaps Tuckerman feels nostalgia for a lost world of pioneers and trappers; but more pointedly, he seems to question whether change and "progress" always offer improvements over what had existed since time immemorial.

Walt Whitman meditates on time, change, and ways of transcending them in "Crossing Brooklyn Ferry" (1856, rev. 1881; originally titled "Sun-Down Poem"). The poem originated in Whitman's love of crossing by ferry from Brooklyn to Manhattan. It describes a single crossing at sundown, the ferry filled with many hundreds of passengers. Whitman observes them, but his expansive thoughts are not limited to them. Instead, his imagination ranges freely in time, as he directly addresses all those who will cross in future times—fifty years, a hundred years, or even many hundreds of years into the future. The poem, thus, stresses the universality of human experience across time. Whitman notes how later generations will feel much the same emotion he does while gazing "on the river and sky" (line 22). Throughout, despite the presence of the ferry and the New York skyline, Whitman stresses the overarching presence of nature, which more than anything represents the continuity between present and future. The water beneath him represents the flowing of time; thus, when he mentions the "current rushing so swiftly" (line 10), a reader can see from the context that it refers to both water and time. The time of day—sundown—also symbolizes change; it is a glorious time, full of beauty ("Gorgeous clouds of the sunset!"), but also the prelude to darkness.

The "dark patches" of section six will fall, but Whitman again consoles the reader with the universal constants in human nature: he, too, knew these patches and felt in himself unworthiness and even evil. Whitman has already insisted that time, place, and distance "avail not": they are bridged not only by the ferry but also by the poem, the ferry of Whitman's thought. In part, the poem is concerned with the almost miraculous way in which writing bridges the gap between readers of different eras. "Closer yet I approach you," Whitman writes—for as the ferry moves through space, the poem moves through time, and both of these motions are implied in Whitman's claim. The climax of the poem may be seen to occur in line 97, in which the poet "fuses" with the reader and "pours my meaning into you." Time has been momentarily erased at this juncture, for Walt Whitman in 1856 has made direct contact with readers far into the distant future, as long as his poetry endures. Whitman anticipates these "generations after me" and their own journeys on the ferry. He knows and even wills the inevitability of change: "Flow on, river!" But at the same time he would like for the present moment to stretch into eternity: "Suspend here and everywhere, eternal float of solution!" The tension between these two seemingly unreconcilable positions is fruitfully maintained and paradoxically resolved in the image of the ferry itself, which comes to represent both time and change and "eternity," or that which endures through time and change. The ferry will continue to move through time, ushering generation after generation from shore to shore, but it, along with the natural scenery and the poem itself, will also connect the experience of the present to that of the distant future. All "furnish [their] parts toward eternity."

Edwin Arlington Robinson's "Mr. Flood's Party" (1921) steps down from the cosmic heights of Whitman's lyric to portray the life of a single old man in relation to his past—much as "The Last Leaf" does, but in a much more sympathetic and penetrating manner. Many of Robinson's poems poignantly address the theme of time and change—notably the two sonnets "The Clerks" and "The Sheaves"—but none more powerfully than does "Mr. Flood's Party." The poem begins with a symbolic and syntactically complex sentence. If we parse the sentence, we find that the subject and verb are, quite simply, "Eben Flood . . . paused." The poem begins in a time of hesitation, with old Eben standing on a hill, poised between his "forsaken" hermitage and Tilbury Town (a fictional version of Gardiner, Maine—Robinson's boyhood home—which provides the setting for a number of his works). In thematic terms, nothing could be more significant, for Eben stands between and overlooking his past (the town) and his present (the isolated hermitage). The hermitage, we must also realize, holds "as much as he should ever know / On earth again of home"—in other words, it is his only foreseeable future. We have caught up with Mr. Flood at a telling moment in his long life.

In the stanzas that follow, Mr. Flood converses with himself, as he grows more and more drunk from the liquor in his jug, until finally he suffers from double vision—the "two moons" of line 47. He acknowledges that his days are numbered ("we may not have many more [harvest moons]") and even more explicitly introduces the theme of time with an allusion to Edward FitzGerald's *Rubáiyát of Omar Khayyám*, an extremely popular Victorian poem, in line 11. "The bird is on the wing," he quotes, or in other words, "time flies." (*Tempus fugit* is a complementary theme to *carpe diem*, derived likewise from the Latin poets.) Time has left the old man little. Mr. Flood, we quickly realize, has gone to Tilbury Town simply to fill his jug—a sad errand, especially when we realize it is his only reason for going to town these days. The full situation becomes clear in stages; as the third stanza informs us, in an earlier time, Mr. Flood was honored in the town by friends. But "many a change has come" since then. We soon realize that Mr. Flood's tragedy is that he has outlived his time. The time, town, and people he knew—all are gone. He has only himself to drink and talk with "amid the silver loneliness / Of night," as Robinson memorably describes it. The final stanza asserts that "not much" is ahead of Mr. Flood; this is true in a double sense, in terms of the time left to him and the quality of his existence. Behind him, in the town, are only strangers who "would have shut the many doors / That many friends had opened long ago." The power of the poem's accumulated images and implications makes the reader feel the terrible alienation of Flood's life. The narrative expands our capacity to sympathize with the human condition. Robinson has penned a generous and humanizing poem.

In the poems to be discussed next, we may discover another reason for the pervasiveness of the themes of time and change in American poetry—namely, the modern, empirical understanding of the world in evolutionary terms, as revealed by geology, biology, and physics. All the modern sciences have demonstrated that time is dwarfingly immense and that all things decay and die, even mountains, species, and stars. This sense of the transience of all things deeply permeates the poems of Robert Frost, such as "The Oven Bird" (1916)—an unusually constructed sonnet that may initially seem to be an enigmatic poem. The first thing one needs to know is that the ovenbird is an actual kind of bird (*Seiurus aurocapillus*), a small olive-brown member of the wood warbler family, distinguished by its orange crown and loud voice, which Frost mentions in the poem. The bird builds its oven-shaped nest on the ground. The sonnet—as do other poems such as "What the Thrush Said" by John Keats, "Out of the Cradle Endlessly Rocking" by Walt Whitman (discussed under "Poetry"), and "Nightingales" by Robert Bridges—"translates" the bird's song. The ovenbird, apparently a practicing phenologist, first says "that for flowers / Mid-summer is to spring as one to ten," a potentially perplexing claim that means, simply, that there are approximately ten times as many flowers in spring as there are in mid-summer. The assertion introduces the themes of change and diminishment, which the poem develops further. The bird (in Frost's translation) next says that the petals have all fallen. At this point, we arrive at the ninth line, or the "turn" in the sonnet—the conventional point in this form at which the "argument" of the poem shifts. Frost uses the turn very cleverly, for it is at this point that the season turns from summer to fall. The ovenbird continues to document the change of the seasons: dust from rural highways, he says, has covered virtually everything. At the very end of the poem he poses the question, What are we to make of a diminished thing? To understand the full ramifications of this query, we need to understand that Frost often creates analogies, implicit or otherwise, between times of day, seasons of the year, and cycles of life. The point is that Frost's "diminishment" need not be taken as referring only to autumn; autumn stands here for any moment of precipitous decline (twilight, old age, the mythic fall of man, etc.). The bird simply asks, What are we to make of such a sad state of affairs?

A further interpretation, which extends the theme of time and change in another direction, can be placed alongside what we have already established. The bird is a "singer" who takes for its topic the changing of seasons. It also knows, paradoxically, "in singing not to sing." If we acknowledge that a poet is a kind of singer (in the past, much lyric poetry was meant to be sung) and that the poet who wrote this particular poem is known both for writing about the changing of seasons and for combining traditional verse rhythms with colloquial speech ("in singing not to sing"), then we might identify the bird with Frost himself. In fact, it may be useful to view the sonnet as an answer to the question, "If you could be a bird, Mr. Frost, any bird, which would you be?" The literary critic Harold Bloom has written a great deal about "the anxiety of influence," or the ways in which poets struggle with the accomplishments of the poets who preceded them. Perhaps Frost is writing here about his own belated position in the history of poetry. If so, he presents himself as the poet of the autumn of the tradition—whereas such precursors as Shakespeare and Keats were presumably poets of the spring—trying to make the best of his situation. If we accept this interpretation, then the poem's themes of time and change apply as much to the poet and to poetry itself as to the changing of seasons or anything else.

Frost's "Nothing Gold Can Stay" (1923) distills the themes of time and change even further. In eight lines, the poem presents an entire cosmology, employing the kind of compressed hyperbole we associate with Emily Dickinson's work. It also makes explicit the analogies between days, seasons, and life cycles that "The Oven Bird" only implied. Dawn lapses into day; leaves fall with the changing of seasons; humanity fell from the paradise of Eden. Again, this poem concerns negative changes, or diminishment. According to Genesis, death (and knowledge) entered the world after Adam and Eve ate of the apple, thus providing the Western world with its proverbial, archetypal story of innocence and experience. Frost uses the story as a symbol to indicate that in this imperfect world, the only world we know, "Nothing gold"—whether dawn (literally golden) or a flower (literally or metaphorically golden) or innocence (metaphorically golden)—"can stay." Gold in the poem represents all things good and yet also transient—and in Frost's world, all things are transient. The poem is a marvel of compression, and formally, too, it contains riches for the reader to discover, particularly in its abundant sound patterns.

A subtler, more subdued poem than either "The Oven Bird" or "Nothing Gold Can Stay," "Spring Pools" (1928) presents an apparently simple picture of flowers beside forest pools. But this, too, is a dark poem—note that the words "dark" and "darken" both appear in the text. It records, like the earlier poems, seasonal changes. The pools and flowers will soon be gone, and in a very particular manner: the pools will be sucked up by the roots of the trees as they bring forth their summer foliage, and the flowers will therefore die for lack of water. Frost uses complex mirrorings in the poem to suggest the whole process of transformation of one thing into another. For example, each of the six-line stanzas forms a single, syntactically complex sentence. The subject of the first is "pools," whereas the subject of the second is "trees." As the pools are becoming part of the trees, the stanzaic and syntactic structures underscore the poem's basic argument. One sees something similar, on a smaller scale, in line 11: "These flowery waters and these watery flowers" again gives us a mirror image that implies how one thing can be a vital part of another. The poem depicts the momentary beauty of spring, but only to teach us a dark lesson: that one season comes into being as the destruction of its predecessor. In fact, the end of the poem reminds us that the pools themselves were formed from "snow that melted only yesterday." The pools and flowers result from the destruction of the snow, and the leaves result from the destruction of the pools and flowers: "Thus," as Bryant put it, "change the forms of being." Frost's originality derives from making natural processes feel sinister. The destruction of beautiful but seemingly trivial pools and flowers comes to stand for all the forms of being, from our own to those of stars, born from the deaths of other stars. As with many Frost poems, the appearance of simplicity is deceptive; these pools are deep.

It may appear paradoxical to discuss a poem that lacks a verb under the rubric of "Time and Change," but Ezra Pound's "In a Station of the Metro" (1916) can be understood as a picture of the return of spring. This tiny yet justly famous poem represents the quintessence of imagism, a short-lived but influential poetic movement that attempted to "purify" poetry by divesting it of ideas and rhetoric and indeed anything besides the emotional and intellectual resonance of imagery. Pound drew inspiration from a traditional Japanese form, the haiku—a very brief three-line poem that specifies a season and generates emotion through the objective presentation of natural imagery. Pound does not observe all the traditional features of the haiku, but if we view the title, which certainly contains essential information, as part of the poem, we have three lines of poetry. Also, we can discern a season—spring—from the presence of the petals. The element of time and change, and indeed the entire meaning of the poem, is implied by the juxtaposition of two images: the crowd at the metro station and the petals. Visually, it is not difficult to note similarities between these images: white faces against the dark background of the underground station and petals (very likely white) against the black bough. But does the comparison end there? Probably not.

The word "apparition" in the first line suggests both a sudden appearance and a spectral presence. This double meaning is decisive for one interpretation of the poem, for if the people at the Paris metro are indeed ghostly, then the station itself can be seen as a kind of modern-day equivalent of Hades, or the underworld. Pound often drew on Greek mythology in his poetry: to take one obvious example, the first in his long series of *Cantos* partially retells the story of Ulysses. "In a Station of the Metro" can be seen as alluding to another myth, that of Persephone, the daughter of Demeter, goddess of agriculture. The myth is a familiar one: Hades, ruler of the underworld, carried Persephone away to his infernal kingdom and forced her to become his queen. Zeus, to appease Demeter's grief, permitted Persephone to return for half the year to her mother's side. Demeter's joy at the return of her daughter brings with it the spring and the summer; her grief at Persephone's departure for the other half of the year ushers in autumn and winter. This, in other words, is the Greek myth of the seasons. In Pound's poem, the people return to the earth's surface from the underworld of the metro; their return, analogous to the return of spring, is indicated by the petals on the bough. The poem can be seen as a modern, much compressed rewriting of the Greek myth. Paradoxically, it depicts change through two static images.

William Carlos Williams wrote a longer and more explicit poem about the coming of spring, "Spring and All" (1923). The feeling here is more celebratory than in Frost's dark poems about the changing of the seasons. The rebirth of life at the coming of spring is the subject, although the poem seems to begin rather incongruously with the image of a road "to the contagious hospital." Similarly to Pound, Williams juxtaposes natural imagery with a human construction, and to much the same end. Williams's contagious hospital, in the same manner as Pound's Hades-like metro station, makes us aware of the presence of death—the necessary complement of birth and rebirth. Both poems quite deliberately show us the two sides of the coin of life, although in the beginning, the whole scene in Williams's poem appears to belong to the kingdom of death. In addition to the hospital, we see muddy fields with dead weeds and feel the presence of a cold wind; images of lifelessness accumulate. But there are "patches of standing water," similar to Frost's spring pools—in other words, a sign of thaw, a source of life. The discerning eye of the poet sees, finally, not death, but the "sluggish / dazed" approach of spring, a time of "profound change" and difficult yet hopeful births. The power of this poem (and of Pound's) is that through its arrangement of imagery, it makes us keenly feel the significance of spring's annual triumph over death.

Archibald MacLeish's "You, Andrew Marvell" (1930) takes us back to the darker side of change. The title references the seventeenth-century English poet who penned the classic seduction poem "To His Coy Mistress," wherein the speaker famously says, "at my back I always hear / Time's wingèd chariot hurrying near." MacLeish's poem, with breathlessly light punctuation, presents this idea of time as an encroaching pursuer through the image of night's shadow falling across the world. In the first stanza, the speaker feels that even in the security of noon, night is coming, creeping somewhere across the other side of the globe.

The poem then depicts night's shadow engulfing Ecbatan of ancient Persia and then passing westward across Kermanshah, Baghdad, Palmyra, Crete, Sicily, and then Spain and the west coast of Africa. Not only does this trajectory roughly trace the thirty-fifth parallel across the Middle East, Europe, and northern Africa, but it also symbolically represents the development and decline of Western civilizations. There is an old saying that the course of empire runs westward. Historically, the highest peaks of Western civilization have been Mesopotamia, then Greece, then the Roman Empire, and then western Europe. The direction of civilization is exactly that of night's shadow in the poem. As in some of Frost's poems, the cycle of the day symbolically suggests larger cycles, in this case the rise and fall of Western empires. MacLeish, who along with many others felt pessimistic about the future of Western civilization after World War I, compresses the history of the West into a single night.

A fair question a reader might pose when confronted with Elizabeth Bishop's "At the Fishhouses" (1955) is, Where is the poem's center? Is the poem about the fishhouses themselves, or the memorable seal who "was curious" about the poet, or the cold seawater, described at the end of the poem? The focus keeps shifting, suggesting that perhaps change itself is the poem's operative principle. First, we meet an old man, whose very presence serves as a reminder of time's passage. He had been a friend of the poet's (presumably deceased) grandfather. The poet and the old man discuss "the decline in the population." The blade of the old man's knife "is almost worn away" with all the scaling it has performed. The ironwork of the capstan "has rusted." Bishop, with her usual descriptive brilliance, sets the scene vividly before us, but part of what her sharply etched detail reveals is that the effects of time and change are everywhere present. Bishop revels in surfaces that conceal depths, and so it is fitting that the poem—after the charming interlude with the seal—concludes with the image of seawater, which here quite overtly symbolizes change. The water, Bishop asserts, resembles an image of knowledge: "clear, moving, utterly free." What captivates Bishop most is the water's freedom of movement, which she twice describes as "flowing." It, like knowledge, is historical and ever-changing; change, the poem asserts, is the essence of both the world and our knowledge of the world.

Of all contemporary poets, none seemed more preoccupied with the themes of time and change than A. R. Ammons, whose early training, we should note, was in the sciences. His fascination with change and motion is apparent not only in the titles and content of his poetry, but also in his flowing free-verse lines and unorthodox use of punctuation. (He loves colons, which imply equivalence and the flowing of one thing into the next, but is wary of full stops.) One of Ammons's most characteristic poems, "Corsons Inlet" (1965), which has been accepted both as a modern classic and as a manifesto of the free-verse style, records a walk on a southeastern New Jersey beach. During the walk, the poet feels his mind liberated from the rigid forms of thought into the "formlessness" of perception. The shape of the poem itself, which constantly fluctuates on the page, approximates the complex, ever-changing landscape that the poet sees: dunes blowing in the wind, irregular clusters of plants, a shifting waterline, a flock of tree swallows, and so forth. The poem, Ammons asserts, has a "geography" of its own. Its protean lines vary from the extremely short (one line is simply the word "as") to the relatively long (up to sixteen syllables), mimicking the chaos of the beach. Death, in the poem, is simply one manifestation of change, as smaller orders are assimilated into larger orders, themselves merely temporary formations. The only constant is flux itself, and there is no way of gaining access to what Ammons symbolizes by the only two capitalized words in the poem, besides "I": "Overall" and "Scope." Ammons rejects such static, Platonic ideals for a Heraclitean view of the world—as something that constantly flows. "Corsons Inlet" concludes with a meaningful tautology that distills the poem's vision, for the new walk of the next day will indeed be completely new, in a sense whose full philosophical implications have been made clear by the poem's wealth of images and ideas.

Of all the poems discussed in this section, "Corsons Inlet" is the one that, on a formal level, harmonizes most completely with the theme of change. Ammons has given himself and his art over to the power of change itself. In contrast, Robert Frost, who disliked free verse, used form as a bulwark against the forces of change that Ammons embraces. In his poem "Reluctance," Frost considered it to be "a treason / To go with the drift of things"; Ammons, on the other hand, finds the experience "liberating." Between the two we see the wide range of responses American poets have formulated to the challenges posed by time and change.

Two more recent poems on these themes, both more "Frostian" than "Ammonsian," are Brad Leithauser's "Old Bachelor Brother" (1990) and Timothy Steele's "Aurora" (1995). Leithauser's poem describes an unexpected transformation at a wedding ceremony. The speaker of the poem calls attention to his brother, standing as a member of the groom's party and awaiting a replay of the previous night's tedious rehearsal. The real thing, however, proves to be a wholly different type of experience, rising to the occasion of the important social ritual being enacted. The narrator notes several differences: the crowd, the bright stained-glass windows, the organ playing the music of the great English composer Henry Purcell (1659–1695); but for the brother, the most important difference is the transfiguration of the marching women. As they enter through the church doors, the women are lit from behind by sunlight.

(The fact that the wedding takes place on a brilliant day has already been established by the description of the stained-glass windows.) The flooding light, an image charged here with spiritual and sexual significance, seems to place halos on each woman and also to make all the women appear younger, unfamiliar, and desirable. The allusion to Moses parting the Red Sea (and perhaps to the Pentecost as well) reinforces the seemingly supernatural aspect of the transformation; but the poem's poignance derives from the subtle way it makes us feel the longing of the old bachelor brother for the "passionate anonymity" of the women. Their illusory regression to girlhood makes us more acutely aware of the brother's age. We also become aware of the untested possibilities of his bachelor life. At the beginning of the poem, the narrator sardonically remarks that the brother's position is "thankfully / uncentral" (i.e., that he is glad not to be the groom himself); but by the end, the brother perhaps wishes he could arrive—or had previously arrived—at such a central position with one of these women. Reality will undoubtedly set in again, and the women will once more become those more ordinary people the brother has known. Yet the poem perhaps suggests that love, or at least the possibility of love, is born in such moments, wherein time seems to reverse itself, and change, however fleeting, transfigures the mundane. The fact that in some sense this moment is an illusion seems unimportant, since as an experience and as a feeling it is wholly authentic for the brother.

Steele's "Auora," a gorgeous poem, concerns the transformation that comes over the lives of cities and individuals as the day awakens. It is, in effect, MacLeish's "You, Andrew Marvell" in reverse. As Aurora is the Greek goddess of the dawn, we can assume that the person addressed in the opening line and indeed throughout the poem is she. Line 22, which begins "Goddess, . . ." seems to confirm this hypothesis, although it is quite possible to see the poem's central female figure in dual terms, both as a goddess who represents the dawn and as a normal woman who wakes in the morning and brushes her hair and stares into the mirror, like most of us do. Such naturalistic details suggest a transposition of the mythic into the present, as we find in James Joyce's novel *Ulysses* or in R. S. Gwynn's contemporaneous "Among Philistines" (discussed under "Civilization"). Unlike Gwynn's poem, however, Steele's is evocative rather than narrative. Instead of a story line, we are given ordinary-seeming images, but images charged by the wonder of moments that only the jaded could take for granted—such as when the sunlight of a new day first strikes a windowpane or when doves suddenly dive from the roofs of tall buildings. The day resumes and with it, both life and ideas. The poem's narrative voice exhorts the symbolic, life-affirming woman to draw back the drapes and let in the flooding light of the sun—in much the same way that Aurora was said to open the gates of the east and so let free the light of day. Steele's poem celebrates and indeed—insofar as this is possible in words—re-creates the moment of transformation that Thoreau described as "the most memorable season of the day."

∽∿∾

"The Prairies," William Cullen Bryant

AAL-1; APN-1; ATL-1; ColAP; HAL-1; HoAL-1; NAL-1; NOBA; OxBA

"The Last Leaf," Oliver Wendell Holmes

AAL-1; ATL-1; HAL-1; HoAL-1

"My Lost Youth," Henry Wadsworth Longfellow

AAL-1; APN-1; ATL-1; HoAL-1; LPTT; NAL-1; NOBA; OxBA; TFi

"Days," Ralph Waldo Emerson

AAL-1; APN-1; ATL-1; ColAP; HAL-1; HoAL-1; NOBA; NoP-4; OxBA; TFi

"And Change, with hurried hand, has swept these scenes," Frederick Goddard Tuckerman

APN-2; HAL-1; HoAL-1; NOBA

"Crossing Brooklyn Ferry," Walt Whitman

AAL-1; APN-1; ATL-1; ATL-2; ColAP; HAL-1; HAL-2; HoAL-2; NAL-1; NoAM; NOBA

"Mr. Flood's Party," Edwin Arlington Robinson

AAL-2; APT-1; ATL-2; ColAP; HAL-2; HoAL-2; LPTT; MAP; NAL-2; NoAM; NOBA; NoP-4; OxBA; SoSe-9; TFi; WeW-4

"The Oven Bird," Robert Frost

AAL-2; APT-1; ATL-2; HAL-2; HoAL-2; MAP; NAL-2; NoAM; NOBA; NoP-4; OxBA; SoSe-9

"Nothing Gold Can Stay," Robert Frost

AAL-2; APT-1; ColAP; HoAL-2; MAP; NAL-2; NOBA; SoSe-9; VGW

"Spring Pools," Robert Frost

APT-1; ColAP; NAL-2; NoAM; NOBA; OxBA

"In a Station of the Metro," Ezra Pound

AAL-2; APT-1; ATL-2; ColAP; HAL-2; HoAL-2; MAP; NAL-2; NoAM; NOBA; NoP-4; OxBA; TFi; VGW; WeW-4

"Spring and All" (aka "By the road to the contagious hospital"), William Carlos Williams

> AAL-2; APT-1; ATL-2; ColAP; HAL-2; HoAL-2; MAP; NAL-2; NoAM; NOBA; OxBa; TFi

"You, Andrew Marvell," Archibald MacLeish

> APT-1; ATL-2; ColAP; HoAL-2; NoAM; NOBA; NoP-4; OxBA; TFi; WeW-4

"At the Fishhouses," Elizabeth Bishop

> APT-2; ATL-2; CoAP; HAL-2; HCAP; HoAL-2; MAP; NAL-2; VCAP

"Corsons Inlet," A. R. Ammons

> AAL-2; ATL-2; CoAP; ColAp; HoAL-2; MAP; NAL-2; NoAM; NOBA; NoP-4; VCAP

"Old Bachelor Brother," Brad Leithauser

> NoP-4; RA

"Aurora," Timothy Steele

> DiPo

Tradition and Heritage

> What thou lov'st well is thy true heritage.
>
> Ezra Pound, "Canto LXXXI"

In 1782, J. Hector St. Jean de Crèvecoeur helped to create one of the enduring and mythic symbols of American culture. He wrote: "Here [in America] individuals of all nations are melted into a new race of men, whose labors and posterity will one day cause great changes in the world." By the time Israel Zangwill popularized the image of a culture "melting" together in his 1909 play *The Melting Pot*, Crèvecoeur's prophecy that America would "cause great changes in the world" was well on its way to being fulfilled; but the extent to which mainstream American culture, with its notoriously poor treatment of certain races and ethnic groups, could be regarded as an authentic "melting pot" remained open to question. A melting pot implies a single monolithic culture that arises from a fluid intermixture of diverse cultural strands and traditions. The actual heterogeneous state of American culture, with its various marginalized subcultures, has led some commentators to propose the quilt as a more apt symbol for the reality of America's cultural diversity. The many different strands of American culture intertwine in complex chains of influence, orthodoxy, and fruitful discontinuity, even as they resist complete assimilation into a single, coherent tradition. The poems discussed in this section represent the heterogeneous nature of American culture and its disparate sources in the cultures of Europe and Africa, as well as those of Native Americans.

Philip Freneau, who was extremely interested in establishing a unique American cultural tradition, was fascinated by the Native Americans. White settlers had tended to demonize or to belittle the cultures of the peoples whose land they rapidly annexed—a glaring example of the failure of the melting pot symbol—but Freneau belonged to a more liberal intellectual elite that was becoming increasingly interested in the vanishing cultures of the Native Americans. The rise of romanticism, with its emphasis on the important connection between freedom and nature, made it possible for white settlers to view Native Americans in a more positive light, as possessing valuable traits that "civilized" Europeans had, much to their detriment, lost. Freneau's poem "The Indian Burying Ground" (1788) entertains the notion that the West has something important to learn from the Native Americans. Despite the genuine interest it evinces in another culture, Freneau's poem does still retain a distinct vestige of Western condescension, evident when he characterizes the indigenous peoples as "a ruder race" (line 24) and as childlike (line 28), and when he describes them as "many a barbarous form" (line 31). The poem also tends to refer to "the Indian," as if all Native Americans belonged to a single culture with the same cultural practices, rather than there being many different cultures. Nonetheless, the poet's general attitude of humble and curious sympathy does represent a positive step forward.

The poem's opening stanzas implicitly contrast the relative indifference of westerners to the posture of their dead with the carefully arranged seated postures and elaborate accessories that characterize certain Native American burials. The poet sides with the Native Americans against the "learned" authorities of the West as to the symbolic importance of burial practices. Unfortunately, however, the burial sites seem to be about all that is left of these Native American societies. Their mysterious, spectral presence, a source of both awe and superstitious dread, leads toward the poem's almost unwilling celebration of forces that transcend rational apprehension. Nonetheless, the brutal fact of cultural displacement is driven home in the seventh stanza by the reference to shepherds who still admire the ancient elm in whose shade the Native American once "played." The final stanzas assert that even though the Native Americans have been displaced, their culture still haunts the land. A hunter still pursues a deer, even though each is "a shade." These lines can be interpreted as a metaphor for the enduring cultural influence of the Native Americans. Even as they are being driven from their lands, their way of life influences those who would replace them. Thus, "long shall timorous fancy see" the form of their civilizations, in such various manifestations, as the names of places and in words like "canoe" and "moccasin," assimilated to modern English. The impact of the Native Americans on the imagination of their successors is, according to Freneau, not negligible (a theme later developed in Robert Francis's poem "Like Ghosts of Eagles"). Freneau seems to have stumbled upon the

Freudian notion that what one attempts to repress will come back to haunt one. As a child of the Enlightenment, Freneau placed the highest value on "Reason," but in the conclusion of this poem, he maintains that even reason will have to "bow the knee" before the shadowy, irrational influence exerted on the Western mind by the Native Americans. Nevertheless, Freneau offers the veneration of shadows, rather than any kind of protest against the reality of displacement and persecution. Despite its failure to adopt an adequate ethical stance, the poem does suggest that Native American culture contains valuable elements and thus sets the stage for the more enlightened attitudes that have belatedly changed our perceptions of American history.

American poets have often examined their European heritage in an effort to gauge what from the past is usable and what should be rejected. American literature, in part because it is written in English, seemed initially to be a branch of the great tradition of English literature, with its thousand-year history of achievement, from *Beowulf* to Chaucer to Shakespeare to Wordsworth and beyond. In the nineteenth century, as America's cultural flowering began in earnest, poets were confronted with two basic options: (1) to write more or less as English writers, or (2) to attempt to establish a specifically American literary tradition—whatever that might mean. The poets who adopted the latter option, who elected to break, as much as possible, with tradition—such as Emerson, Whitman, and Melville—have received the greater posthumous glory. Their prose statements on the subject of literary tradition, notably Emerson's "The American Scholar," Whitman's preface to *Leaves of Grass*, and Melville's "Hawthorne and His Mosses," all celebrate the possibility of discontinuity with English literature. As Melville forcibly puts it, "we want no American Goldsmiths; nay, we want no American Miltons. . . . Let us boldly contemn all imitation." Despite their nationalist rhetoric, Emerson, Whitman, and Melville were all, of course, deeply indebted to English literature—to Shakespeare, Milton, and the romantics especially—but all deliberately chose to move in progressive directions that extended the literary tradition rather than within its safely circumscribed borders. In this sense, they are paradoxically closer to the nonconformist spirit of such great English writers as Milton, Blake, and Shelley than are the less progressive writers—"Poets of the Tradition," as one anthology labels them—such as Henry Wadsworth Longfellow, John Greenleaf Whittier, Oliver Wendell Holmes, and James Russell Lowell. Directly influenced by English neoclassicism and the more conservative side of romanticism, the popular "fireside" or "schoolroom" poets elected to work within the framework of traditional forms and themes. Their antithetical relationship to the more radical writers highlights certain important aspects of tradition, including the possibility of stagnation, the need for renewal, the danger of being overwhelmed by the great achievements of the past, and the complementary danger of writing in ignorance of the past.

Of the more conservative poets, the most accomplished surely is Longfellow, whom Henry James once praised for his ability to balance European and American cultural traditions. Longfellow was a poet steeped in European literature and languages, but he utilized European forms to write of American subjects. Like the great composer Brahms, who complained of having to follow in the footsteps of a giant like Beethoven, Longfellow was shadowed by what he described in "The Day Is Done" as "the bards sublime / Whose distant footsteps echo / Through the corridors of Time." Longfellow did not equal the achievements of these "bards sublime," but toward the end of his career, he celebrated two of the greatest of them in a pair of sonnets written in 1873: "Chaucer" and "Milton." Both are homages to the great tradition Longfellow and many other American poets have sought to perpetuate, and no form could be more appropriate for such homages than that of the sonnet, the most honored and traditional of all Western poetic forms.

"Chaucer" pays tribute to the power modern English poetry's founder still has to vividly re-create for the imaginative reader his bustling fourteenth-century world. In an effort to capture something of the flavor of Chaucer's time and language, Longfellow deliberately employs anachronistic verb forms in the poem, such as "laugheth" and "writeth." Chaucer himself is depicted as a high-spirited old man, perpetually bemused by the variousness of life and assiduously recording it "in a book like any clerk." (Clerk here means "scholar" and alludes to the Clerk of Oxenford, one of the pilgrims from Chaucer's masterpiece, *The Canterbury Tales*. Chaucer wrote these tales in his final years, which is why he appears in the poem as an old man.) After the octave's portrait of the poet at work, the sonnet's sestet focuses on Chaucer's enduring achievement. Longfellow hails him as "the poet of the dawn," in the sense that his work is the gateway through which modern English literature emerged from the Middle Ages. Chaucer was the first major poet to employ Middle English as a literary language, and he also developed such important forms as the pentameter line, heroic couplets, and rhyme royal; in other words, he has a very strong claim to being considered the father of modern English poetry. Nonetheless, Longfellow's highest tribute to his illustrious predecessor is a more personal one. As he reads from Chaucer, Longfellow begins to hear and smell the world the poet describes. From across five centuries, Chaucer's words remain miraculously vital. For what more could a poet hope?

In "Milton," Longfellow employs the sonnet's binary structure in a somewhat different manner. Here the octave and sestet are two parts of an extended simile that compares the epic poetry of John Milton (author of *Paradise Lost, Paradise Regained,* and *Samson Agonistes* and typically regarded as the greatest English poet after Shakespeare) to pounding waves on the shore. The waves are first depicted as "voluminous billows" or "sheeted emerald." The ninth wave, which tradition maintains is usually the greatest of a cycle, strikes the sands "and changes them to gold." The sestet maintains that Milton is like this ninth wave: his powerful imagination transformed ordinary words into gold, which floods the soul as the wave floods the shore. Longfellow hails Milton as an English Mæonides (another name for the Greek epic poet Homer, who, at least according to tradition, was, like Milton, blind). As in the tribute to Chaucer, the language of this poem borrows something from its subject. Longfellow aspires in his description to reach the sublime heights of Milton's own rhetoric. The choice of an extended simile is also not accidental: Milton is justly famous for his own extended similes, a traditional feature of epic poetry. Both of these sonnets evince Longfellow's reverent and thoughtful engagement with the great English poetic tradition, from which American poetry derives.

By contrast, thoughtless adherence to cultural traditions is the main theme of one of Robert Frost's best-known poems, "Mending Wall" (1914). The poem is structured around a dramatic encounter between two men, the poem's speaker and his neighbor who lives "beyond the hill." Each spring, the two repair the stone wall between their properties, which has been damaged by the "frozen-ground-swell" of early spring thaws. The narrator notes, too, that "The work of hunters is another thing" that damages the wall, but not the principal thing that draws the neighbors together. The two men bring distinctly different attitudes to bear on the work of repairing the wall. To the simpleminded neighbor from beyond the hill, the only thing of importance is that, as he repeats twice, "Good fences make good neighbors." Careless readers may assume that this statement represents the moral of the poem, especially since it concludes with these words; but in fact, the meaning of the poem is much more nuanced. It is neither a celebration of walls nor a simple diatribe against walls, rather, it is a subtle examination of the nature of tradition. The mischievous narrator has his own twice-repeated statement that "Something there is that doesn't love a wall." Literally, this "something" is the personified process of erosion, which works its secret ministry in so undetectable a manner as to set the stage for the narrator's joke that magical forces—"Elves," to be precise—are responsible for the decay of the wall; but as the narrator finally admits, "it's not elves exactly." The way that the wall, an imposition of human will and order, stands in opposition to natural forces that tend toward entropy and decay represents an instance of one of Frost's favorite themes: the ultimately futile struggle of humans against nature, which he explores most notably in "The Wood-Pile" (discussed under "Nature"). Here, this opposition is an important structural element, though secondary to the more important opposition between the attitudes the two men adopt toward tradition.

To the narrator, mending time is "just another kind of outdoor game." In this capriciously playful spirit, the narrator attempts to "put a notion" in his neighbor's head. In other words, he wants to see if he can convert the neighbor to thinking about repairing the wall the way he does, as a useless tradition. The narrator does not have an ideological bias against walls per se, as is indicated by his recognition of their necessity "Where there are cows," but he does object to a wall that divides properties containing only trees. The narrator owns an apple orchard, whereas his neighbor "is all pine." "My apple trees," he says, in his mischievous manner, "will never get across / And eat the cones under his pines." The narrator wants the neighbor to question why the walls make good neighbors, but his efforts prove to be futile. Armored by obtuse stubbornness, the neighbor is pictured as moving "in darkness . . . Not of woods only and the shade of trees"; in other words, the neighbor also moves in a kind of mental darkness requisite for the unquestioning maintenance of outworn traditions. Mindlessly, he repeats the saying of his father (and perhaps his father's father and so forth). The poem almost seems to illustrate a passage from Thoreau's journal dated March 4, 1852:

How little use is made of reason in this world! You argue with a man for an hour, he agrees with you step by step, you are approaching a triumphant conclusion, you think that you have converted him; but ah, no, he has a habit, he takes a pinch of snuff, he remembers that he entertained a different opinion at the commencement of the controversy, and his reverence for the past compels him to reiterate it now.

Frost's poem ends with just such a blind reiteration, but its intention, clearly, is not to validate the neighbor's statement but to make the reader examine the nature of tradition. The idea that traditions are irrationally and thoughtlessly maintained applies to innumerable things beyond the wall depicted in the poem (e.g., politics and religion); thus, the poem's meaning widens outward like ripples from a pond.

Tradition is often problematic, and never more so than for those caught between two cultures. In the 1920s, black poets began to respond in vital ways to their dual cultural heritage, at once both African and American. They posed several important questions: To what extent was their own culture continuous with that of Africa? How far had their culture been transformed by their experience in America, and what from that experience should they be willing to accept? Should they express their ideas and experience through Western forms or try to invent their own? Should they write primarily as blacks or simply as Americans? Was there such a thing as a single black culture or experience? Langston

Hughes, Claude McKay, and Countee Cullen, three of the most prominent figures of the Harlem Renaissance, answered these questions in somewhat different ways. Their responses to these issues of identity, heritage, and power continue to resonate within the work of African-American poets today. Hughes, the least traditional of the three in terms of his handling of poetic form, as well as the most politically radical, posits a strong connection between Africa and America and between past and present in his brief but seminal poem "The Negro Speaks of Rivers" (1921). The poem seems to be written less from the perspective of Hughes himself than from that of the "soul" or "consciousness" of black people in general; thus, it conceives of black experience as something distinct and deeply shared. It chronicles the history of black experience specifically in relation to the various rivers that have been an integral part of that history. By moving from the Euphrates to the Congo to the Nile to the Mississippi, Hughes traces a mythical and historical lineage of African-American cultural traditions, from the Garden of Eden (which supposedly existed in the vicinity of the Euphrates) to modern America. The reference to Abraham Lincoln in conjunction with the Mississippi serves as a reminder of both slavery and eventual emancipation, a movement *per aspera ad astra* (through suffering to the stars) that is symbolized by the "muddy bosom" of the river suddenly turning "all golden in the sunset." Experience of adversity has made a certain kind of profundity possible. Neither angry nor resentful in tone, the poem concludes by reiterating the primal connection between the black soul and the deep, dusky, ancient rivers.

Hughes's seemingly mellow, universalizing poem stands in contrast to the more bitter feelings of diminishment and alienation expressed in McKay's sonnet "Outcast" (1922). Instead of seeing a degree of continuity between the Congo and the Mississippi, McKay feels that his spirit is in bondage to his body, which in turn is imprisoned by "the great western world." He longs for the cultural traditions (represented by "forgotten jungle songs") and the "darkness" and "peace" of Africa. Instead of enjoying that heritage, he bends his knees to "alien gods," a reference to the way so many blacks converted to Christianity. (McKay himself converted to Catholicism in 1944.) Capitulation to alien traditions has taken "Some vital thing" from him, namely the cultural heritage and experience of his ancestors. He compares himself to a "ghost" that walks the earth as "a thing apart." Alienation is depicted here as the inevitable consequence of being born far from the land of one's ancestors, into a world ruled by "the white man's menace." The emotions McKay explores here are ones that would later compel Malcolm Little to change his name to Malcolm X (the "X" denoting his lost African surname). A powerful, unresolved tension exists in this poem between its form—a deeply traditional European sonnet, such as Longfellow had used to celebrate the achievements of Chaucer and Milton—and its content, which expresses longing for the cultural traditions of Africa. McKay articulates his loss of one heritage through the traditional form of another, which on some level seems to imply at least the possibility of reconciliation and reintegration. On the other hand, the tight form of the sonnet might be identified with the prison of the Western world, which confines the poet's spirit, and thus might be seen as an emblem of the poet's fractured identity. In any event, the poem is far less at ease with the reality of cultural dislocation than is "The Negro Speaks of Rivers."

Cullen's "Heritage" (1925) stands somewhere between the visions of Hughes and McKay. A significantly longer poem (128 lines), it has more room to develop and qualify its ideas. Most basically, the poem is an answer to the question of its opening line: "What is Africa to me . . . ?" Cullen's imagery suggests polarized, contradictory answers to the question (e.g., sun/sea, men/women). Alienation and longing, as expressed by McKay, are present in Cullen's reminder that he is *three centuries removed / From the scenes his fathers loved.*" Cullen's response to contradiction and dislocation is to "lie," as he repeats three times in the second stanza and twice more in the fourth. The meaning of the word is ambiguous: it could signify either "lie down" (i.e., become passive) or not tell the truth (to others or himself). Contradictions mount, as he simultaneously longs for the sound of "wild barbaric birds / Goading massive jungle herds" and jams his thumbs into his ears in a futile effort not to hear "Great drums throbbing through the air." He explicitly defines his state of mind in contradictory terms as that of "distress, and joy allied." The second stanza concludes with strong indications that such a state cannot be maintained—something will have to give. All the "dark blood dammed within" cannot remain so forever.

Part of the problem, for Cullen, is that Africa has become merely a picture book to the African American, who yearly forgets the wildness of the so-called "dark continent." Stanza three develops a contrast between the tameness of America (two lines begin with the words "Here no . . .") and the dangerous wildlife of Africa, imaged as bats, cats, snakes, and "leprous flowers." These teeming, virile images of beauty and deadliness color the return to self-portraiture in the fourth stanza. A conjunction of urban America and the African jungle is enacted in images such as "cruel padded feet / Walking through my body's street." The suggestion here, though, is again of dislocation, of Africa imported to an alien context in which it can never be at home or at ease. Rain, in this stanza, assumes an importance similar to that of the rivers in Hughes's poem: it belongs to the realm of racial memory and identity formation. But as the final stanza demonstrates, that identity has been inescapably complicated by exposure to Western cultural traditions.

As a Christian, Cullen cannot honor the "Quaint, outlandish heathen gods" of Africa. Like McKay, he worships "alien gods" ("Father, Son, and Holy Ghost"), but in his recognition of his "double part" in American culture, he transcends both the sullenness of McKay's position in "Outcast" and the uncritical stance of those who accept Christianity strictly on its own terms. The relation between African Americans and Christian theology—one of the dominant cultural traditions of the West—has been a complicated one. It is a prime example of the shifting, tangled nature of heritage and culture in America. Some blacks, like the poet Phillis Wheatley (who wrote before the War of Independence and thus is not included in this guide), have gratefully and rather passively accepted the religion of the dominant culture, even seeing in it—as she expresses in the widely anthologized poem "On Being Brought from Africa to America"—a kind of redemptive compensation for the trials of slavery and racism. Whites, on the other hand, as Robert Hayden points out in "Middle Passage" (discussed under "Freedom & Slavery"), often saw Christianity as a way of rationalizing the slave trade: they were saving souls, not simply trafficking in human stock. Due in part to such hypocrisy, other blacks have rejected Christianity altogether as the false religion of their oppressors. Elijah Muhammad and the Black Muslims, for instance, referred to Christianity as "the religion of white devils." Langston Hughes also emphatically rejected Christianity in his poem "Goodbye Christ" (1932). Later, the radical black nationalist poet Amiri Baraka updated Hughes's position in his "When We'll Worship Jesus" (1972), which opens by stating that black radicals will worship Jesus when he does something for them, like blow up the White House.

In "Heritage," Cullen attempts to find a cultural solution between the extremes of passive assent and separatist rejection, so he envisions a Christ with "Dark despairing features" and "dark rebellious hair." He had already ridiculed the Africans for making gods in their own image (line 88), but here, with the knowledge that creating divinity in one's image is hardly to be escaped, he follows the same impulse and fashions in his mind's eye a black Christ that represents the confluence of Western and African traditions and that also, in some sense, represents an effort to resolve the poem's various contradictions. Cullen would later, in 1929, publish a collection entitled *The Black Christ and Other Poems*, which develops the theological position further. Here, he backs away from the full implications of his vision and concludes by seeking humility and by praying for forgiveness "if my need / Sometimes shapes a human creed." Neither a complete statement nor a fully coherent poem, "Heritage" nonetheless raises major issues and contains some powerful imagery.

Inspired in part by the example of black poets who have celebrated their own cultural heritages (such as jazz, which the contemporary poet Michael S. Harper has often written about), poets representing and celebrating other minority heritages, particularly those of Asian Americans, Hispanic Americans, and Native Americans, have stepped forward and come to prominence in the past few decades. This chapter began by focusing on an early and somewhat distorted (however well meaning) view of Native American culture as seen by a white poet, so it is fitting that it should conclude with a contemporary view of Native American culture by a poet who belongs to the Acoma Pueblo Community in Albuquerque, New Mexico: Simon J. Ortiz. Native American literature in the English language that employs traditional European genres and forms first acquired widespread attention with the publication of N. Scott Momaday's Pulitzer-Prize–winning novel *House Made of Dawn* (1968). From that time forward, Native American literature has undergone a veritable renaissance with the emergence of such acclaimed writers as Leslie Marmon Silko, Joy Harjo, Louise Erdrich, Sherman Alexie, and Ortiz, whose "Passing through Little Rock" (1976) is a characteristic statement about both the sorrows of a lost heritage and the will for cultural renewal.

The poem consists of three parts: an opening observation, a brief dramatic dialogue, and a concluding lyrical expression of desire that arises from the first two parts. The Little Rock of the poem's title is not the well-known city in Arkansas but rather a "crummy town" in Arizona and an emblem of what American civilization has become in modern times. It has, for example, converted the names of the Native American tribes that formerly inhabited the region—the Quapaw and the Waccamaw—into "billboard words." Ortiz's observation is a comment on capitalist commodification, which inauthenticates and trivializes cultural traditions by assigning them dollar values and incorporating them into the rhetoric of advertising (e.g., on billboards). Ortiz's complaint also indicates a quite different sense of cultural dislocation than one finds in the writing of African-American poets like Claude McKay. Native Americans were not taken from their homeland; rather, their homeland was taken from them. So here, the dislocation is principally temporal rather than geographical. This opening statement about the derogation of the tribal names is succeeded by a brief exchange, possibly between the poet and a bartender. The shifting pronouns, as in a Bob Dylan song, make it difficult to be sure that the "he" of line 7 is the same person as the "I" of line 9, but that is one possible interpretation. In any event, the first speaker indicates that he is worrying a lot lately. The second speaker attributes that worry to age, perhaps emphasizing that cultural self-consciousness is an inevitable product of maturation. The final seven lines of the poem formulate a response to both the trivialization of Native American culture (symbolized by the billboards) and the problems of age and fear. The speaker longs to discover a haven from the polluted, commercialized landscape of modern America, a place where there would be "a clean river" and the sounds of the earth when it was new. What Ortiz ultimately longs for is the rebirth of his rightful heritage and the relative harmony it was supposed to enjoy with unspoiled, uncommodified nature.

⸎⸜⸝⸎

"The Indian Burying Ground," Philip Freneau

AAL-1; ATL-1; ColAP; HAL-1; HoAL-1; NAL-1; NOBA; NoP-4; OxBA; TFi

"Chaucer," Henry Wadsworth Longfellow

AAL-1; APT-1; ATL-1; HAL-1; HoAL-1; NOBA; OxBA; TFi

"Milton," Henry Wadsworth Longfellow

AAL-1; ATL-1; HAL-1; HoAL-1

"Mending Wall," Robert Frost

AAL-2; APT-1; ATL-2; HAL-2; HoAL-2; MAP; NAL-2; NoAM; NOBA; NoP-4; OxBA; SoSe-9; TFi; VGW; WeW-4

"The Negro Speaks of Rivers," Langston Hughes

APT-2; ATL-2; ColAP; HAL-2; HCAP; HoAL-2; MAP; NAL-2; NoAM; NOBA; TFi; WeW-4

"Outcast," Claude McKay

APT-1; MAP; NAL-2; NoP-4

"Heritage," Countee Cullen

AAL-2; APT-2; ATL-2; ColAP; HAL-2; HoAL-2; MAP; NAL-2; NoAM; NoP-4

"Passing through Little Rock," Simon J. Ortiz

NAL-2

Truth and Appearances

Truth, *n.* An ingenious compound of desirability and appearance.
Ambrose Bierce, *The Devil's Dictionary*

Each day we seem to see the sun rise and set. The earth seems fixed beneath our feet, but spins on its axis, hurtles round the sun, and is being drawn through the Milky Way—all at tremendous speeds. We swat at insects out of fear that one might land on us, while an army of microorganisms clambers over our skin. We sit outside on a warm cloudy day, safe from sunlight, but are soon burned by ultraviolet rays. We do not detect the pesticides that give us cancer forty years later or the thought, for good or ill, behind the mask of a stranger's face. A smile may conceal malice, and a stingray may glide beneath the next wave's beautifully gleaming crest. The world our senses bring to us is, in short, often more a matter of appearance than reality. As Emerson states in his essay "Illusions": "The senses interfere everywhere, and mix their own structure with all they report of." Our senses are limited by their structure and scope and by perspective. They fail to detect not only things that are hidden or very small or very faint, but also the enormities of time and space. We cannot learn directly from our senses the truths of science: we need microscopes, telescopes, and other types of equipment to assist the senses, as well as inference and intuition. Meanwhile, much of what we take for granted as "reality" is in fact illusion; life, as Edgar Allan Poe once noted, is often but "A Dream within a Dream."

Emerson, who in this respect concurred with his nemesis Poe, constructed a mythic allegory of truth and appearance in his remarkable poem "Uriel" (1847), which unveils the relation between power and illusion. In a time before time, the celestial wanderer Said (or "Seyd" in later editions), who quite possibly stands for Emerson himself, overhears the gods, still young, discussing the nature of order and appearances. One god, Uriel (whose name means "fire of god"; Emerson derived it from Milton), with a kind of Promethean voice, interrupts the conversation and tells the other gods, in effect, that the universe is both chaotic ("Line in nature is not found") and contradictory ("Evil will bless, and ice will burn"). The other gods, however, react with displeasure to this news: they seem to have a vested interest in maintaining certain appearances and traditions. Uriel, enlightened and embittered, withdraws like a fallen angel from paradise into a cloud that represents the private space wherein truth may be maintained safely from the politicized falsehoods of society. The gods quickly forget Uriel's words, but from time to time some event or aspect of nature shames "the angels' veiling wings" and reveals that Uriel spoke truthfully. Although the poem alludes to the brouhaha occasioned by Emerson's "Divinity School Address" (discussed more fully under "Skepticism and Belief"), it is also a universal parable about challenging established assumptions and hierarchies with ideas that are unsettlingly complex and that offer no justification for egotism or the wielding of power. Uriel tells the gods that the universe they have faith in is but an illusion. Ideas of order and false antitheses may allow the gods to rule, but they do not, according to Uriel, describe the fundamental characteristics of the universe itself. Uriel adopts a distinctly Eastern philosophical perspective on the nature of reality that derives (as the presence of the Eastern sage Said already hints at) from the doctrines of Hinduism and Buddhism. Time itself is an illusion, Uriel claims, for in the end, all opposites will be reconciled (e.g., "good of evil born"). Such a premise destroys the foundations of worldly action and leads to Uriel's contemplative withdrawal. Uriel's peers, however, are unable or unwilling to accept so rigorous, transcendent, and austere a view of reality, for to do so would mean the abdication of their pursuits, such as conquest (the war gods) and rulership (Hades). The gods (whom we may understand as authority figures of any type) lord over the world, but cower from the true nature of things.

Emerson's "Brahma" (1857) can be read as a companion piece to "Uriel." The speaker of the poem is Brahma himself—the supreme spirit of Hindu theology, whose presence makes the Eastern overtones of Emerson's thought explicit. Brahma first denies the reality of death ("the red slayer"), for death is but the gateway to rebirth. All organic matter is merely recycled or reincarnated, as Whitman truly understood when he imagined himself reborn as grass at the conclusion of *Song of Myself* (discussed under "The Self"). In Emerson's poem, Brahma collapses other oppositions—far and near, shadow and sunlight, fame and shame—in a similar manner. What he insists on is an underlying unity to all things. Individuality and separateness are illusions of time; in eternity, all is reconciled into a oneness represented by Brahma himself. At the end of the poem, Brahma hints that the truth-loving, humble soul has a better chance of finding this wisdom of unity than do even the "strong gods" (harking back to "Uriel") and "the sacred Seven" (or the highest saints of Hinduism). To find Brahma, the aspirant has to "turn thy back on heaven," or in other words, to reject so partial and antithetical a concept as heaven (which implies its opposite, hell) in favor of an acceptance of totality. Parts are mere appearance; truth can only be found in the whole. Note that Emerson also explores this idea in the poem "Each and All" (discussed under "Art & Beauty").

Emily Dickinson's terse "I like a look of Agony" (#241, c. 1861) approaches the problem of discerning truth from appearance at the level of human behavior. This ironic poem begins with a typically bizarre and unsettling assertion, which the speaker supports by arguing that only in moments of agony or death can we be sure that the outer appearance of a person accords with the inner state of mind. Deception is always possible, except in extremity—thus, the poem does not celebrate sadism but rather the speaker's love of truth. The poem takes a dim view of human nature, not unlike that arrived at by Young Goodman Brown at the end of Hawthorne's famous tale. If the Hawthorne tale is any indication, alienation and gloom are the price of such a rigorous mistrust of the human heart. This dark side of the knowledge of the truth becomes the explicit subject of another eight-line Dickinson poem, "Tell all the Truth but tell it slant—" (#1129, c. 1868). Instead of focusing on the devious nature of humanity, this poem addresses the dangers attending the disclosure of truth. The speaker favors an oblique telling of the truth that dazzles "gradually" rather than blinds instantaneously. The nature of truth is such that an incremental approach to it is less shocking and damaging than a sudden confrontation. Dickinson strongly implies that to let go of our illusory notions all at once would be psychologically traumatic and beyond the normal powers of our endurance. Before the truth, we are like children, stunned and terrified by lightning. And so "Success in Circuit lies": the suggestion or the implication can be far more pleasing and instructive than the bald statement. The poem can certainly be seen as describing the indirect method favored by Dickinson in much of her work.

Stephen Crane, a poet whose brevity can make even Dickinson seem long-winded, depicts in his "I saw a man pursuing the horizon" (1895) an extraordinarily terse dramatic encounter between two men representing different perspectives on life. The poem's narrator represents a realistic point of view, whereas the man he sees pursuing the horizon represents an indefatigable idealism. The idealist runs after the horizon, despite the fact that it continually recedes from him. The horizon, by definition, is a place one cannot reach. Chasing it is like chasing a rainbow. But the idealist (or fool, depending on how you look at it) disregards the narrator's advice. He would rather pursue an impossible dream than learn to live without such a dream. Crane's allegorical poem raises some interesting questions about different character types and different ways of living one's life.

George Santayana's "Sonnet XXV" ("As in the midst of battle," 1895) presents a tightly structured argument on the nature of truth, appearance, and disillusionment. The first six lines consist of three similes (the first a kind of double simile), each beginning with the word "As." Each simile develops a scenario wherein something positive emerges from what appears to be a wholly negative situation (as in Emerson's "good of evil born"). Thoughts of love may occur during battle; mirth arises from sin; inheritance follows death; and plant life spouts from the crevices of a tomb. All four of these possibilities are then compared to the happiness that all people may find in the "great disaster of our birth." The illustrative images of the sonnet's octave seemingly allow for authentic joy to exist even within Santayana's extremely dark vision of life. This position, however, is then grimly modified by the sestet. During one's innocent youth, the "iron heaven," which the poem associates with reality and truth, is hidden by the splendor of the morning. Evening, likewise, "woos us" to transform what grief we may have into song ("idle catches"). The illusory consolations of art and nature, however, are then brushed aside by the poem's pessimistic conclusion as mere products of youthful idealism. When we "wake" from the "trance" of summer into a true autumnal maturity, all we find are "Despair before us, vanity behind." What had seemed like hope turns out, on closer inspection, to be mere vanity. Stripped of illusions, one is left only with despair. The truth, in other words, is something we spend most of our lives hiding from; we delude ourselves so as not to have to confront our true insignificance. Santayana's poem depicts as dark a view of life as Dickinson's "I like a look of Agony" and reminds us why it is sometimes asserted that certain illusions are necessary for life and well-being.

In "We Wear the Mask" (1896), Paul Laurence Dunbar develops a related notion that again bears affinities with Dickinson's "I like a look of Agony." Dunbar comments wisely on one fundamental aspect of the human condition: the discrepancy between the public self and the private self. The public self "grins and lies," paying its debt to "human guile" of the type Dickinson had dissected; inside, however, one may be "torn and bleeding." Dunbar closes his first stanza by acknowledging the subtleties of human deceit. The reader should remember that Dunbar's status as an African American probably helps determine (and intensify) his choice of subject matter and imagery, for he is perhaps thinking foremost of blacks masking their true identity in a white world. The second stanza complicates the argument by posing a rhetorical question: Why would anyone even want the world to know their true inner selves? Wearing a mask becomes the very price and condition of social existence. The implication seems to be that the fragility of identities requires such deception, although one could also infer an ironic reading that primarily laments the underlying cruelty and indifference inherent in human relations. In the third stanza—which corroborates the ironic reading—Dunbar introduces a religious note that strengthens the idea of the duality of the self by drawing upon the Platonic-Christian tradition of a soul separable from the body. If this intangible soul represents the authentic self, then the "clay" of both earth and body is indeed bound up with a false world of appearances, beyond which one cannot penetrate in this life. The world becomes associated, as in Poe's work, with the realm of dream, from which the spirit will ultimately find its liberation. In this world, however, the mask cannot be transcended, and so the poem ends with a bleak reiteration of its title-refrain. Despite its grim conclusion, Dunbar's lyric is a kind of prayer of hope, conceived within the dualistic tradition of Christian theology wherein material reality is often equated with illusion and intangible spirituality is equated with truth.

William Meredith, like Santayana before him, employs the sonnet form (if somewhat irregularly) for philosophical purposes in his "Sonnet on Rare Animals" (1958). The poem concerns how the very act of looking for something alters it. Meredith, thus, might be said to have written a poem loosely modeled on Heisenberg's famous uncertainty principle. The sonnet begins with two specific instances that illustrate its central idea. In the first instance, the poet brings a companion (or companions—an unspecified "you") out to a clearing to see deer that, apparently, do not typically take fright at his solo approach. But numbers multiply the anxiety of the deer, who are off with only the sound of their departure left to the contemplation of the would-be observers. Likewise, the poet tried to point out to sunbathers the fins of sharks within a coral reef. He spoiled the bathers' fun (they would no longer enter the water), but he failed to compensate them with the excitement of seeing the sharks themselves. In a sense, the situation reverses that of the opening, for here the humans fear the animals rather than the other way around. These cases are merely two instances where the poet has alarmed animals (or humans) without producing satisfactory results. In turn, the business of finding (or not finding) rare animals is simply an illustration of a larger idea, which involves also poetry and love: "when you point you lose them all." In other words, some of the most deeply satisfying things of this life have a fleeting essence that resists too deliberate scrutiny. The rarest things have an appearance that can be discerned only in moments of grace or intuitive understanding. When deliberately sought, they vanish like phantoms, as if they were merely illusions in the first place; but in fact, they are not illusions—it is merely the type of looking that determines their solidity. Reality, in this sense, possesses a fundamentally subjective aspect that is best approached, as Dickinson suggested the truth be approached, indirectly.

Robert Francis, a greatly underappreciated American poet, takes the game of baseball as his metaphor for the nature of truth and appearance in the brief, incisive, masterfully composed poem "Pitcher" (1960). Francis concentrates on the art of the pitcher, which is another version of Dickinson's art of revealing the truth by degrees. Throughout the poem, Francis realizes his ideas in the poem's very form, employing metrical substitutions, additional words, and near rhymes that all exemplify the indirect approach adopted by his pitcher. For example, the extra word "at" at the end of line 2 enacts the idea of not hitting the thing for which one should be aiming, in this case the word "aim" itself (which also concluded the preceding line). Each "seeming aberration" of both the pitcher and the poet is in fact "willed" (a deliberate near rhyme with the etymologically related word "wild"). Throughout, Francis—like his pitcher—avoids the obvious ways of doing things in the name of art and skill. The reader of poetry, like the batter, must be caught off guard; the line, for Francis, is like a curve ball or knuckle ball that moves erratically and unexpectedly toward its inevitable destination. If it moves successfully, it constitutes a strike. For the pitcher, as for the poet, "Success in circuit lies." In the end, however, the artful appearance discloses the truth—even if the dumbfounded batter understands all of this too late. The reader, on the other hand, will have lost no precious points from a batting average but will have gained a moment of vertiginous, delighted surprise at the poet's dexterous, imaginative performance. Surely, Francis's pitcher must be seen as a cousin of Richard Wilbur's "Juggler" (discussed under "Art & Beauty")—and just as surely, both characters devised by these Massachusetts poets pay homage to the dazzling performance and ideas of Emily Dickinson.

ᴇᴦᴪᴖᴏ

"Uriel," Ralph Waldo Emerson
    AAL-1; APN-1; ATL-1; HAL-1; HoAL-1; NAL-1; NOBA; OxBA
"Brahma," Ralph Waldo Emerson
    AAL-1; APN-1; ATL-1; ColAP; HAL-1; HoAL-1; NOBA; NoP-4; OxBA; TFi
"I like a look of Agony," Emily Dickinson
    AAL-2; APN-2; ATL-2; HAL-1; HAL-2; HoAL-2; NAL-1; NoP-4

"Tell all the Truth but tell it slant—," Emily Dickinson

    AAL-2; APN-2; ATL-2; ColAP; HAL-1; HAL-2; HoAL-2; MAP;
NAL-1; NoAM; NOBA; NoP-4; WeW-4

"I saw a man pursuing the horizon," Stephen Crane

    AAL-2; APN-2; HAL-2; HoAL-2; NOBA; NoP-4

"Sonnet XXV" ("As in the midst of battle"), George Santayana

    APN-2

"We Wear the Mask," Paul Laurence Dunbar

    APN-2; ATL-2; HAL-2; HoAL-2; MAP; NoP-4

"Sonnet on Rare Animals," William Meredith

    HAL-2

"Pitcher," Robert Francis

    APT-2; WeW-4

War

There is many a boy here today who looks on war as all glory, but, boys, it is all hell.

> William Tecumseh Sherman, speech before the
> Grand Army of the Republic Convention

From the time of the *Iliad* to that of Wilfred Owen and beyond, poets have often been moved to write about man's greatest evil perpetrated against himself: war. Almost every war occasions poetry—sometimes a notable amount of high quality poetry, as in Great Britain during World War I. In America, all our major armed conflicts have inspired poetry, although little of it, with the notable exception of the best Civil War poetry, has proved to be of enduring quality. America's independence was won through war, but the nation's literary traditions were as yet unestablished. The only contemporaneous poem on the War of Independence anthologized with any regularity is Philip Freneau's "To the Memory of the Brave Americans" (1781), a patriotic elegy for General Nathanael Greene and the men who fought under him at Eutaw Springs. Interesting as it is from a historical perspective, the poem can hardly be called a major contribution to American poetry, or even one of Freneau's finer productions. It would be another fifty-six years before Ralph Waldo Emerson would compose the most memorable poem pertaining to the War of Independence—the "Concord Hymn," with its famous "shot heard round the world" line (discussed under "Memory"). The War of 1812, specifically the British bombardment of Baltimore, inspired one extremely famous American poem: Francis Scott Key's rousingly patriotic "Defence of Fort McHenry" (1814). Sung to the tune of an old Eng-

235

lish drinking song, its first stanza is known to every American as "The Star-Spangled Banner."

The first poem by an American on the nature of war that endures as a significant literary achievement is probably Joel Barlow's "Advice to a Raven in Russia" (1812). The poem, rather atypically, concerns a war that does not involve either American soil or American troops: the Napoleonic Wars and specifically Napoleon's 1812 campaign in Russian. Barlow's interest in the subject derives from personal experience: he had been dispatched by President Madison to persuade Napoleon to sign a new trade treaty with the United States. When he arrived in France in 1811, he found that Napoleon was away on his Russian campaign and was forced to set off on a difficult journey to Lithuania. Finally, Barlow, in deep shock after witnessing the catastrophic carnage of the war, wrote "Advice to a Raven in Russia"—a powerful antiwar statement. Barlow, however, died of pneumonia before the poem could be published. It was discovered among his posthumous papers, and a corrupt version was published in 1843. Not until 1938 did the authentic version finally see the light; it has since become, along with "The Hasty Pudding," one of Barlow's two most celebrated works.

As befits its serious subject matter, "Advice to a Raven in Russia" is written in heroic couplets. It is conceived as an apostrophe to a raven, the "Black fool" of the opening line. A carrion bird, the raven follows Napoleon's armies, feeding in the wake of their devastation. Barlow's ironic "Advice" to the raven is to head for more hospitable climates, such as one finds in southern Europe; for there, too, Napoleon's armies were wreaking their havoc in the Peninsular War of 1808–1814. The raven would find sunshine and warmth, in addition to more delectable corpses. As Barlow bitterly notes, Napoleon's soldiers "Please best their master when they toil for you." Conscription merely becomes a means of harvesting troops for the raven's insatiable appetite. The poem projects a deep sense that civilization itself has been betrayed by Napoleon's mad and far-reaching ambitions. Even a raven will not be able to fly further than Napoleon's battle flags (the "bandrols" of line 30) have been extended. With scathing irony, Barlow contends that the raven merely provides a service by cleaning up the messy corpses; but here in the great North, where the bodies of the slain are "marbled through with frost," the corpses do not stink and are frozen too solid for even the raven to pick apart. The poem's conclusion summarizes the "Advice," prophecies further carnage, and calls for "Earth's total vengeance" to be directed against Napoleon ("the monster") to end the madness of his wars. Barlow's scathing poem, which makes effective use of the raven as both image and symbol well before Poe (and in a more naturalistic manner), stands as the first in a series of antiwar statements by American poets.

It would be another two generations before the poets and indeed all Americans would witness such carnage on their own soil.

America's distinctive literary culture was largely established in the decades leading up to the American Civil War (1861–1865). James Fenimore Cooper, Washington Irving, William Cullen Bryant, Ralph Waldo Emerson, Nathaniel Hawthorne, Henry Wadsworth Longfellow, Edgar Allan Poe, Henry David Thoreau, Walt Whitman, and Herman Melville all produced significant works in the years between 1820 and 1860. The Civil War then marked a hiatus in the development of America's burgeoning literary culture. Cooper, Irving, and Poe had died before its outbreak; Hawthorne and Thoreau died during the war (but not because of it); Bryant and Emerson had achieved their most significant works in the prewar years; and Longfellow, with the exception of a few minor poems like "Killed at the Ford" and "The Cumberland," did not find the war to be a subject congenial to his particular talents. That left Whitman and Melville to grapple seriously with the horrors and significance of a war in which over 600,000 American men died. Shortly after the end of the war, Whitman brought out a new volume of poetry titled *Drum-Taps* (1865), which was later incorporated into his life's work, *Leaves of Grass* (1855–1892). At approximately the same time, Melville, who had given up his fruitful but unfortunately not lucrative career as a fiction writer, first turned his hand to writing poetry with *Battle-Pieces and Aspects of the War* (1866). Even though other poets, such as Henry Timrod, Thomas Bailey Aldrich, and Francis Orrery Ticknor, produced Civil War verse, it is these two volumes, *Drum-Taps* and *Battle-Pieces*, that constitute the major poetic response to the Civil War. The two volumes differ in every respect, and so complement one another in a variety of ways. Whitman, who had witnessed the war's horrors firsthand as a nurse and a correspondent, wrote documentary poetry that dealt with highly individualized episodes and scenes. Melville, who had followed the war from a safer distance, wrote in a much more general and philosophical spirit and focused, like a historian, on the war's major events. Whitman, in other words, recorded a private history of the war, Melville a public.

Whitman's Civil War poems have a remarkable range, from the jingoism and martial rhythms of "Beat! Beat! Drums!" to the terse imagism of "Cavalry Crossing a Ford" to the poignancy of the dramatic monologue "Vigil Strange I Kept on the Field One Night." A poem that is representative of Whitman's typical documentary style is "A March in the Ranks Hard-Prest, and the Road Unknown" (1865), which depicts a bleak view of war's carnage. In a shadowy old church, converted into "an impromptu hospital," the poet nurses a young soldier in danger of bleeding to death and surveys a scene that he claims surpasses "all the pictures and poems ever made." The poet's senses are flooded with blood, death, ether, and cries of agony. He faithfully, unflinchingly records it all, as a kind of moral obligation. Whitman, functioning almost like a roving camera eye, allows the images, sounds, and odors to speak for themselves; this, the poem asserts, is the truth of warfare, not slogans or flags or abstract causes. Whitman's attention returns to the boy he had bandaged, right at the moment of his calm death. There is nothing more to be done and no possibility, in this context, of mourning, so Whitman proceeds "forth to the darkness," resuming the march, off to confront whatever unknown carnage lies ahead. The poet stoically faces the horrors of war; he does not judge or protest, but merely bears witness, knowing that the authenticity of his images will penetrate more deeply than would any abstract argument.

"Reconciliation" (1866), a brief poem that seems to summarize Whitman's feelings about the war, echoes the famous words of President Lincoln's second inaugural address: "With malice toward none; with charity for all." The poem is divided into two sections of three lines each, connected by a semicolon. The first celebrates the ending of the war in a general way; the second provides a symbolic image that indicates in what spirit that ending should be accepted. The war over, it is time not for blame or hatred but for, as the title indicates, that "Word over all": "Reconciliation." Whitman celebrates the fact that the war's "deeds of carnage must in time be utterly lost." He attempts to provide reassurance to the weary nation by placing the bald, glaring facts of the present moment in a cosmic context. In the second part, the poet views a dead foeman, "divine as myself," and, in a gesture of reconciliation, lightly kisses the corpse. The act symbolizes the spirit of forgiveness and the need to deal with the conquered enemy even-handedly and without malice.

Melville's better-known Civil War poems include symbolic pieces about the war's onset, such as "The Portent" and "Misgivings," as well as topical poems that address the events of specific battles, such as "Malvern Hill" and "The March into Virginia" (discussed under "Innocence & Experience"). Perhaps Melville's most trenchant statement about the significance of the Civil War is "A Utilitarian View of the Moniter's Fight" (1866), which principally gauges the implications of the war's modernity. To understand the poem, it is useful to know that the American Civil War brought into use many new efficient and destructive technologies, from repeating rifles, barbed wire, and trenches to railroad transport and the telegraph. The carnage of the war can, in part, be blamed on American ingenuity turned against itself. Melville's poem concerns perhaps the most publicized new technology employed in the war, the ironclad vessel. On May 9, 1862, the Union *Monitor* had engaged the Confederate *Merrimack* in an inconclusive battle at Hampton Roads, Virginia. Melville saw in this skirmish between ironclads an inkling of war's faceless future. The poem commemorating the battle opens with a stanza that reflects on how a plain poetry will be apt to capture the spirit of war as it is now waged, without "Orient pomp." Melville's own sparsely rhymed, heavily enjambed lines exemplify this idea. War is now a matter of "mechanic power / Plied cogently" and devoid of "passion." The fame of the ironclads' engagement precludes lengthy description; Melville dispatches the battle itself in the fourth stanza, with an allusion to Emerson's "Concord Hymn" in line 21 ("Still ringeth round the world—"). The gist of the poem's message is contained in the concluding stanza, which adopts a prophetic stance. War and warriors have been changed forever into a matter of devices and those who operate them. War, paradoxically, is now "Less grand than Peace," as it has become a kind of factory work with a steadier rate of mortality. The concluding image of the singe that "runs through lace and feather" signals the end of chivalric warfare, which has been antiquated by the machine. Melville's intention would seem to be not to glorify past wars but to note the change in how human brutality manifests itself. His prophecy that wars would become increasingly mechanized has been more than fulfilled by the conflicts of the twentieth century, perhaps most notably by the Persian Gulf War.

Another of Melville's powerful and topical Civil War poems is "Shiloh: A Requiem" (1866). On the morning of Sunday, April 6, 1862, Confederate forces struck General Grant's army at Shiloh, a Baptist church along the Tennessee River. The engagement turned into the most costly yet in the war, with combined casualties approaching 25,000—more than the total dead and wounded of the War of Independence, the War of 1812, and the Mexican War combined. Americans had never faced carnage on this scale, although even deadlier battles, such as Gettysburg, lay ahead. Melville's poem, in a single complex sentence, contrasts the beauty of the natural surroundings with the unexampled carnage of the battle. The poem opens and closes with the image of swallows circling over the fields. They seem to suggest nature's indifference to the battle, the continuity of natural processes, and perhaps the cyclic nature of life and death. A further ironic contrast is indicated by the presence of the church as the focal point of this "Sunday fight": the war is thus presented as a desecration of all civilized and religious ideals. The differences between the men who died in the presence of nature and the church, sending up "many a parting groan / And natural prayer," were resolved in death, an idea obviously related to that of Whitman's "Reconciliation." In their final moments, thoughts of fame or country were far from them. The poem's most powerful line, a parenthetical aside, asserts: "What like a bullet can undeceive!" Ironically, it has been death that has freed them from the deceptions of glory and patriotism. Only war, impersonal and abstract, has created the illusion of enmity between them. Melville implies here what Thomas Hardy would state in the first stanza of a later war poem, "The Man He Killed": that had the men "but met / By some old ancient inn," they would have made sociable companions. Instead, they lie dead, as the swallows continue to wheel overhead.

Among later writers on the Civil War, Stephen Crane stands out as the most notable. His short novel *The Red Badge of Courage* (1895) so impressed veterans that many assumed Crane had seen action himself; in fact, he had been born six years after the conflict had ended. "Do not weep, maiden, for war is kind" (1899) is, like much of Crane's writing, an exercise in savage irony. The poem does not have to be seen as being specifically about the American Civil War, but it is certainly informed by that tragedy. The poem's refrain that "War is kind" rings more hollowly with each repetition and is rapidly undermined by the poem's unsparing images of death. Phrases that glorify destruction—"the virtue of slaughter" and "the excellence of killing"—magnify the irony further, until one begins to feel the poet's smoldering contempt for his subject. Throughout, the poem addresses the survivors—a maiden who loses a lover, an infant who loses a father, a mother who loses a son—reminding us of the individual tragedies represented by each death on that "field where a thousand corpses lie." Counterpoised against all the destructive imagery, a touching and surprising simile in the final stanza compares the humility of a mother's heart to "a button," as she surveys the shroud of her slaughtered son. The domestic note sounded by the button rings just right, for it conjures up all the traditional cares and duties of motherhood that will be discharged no more. By juxtaposing two perspectives—those of impersonal rhetoric and of personal sorrow—Crane's irony humanizes the staggering meaning of war's costliness.

The Civil War remains America's most shattering conflict for two reasons: it pitted Americans against Americans, and it was fought on American soil. America's involvement in the two world wars of the twentieth century, by contrast, lacked such immediacy and, for whatever precise reason, did not elicit from American poets a significant number of enduring works. Perhaps the wars seemed too far away, perhaps the individuals who might have written the major poems were killed in combat or were not situated so as to assimilate the experience in a meaningful way, or perhaps war had become too dauntingly large and too mechanistic for poetry to digest. The latter possibility seems unfounded, particularly given the high level of quality of English verse written about World War I. The achievements of Edward Thomas, Siegfried Sassoon, Rupert Brooke, Isaac Rosenberg, Ivor Gurney, and, above all, Wilfred Owen dwarf those of their American counterparts—which is perhaps hardly surprising, given the proximity of the two nations to the center of the conflict. Several of these British poets died in the war, "For"—as Ezra Pound bluntly put the matter in "Hugh Selwyn Mauberley"—"an old bitch gone in the teeth, / For a botched civilization." Europe was left in shambles, while the United States emerged definitively as one of the great powers of the world.

Since Robert Frost's great poem "Not to Keep" is neither well known nor widely anthologized (nor are Alan Seeger's "Rendezvous," Edna St. Vincent Millay's "Conscientious Objector," and Archibald MacLeish's "The Silent Slain") and since John McCrae, who wrote the rousing, much-recited "In Flanders Fields," was a Canadian, the closest we have to a classic American lyric on the Great War is probably Carl Sandburg's "Grass" (1918). The poem is less centrally concerned with the specific events of the war than with the transitory nature of all flesh. For Sandburg's purposes, the carnage of war simply multiplies and thus makes more apparent the decomposition and organic transformation of the human body after death. Written from the point of view of the grass that grows from and covers over the piles of the dead, the poem mentions famous battlefields from the Napoleonic Wars, the American Civil War, and World War I, thereby implying a depressing continuity of slaughter and warfare. Yet the mood of the poem is far from somber. Essentially Whitmanesque both in tone and in its central trope, the poem strives to put the horrors of the past into perspective and implicitly advocates that the living must carry on with the business of life. The natural cycle of the grass covers over even the most desolate carnage of battlefields, so that in time they become indistinguishable from ordinary fields. The poem echoes the conclusion of Whitman's *Song of Myself*—where the poet imagines himself transformed into grass after his death—but applies its personal theme to public events. Behind the visions of both Sandburg and Whitman is the biblical passage from Isaiah 40.6: "All flesh is grass, and all the goodliness thereof *is* as the flower of the field."

Two brief, intense American poems about World War II have become classics: Randall Jarrell's "The Death of the Ball Turret Gunner" (1945) and Richard Eberhart's "The Fury of Aerial Bombardment" (1947). Both focus on the war in the air—a new stage in war's technological evolution, which began with the triplanes of World War I and was taken to wholly new levels of strategic importance and sophistication in World War II. Thus, both poems, in that they document the mechanical dehumanization of warfare, stand as legitimate heirs to Melville's "A Utilitarian View of the Monitor's Fight." Jarrell's stark, powerful little poem is narrated from the point of view of a hapless gunner, who is presented as both mechanical operative and, more figuratively, unborn fetus. The poem emphasizes both the brevity of his life and the inhumanity of his confinement. In a sense, he is never born, for he passes directly from his "mother's sleep" to the "belly" of the state. Literally, this belly is, as Jarrell's note to the poem specifies, a plexiglass sphere on the underside of a B-17 or B-24 bomber. Figuratively, since the antecedent of "its" in line 2 is "state," the boy has been swallowed whole by the state itself.

The boy is both the unborn child and the devoured morsel of the nation, a meaningful juxtaposition of contrasting imagery that suggests both the innocence of individual soldiers and the rapacity of warring nations. As the plane gains altitude, the boy's fur coat freezes. Six miles above the earth, he feels that he has been removed from the "dream of life" but ironically wakens only to find the "the nightmare fighters." If, as the cliché would have it, "life is but a dream," war is but a nightmare. The shocking last line of the poem says everything that needs to be said about the dehumanizing effects of modern warfare. To die six miles above the earth, torn to shreds by enemy flak, and to have one's scattered remains washed out of a plexiglass shell with a steam hose is to be as far from any sane "dream of life" as is possible. The ball turret gunner is at last delivered from the state's belly—as an abortion.

Eberhart's "The Fury of Aerial Bombardment," a more overtly philosophical poem, ponders God's silence in the face of human evil as well as the technological advances humans have made without making commensurate moral strides. It is now possible, the poem notes, to kill as did Cain, but on a massive scale. The "ancient furies" still burn in "man's fighting soul." The questions posed by the poem's third stanza, concerning God's indifference and man's compulsive stupidity and brutality, remain unanswered. The concluding stanza, instead, veers away from these abstract musings and lands in a starkly concrete world inhabited by the names of actual men who died in combat ("Van Wettering" and "Averill") and the technical names of the parts of a .50-caliber Browning machine gun ("the belt feed lever" and "the belt holding pawl"). The contrast reminds us of the different sides of Eberhart's own experience, as he was both a philosophically minded and somewhat unorthodox Christian and, for one summer during World War II, an aerial gunnery instructor. The conclusion anchors the big questions about war, God, and existence in the specificity of the actual world. Those questions are prompted by and only have meaning in relation to specific events and specific deaths. The men die; the questions remain.

America's next major conflicts were the Korean War (1950–1953) and the Vietnam War (1965–1973)—both technically "police actions" even though in the two conflicts combined, 91,000 Americans died in battle and 373,000 more were either wounded or missing in action. Thomas McGrath pays tribute to those casualties in his "Ode for the American Dead in Asia" (1964, rev. 1968). McGrath's original title for the poem had been "Ode for the American Dead in Korea," but he changed it in the year of the infamous Tet Offensive, when North Vietnamese troops violated a New Year's truce to mount a surprise attack on American and South Vietnamese forces. Consisting of three sonnets, McGrath's poem, in measured, formal language (appropriate for the dignified nature of an ode), pays tribute to the average men who served as canon fodder in the two Asian wars. Their corpses litter the rice paddies and the hills, where they fought in a war they neither wanted nor understood. McGrath takes a dim view of the authorities that sent them there, the "safe commanders" and, more ironically, "distinguished masters" who, according to line 22, confirmed the soldiers in their ignorance. The state molded the soldiers and the church blessed them; they went off to war as the victims of a bravery and ignorance inculcated by their own culture to serve its selfish ends. The attention to nature in the second and third stanzas leads toward comparisons between the brief lives of fish, moles, and a lone crow and those of the soldiers. God, as in Eberhart's "The Fury of Aerial Bombardment," appears utterly indifferent to all these deaths, which flutter past, in a striking image, like confetti in his peripheral vision. The soldiers are mourned in public, but principally for political reasons. Genuine public sorrow must wait for "another year." The poem concludes by returning to the opening image of the soldiers dead amid the rice fields and hills of Asia. Like all the major American poems on this theme since the time of Joel Barlow, it unambiguously denounces its subject.

This survey of American wars and the poems they have inspired concludes with Carolyn Kizer's "On a Line from Valéry" (1996), subtitled "The Gulf War." As the title suggests, Kizer takes her departure from the work of the influential French poet Paul Valéry (1871–1945). She faithfully translates his line "Tout le ciel vert se meurt. Le dernier arbre brûle" from the poem "La Fileuse" (The Spinner) as "The whole green sky is dying. The last tree flares." The poem is aptly cast in a traditional French form, the villanelle; however, following the precedent of other "incremental" villanelles, such as Elizabeth Bishop's "One Art" (discussed under "Loss") and Julia Alvarez's "Woman's Work" (discussed under "Family Relations"), Kizer does not feel obliged to repeat the line from Valéry or her third line verbatim, but rather spins out several variations based fairly closely on them. The poem thereby "evolves," avoiding the static effect sometimes produced by English-language villanelles.

It engages its ostensible subject—the Persian Gulf War of 1990–1991 between the United States and Iraq—only obliquely. In terms of the development of warfare, the Gulf conflict represents, as mentioned earlier, the most complete fulfillment of Herman Melville's prophecy that war would become increasingly mechanized and dehumanized. A complete mismatch of technological might, the Gulf War inflicted only 146 casualties (including twelve women) on the U.S. forces, whereas approximately 100,000 Iraqis were killed. As the Western media packaged the conflict as a kind of video-game entertainment, the American public remained quite insulated from the authentic horrors of the Gulf War. Kizer's poem reflects this sense of distance, with its vague, quasi-symbolist, apocalyptic imagery that alludes, at one point near the conclusion, to the possibility of nuclear winter. Kizer alludes also to T. S.

Eliot's wartime poem "Little Gidding," the fourth of the *Four Quartets*, in line 2, but without holding forth any promise of transcendence, such as Eliot found in the fire and the rose. The rose of fire, in Kizer's poem, may be beautiful, but it blossoms beneath a poisonous atmosphere. The doom-laden mood reflects not elation over a national victory (for who could be elated over such a lopsided, mechanized slaughter?) but repugnance for the monstrous destructive forces humans have unleashed against other humans and against the natural world. The poem evokes the monstrous threats of the modern military arsenal (such as air strikes and poisonous gas) and places them within the context of the entire dismal and unending history of warfare.

❧✦❧

"Advice to a Raven in Russia," Joel Barlow

> APN-1; ATL-1; ColAP; HAL-1; HoAL-1; NOBA; OxBA

"A March in the Ranks Hard-Prest, and the Road Unknown," Walt Whitman

> AAL-1; ATL-1; ATL-2; HAL-1; HAL-2; HoAL-1; HoAL-2; NAL-1; OxBA

"Reconciliation," Walt Whitman

> AAL-1; APT-1; ATL-1; ATL-2; HAL-1; HAL-2; HoAL-1; HoAL-2; NAL-1; NoP-4; OxBA; WeW-4

"A Utilitarian View of the Monitor's Fight," Herman Melville

> AAL-1; APN-2; ATL-1; ColAP; HAL-1; NAL-1

"Shiloh: A Requiem," Herman Melville

> AAL-1; APN-2; ATL-1; ColAP; HAL-1; HoAL-1; LPTT; NOBA; NoP-4; OxBA

"Do not weep, maiden, for war is kind," Stephen Crane

> AAL-2; APN-2; ATL-2; HoAL-2; LPTT (under title "War Is Kind"); NOBA

"Grass," Carl Sandburg

> AAL-2; ATL-2; ColAP; HAL-2; HoAL-2; MAP; NAL-2; NoAM; NOBA; NoP-4; OxBA; TFi

"The Death of the Ball Turret Gunner," Randall Jarrell

> AAL-2; CAPP-6; ColAP; HAL-2; HoAL-2; MAP; NAL-2; NoAM; NOBA; NoP-4; OxBA; SoSe-9; TFi; VCAP; VGW

"The Fury of Aerial Bombardment," Richard Eberhart

> APT-2; ColAP; NoAM; NoP-4; TFi; VGW

"Ode for the American Dead in Asia," Thomas McGrath
    MAP; VGW (as "Ode for the American Dead in Korea")
"On a Line from Valéry," Carolyn Kizer
    CAPP-6

Biographical Sketches

ളᢙᢙᡐᢀ

JULIA ALVAREZ (1950–) was born in New York City, although her
family moved to the Dominican Republic shortly after her birth.
When she was ten, her family returned to the United States because
of Alvarez's father's involvement in an unsuccessful attempt to over-
throw General Rafael Trujillo's dictatorship. Alvarez graduated from
Middlebury College in Vermont and received an M.F.A. in creative
writing from Syracuse University. Her first book of poems, *Home-
coming*, was published in 1984 and was followed by *The Other Side*
in 1995. Alvarez has also published two novels. Her work focuses
on Latina culture, gender roles, and identity. Currently, she teaches
at Middlebury College.

A[RCHIE]. R[ANDOLPH]. AMMONS (1926–2001) was born in a farmhouse four miles outside of Whiteville, North Carolina. He studied
biology and chemistry—subjects that greatly influenced his poetry—
at Wake Forest College and only later studied English literature at
Berkeley. Ammons worked for one year as an elementary school
principal in Cape Hatteras and spent the next decade as an executive
for a glassmaking firm. From 1964 he taught creative writing at Cornell University. Ammons had begun writing poetry years earlier
while serving on a navy destroyer in the South Pacific during World
War II. His first book of poems, *Ommateum* (a term that describes
the compound structure of an insect's eye), appeared in 1955. Ammons published prolifically; his work includes a number of book-
length poems, such as *Tape for the Turn of the Year* (1965), *Sphere: The
Form of a Motion* (1974), *Garbage* (1993), and *Glare* (1997), and collections, such as *Expressions of Sea Level* (1964), *Corsons Inlet* (1965),
Northfield Poems (1966), *Uplands* (1970), *Diversifications* (1975), *The*

Snow Poems (1977), *A Coast of Trees* (1981), *Lake Effect Country* (1983), and *Sumerian Vistas* (1987). He won two National Book Awards. Ammons wrote in a free-verse style whose form and subject matter extend the transcendental tradition of Emerson and Whitman and evidence the influence of Stevens and Williams. *The Selected Poems: Expanded Edition* (1986) provides an excellent introduction to his shorter work.

MAYA ANGELOU (1928–) was born Marguerite Johnson in St. Louis, Missouri. After being raped at the age of eight by her mother's boyfriend, she went through a nearly five-year period of muteness. She was given the name "Maya Angelou" in her early twenties when she started working as a dancer. Later, she began a theatrical career by appearing in Gershwin's *Porgy and Bess* on an international tour sponsored by the State Department. Angelou has since written and directed for both stage and screen and was nominated for an Emmy Award for her performance in the television miniseries *Roots*. She was also active in the Civil Rights movement and, at the request of Martin Luther King, Jr., served as a coordinator for the Southern Christian Leadership Conference. Angelou is best known as a commentator on black American culture, particularly the situation of black women. Her most widely known work is undoubtedly her best-selling autobiography, *I Know Why the Caged Bird Sings* (1969). Her collections of poetry include *Just Give Me a Cool Drink of Water 'fore I Diiie* (1971), *Oh Pray My Wings Are Gonna Fit Me Well* (1975), *And Still I Rise* (1978), and *Shaker, Why Don't You Sing?* (1983). In 1981 Angelou received a lifetime appointment as Reynolds Professor of American Studies at Wake Forest University. She wrote and recited a poem at the inauguration of President Bill Clinton in 1993. *The Complete Collected Poems of Maya Angelou* appeared in 1994.

JOEL BARLOW (1754–1812) was born in Redding, Connecticut Colony. He attended Dartmouth and Yale, where he became associated with the so-called Connecticut Wits—a group of eighteenth-century poets, including Timothy Dwight and John Trumbull, with conservative literary, political, and religious values. Barlow served as a chaplain during the War of Independence. Afterward, he studied law and was admitted to the bar in 1786. In 1786–1787 he serialized *The Anarchiad*, a satire on democratic liberalism, and in 1787 he brought out the first version of his unsuccessful national epic *The Vision of Columbus*, which he later revised, expanded, and retitled *The Columbiad*. He lived periodically in France for seventeen years, and contact with European intellectuals, along with a new appreciation for the writings of Thomas Paine and Thomas Jefferson, transformed him into a champion of democratic and progressive causes. He was eventually awarded French citizenship for his pamphlet *A Letter to the National Convention of France* (1792), which defended the French Revolution. During the Reign of Terror, Paine entrusted Barlow with the manuscript of *The Age of Reason*, which Barlow arranged to have published in 1794. Barlow returned to America in 1804 and settled near Washington, D.C. He died of pneumonia while attempting, at President Madison's behest, to contact Napoleon, in order to negotiate a trade agreement with the United States. Barlow's posthumous literary reputation rests principally on two works, the mock-heroic epic "The Hasty Pudding" (1796) and the bitter antiwar poem "Advice to a Raven in Russia" (1812).

WENDELL BERRY (1934–) was born in Port Royal, Kentucky. He was educated at the University of Kentucky and taught there after holding posts at Stanford and New York universities. In 1977 he left teaching to concentrate on farming and writing. His first book, a long poetic eulogy for President Kennedy entitled *November Twenty-six, Nineteen Hundred Sixty-three*, was published in 1964. His first collection of poems, *The Broken Ground*, appeared the same year. Later collections include *Openings* (1968), *Farming: A Handbook* (1970), and *Clearing* (1977). He is also well known for prose works on agriculture and ecology, most notably *The Unsettling of America* (1977).

ELIZABETH BISHOP (1911–1979) was born in Worcester, Massachusetts. After the death of her father in 1911 and the permanent hospitalization of her mother for mental illness in 1917, she was raised by maternal grandparents in Nova Scotia, paternal grandparents in Worcester, and an aunt near Boston. She attended Vassar College, where she met and received encouragement from Marianne Moore. Later, she became close friends with Robert Lowell. Her first volume of poetry, *North and South*, appeared in 1946. Six years later she settled in Rio de Janeiro with Lota de Macedo Soares, a Brazilian architect. *Questions of Travel* (1965) contains a number of poems that derive from her experience of Brazil. Soares committed suicide in 1967, and Bishop finally left Brazil in 1970. She returned to Boston and taught for several years at Harvard. Her collection *Poems: North & South—A Cold Spring* (1955) won the Pulitzer Prize, and her *Complete Poems* (1969) won the National Book Award. Her final and possibly greatest volume was *Geography III* (1976), which includes "In the Waiting Room," "The Moose," and the famous villanelle "One Art." Bishop is valued as a skilled observer (she was a talented amateur painter), and her subdued, carefully crafted work has grown in reputation through the years, becoming a model for many contemporary poets.

GWENDOLYN BROOKS (1917–2000) was born in Topeka, Kansas, and raised and educated in Chicago. Her first collection, *A Street in Bronzeville* (1945), established her primary concern with everyday black urban life. In 1949 Brooks became the first black poet to win the Pulitzer Prize, for her collection *Annie Allen*. Perhaps her most celebrated single volume is *The Bean Eaters* (1960), which includes the brief, widely anthologized poem "We Real Cool." Brooks succeeded Carl Sandburg as poet laureate of Illinois in 1969. After 1967, when she attended the Second Black Writers' Conference at Fisk University, her work reflected the political concerns of militant activists and became less formal and more improvisatory in style. Her later volumes include *In the Mecca: Poems* (1968), *Riot* (1969), *Aloneness* (1971), *Beckonings* (1975), *To Disembark* (1981), and *The Near-Johannesburg Boy and Other Poems* (1986). Her collected poems, under the title *Blacks*, appeared in 1987.

STERLING BROWN (1901–1989) was born in Washington, D.C., the son of a minister and a professor of religion. Brown earned his M.A. at Harvard in 1923 and later taught at Virginia Seminary and College, Fisk University, Lincoln University, and then for fifty years at Howard University, where his father had also worked. Brown became an expert in the fields of black folklore, black literature, and black music. The first of his relatively few published poetry collections was *Southern Road* (1932). His work, characterized by rural settings and social protest, frequently employs dialect and folk forms, such as the ballad and the work song. Brown deliberately distanced himself from the poetry movement in Harlem, which he saw as "the show-window" of black American experience. Robinson, Dunbar, Frost, and Sandburg were important influences on his poetry. His *Collected Poems* appeared in 1980.

WILLIAM CULLEN BRYANT (1794–1878) was born in Cummington, Massachusetts. A precocious youth, he began writing poetry at the age of nine. His first published work was a satire on the Jefferson administration entitled "The Embargo," published in 1808 when he was only fourteen. He completed the first version of what may be his most famous poem, "Thanatopsis," at the age of sixteen. Bryant withdrew from Williams College without taking a degree, was admitted to the bar, and began practicing law in Great Barrington, Massachusetts. He married Frances Fairchild in 1821, the same year he brought out his first major collection, simply titled *Poems*. In 1825 he gave up law, which he despised, to pursue a literary career in New York City. He befriended the novelist James Fenimore Cooper and the painters Thomas Cole and Asher B. Durand (the latter of whom depicted Bryant and Cole in the famous painting *Kindred Spirits*). In 1829 Bryant became editor-in-chief of the New York *Evening Post*, a position he held for the rest of his life. He also became a noted public speaker and championed various progressive causes, including international copyright protection, opposition to the death penalty, free trade, free speech, workers' rights, and abolition. He helped organize the Republican Party and advised Abraham Lincoln on cabinet appointments. Rejecting his early Calvinist training, he also became a leader in the Unitarian movement. Bryant traveled widely in America, Europe, and the Middle East, and made the acquaintance of many important literary figures, including Walter Savage Landor, Hawthorne, Longfellow, Dickens, and the Brownings. New collections of his verse appeared in 1832, 1842, 1844, 1846, 1854, 1864, and 1876. Late in life he produced blank verse translations of the *Iliad* (1870) and the *Odyssey* (1872). He died from injuries suffered in a fall during a public ceremony at the unveiling of a statue of Mazzini in Central Park. His poetry was strongly influenced by Wordsworth and the romantic movement, although it also exemplifies a neoclassical restraint, commitment to reform, and careful observation of American landscapes. Bryant was widely regarded as the greatest American poet before Longfellow.

HART CRANE (1899–1932) was the only child of the candy manufacturer who invented the Life Saver. He was born in Garrettsville, Ohio, although he spent most of his life in Cleveland and New York City. In his youth, he worked at a munitions factory and an advertising firm and as both a shipping clerk and a reporter. In 1924 he moved into a building with a close view of the Brooklyn Bridge, which would later become a central symbol in his work. His first published collection, *White Buildings*, appeared in 1926. His major work, *The Bridge*, an optimistic counterstatement to Eliot's *The Waste Land* and an attempt to forge an epic myth from American experience, followed in 1930. Crane employed modernist techniques but considered his poetry to be a continuation of Whitman's effusive, affirmative, visionary work. He sailed to Mexico with the intention of writing another long poem, but disappointed by the critical reception of *The Bridge* and afflicted by the feeling that he had squandered his talent, he committed suicide by jumping overboard on his way back to the United States. His *Collected Poems* was published posthumously in 1933.

STEPHEN CRANE (1871–1900) was born in Newark, New Jersey. He attended Syracuse University, where he distinguished himself principally as a baseball player. In 1891 he began work as a journalist, sharpening his powers of observation and gathering material for his later literary work. Best known for his fiction, Crane published the radical naturalist novella *Maggie: A Girl of the Streets* at his own expense in 1893 and followed it with his masterpiece, the impressionist Civil War novel *The Red Badge of Courage* (1895), and several classic short stories, such as "The Open Boat," "The Bride Comes to Yellow Sky," and "The Blue Hotel." His experimental free-verse poetry was collected in two volumes, *The Black Riders and Other Lines* (1895) and *War Is Kind* (1899). Crane's work is characterized by technical innovation, savage irony, and violent subject matter. In 1899 he and his companion Cora Taylor settled in southeastern England, where they got to know the two contemporary writers Crane most admired, Henry James and Joseph Conrad. A year later Crane died in Germany of tuberculosis. In his meager twenty-eight years, he wrote feverishly—often to pay off debts—producing a large quantity of material that, though highly uneven in quality, has proved to be extremely influential.

ROBERT CREELEY (1926–) was born in Arlington, Massachusetts. As a child, he lost both his father and his left eye. He dropped out of Harvard after a year to join the American Field Service in India and Burma. He returned to Harvard, but left once more to take up subsistence farming in New Hampshire and to travel to France and Spain. A voluminous correspondence with the iconoclastic poet Charles Olson eventually brought Creeley to the short-lived, experimental Black Mountain College in North Carolina, where he completed a B.A., taught, and edited the *Black Mountain Review*. Creeley and Olson became central figures in the so-called Black Mountain school of poets that included Denise Levertov and Paul Blackburn. Later, when Black Mountain College closed, Creeley traveled to San Francisco where he met Allen Ginsberg and other beat writers, whose spontaneous, free-form aesthetics jibed with Creeley's own. Creeley writes in a terse, minimalist, monosyllabic, heavily enjambed style that derives in large measure from the work of William Carlos Williams. His collections include *You* (1956), *For Love: Poems 1950–1960* (1962), *Words: Poems* (1967), *Pieces* (1968), *Later* (1979), and *Windows* (1990). He has taught at several universities, including the State University of New York at Buffalo, and has been married three times.

COUNTEE CULLEN (1903–1946) was born in Louisville, Kentucky, and reared by middle-class foster parents in Harlem. He won a citywide poetry contest as a schoolboy and published his influential first volume, *Color* (1925)—which contains such widely anthologized poems as "Yet Do I Marvel," "Incident," and "Heritage"—while still an undergraduate at New York University. The following year he earned an M.A. from Harvard. In 1927 he published two more volumes, *Copper Sun* and *The Ballad of the Brown Girl: An Old Ballad Retold*. His precocity established him as "the black Keats"—and indeed Keats's themes of truth and beauty, along with his technical proficiency, do find an echo in Cullen's work. (The connection is further strengthened by the fact that Keats was Cullen's favorite poet, and that Cullen wrote an epitaph titled "For Keats, Apostle of Beauty.") Along with Claude McKay, Cullen represented the formal side of Harlem Renaissance poetry, in contradistinction to the freer jazz-inspired style employed by Langston Hughes. He always wanted to be known "as a poet and not as a Negro poet," but he certainly did not eschew themes of injustice and racial prejudice. He married Nina Yolande Du Bois, daughter of W. E. B. Du Bois, in 1928, but the marriage lasted only two years. Cullen's popular reputation declined after the publication of a controversial volume entitled *The Black Christ and Other Poems* in 1929. In his remaining years he published a novel, two collections of children's stories, and a translation of Euripides' *Medea* along with original sonnets and short lyrics. From 1934 he taught English and French at Frederick Douglass Junior High School. He married again in 1940.

E[DWARD]. E[STLIN]. **CUMMINGS** (1894–1962) was born in Cambridge, Massachusetts and educated at Harvard. During World War I, he drove an ambulance and was unjustly detained for three months in Normandy, an event that serves as the basis for his first book, *The Enormous Room* (1922). In the 1920s and 1930s he lived in both New York City and Paris, where he met Ezra Pound (whose early work had deeply influenced him), Archibald MacLeish, and Hart Crane. He simultaneously pursued careers as a painter and a poet, devoting himself in both fields to the avant-garde. *Tulips and Chimneys*, his first volume of poetry, was published in 1923, to be followed by eleven more collections. A two-volume *Complete Poems* appeared in 1968. Cummings experimented radically with typography and syntax, although he often employed rhymes (sometimes in eccentric patterns) and traditional forms like the sonnet. His modernist techniques and scathing attacks on middle-class values only seemingly enhanced the popularity of his poetry, which easily outstripped that of his largely neglected painting. Cummings's work has deep roots in the transcendentalist tradition of Emerson, as one easily discerns from his iconoclastic attitude toward politics and religion and his deep love of individualism and nature. The commonly held notion that Cummings had his name legally changed to lowercase letters is false.

J[AMES]. V[INCENT]. **CUNNINGHAM** (1911–1985) was born in Cumberland, Maryland, although he came to view himself as a westerner. He grew up in Montana, worked for the Denver Stock Exchange at the time the market crashed in 1929, and, with the assistance of Yvor Winters, enrolled at Stanford, where he studied classics and mathematics and began writing poetry. Eventually, he received a doctorate in English for a dissertation on Shakespeare's tragedies. His two major collections of verse are *The Helmsman* (1942) and *The Judge Is Fury* (1947). He continued to write verse at a slow pace after 1947, particularly epigrams. *The Poems of J. V. Cunningham*, edited by Timothy Steele, appeared in 1997. Cunningham's is a severe, compressed, plain style that employs traditional meters. His poetry is often darkly humorous and unsparingly satirical and frequently attains both a rare concentration and seriousness of purpose. As an epigrammatist, his only peers in English are Ben Jonson, Robert Herrick, and Walter Savage Landor. Cunningham taught at several universities, including Hawaii, Chicago, Harvard, Virginia, and Brandeis, and was married three times.

JAMES DICKEY (1923–1997) was born in Atlanta, Georgia. He became a high-school football star and served as a pilot in the Air Force during World War II. After the war, he earned his B.A. and M.A. from Vanderbilt. His first book of poems, *Into the Stone and Other Poems*, was published in 1960. His other collections include *Drowning with Others* (1962), *Helmets* (1964), *Buckdancer's Choice* (1965), *The Zodiac* (1976), and *The Whole Motion* (1992). He frequently wrote about life in the southern backwoods, as in what is surely his best-known work, the novel *Deliverance* (1970), which he helped adapt into a popular film directed by John Boorman. Dickey was known as a flamboyant, self-promoting personality, who loved hard drinking and motorcycles.

EMILY DICKINSON (1830–1886) died in the house where she was born in Amherst, Massachusetts. Hers was an affluent family, her father being a state legislator, U.S. congressman, and judge. Dickinson seems to have been severely agoraphobic and rarely ever left home. Her one lengthy absence from her father's house—the year she attended Mt. Holyoke Female Seminary, only ten miles away—left her pining for her *"own* DEAR HOME." In her youth she was terrorized by fire-and-brimstone sermons, although she later adopted a highly ambivalent view toward conventional religion. She became noted for eccentric behavior, such as always dressing in white and dangling sweets on a string from a second-story window for the local children to grasp. After 1848, she rarely received visitors and rarely left her house. She became known as "the Myth." Dickinson began writing poetry around 1850, and starting in 1858, at which time her productivity greatly increased, she began collecting her poems in small, hand-sewn booklets. A large number of her poems are written in the same measure as the hymns she sang at church. Her most characteristic punctuation is a dash, and her most distinctive—and subsequently influential—technical device is a near rhyme. In substance, her poetry is elliptical and extremely original. Her lack of a wide experience of the world forced her to turn inward, where she probed deeply into issues of perception, terror, faith, loss, and death. Of her 1,775 poems, only 7 were published during her lifetime. Dickinson's posthumous reputation owes much to the industry of Mabel Loomis Todd, who lectured on her work and edited several volumes of her poetry—although she, like most of Dickinson's early editors, frequently conventionalized the idiosyncratic punctuation, meter, rhymes, diction, and sentiments. Not until 1955 were Dickinson's collected poems available in their original form.

HILDA DOOLITTLE (1886–1961) was born in a Moravian community in Bethlehem, Pennsylvania. She attended Bryn Mawr College in 1905, where she met Marianne Moore and Ezra Pound, with whom she was briefly engaged in 1907. Pound remained a friend and a major influence in her life and arranged to have her early work published under the *nom de plume* H. D., Imagiste. Her work appeared in the original imagist anthologies, and she became a key figure in the movement, exemplifying its tendencies with her unrhymed, unmetered, spare, impersonal verse and austere natural imagery. From 1911 she lived in Europe. Her first collection, *Sea Garden*, appeared in 1916 and was followed by *Hymen* (1921), *Heliodora and Other Poems* (1924), and *Red Roses for Bronze* (1931). She was married to the British imagist poet Richard Aldington from 1913 to 1937, although she also had affairs with D. H. Lawrence and the composer Cecil Gray, with whom she conceived a child. Later, she formed an intimate relationship with the novelist Bryher (Annie Winnifred Ellerman). In 1933 she was psychoanalyzed by Freud, an experience that enhanced her interest in symbolism. Her most significant later publication is the trilogy inspired by the bombing of London, consisting of *The Walls Do Not Fall* (1944), *Tribute to the Angels* (1945), and *The Flowering of the Rod* (1945). She often translated or wrote poems inspired by her favorite Greek writers, notably Sappho and Euripides. Her long poem *Helen in Egypt*, a feminist revision of the familiar Trojan War epic told from Helen's point of view, was published the year after her death, and her *Collected Poems* appeared in 1983.

RITA DOVE (1952–) was born in Akron, Ohio and educated at Miami University in Ohio, the University of Tubingen in Germany, and the University of Iowa, where she earned an M.F.A. She has taught at Arizona State University and the University of Virginia. Dove's early poetry collections include *The Yellow House on the Corner* (1980) and *Museum* (1983). Her Pulitzer Prize–winning collection *Thomas and Beulah* (1986) chronicles the lives of the author's maternal grandparents in the Deep South and the movement of millions of black Americans north in the early decades of the twentieth century. Subsequent collections include *The Other Side of the House* (1988), *Grace Notes* (1989), and *Mother Love* (1995), which recasts the myth of Demeter and Persephone in a modern context. In 1993, Dove became the youngest person ever appointed poet laureate of the United States.

PAUL LAURENCE DUNBAR (1872–1906), a son of former slaves, was born in Dayton, Ohio. Dunbar's father escaped to Canada with the assistance of the Underground Railroad, but returned to the United States to enlist in a black regiment of the Union Army. Dunbar himself became the first black writer to support himself by writing and the first black poet after the Civil War to attain national prominence. He attended a white high school, where he demonstrated a talent for writing. While he worked as an elevator operator, he published his first volume of poetry, *Oak and Ivy* (1893), at his own expense and sold copies to his passengers to cover the cost. His lot improved when Frederick Douglass secured a job for him at the Columbian Exposition in Chicago. Later he worked as an assistant in the reading room of the Library of Congress. His second volume, *Majors and Minors* (1895), received a favorable review from the influential novelist and critic William Dean Howells, who wrote an introduction to Dunbar's third book, *Lyrics of Lowly Life* (1896). His later collections include *Lyrics of the Hearthside* (1899), *Lyrics of Love and Laughter* (1903), and *Lyrics of Sunshine and Shadow* (1905). Dunbar also wrote four novels and four short-story collections and lectured widely in the United States and England. Booker T. Washington dubbed him "the poet laureate of the Negro race." His work anticipates such later developments in black American poetry as the Harlem Renaissance. Like Claude McKay and Countee Cullen after him, Dunbar employed formal techniques of versification. His extensive use of dialect also anticipates the work of Sterling Brown. When he died of tuberculosis at the age of thirty-three, he was one of the most popular poets in the United States.

RICHARD EBERHART (1904–) was born in Austin, Minnesota. He was educated at Dartmouth, Cambridge, and Harvard. He tutored the son of the King of Siam and taught at St. Mark's School outside of Boston, where Robert Lowell numbered among his pupils. In World War II he served as an aerial gunnery instructor, an experience he drew upon in what may be his best-known lyric, "The Fury of Aerial Bombardment." After the war, he became vice president of his father-in-law's floor wax company before turning to an academic career. He taught at the University of Washington, the University of Connecticut, Wheaton College, and Princeton before being appointed poet-in-residence at Dartmouth. His many volumes of poetry include *A Bravery of Earth* (1930), *Burr Oaks* (1947), and *The Quarry* (1960). His *Collected Poems* (1976) won the National Book Award. Eberhart's style can be described as lyrical, contemplative, and metaphysical. He is often at his best in ruminations on transience and death, such as "For a Lamb" and "The Groundhog." William Blake exerted a decisive influence on both the deceptive simplicity of his presentation and his thematic concerns.

T[HOMAS]. S[TEARNS]. ELIOT (1888–1965) was born to a prominent New England family in St. Louis, Missouri. He entered Harvard in 1906, where he studied Latin, Greek, Sanskrit, German, French, and philosophy, and his teachers included Irving Babbitt, Josiah Royce, Bertrand Russell, and George Santayana. Later, he studied at the Sorbonne and Oxford and wrote a doctoral thesis on the English philosopher F. H. Bradley. He moved to England in 1914 and married Vivien Haigh-Wood in 1915. After working as a teacher in a grammar school, he took a position at Lloyds Bank, where he remained from 1916 to 1925. In 1917, with assistance and encouragement from Ezra Pound, he published his first volume of poetry, *Prufrock and Other Observations*, which is often said to have initiated modernism in poetry. It was followed by *Poems* (1919), which includes "Gerontion," a kind of prelude to his best-known and most revolutionary work, *The Waste Land* (1922), written largely during a nervous breakdown and edited by Pound. Although Eliot himself later dismissed *The Waste Land* as "a personal and wholly insignificant grouse against life," its fragmentary, allusive manner helped to define the nature of poetic modernism. Eliot became a highly influential critic with such essays as "Tradition and the Individual Talent" and "The Metaphysical Poets." He introduced such concepts as "the objective correlative" and "the dissociation of sensibility" and, along with Pound, exerted an enormous influence over how the literature of the past was evaluated. He left Lloyds Bank and joined the publishing firm Faber and Faber in 1925, where he became the virtual arbiter of British literary taste. In 1927 he joined the Church of England and became a British subject, later declaring himself a "classicist in literature, royalist in politics, and anglo-catholic in religion." After the nihilistic crisis of "The Hollow Men" (1925), Eliot's later poetry—beginning with "Journey of the Magi" (1927) and "Ash Wednesday" (1930)—affirms a Christian vision of reality. His poetic career culminated with the *Four Quartets* (1943), which Eliot considered to be his masterpiece. He wrote several books on culture and Christianity; several verse dramas, including *Murder in the Cathedral* (1935); and a charming book of verse for children, *Old Possum's Book of Practical Cats* (1939). In 1948 he received both the Nobel Prize for literature and the Order of Merit. Eliot separated from Vivien Haigh-Wood in the early thirties, but never divorced her. She died in 1947, and Eliot married Valerie Fletcher in 1957.

RALPH WALDO EMERSON (1803–1882) was born in Boston. He graduated from Harvard and was ordained pastor of the Second Church of Boston in 1829. Later that same year, he married Ellen Tucker, who, like Emerson, had already contracted tuberculosis. She died in 1831 at the age of nineteen, leaving Emerson a legacy that amounted to a small fortune. The following year, he resigned from his ministerial position, principally because he no longer believed in administering the sacrament, and sailed to Europe, where he met Walter Savage Landor, John Stuart Mill, Samuel Taylor Coleridge, William Wordsworth, and Thomas Carlyle. In 1834 he settled in Concord and a year later married Lydia Jackson. Soon an intellectual circle developed around him—including Margaret Fuller, A. Bronson Alcott, and Orestes Brownson—which would develop into the Transcendental Club. Later, he befriended such illustrious neighbors as Hawthorne, who moved into the house of Emerson's ancestors, and Thoreau, who built his famous Walden cabin on property owned by Emerson. In 1836 Emerson anonymously published the influential pamphlet *Nature*, which became a kind of manifesto of the transcendentalist movement. Emerson is best known for the essays and lectures he produced between 1837 and 1844, such as "The American Scholar," "The Divinity School Address," "Self-Reliance," and "The Poet." The latter work, with its call for an organic notion of form, set the stage for Walt Whitman and the rise of free verse. Emerson's own verse, published in *Poems* (1847) and *May-Day and Other Pieces*

(1867), often exhibited irregular rhythms and near rhymes (which Dickinson would use even more extensively), as well as a kind of rugged compression. He revised some of his work for a volume of *Selected Poems* published in 1876. The influence of his ideas on subsequent developments in American literature is incalculable.

ROBERT FRANCIS (1901–1987) was born in Upland, Pennsylvania, and raised in New Jersey, Long Island, and Massachusetts. He was educated at Harvard, taught preparatory school for several years in Beirut, Lebanon, and settled in Amherst, Massachusetts, where he supported himself by teaching and giving violin lessons. He lived in rural solitude from 1926 onward, and from 1940, he lived in a one-man house called Fort Juniper, cultivating a life of Thoreauvian simplicity. He first met Robert Frost in 1933, who became a friend to Francis and was sympathetic to his work. Francis's volumes of poetry include *Stand with Me Here* (1936), *Valhalla and Other Poems* (1938), *The Sound I Listened For* (1944), *The Face against the Glass* (1950), *The Orb Weaver* (1960), *Come Out into the Sun* (1965), and *Like Ghosts of Eagles* (1974). He also published an autobiography, *The Trouble with Francis* (1971). His *Collected Poems* appeared in 1976. Francis wrote in a subdued style that focuses on natural imagery and is rife with metrical felicities. Francis has an excellent claim to being one of America's most unjustly underappreciated poets.

PHILIP FRENEAU (1752–1832) was of Huguenot descent. He was born in New York City and educated at the College of New Jersey (now Princeton), where James Madison was his roommate. With his classmate Hugh Henry Brackenridge, who became one of America's first novelists, he composed a poem read at commencement, entitled "The Rising Glory of America." After graduation, he worked as a teacher and then as a secretary on a plantation in the West Indies. During the War of Independence, he served in the Monmouth Militia of New Jersey. He was captured by the British in 1780 and received brutal treatment aboard a prison ship aptly called the *Scorpion*, which provided the background for his poem "The British Prison Ship." After the war, he settled in Philadelphia and worked variously as a journalist, a postal clerk, and a master of trading ships. His first major collection of verse, *The Poems of Philip Freneau Written Chiefly During the Late War*, appeared in 1786. In 1790 he married Eleanor Forman, with whom he had four daughters. Thomas Jefferson hired him as a translator for the State Department in 1791, where he remained despite earning the enmity of President Washington for his radically democratic political views. In later years, he worked as a printer and bookseller in New Jersey and as a ship captain. His most significant later volume was *A Collection of Poems on American Affairs* (1815). Freneau's poetry remained indebted to British neoclassicism despite its American subject matter, but did, however, anticipate the romantic movement. Freneau is notable as a satirical poet, a nature poet, and a poet of ideas, and has deservedly been called the father of American poetry. Nonetheless, his later years were difficult, and he failed to attain adequate recognition in his own time. Impoverished and nearly forgotten, he died of exposure when caught in a blizzard while walking home.

ROBERT FROST (1874–1963), despite being closely identified with the rural landscape of New England, was born in San Francisco, where he lived until the age of eleven. He attended both Dartmouth and Harvard, but failed to take a degree. He began sending out verse in quantity in 1890, but very few of his poems were accepted before 1913. He married Elinor White, the co-valedictorian of his high school, in 1895, and they had four children. He taught school and ran, without great success, a farm in Derry, New Hampshire. Following the deaths of his mother, his son Elliott, and his daughter Elinor, Frost fell into a profound depression and contemplated suicide. He made a new start in 1912, when he and his family moved to England. There, Frost published his first book of poetry, *A Boy's Will* (1913). It was favorably reviewed by Ezra Pound, who found Frost to be a "VURRY Amur'k'n talent" and helped him get his second and perhaps finest book, *North of Boston*, published the following year. Frost also became close friends with Edward Thomas, who, with Frost's encouragement, developed into a superb poet in his own right, despite the fact that he was killed in action in 1917. After the success of his second book and the outbreak of World War I, Frost returned to America and bought another farm in New Hampshire. He taught at Amherst, Wesleyan, Michigan, Dartmouth, Yale, and Harvard. His later collections, each of which includes at least a handful of classic lyrics, are *Mountain Interval* (1916), *New Hampshire* (1923), *West-Running Brook* (1928), *A Further Range* (1936), *A Witness Tree* (1942), and *A Steeple Bush* (1947). He won four Pulitzer Prizes, more than any other American poet. Venerable and revered, Frost read "The Gift Outright" at John F. Kennedy's inauguration in 1961. His last—and perhaps weakest—collection, *In the Clearing*, appeared the year before he died. Frost forged a style that combines American speech patterns with traditional metrical forms. He rejected free verse as being like playing tennis without a net and saw the work of poetry as creating a "momentary stay against confusion." His poems appeal broadly because of their natural imagery, memorable phrasing, and apparent simplicity, but their hidden depths and technical ingenuity reward careful study.

ALLEN GINSBERG (1926–1997) was born in Newark, New Jersey. He was expelled from Columbia University in 1945 for sketching obscene drawings and phrases in the dust of his dormitory window. Ginsberg subsequently supported himself as a messman, a welder, a night porter, a dishwasher, a market researcher, and a book reviewer for *Newsweek*. He lived with William S. Burroughs and Jack Kerouac, fellow "beats" as Kerouac dubbed them, punning on "beaten down" and "beatified." In 1948 Ginsberg finished his degree at Columbia, but also had to plead insanity to avoid prosecution as an accomplice to theft. He and Kerouac moved to San Francisco in 1954, where Lawrence Ferlinghetti's City Lights Press published *Howl and Other Poems* (1955), a volume that made Ginsberg the leading beat poet and brought him further obscenity charges. He employed an extremely long, tumbling free-verse line that built on the work of the poets who influenced him most: Blake, Whitman, and Williams. His later work includes *Kaddish and Other Poems* (1961), *Reality Sandwiches* (1963), *Planet News* (1968), and *The Fall of America* (1972). Ginsberg was an outspoken critic of the commercialism, complacency, and conformity of postwar America. Like the other beats, he sought an alternative (and sometimes destructive) lifestyle rooted in mysticism, experimentation, and absolute freedom. He became an icon of the counterculture movement and was a public advocate of Zen Buddhism, hallucinatory drugs, homosexuality, and civil rights.

DANA GIOIA (1950–) was born in Los Angeles. He received a B.A. and an M.B.A. at Stanford and an M.A. at Harvard, where he studied with Robert Fitzgerald and Elizabeth Bishop. From 1977 to 1992 he worked as an executive at General Foods in New York City, during which time he also published poems, essays, and reviews. Since 1992 he has devoted himself full time to freelance writing. His poetry collections include *Daily Horoscope* (1985), *The Gods of Winter* (1991), and *Interrogations at Noon* (2001). These volumes, in conjunction with the essay collection *Can Poetry Matter?* (1992), have made him a leading figure in the so-called new formalist movement. Gioia has edited the stories of Weldon Kees and numerous anthologies, has translated the work of Seneca, Eugenio Montale, and Nina Cassian, and has written the opera libretto *Nosferatu*.

EMILY GROSHOLZ (1950–) was born in the suburbs of Philadelphia. She received her B.A. at the University of Chicago in 1972 and her Ph.D. in philosophy at Yale in 1978. She is currently Professor of

Philosophy and African-American Studies at Penn State University and is married to the medieval scholar Robert Edwards. Grosholz has published four books of poetry: *The River Painter* (1984), *Shores and Headlands* (1988), *Eden* (1992), and *The Abacus of Years* (2001). She has edited *W. E. B. Du Bois on Race and Culture* (1996) and *Telling the Barn Swallow: Poets on the Poetry of Maxine Kumin* (1997) and serves as an advisory editor for the *Hudson Review*.

R. S. GWYNN (1948–) was born in Eden, North Carolina. He received his B.A. in 1969 from Davidson College, where he played football and distinguished himself as a creative writer. He earned both an M.A. and an M.F.A. at the University of Arkansas. He has taught at Southwest Texas State and Lamar universities. His poetry collections include *Bearing and Distance* (1977) and *The Drive-In* (1986). He has also published a satirical poem about contemporary poetry entitled *The Narcissiad* (1982). His best work from 1970 to 2000 has been collected in *No Word of Farewell* (2001). Gwynn is noted as a master of formal technique and as a humorous, scathing satirist.

ROBERT HASS (1941–) was born in San Francisco and raised in San Rafael, California. He earned a B.A. at St. Mary's College and a Ph.D. from Stanford, where he studied with Yvor Winters. He has taught at the State University of New York at Buffalo, St. Mary's College, and the University of California at Berkeley. His collections include *Field Guide* (1973), *Praise* (1979), and *Human Wishes* (1989). The relationship between language and material reality is a principal concern in his poetry. He has also published critical essays, notably *Twentieth Century Pleasures: Prose on Poetry* (1984), as well as translations both of the Nobel Prize–winning Lithuanian poet Czeslaw Milosz and of classic haiku poetry. In 1995 Hass was appointed poet laureate of the United States.

ROBERT HAYDEN (1913–1980) was born Asa Bundy Sheffey in Detroit, Michigan. He was raised by foster parents William and Sue Ellen Hayden after his biological parents separated. He was educated at Detroit City College (now Wayne State University) and the University of Michigan, where he studied with W. H. Auden. Starting in 1936, he researched black folklore and the Underground Railroad—subjects that would leave a mark on his poetry—for the Federal Writer's Project. In 1940 he married the concert pianist Erma Inez Morris. He taught at Fisk University and the University of Michigan. His poetry collections include *Heart-Shape in the Dust* (1940), *Figures of Time* (1955), *A Ballad of Remembrance* (1962), *Words in the Mourning Time* (1970), *The Night-Blooming Cereus* (1972), and *Angle of Ascent*

(1975). His work evinces a debt to Yeats's imaginative engagement with history and Eliot's modernist techniques, such as the collage employed in his most famous poem, "Middle Passage" (1962). Hayden has also published a play about Malcolm X and a collected volume of prose and has edited several anthologies. He won the First World Festival of Negro Arts prize for poetry in Dakar, Senegal in 1966, and in 1976 he became the first black poet to be appointed poetry consultant to the Library of Congress.

OLIVER WENDELL HOLMES (1809–1894) was born in Cambridge, Massachusetts. He graduated from Harvard in 1829 and entered Harvard Law School, but left to study medicine in Paris, before returning to take his M.D. at Harvard in 1836. He worked as a professor of anatomy at Dartmouth from 1838 to 1840. In 1840 he turned to general practice in Boston and married Amelia Lee Jackson, with whom he had three children, including Oliver Wendell, Jr., who became a justice for the United State Supreme Court from 1902 to 1932. From 1847 to 1882 he worked as Parkman Professor of Anatomy and Physiology at Harvard Medical School. He helped to found the American Medical Association and also conducted important medical research, including a landmark study of puerperal fever, which helped reduce the risk of mortality during childbirth. Holmes also maintained an active literary career, publishing numerous humerous essays, three novels, and three biographies (including one of Emerson). He was also a noted lecturer and famous as both a conversationalist and an after-dinner speaker. His poetry collections include *Poems* (1836), *Songs in Many Keys* (1862), *Songs of Many Seasons* (1875), *The Iron Gate* (1880), and *Before the Curfew* (1887). In 1857 he helped to found the *Atlantic Monthly*. His friends included such notable writers as Emerson, Hawthorne, Longfellow, Whittier, James Russell Lowell, and William Dean Howells.

ANDREW HUDGINS (1951–) was born in Killeen, Texas, and grew up in Montgomery, Alabama, where he witnessed the civil rights turmoil of the sixties. He was educated at the University of Alabama, the University of Iowa (where he earned an M.F.A.), Syracuse University, and Stanford. He has taught at Baylor University, the University of Cincinnati, and Princeton. His volumes of poetry include *Saints and Strangers* (1985), *After the Lost War* (1988), *The Never-Ending* (1991), *The Glass Hammer* (1994), and *Babylon in a Jar* (1998). He has also published a book of essays, *The Glass Anvil* (1997). His work, which has won numerous awards, is noted for its formal elegance and profound concern with religious issues.

LANGSTON HUGHES (1902–1967) was born in Joplin, Missouri and raised in Kansas, Illinois, and Ohio. He attended Columbia University in 1921–1922 and subsequently worked as a sailor on a freighter to West Africa, a doorman and bouncer in Paris, and a busboy in New York City. He became a crucial member of the Harlem Renaissance movement of the late 1920s and a friend of Countee Cullen. He first came to notice as a poet when his "The Negro Speaks of Rivers" was published in *Crisis* in 1921. Eleven of his poems appeared in Alain Locke's pioneering anthology *The New Negro* (1925), and his first collection, *The Weary Blues*, appeared the following year. It was followed by further volumes, including *Fine Clothes to the Jew* (1927), *Shakespeare in Harlem* (1942), *Fields of Wonder* (1947), and *Montage of a Dream Deferred* (1951). His poems focus on the plight of urban blacks and draw upon the rhythms of jazz, blues, and street language. He also wrote novels, short stories, plays, essays, and memoirs, and edited several anthologies. Hughes received a B.A. from Lincoln University in Pennsylvania in 1929 and taught creative writing at Atlanta University in 1947. In 1949–1950 he was appointed poet-in-residence at the University of Chicago. Because of his support of the Republican side during the Spanish Civil War and his affiliation with the American Communist Party, he was summoned to testify before Senator Joseph McCarthy's House Un-American Activities Committee in 1953. He was listed by the F.B.I. as a security risk and prevented from traveling outside the United States until 1959. His *Collected Poems* appeared posthumously in 1994.

RANDALL JARRELL (1914–1965) was born in Nashville, Tennessee and educated at Vanderbilt University, where he studied with John Crowe Ransom. He taught at Kenyon College, where he roomed with fiction writer Peter Taylor and poet Robert Lowell, as well as at the University of Texas, Sarah Lawrence College, and the Women's College of the University of North Carolina at Greensboro. His first volume of poetry, *Blood for a Stranger*, appeared in 1942. Jarrell served in the U.S. Army Air Corps from 1942 to 1946, and his next two volumes, *Little Friend, Little Friend* (1945) and *Losses* (1948), feature some of the best American poetry that came out of World War II. His later collections include *The Seven-League Crutches* (1951), *The Woman at the Washington Zoo* (1960), which won the National Book Award, and *The Lost World* (1965). He cultivated a colloquial style and focused principally on what he called the "dailiness of life." Jarrell was also an influential critic, who helped establish the reputations of Bishop and Lowell, and who reassessed the work of Whitman and Frost. He held editorial positions at the *Nation*, the

Partisan Review, the *Yale Review*, and the *American Scholar*, and translated Chekhov, Goethe, and Grimm's fairy tales. He was killed in an automobile accident.

ROBINSON JEFFERS (1887–1962) was born in Pittsburgh, the son of a minister and a classical scholar. Jeffers knew Latin and Greek by the age of ten. He received his B.A. at Occidental College in Los Angeles and pursued graduate work in medicine at the University of Southern California and in forestry at the University of Washington. His first volume of poetry, *Flagons and Apples*, was published at his own expense in 1912. At USC he met Una Kall Custer, who was married at the time; they fell in love, she divorced, and they were married in 1913. In 1914 the couple moved to Carmel, California, where Jeffers built a stone cottage overlooking the sea called Tor House and a two-and-a-half-story stone tower. Jeffers dedicated himself from this point forward to writing poetry and attracted serious critical and popular attention with the volumes *Roan Stallion, Tamar, and Other Poems* (1925), *The Women at Point Sur* (1927), *Cawdor* (1928), *Dear Judas* (1929), *Descent to the Dead* (1931), *Thurso's Landing* (1932), *Give Your Heart to the Hawks* (1933), *Solstice* (1935), *Such Counsels You Gave to Me* (1937), and *Be Angry at the Sun* (1941). Jeffers employed a long free-verse line derived from Whitman's work, and developed a philosophical stance he called inhumanism. He attacked the greed, self-absorption, shortsightedness, and corruption of modern civilization, against which he counterpointed the primal values of the natural world. Jeffers's adaptation of Euripides' *Medea* was produced on Broadway in 1947. His criticisms of American involvement in World War II and of political leaders prompted his publisher, Random House, to include a disclaimer in the controversial volume *The Double Axe* (1948). His final poems were collected in *The Beginning and the End* (1963). Although his relentless misanthropy eventually disenchanted many contemporary readers, his work's call for a radical reevaluation of the place of humans in the cosmos has become a major source of inspiration to the environmental movement.

CAROLYN KIZER (1925–) was born in Spokane, Washington and educated at Sarah Lawrence College, Columbia University, and the University of Washington, where she studied with Theodore Roethke. She founded the quarterly *Poetry Northwest* in 1959 and, from 1964–1965, worked for the U.S. State Department in Pakistan. From 1966–1970 she served as the first director of the Literature Program for the National Endowment for the Arts. Since 1970 she has been a professor, visiting professor, or poet-in-residence at a number of American universities. Her collections of poetry include *Poems* (1959), *The Ungrateful Garden* (1961), *Knock upon Silence* (1965), *Midnight Was My Cry* (1971), *Mermaids in the Basement: Poems for Women* (1984), *Yin* (1984), which won the Pulitzer Prize, and *The Nearness of You* (1986). Kizer is noted for her feminist themes and her alternate use of formal and free verse. She has made numerous translations, notably of the work of Chinese poets.

STANLEY KUNITZ (1905–) was born in Worcester, Massachusetts, and educated at Harvard. He has taught at Bennington College, Potsdam State Teachers College, the New School for Social Research in New York, the University of Washington, Queens College, Brandeis, Columbia, and Yale. His poetry collections include *Intellectual Things* (1930), *Passport to the War* (1944), *The Testing-Tree* (1971), *The Wellfleet Whale and Companion Poems* (1983), and *Passing Through* (1995), which won the National Book Award. He also won a Pulitzer Prize in 1959 for his *Selected Poems, 1928–1958*. Kunitz has translated the work of the Russian poets Anna Akhmatova, Andrei Voznesensky, and Yevgeny Yevtushenko and has edited eight dictionaries of literary biography. In 2000 his *Collected Poems* appeared, and—at the age of 95—he was appointed poet laureate of the United States.

EMMA LAZARUS (1849–1887) was born in New York City to a Sephardic (Spanish Jewish) family and educated at home. She learned German, French, and Italian at an early age, and published a volume of *Poems and Translations* (1867), all of which she wrote between the ages of fourteen and sixteen. She sent a copy to Emerson, whom she then met in 1868. He subsequently provided extended critical advice on her work. Her second volume, *Admetus and Other Poems*, appeared in 1871. She translated the German poet Heinrich Heine and medieval Hebrew poetry from German versions. She also contributed to Jewish causes, providing refugee relief to immigrants fleeing from persecution and writing articles on their behalf. She wrote her sonnet "The New Colossus," the poem for which she is best remembered, in support of a fund-raising campaign for the pedestal of the Statue of Liberty. In 1883 she traveled to Europe and met Robert Browning and William Morris. She returned to Europe for an extended visit in 1885–1887, but was seriously ill by the end, and died shortly after her return to America of cancer. A two-volume edition of her poems, edited by her sisters, was published posthumously in 1889.

LI-YOUNG LEE (1957–) was born in Jakarta, Indonesia, to Chinese parents. Lee's father had been personal physician to Mao Tse-tung and was held in Indonesia as a political prisoner. In 1959 the family fled, traveling to Hong Kong, Macau, Japan, and finally to the United States, where Lee's father became a Presbyterian minister in western Pennsylvania. Lee studied at the University of Pittsburgh, the University of Arizona, and the State University of New York at Brockport. He has worked as an artist for a fashion-accessories company in Chicago and has taught at Northwestern and the University of Iowa. His collections of poetry include *Rose* (1986) and *The City in Which I Love You* (1990). Both the powerful figure of his father and his Asian background play important roles in his sensuous poetry.

BRAD LEITHAUSER (1953–) was born and raised in Detroit. He took a law degree at Harvard and worked for three years as a researcher in Japan. He has subsequently lived in Italy, England, Iceland, and France. Currently, he is Emily Dickinson Lecturer in the Humanities at Mount Holyoke College in Massachusetts. His poetry collections include *Hundreds of Fireflies* (1982), *Cats of the Temple* (1986), *The Mail from Anywhere* (1990), and *The Odd Last Thing She Did* (1998). He has also published novels and essays and has edited *The Norton Book of Ghost Stories*. He is married to the poet Mary Jo Salter.

DENISE LEVERTOV (1923–1997) was born in Ilford, Essex, England and worked as a civilian nurse during World War II. Her first volume of verse, *The Double Image*, appeared in 1946. She settled in New York City in 1947 and became a naturalized citizen of the United States in 1955. From 1956 to 1959 she lived in Mexico. After returning to the United States, she became poetry editor of the *Nation* and taught at various institutions, including Vassar, MIT, Tufts, and Stanford, from 1982 to the time of her death. Her many later volumes, which evince the influence of Doolittle, Pound, and Williams as well as affiliations with "Black Mountain" poets such as Creeley and Robert Duncan, include *Here and Now* (1957), *Overland to the Islands* (1958), *The Jacob's Ladder* (1961), *The Sorrow Dance* (1967), *Relearning the Alphabet* (1970), *Footprints* (1972), *Life in the Forest* (1978), *Candles in Babylon* (1982), *A Door in the Hive* (1989), and *Evening Train* (1992). She typically wrote in a visionary mode, although during the time of the Vietnam War her work took on a distinctly political cast. She also published essays and a translation of the Buddhist work *In Praise of Krishna: Songs from the Bengali* (1967).

HENRY WADSWORTH LONGFELLOW (1807–1882) was born in Portland, Maine and attended Bowdoin College, where Nathaniel Hawthorne was a classmate. Longfellow's graduation speech, "Our Native Writers," called for the establishment of a national literature.

He studied abroad for three years in France, Spain, Italy, and Germany, after which time he assumed the position of Chair of Modern Languages at Bowdoin. In 1831 he married Mary Storer Potter, who died in 1835—the year that Longfellow was appointed Smith Professor of Modern Languages at Harvard. He became famous as a poet with the publication of "A Psalm of Life" in 1838. His first collection, *Voices of the Night*, appeared in 1839 and was followed by *Ballads and Other Poems* (1841) and *Poems of Slavery* (1842). In 1843 he married Fanny Appleton, with whom he had six children. In 1945 he published two new collections, *Poems* and *The Belfry of Bruges and Other Poems*, and an anthology, *The Poets and Poetry of Europe*, which contained work from ten languages, much of it translated by Longfellow himself. His long narrative poems *Evangeline* (1847) and *The Song of Hiawatha* (1855), whose meter was derived from the Finnish epic *The Kalevala*, proved to be immensely popular. Longfellow retired from Harvard in 1854 to devote himself full time to writing. His later collections include *Tales of a Wayside Inn* (1863), which contains "Paul Revere's Ride" and is loosely modeled on Chaucer's *Canterbury Tales; Flower-de-Luce* (1867), *Three Books of Song* (1872), *Aftermath* (1873), *The Hanging of the Crane* (1874), *The Masque of Pandora and Other Poems* (1875), *Kéramos and Other Poems* (1878), *Ultima Thule* (1880), and *In the Harbor* (1882). He also translated Dante's *Divine Comedy* in 1865–1867. He became partially blind in 1843 and was badly injured when in 1861 he tried, futilely, to prevent his second wife from burning to death. This latter tragedy occasioned his famous sonnet "The Cross of Snow," published posthumously in 1886. Longfellow was a master of modern languages and of poetic rhythms and forms. Although his reputation went into decline in the twentieth century when critics promoted the more experimental work of Whitman and Dickinson, he was by far the most popular American poet of the nineteenth century. A more balanced appraisal of his achievement is only now becoming possible.

ROBERT LOWELL (1917–1977) was born in Boston to a distinguished family. He was related to two earlier American poets: James Russell Lowell and Amy Lowell. He was educated at Harvard and Kenyon College, where he studied with John Crowe Ransom and Allen Tate and befriended Randall Jarrell and the fiction writer Peter Taylor. After graduation, he taught at Louisiana State University, where his colleagues included Robert Penn Warren and Cleanth Brooks. From 1943 to 1944 he was imprisoned as a conscientious objector to World War II. His first major work, *Lord Weary's Castle*, won the Pulitzer Prize in 1947. He turned away from the more oblique and formal style of his early work with *Life Studies* (1959), which won the National Book Award and which helped to establish the so-called confessional school of modern poetry. Lowell championed civil rights and antiwar causes in the sixties, and the poetry of his next collections, *For the Union Dead* (1964), *Near the Ocean* (1967), and *Notebook 1967–68* (1969), reflects these political concerns. His later work includes *The Dolphin* (1973), which won him a second Pulitzer Prize, and *Day by Day* (1977). Lowell also produced loose translations and dramatic adaptations of short stories by Hawthorne and Melville. He held teaching positions at Harvard, Oxford, and Essex. He was married three times to other writers, including the novelist Jean Stafford, his first wife.

ARCHIBALD MACLEISH (1892–1982) was born in Glencoe, Illinois and educated at Yale and Harvard Law School, where he graduated at the top of his class. He also served in World War I and was promoted to the rank of captain. He published his first collection of poetry, *Tower of Ivory*, in 1917. He practiced law in Boston for two years, but moved to France in 1923 to devote himself full time to writing. Subsequent books of poetry include *The Happy Marriage* (1924), *The Pot of Earth* (1925), and *Streets in the Moon* (1926). His early work owes much to the example of T. S. Eliot, Ezra Pound, and the imagist movement. MacLeish returned to America in 1928 and published *New Found Land* (1930), which includes the famous poem "You, Andrew Marvell," and *Conquistador* (1932), a long poem about Mexico that won the Pulitzer Prize. He worked as an editor for *Fortune* from 1929 to 1938, as Librarian of Congress from 1939 to 1944, as Assistant Secretary of State from 1944 to 1945, and as Boylston Professor of Rhetoric and Oratory at Harvard from 1949 to 1962. His concern for liberal democracy is reflected in much of his later work. MacLeish also helped secure the release of Ezra Pound from St. Elizabeth's mental hospital. He published many later collections of poetry and verse drama, winning further Pulitzer Prizes for his *Collected Poems* (1952) and for his modernized version of the book of Job, *J. B.* (1958).

CHARLES MARTIN (1942–) was born in New York City and educated at Fordham University and the State University of New York at Buffalo, where he earned a Ph.D. He taught at Notre Dame College of Staten Island and currently teaches both at Queensborough Community College and in writing seminars at John Hopkins University. His volumes of poetry include *Room for Error* (1978), *Passages from Friday* (1983), and *Steal the Bacon* (1987).

EDGAR LEE MASTERS (1869–1950) was born in Garnett, Kansas and raised in Petersburg and Lewistown, Illinois, near the Spoon River. He practiced law in Chicago from 1891 to 1920 and was a partner of Clarence Darrow from 1903 to 1911. He married Helen Jenkins in 1898, the same year he published his first volume of poetry, *A Book of Verses*. By far his most famous volume is *Spoon River Anthology* (1915), a collection of 245 free-verse dramatic monologues spoken from beyond the grave. His later collections, including *Songs and Satires* (1916), *Toward the Gulf* (1918), and *Domesday Book* (1920), never recaptured the popular and critical success of *Spoon River Anthology*. Masters was divorced from Jenkins in 1923 and married Ellen Coyne in 1926. In addition to his many volumes of poetry, he also wrote novels, plays, an autobiography, and biographies of Lincoln, Whitman, and Twain.

THOMAS MCGRATH (1916–1990) was born near Sheldon, North Dakota and educated at the University of North Dakota, Louisiana State University, New College, and, as a Rhodes Scholar, Oxford. He served in the U.S. Air Force during World War II, after which time he became active in the Communist Party in Los Angeles. In 1953 he was summoned before the House Un-American Activities Committee and refused to answer questions, which led to his being fired from Los Angeles State College and blacklisted. He supported himself through various types of work, including screenwriting, until he finally secured another academic position—at the C. W. Post Campus of Long Island University—in 1960. He taught subsequently at North Dakota State University and at Moorehead State University in Minnesota. Parts one and two of his book-length poem *Letters to an Imaginary Friend* appeared in 1962, part three in 1985; the poem in its entirety was published posthumously in 1997. His *Selected Poems* were also published posthumously in 1998.

CLAUDE MCKAY (1890–1948) was born in Jamaica, the youngest in a family of eleven children. He was apprenticed as a cabinetmaker and a wheelwright, but his life changed when he met the English linguist Edward Jekyll, who encouraged him to write poetry. McKay published two volumes, *Songs of Jamaica* and *Constab Ballads*, in Jamaican dialect in 1912, the same year that he immigrated to the United States. He attended Tuskegee Institute in Alabama and Kansas State Teachers College before moving to Harlem in 1914. He supported himself at odd jobs and published a volume of poems under the pseudonym Eli Edwards, titled *Seven Arts* in 1917. His most important collection, *Harlem Shadows* (1922), helped to initiate the Harlem Renaissance. McKay, like Countee Cullen, wrote in meter, employing the sonnet form for some of his most significant statements, including the rousing "If We Should Die" (which Winston Churchill recited during a speech against the Nazis during World War II) and the more subdued and artful "Harlem Dancer." McKay lived abroad in the Soviet Union, France, Spain, and Morocco between 1922 and 1934. He published novels, short stories, a sociological study of Harlem, and an autobiography. His health deteriorated in the 1940s. He converted to Catholicism in 1944 and worked for the Catholic Youth Organization in Chicago.

HERMAN MELVILLE (1819–1891) was born and raised in New York City. He sailed for the South Seas in 1841 aboard the *Achushnet*, a whaling vessel, but jumped ship in the Marquesas Islands, where he lived for a time among cannibals. He escaped to Tahiti, was involved in a ship mutiny, and later served aboard the frigate *United States*. His popular early fiction, *Typee* (1846) and *Omoo* (1847), is based on his South Seas adventures. Melville married Elizabeth Shaw, daughter of Massachusetts Chief Justice Lemuel Shaw, in 1847. They had four children. Melville's more ambitious and allegorical third novel, *Mardi* (1849), failed commercially. He wrote two further novels, *Redburn* (1849) and *White-Jacket* (1850), in rapid succession to support his family. In 1850 he moved to the farmhouse Arrowhead near Pittsfield, Massachusetts, wrote a famous review of Nathaniel Hawthorne's work, "Hawthorne and His Mosses," and befriended Hawthorne, writing him some of the liveliest and most revealing letters in American literary history. Melville's masterpiece *Moby-Dick*, deeply influenced by both Hawthorne and Melville's reading of Shakespeare, appeared in 1851 but was not a success. After the commercial and critical failure of three more novels, *Pierre* (1852), *Israel Potter* (1855), and *The Confidence-Man* (1857), and a brilliant collection of short stores, *The Piazza Tales* (1856), Melville fell into a depression and retired from full-time writing at the age of thirty-seven. From 1857 to 1860 he lectured on travels to Italy and the South Seas, but without success. In 1863 he returned with his family to New York City, where he was eventually appointed deputy inspector of customs. Only at this point did he turn his hand to poetry, producing the classic collection of Civil War poems *Battle-Pieces and Aspects of the War* in 1866. A long poem, *Clarel*, based on his trip to the Holy Land in 1856–1857, followed a decade later. Two further volumes of poetry, both quite short, appeared in his final years, *John Marr and Other Sailors* (1888) and *Timoleon* (1891). His famous short novel *Billy Budd, Sailor*, begun as a headnote to the poem "Billy among the Darbies," was discovered among his papers and published posthumously in 1924, facilitating the spectacular reevaluation of Melville's reputation that placed him securely in the forefront of American literature. His dense, awkward, cerebral poetry has been overshadowed by his prose, but has increasingly come to be valued in its own right.

WILLIAM MEREDITH (1919–) was born in New York City and educated at Princeton. He worked as a reporter for the *New York Times* and served in the U.S. Navy in World War II, during which time he wrote much of his first volume of poems, *Love Letter from an Impossible Land* (1944). After the war, he taught at Princeton, the University of Hawaii, and Connecticut College. His later collections include *Ships and Other Figures* (1948), *The Open Sea and Other Poems* (1958), *The Wreck of the Thresher* (1963), *Hazard, the Painter* (1975), *The Cheer* (1980), and *Effort at Speech: New and Selected Poems* (1997), which won the National Book Award. His work, which was influenced by Frost and W. H. Auden, is noted for its formal grace and concern with civilized values. He has also published a libretto, opera criticism, and translations of the French poet Guillaume Apollinaire. In 1983 a stroke left Meredith with partial aphasia (which explains the title of his most recent collection), but he has continued to write poems.

JAMES MERRILL (1926–1995) was born in New York City, the son of Charles Merrill, a founding partner of the investment firm Merrill Lynch. He attended Amherst, where he wrote a thesis on the work of Marcel Proust, whose concern with memory deeply influenced Merrill's poetry. Other important literary influences on Merrill's work include Henry James, William Butler Yeats, Wallace Stevens, and W. H. Auden, whose metrical virtuosity Merrill emulated. Merrill served for a year in the U.S. Army during World War II. In 1954 he settled in Stonington, Connecticut, and subsequently spent much time in both Florida and Greece, traveling with his lifelong partner David Jackson. His volumes of poetry include *Jim's Book* (1942), *The Black Swan* (1946), *First Poems* (1951), *Short Stories* (1954), *The Country of a Thousand Years of Peace* (1959, revised 1970), *Water Street* (1962), *Nights and Days* (1966), *The Fire Screen* (1969), *Braving the Elements* (1972), *The Yellow Pages* (1974), *Late Settings* (1985), *The Inner Room* (1988), and *A Scattering of Salts* (1995). His major work is a trilogy, based on extensive use of a Ouija board, consisting of "The Book of Ephraim" from *Divine Comedies* (1976), *Mirabell: Book of Numbers* (1978), and *Scripts for the Pageant* (1980). The three parts were collected together along with a coda, "The Higher Keys," as *The Changing Light at Sandover* (1986). His work won two National Book Awards and a Pulitzer Prize. Merrill's detractors resent his leisured life and precious, esoteric style, and scoff at the notion of a great epic based on a Ouija board; his admirers, on the other hand, value him as a formal master and a visionary poet in the tradition of Dante and William Blake.

W[ILLIAM]. S[TANLEY]. MERWIN (1927–) was born in New York City and raised in Union City, New Jersey, and Scranton, Pennsylvania. He graduated from Princeton, where he studied with John Berryman and R. P. Blackmur. He traveled abroad before returning to America to work as poetry editor of the *Nation* from 1951 to 1953. Since then, he has lived in Mexico and France and currently lives in Hawaii. His early poetry, collected in *A Mask for Janus* (1952), *Green with Beasts* (1956), and *The Drunk in the Furnace* (1960), is formal in style and impersonally draws upon mythical and archetypal subject matter. Starting with *The Moving Target* (1963) and *The Lice* (1967), Merwin began employing a freer, more surrealist and autobiographical style. Merwin won the Pulitzer Prize for *The Carrier of Ladders* (1970). His later work includes *The Compass Flower* (1977), *Finding the Islands* (1982), *The Rain in the Trees* (1988), *Travels* (1993), and *The Vixen* (1995). Merwin possesses extensive knowledge of foreign languages and has translated poetry from Greek, Latin, Sanskrit, French, Spanish, Portuguese, Chinese, and Japanese.

EDNA ST. VINCENT MILLAY (1892–1950) was born in Rockland, Maine. She first received acclaim as a poet when "Renascence" was published in *The Lyric Year* in 1912. After graduating from Vassar in 1917, she moved to Greenwich Village, where she and her poetry came to symbolize the rebellious, sexually liberated "flaming youth" of the 1920s. Her early collections include *Renascence and Other Poems* (1917), *A Few Figs from Thistles* (1920), *Second April* (1921), and *The Ballad of the Harp Weaver* (1922), which won the Pulitzer Prize. She became friends with the influential critic Edmund Wilson, married Eugene Boissevain in 1923, and was awarded an honorary doctorate from Tufts in 1925. She also became involved in various political causes, including protests against the execution of anarchists Sacco and Vanzetti in 1927, which later became the subject of a number of her poems. In addition to her poetry, Millay published plays and wrote the libretto to Deems Taylor's opera *The King's Henchman* (1927). Her later poetry collections include *The Buck in the Snow* (1928), the sonnet cycle *Fatal Interview* (1931), *Wines from These Grapes* (1934), *Conversation at Midnight* (1937), *Huntsman, What Quarry?* (1939), *Make Bright the Arrows* (1940), and *The Murder of Lidice* (1942). She translated Baudelaire's *Flowers of Evil* with George Dillon in 1936 and her *Collected Poems* appeared posthumously in 1956. Addicted to both drugs and alcohol and recently widowed, she died when she broke her neck in a fall down a dark flight of stairs. Millay worked frequently in the sonnet form, employed traditional poetic diction, and was her generation's most celebrated poet of love—a subject she treated at times passionately and at other times satirically.

CLEMENT MOORE (1779–1863) was born in New York City and educated at Columbia. He taught biblical studies as well as Greek and Oriental literatures at the General Theological Seminary. He was a serious student of Hebrew and published a two-volume *Compendious Lexicon of the Hebrew Language* in 1809. As a poet, he is remembered for his beloved "A Visit from St. Nicholas," which he wrote in 1822 for his family. Unknown to Moore, a houseguest copied the poem down and had it published anonymously in the *Troy Sentinel* in 1823. Not until 1837 was Moore's authorship publicly revealed. Moore published the poem, along with others, in his *Poems* of 1844.

MARIANNE MOORE (1887–1972) was born in Kirkwood, Missouri, and educated at Bryn Mawr College and Carlisle Commercial College. In 1919 she moved to New York City, where she devoted herself to writing poetry and criticism while working as a teacher, secretary, and librarian. Her first volume, *Poems*, was published in England in 1921 without her knowledge by Hilda Doolittle and Bryher, both of whom she had befriended at Bryn Mawr. It was followed in 1924 by *Observations*, which includes some of Moore's best-known works, such as "Poetry" and "The Fish." From 1925 to 1929 she edited the influential literary journal *The Dial*. Her later volumes include *The Pangolin and Other Verse* (1936), *What Are Years* (1941), and *Nevertheless* (1944). She also translated the fables of La Fontaine. Moore's *Collected Poems* (1951) won the National Book Award, Pulitzer Prize, and Bollinger Prize. She revised her earlier work, sometimes drastically, for her *Complete Poems* of 1967, but many readers prefer the original versions. Her work is noted for acute observation, wit, ornate language, and baroque stanzaic forms determined by a syllabic prosody.

HOWARD NEMEROV (1920–1991) was born and raised in New York City and educated at Harvard. He served in both the Royal Canadian Air Force and the United States Air Force during World War II. After the war, he taught at Hamilton College, Bennington, Brandeis, and Washington University in St. Louis. His first book, *The Image and the Law* (1947), featured a witty, ironic, erudite style influenced by T. S. Eliot, W. H. Auden, and seventeenth-century metaphysical poetry. His later work, which includes *The Salt Garden*

(1955), *Mirrors and Windows* (1958), *The Blue Swallows* (1967), *Gnomes and Occasions* (1973), and *The Western Approaches* (1975), tended to be looser in texture and more accessible, while retaining its formal style and satirical edge. His *Collected Poems* (1977) won the Pulitzer Prize and the National Book Award. Nemerov's final collections include *Sentences* (1980) and *War Stories* (1987). He was appointed the third poet laureate of the United States in 1988. Nemerov also produced novels, short stories, and critical essays.

FRANK O'HARA (1926–1966) was born in Baltimore and raised in Grafton, Massachusetts. During World War II, he served in the navy in the South Pacific. He was educated at Harvard and the University of Michigan and settled in New York City in 1951, where he became deeply involved in the avant-garde art world. He worked as editor and critic for *Art News* and as a curator for the Museum of Modern Art. O'Hara met and promoted the work of such abstract expressionist painters as Willem de Kooning, Franz Kline, and Jackson Pollack. His own style in poetry—casual and associative, campy and full of references to popular culture—is modeled to some degree on the spontaneous work of these artists. His collections include *A City Winter and Other Poems* (1952), *Meditations in an Emergency* (1957), *Odes* (1960), *Lunch Poems* (1964), and *Love Poems* (1965). O'Hara became a central figure of the so-called New York school of poets, which included John Ashbery and Kenneth Koch. He was killed when a beach buggy struck him at night on Fire Island. His *Collected Poems*, including many poems not published previously, appeared posthumously in 1971.

MARY OLIVER (1935–) was born in Maple Heights, Ohio and educated at both Ohio State University and Vassar College. She has taught at Sweet Briar College in Virginia, Duke, and Bennington. Her collections include *No Voyage and Other Poems* (1963), *Sleeping in the Forest* (1978), *The Night Traveler* (1978), *Twelve Moons* (1979), *American Primitive* (1983), which won the Pulitzer Prize, *Dream Work* (1986), *House of Light* (1990), and *West Wind* (1997). Her *New and Selected Poems* of 1992 won the National Book Award. Oliver's poetry is rooted in her observations of and response to the natural world, and shares certain traits with the work of Frost, Roethke, and James Wright. She has also published crticial essays, along with *A Poetry Handbook* (1994) and *Rules for the Dance: A Handbook for Writing and Reading Metrical Verse* (1998).

SIMON J. ORTIZ (1941–) was born and raised in the Acoma Pueblo Community in Albuquerque, New Mexico. He attended a Bureau of

Indian Affairs school, where he was punished for speaking his native language, Keresan. He enrolled at Fort Lewis College, but then served in the U.S. Army from 1962 to 1965. He resumed his higher education at the University of New Mexico and the University of Iowa, where he received an M.F.A. He has taught at San Diego State University and the University of New Mexico. His collections of poetry include *Going for Rain* (1976), *The Good Journey* (1977), *From Sand Creek* (1982), *Woven* (1992), and *After and Before the Lightning* (1994). His work laments the contemporary environmental crisis and focuses on other issues relevant to contemporary Native American life. Ortiz has also published fiction and essays.

SYLVIA PLATH (1932–1963) was born in Boston and educated at Smith College and Newham College, Cambridge, where she met her husband, the English poet Ted Hughes. Plath suffered a breakdown, attempted to commit suicide, and was hospitalized for six months in 1953. She drew upon these events for her popular novel *The Bell Jar* (1963). In 1958 she attended Robert Lowell's poetry seminar at Boston University, where she met fellow poet Anne Sexton. Plath, along with Lowell, Sexton, John Berryman, and W. D. Snodgrass, would go on to help define the confessional mode of contemporary American poetry. *The Colossus and Other Poems*—the only volume of poetry she published during her lifetime—appeared in England in 1960 and in the United States in 1962. Her marriage broke up in 1962, and Plath furiously wrote her final, macabre poems before committing suicide in February 1963 by turning on the gas in her oven. *Ariel* (1965), *Crossing the Water* (1971), and *The Collected Poems* (1981), which was awarded a Pulitzer Prize, all appeared posthumously.

EDGAR ALLAN POE (1809–1849) was born in Boston and raised in Richmond by foster parents, John and Frances Allan. Poe was not legally adopted, but he added his middle name in honor of the Allans. He studied at the University of Virginia, but incurred gambling debts that John Allan refused to honor. In 1827 he quarreled with Allan and moved to Boston, where he anonymously published his first volume of poetry, *Tamerlane and Other Poems*. He enlisted in the army, giving both a false name and an incorrect age, but was dismissed from West Point in 1831 for neglecting his duty. In the meantime, he had partially reconciled with Allan and published a second volume, *Al Aaraaf, Tamerlane, and Minor Poems* (1829). He published another volume, *Poems*, in New York City in 1831 and then settled in Baltimore, where he began publishing essays, reviews, and short stories. In 1836 he married his thirteen-year-old cousin, Virginia. He moved to New York in 1837, then to Philadelphia in 1838, where he worked as editor for *Burton's Gentleman's Magazine* and *Graham's Magazine*. His first collection of short stories, *Tales of the Grotesque and Arabesque*, appeared in 1840. He moved back to New York in 1844, where he worked on the staff of the *Evening Mirror*, in which he published the poem that made him famous, "The Raven." In 1845 the collection *The Raven and Other Poems* appeared. Virginia died of tuberculosis in 1847, and Poe, whose drinking problem had become chronic, returned to Richmond, where he wrote "Annabel Lee" and became engaged to his widowed childhood sweetheart, Elmira Shelton. He stopped in Baltimore on the way back to New York and died near a polling place after breaking his temperance pledge. Poe, who believed poetry should be more concerned with beauty than with truth, experimented with complex stanzaic forms and exerted a great deal of influence on the French symbolists and the English Pre-Raphaelites. His reputation as a poet has typically been greater abroad than at home.

EZRA POUND (1885–1972) was born in Hailey, Idaho and educated at Hamilton College and the University of Pennsylvania, where he studied Romance languages and befriended William Carlos Williams. He taught at Wabash College, Indiana, in 1907, but was fired for allowing a stranded actress to spend the night in his room. He was briefly engaged to the poet Hilda Doolittle, whom he later gave the *nom de plume*, H. D., Imagist. In 1908 he sailed for Venice, where he published at his own expense his first volume of poems, *A Lume Spento*. In September of that year he moved to London, where he renewed his acquaintance with W. B. Yeats (whom he had first met in 1903) and also came to know Ford Madox Ford, James Joyce, Wyndham Lewis, and T. E. Hulme, with whom he helped found the influential imagist movement. Pound's other early collections, which became more experimental and which synthesize disparate influences ranging from Robert Browning to the troubadours to Confucius to Japanese haiku, include *Personae* (1909), *Ripostes* (1912), *Cathay* (1915), and *Lustra* (1916). During these busy years, he married Dorothy Shakespear (1914), edited the anthology *Des Imagistes* (1914), founded with Lewis the journal *Blast* (1914–1915), adapted Japanese Noh plays, published a memoir about the sculptor Henri Gaudier-Brzeska, a friend who was killed in World War I, and helped promote the literary careers of Joyce, Robert Frost, and T. S. Eliot. In 1916 he published the first three "Cantos," the first installment of his long "poem including history" that he had conceived back in 1904 and that would become his major life's work. After World War I, he published two important mid-length poems,

"Homage to Sextus Propertius" (1919) and "Hugh Selwyn Mauberley" (1920), which expressed his disillusionment over the decay of Western civilization. He assisted crucially in the two great modernist works of 1922 by collecting subscriptions for Joyce's *Ulysses* and by editing the manuscript of Eliot's *The Waste Land*. In 1925 he had a daughter with the American violinst Olga Rudge, and the following year he had a son with his wife. Pound published *A Draft of XVI Cantos* in 1925, added eleven more cantos in 1928, and brought the total to thirty in 1930. He also published the influential prose works *ABC of Reading* (1934) and *Guide to Kulcher* (1938). In 1933 he met Mussolini, whose cause he championed in a series of anti-Semitic and anti-American radio broadcasts during World War II. He was captured by the allies in 1945 and held for six months in a prison camp near Pisa. Declared unfit to stand trial for treason, he was confined to St. Elizabeth's mental hospital in Washington, D.C., where he wrote his Bollingen Prize–winning sequence *Pisan Cantos* (1948). During his time at St. Elizabeth's, he received visits from many of the most distinguished modern American poets, including Eliot, Cummings, Moore, Bishop, and Hughes; finally, in 1958, largely through the efforts of Archibald MacLeish, he was released. He returned to Italy, where he continued to work on his *Cantos*, and died in Venice. His role in the development of modernist poetry was decisive, and he more than anyone made English poetry receptive to non-Western influences.

JOHN CROWE RANSOM (1888–1974) was born in Pulaski, Tennessee. He was admitted to Vanderbilt University at the age of fifteen and eventually graduated at the top of his class. Later, he studied as a Rhodes Scholar at Oxford. He taught at Vanderbilt from 1914 to 1937, interrupted by two years of service in World War I. Ransom became a leading figure in the conservative, agrarian "fugitive" movement and established himself as the leading modern southern poet with the collections *Poems about God* (1919), *Chills and Fever* (1924), *Grace after Meat* (1924), and *Two Gentlemen in Bonds* (1927). His poetry, conceived in a kind of neo-metaphysical style, is notable for its irony, wit, and surprising diction. From 1937 to his retirement in 1958, Ransom taught at Kenyon College, where he founded and edited the *Kenyon Review*. In his later years, he turned increasingly from poetry to criticism. His collection of essays *The New Criticism* (1941), an appraisal of the critical work of T. S. Eliot, I. A. Richards, Yvor Winters, and William Empson, inadvertently (and misleadingly) gave a name to the most significant twentieth-century Anglo-American school of literary criticism. Ransom received the National Book Award for his *Selected Poems* (1963).

ADRIENNE RICH (1929–) was born in Baltimore, Maryland and educated at Radcliffe College. Before she graduated, her poetry was selected by W. H. Auden for publication in the Yale Younger Poets series, resulting in her first collection, *A Change of World* (1951). Her second volume, *The Diamond Cutters*, appeared in 1955. Rich increasingly turned away from her early formal work, embracing free verse and frankly exploring feminist and political themes. Her later volumes include *Snapshots of a Daughter-in-Law* (1963), *Necessities of Life* (1966), *Leaflets* (1969), *Diving into the Wreck* (1973), *The Dream of a Common Language* (1978), *A Wild Patience Has Taken Me This Far* (1981), and *An Atlas of the Difficult World* (1991). Rich married the Harvard economist Alfred Conrad in 1953 and had three sons with him. The marriage ended in 1970, and Conrad committed suicide the same year. In 1976 Rich entered into a relationship with Michelle Cliff, with whom she edited the lesbian-feminist journal *Sinister Wisdom*. Rich has taught at Douglass College and Stanford. She has also published numerous collections of prose on feminist themes.

EDWIN ARLINGTON ROBINSON (1869–1935) was born in Head Tide, Maine, and raised in Gardiner, Maine—the model for the Tilbury Town that serves as the setting of many of his poems. He attended Harvard, but his educational career was cut short by the setbacks his family suffered as a result of the 1893 financial crisis. In 1896, Robinson moved to New York City, where he worked as a subway-construction inspector and published his first volume of poems, *The Torrent and the Night Before*. The following year, he revised and expanded the collection, reissuing it as *The Children of the Night*. His third book, *Captain Craig* (1902), caught the attention of President Theodore Roosevelt, who secured Robinson a sinecure at the U.S. Customs House in New York. Robinson held the position until the success of his 1910 collection—*The Town Down the River*, which includes "Miniver Cheevy" and "For a Dead Lady"—gave him some measure of economic independence. Robinson reached the pinnacle of his career in his next four collections: *The Man against the Sky* (1916), which includes "Eros Turannos" and "Bewick Finzer"; *The Three Taverns* (1920), which includes "The Mill"; *Avon's Harvest* (1921), which includes "Mr. Flood's Party"; and *Dionysius in Doubt* (1925), which includes many of his finest sonnets, such as "The Sheaves" and "New England." At his best, Robinson employed a strict formal mastery to dramatize penetrating studies of shattered lives. He also published numerous highly uneven longer poems, most notably his Arthurian trilogy: *Merlin* (1917), *Lancelot* (1920), and *Tristram* (1927). He was influenced by the individualism of Emerson, the character studies of Hawthorne and Henry James, and the tragic vision of Thomas Hardy. Its quality belatedly recognized, Robinson's work was eventually awarded three Pulitzer Prizes.

THEODORE ROETHKE (1908–1963) was born in Saginaw, Michigan, where his father, grandfather, and uncle operated the greenhouses that would become notable images in Roethke's poetry. Roethke was educated at the University of Michigan and, briefly, at Harvard, where he studied with the famous critic I. A. Richards. He taught at Layfayette College in Pennsylvania and then at Michigan State, where he suffered the first of several mental breakdowns that plagued him throughout his adult life. He taught at Penn State from 1936 to 1943, during which time he published his first collection of poems, *Open House* (1941). After a brief stint at Bennington, Roethke taught at the University of Washington from 1947 to the time of his death. He was noted as an inspiring teacher, and his students included the poets Richard Hugo, Carolyn Kizer, and James Wright. Roethke's subsequent volumes of poetry include *The Lost Son* (1948), in which despite an obvious debt to Yeats and Eliot he first arrived at his distinctively ecstatic personal style, *Praise to the End!* (1951), *The Waking* (1953), which was awarded the Pulitzer Prize, and *Words for the Wind* (1958), which won both the National Book Award and the Bollingen Prize. Roethke's final collection, *The Far Field* (1964), which includes the celebrated metaphysical lyric "In a Dark Time," was published posthumously and received the National Book Award.

CARL SANDBURG (1878–1967) was born in Galesburg, Illinois, the son of Swedish immigrants. In 1897 he traveled across America by jumping trains and worked various odd jobs to support himself. He served in the Spanish-American War in 1898, briefly enrolled at Lombard College in Illinois, and worked for the Social Democratic Party of Wisconsin from 1907 to 1912. He married an active socialist, Paula Steichen and had two daughters. The family moved to Chicago in 1912, where Sandburg became acquainted with such literary figures as Theodore Dreiser, Vachel Lindsay, and Edgar Lee Masters. The first volume of Sandburg's extremely popular free verse, *Chicago Poems*, appeared in 1915, and was followed by *Corn Huskers* (1918), *Smoke and Steel* (1920), *Slabs of the Sunburnt West* (1922), *Good Morning, America* (1928), and *The People, Yes* (1936). His *Complete Poems* (1950) was awarded the Pulitzer Prize. Sandburg also wrote a six-volume biography of Abraham Lincoln, a biography of his brother-in-law, the famous photographer Edward Steichen, an autobiography, and children's books. He also compiled two collections of folk songs, *The American Songbag* (1927) and *New American Songbag*

(1950). A radical populist, Sandburg believed in "Simple poems for simple people."

GEORGE SANTAYANA (1863–1952) was born in Madrid, Spain. He did not begin to learn English until he joined his mother in Boston in 1872. He graduated from Harvard, having co-edited the *Harvard Lampoon* (with Ernest Lawrence Thayer and others), studied at the University of Berlin; and then returned to Harvard and completed a Ph.D. in philosophy. He joined the Harvard philosophy faculty, where his colleagues included William James and Josiah Royce and his students included T. S. Eliot and Wallace Stevens. Santayana never relinquished his Spanish citizenship. He left Harvard in 1912 and lived the rest of his life in Europe, principally in Rome. Although best known as a philosopher, he contributed not only to many branches of philosophy, but also to the major literary genres. His most significant works include *The Sense of Beauty* (1896), a treatise on aesthetics; *The Life of Reason* (1905–1906), a five-volume exposition of materialist philosophy; *The Last Puritan* (1935), a best-selling novel that analyzes the lingering influence of Calvinism; and *Persons and Places* (1944–1953), a three-volume autobiography. He also published several early collections of verse, including *Sonnets and Other Verses* (1894) and *The Hermit of Carmel* (1901); a verse play, *Lucifer: A Theological Tragedy* (1899); as well as literary and social criticism, notably *Interpretations of Poetry and Religion* (1900), *Three Philosophical Poets: Lucretius, Dante, and Goethe* (1910), *Philosophical Opinion in America* (1918), *Character and Opinion in the United States* (1920), and *The Genteel Tradition at Bay* (1931).

DELMORE SCHWARTZ (1913–1966) was born in Brooklyn, educated at the University of Wisconsin and New York University, and pursued graduate work at Harvard. He later taught at Harvard and other schools. His first book, *In Dreams Begin Responsibilities* (1939), which included poetry, drama, and fiction, made him famous, although his reputation as a writer subsequently declined. His later works include the verse play *Shenandoah* (1941), the book-length poem *Genesis, Book I* (1943), and short stories. He also translated Rimbaud's *A Season in Hell*. Schwartz served as literary editor of the *Partisan Review* from 1943 to 1955 and of the *New Republic* from 1955 to 1957. His *New and Selected Poems, 1938–1958* appeared in 1959. Brilliant but mentally unstable, Schwartz served as the model for the title character in Saul Bellow's novel *Humboldt's Gift* (1975).

LOUIS SIMPSON (1923–) was born in Jamaica and came to the United States in 1940. He attended Columbia for three years before leaving to serve in the U.S. Army during World War II. After the war, he returned to Columbia, finished his Ph.D., and subsequently taught at Columbia, Berkeley, and the State University of New York at Stony Brook. His early books, *The Arrivistes* (1949) and *Good News of Death and Other Poems* (1955), were written in a formal style. He turned to free verse based on speech rhythms, wherein content determines form, with *A Dream of Governors* (1959) and *At the End of the Open Road* (1963). His later work includes *Adventures of the Letter I* (1971), *Searching for the Ox* (1976), *Caviare at the Funeral* (1980), *The Best Hour of the Night* (1983), *In the Room We Share* (1990), and *There You Are* (1994). He has also written criticism and a biography, *North of Jamaica* (1972).

W[ILLIAM]. D[EWITT]. **SNODGRASS** (1926–) was born in Wilkinsburg, Pennsylvania and began undergraduate studies at Geneva College before serving in the Pacific in the U.S. Navy during World War II. After the war, he studied at the University of Iowa, where he attended Robert Lowell's workshops. Snodgrass has taught at Cornell, the University of Rochester, Wayne State, Syracuse, Old Dominion, and the University of Delaware. His first and most famous volume, *Heart's Needle* (1959), won the Pulitzer Prize and helped, along with Lowell's *Life Studies*, to establish the confessional school of poetry; but unlike the wilder verse of Lowell, Plath, and Anne Sexton, which often took violence and madness as its subject matter, Snodgrass typically wrote low-key formal verse that focuses on the neuroses of an ordinary man. Among his later works are *After Experience* (1968), which includes translations of Rilke; *Remains* (1970), originally published under the pseudonym S. S. Gardons; *If Birds Build with Your Hair* (1979); and *The Death of Cock Robin* (1989). His most ambitious later work is *The Führer Bunker* (1995), a series of dramatic monologues spoken by leaders of the Nazi regime.

CATHY SONG (1955–) was born and raised in Hawaii, the daughter of a Korean-American father and a Chinese-American mother. She was educated at the University of Hawaii, Wellesley College, and Boston University, where she received an M.A. in creative writing. She has taught creative writing at a number of mainland colleges and universities, although she resides permanently in Hawaii. Her first collection of poems, *Picture Bride* (1983), was chosen by Richard Hugo for the Yale Younger Poets series. The clarity, beauty, and visual quality of her writing recalls the poetry of Elizabeth Bishop but also bears an important relation to the work of both the Japanese printmaker Kitagawa Utamaro and the American painter Georgia

O'Keeffe. Song's later collections include *Frameless Windows, Squares of Light* (1988) and *School Figures* (1994).

WILLIAM STAFFORD (1914–1993) was born and raised in Hutchinson, Kansas and educated at the University of Kansas and the University of Iowa, where he earned a Ph.D. He was a conscientious objector to World War II and later joined the pacifist Fellowship of Reconciliation. He taught at Manchester College, San Jose State College, and for many years at Lewis and Clark College in Oregon. He emerged late as a poet, publishing his first two volumes, *West of Your City* and *Traveling through the Dark* in 1961, roughly two decades after such exact contemporaries as Delmore Schwartz and Randall Jarrell had established their reputations. Stafford's poems deal with everyday life and with the open spaces of the midwestern and western landscape. They are written in a style the poet described as "much like talk, with some enhancement," such as near rhymes. After his late start, Stafford published prolifically, producing over forty volumes of verse and several influential critical works, including *Writing the Australian Crawl: Views of the Writer's Vocation* (1978) and *You Must Revise Your Life* (1986).

TIMOTHY STEELE (1948–) was born in Burlington, Vermont. He received his B.A. from Stanford and his Ph.D. from Brandeis. Currently, he is a professor of English at California State University, Los Angeles. Steele, who has emerged as a leading figure of the new formalist movement, has published three brief, carefully wrought collections of verse, *Uncertainties and Rest* (1979), *Sapphics against Anger and Other Poems* (1986), and *The Color Wheel* (1994), all of which exemplify Yvor Winters's dictum: "Write little; do it well." His first two books were reissued, in slightly revised form, as *Sapphics and Uncertainties* (1995). In addition to being a master of metrical forms, Steele is a formidable scholar and prosodic theorist, as his cogently argued study *Missing Measures: Modern Poetry and the Revolt against Meter* (1990) and his comprehensive handbook *All the Fun's in How You Say a Thing: An Explanation of Meter and Versification* (1999) demonstrate. He has also edited the collected poems of J. V. Cunningham.

WALLACE STEVENS (1879–1955) was born in Reading, Pennsylvania and educated at Harvard. He worked as a journalist before entering New York Law School and being admitted to the bar in New York in 1904. In 1916 he joined the legal staff of Hartford Accident and Indemnity Company, where he remained until his death, eventually becoming the firm's vice president in 1934. Stevens began publishing poems in Harriet Monroe's magazine *Poetry* in 1914, but did not bring out his ample and astounding first collection, *Harmonium*— which initially sold fewer than one hundred copies—until 1923, by which time he was forty-four years old. Stevens's poetry is notable for its dazzling verbal brilliance and humor, its eccentric engagement with traditional forms, its modern revision of romanticism, and its obsessive theme of the mind's relation to material reality. His later work, which tends to grow progressively more difficult, discursive, elliptical, and austere, includes *Ideas of Order* (1935), *The Man with the Blue Guitar and Other Poems* (1937), *Parts of a World* (1942), *Transport to Summer* (1947), and *The Auroras of Autumn* (1950), which won the Bollingen Prize. His *Collected Poems* (1954) belatedly brought him recognition as a major figure; it received both the Pulitzer Prize and the National Book Award. Stevens also won a National Book Award for his collection of critical essays *The Necessary Angel: Essays on Reality and the Imagination* (1951).

TRUMBULL STICKNEY (1874–1904) was born in Geneva, Switzerland, the son of a classics professor. He attended Harvard and worked on the staff of the *Harvard Monthly*, to which he contributed the majority of the poems he published in his brief life. Stickney became the first American to receive a doctorate from the Sorbonne, where he studied Greek and Sanskrit. He produced, in collaboration with Sylvain Lévi, a translation of the Bhagavad Gita (which was not published until 1938). He also left unfinished a translation of Aeschylus's *The Persians*. Stickney had many notable friends, including George Santayana and Henry Adams. In 1904 he was diagnosed with a brain tumor. He went blind, but continued to write to the end of his life. *The Poems of Trumbull Stickney* was posthumously published in 1905.

FREDERICK GODDARD TUCKERMAN (1821–1873) was born to a prosperous family in Boston. He attended Harvard, where he was tutored by the minor religious poet Jones Very. Despite trouble with his eye, Tuckerman eventually graduated from the Law School in 1842. He practiced law for a time, but found it distasteful. His inheritence allowed him to retire in 1847 and to devote his life to his principal intellectual passions: botany, meteorology, astronomy, and poetry. Tuckerman settled in Greenfield, Massachusetts, married Hannah Lucinda Jones, and had three children. He became a noted authority on local fauna and began publishing both astronomical observations and poems. In the early 1850s he twice traveled to England, where he formed a close friendship with Alfred, Lord Tennyson. After his wife died in 1857, he lived in virtual seclusion until the end of his life. In 1860 he sent copies of his privately printed

Poems to leading American literary figures, including Emerson, Hawthorne, Bryant, and Longfellow. One result was an extensive correspondence with Hawthorne; but Tuckerman made virtually no further efforts to publicize his work, his diffidence and indifference to the world's opinion closely resembling that of Emily Dickinson, who lived in nearby Amherst (though of course the two never met). Tuckerman, despite his innovative work in the sonnet form and his trained eye for natural detail, is a neglected figure to this day. He did have several notable champions in the twentieth century, including Witter Bynner, who discovered and published many previously unknown Tuckerman poems, Yvor Winters, who regarded Tuckerman as one of the finest poets of the nineteenth century, and N. Scott Momaday, who published Tuckerman's *Complete Poems* in 1965.

WALT WHITMAN (1819–1892) was born in West Hills, Long Island, New York. He worked as a journeyman printer in Brooklyn and later as a teacher, journalist, editor, and carpenter. His early writings, which include novels, short stories, and formal poems, hardly intimate the radical and immensely influential free verse that Whitman would later write, starting with the first volume of *Leaves of Grass*, published anonymously in 1855. Whitman's conception of free verse was influenced principally by the Bible, Italian opera, and Emerson, to whom Whitman sent a copy of the book. Emerson replied in a famous letter that hails Whitman "at the beginning of a great career" and praises *Leaves of Grass* as "the most extraordinary piece of wit and wisdom that America has yet contributed." Whitman shamelessly promoted his work, which proved controversial in both its unorthodox form and its sexual frankness, by writing laudatory anonymous reviews himself and by making unauthorized use of Emerson's letter. Whitman spent the rest of his life revising and expanding *Leaves of Grass*. The 1860 edition incorporated a cluster of poems on heterosexual love called "Enfans d'Adam" (later changed to "Children of Adam") and another on homosexual love called "Calamus." During the Civil War, Whitman visited wounded soldiers at New-York Hospital, surveyed the front in Virginia, and became a volunteer nurse in military hospitals. He translated his war experience into a series of documentary poems entitled *Drum-Taps* (1865), which was expanded after Lincoln's assassination, and incorporated into *Leaves of Grass* in 1867. Whitman was fired from a post in the Department of the Interior when the secretary of the Interior read *Leaves of Grass* and found it indecent; Whitman subsequently worked as a clerk in the Attorney General's office from 1865 to 1873. He brought out new editions of *Leaves of Grass* in 1870 and 1881. He also brought out two signficiant prose works, *Democratic Vistas* (1871) and *Specimen Days* (1882), and suffered from debilitating strokes in 1873 and 1888. A definitive "deathbed" edition of *Leaves of Grass* was completed in 1891–1892. Whitman's influence on twentieth-century free verse, from Carl Sandburg, Ezra Pound, Robinson Jeffers, and Hart Crane to the Black Mountain School and the beats, was immense.

JOHN GREENLEAF WHITTIER (1807–1892) was born in Haverhill, Massachusetts and raised in a devout Quaker household. He worked as a shoemaker and schoolteacher before turning to editing and journalism. His first literary work, *Legends of New England in Prose and Verse*, appeared in 1831. Encouraged by William Lloyd Garrison, he became an ardent and outspoken abolitionist. In 1834 he was elected for one term to the Massachusetts legislature, but paid for his uncompromising antislavery stance in various ways, most dramatically when he was mobbed and stoned in 1835. In 1840 he founded the Liberty Party and made an unsuccessful bid for a U.S. congressional seat as a Liberty candidate in 1842. A collected volume of his verse appeared in 1849. Whittier's conception of his role as poet was deeply influenced both by the romantic pastoralism of Wordsworth and by Milton's political engagement and devotion to the cause of freedom, but his subject matter was determined by his New England background and by the liberal causes he supported. Whittier's later works include *Songs of Labor* (1850), *Home Ballads* (1860), *In War Time* (1864), *Snow-Bound* (1866), which was his greatest popular success, *Among the Hills* (1869), *Miriam and Other Poems* (1871), *Hazel-Blossoms* (1875), *The Vision of Echard* (1878), and *Saint Gregory's Guest* (1886). His devotion to New England regionalism influenced the short-story writer Sarah Orne Jewett, in whose career Whittier took a keen interest. By the end of his life, Whittier was revered as a great American poet, and his seventieth birthday dinner was attended by Emerson, Longfellow, Holmes, Twain, James Russell Lowell, and William Dean Howells. A seven-volume Riverside Edition of his works appeared in 1888–1889.

RICHARD WILBUR (1921–) was born in New York City and educated at Amherst College, where he first came to know Robert Frost. After graduating from Amherst, he took an M.A. in literature at Harvard. He served as a cryptographer in the army during World War II and began to write formal verse as a way of seeking order in the midst of chaos. After the war, he taught at Harvard, Wellesley, Wesleyan, and Smith. Wilbur's collections of verse include *The Beautiful Changes and Other Poems* (1947), *Ceremony and Other Poems* (1950), *Things of*

This World (1956), which won the Pulitzer Prize and the National Book Award, *Advice to a Prophet and Other Poems* (1961), *Walking to Sleep: New Poems and Translations* (1969), *The Mind-Reader* (1976), *New and Collected Poems* (1988), which won him a second Pulitzer Prize, and *Mayflies: New Poems and Translations* (2000). Wilbur's work is eleganty crafted and has typically become more accessible through the years. He also has written the lyrics to Leonard Bernstein's *Candide* (1957), made brilliant and widely performed translations of the dramas of Molière and Racine, and written children's books and volumes of critical essays. He served as the second poet laureate of the United States in 1987–1988. Many readers regard Wilbur as the finest formal lyric poet in American literature since Frost.

WILLIAM CARLOS WILLIAMS (1883–1963) was born in Rutherford, New Jersey, the son of an English father and a Puerto Rican mother of mixed French Basque and Dutch Jewish ancestry. Williams, who was fascinated by his mixed origins, studied medicine at the University of Pennsylvania, where he met Ezra Pound and Hilda Doolittle. After further medical study in New York and Leipzig, Williams returned to Rutherford and practiced medicine for the rest of his life. His specialty was pediatrics, and he delivered more than two thousand babies in his career. Although he spent most of his time in Rutherford, he met James Joyce and Ernest Hemingway on a trip to Europe in 1924 and Wallace Stevens and Marianne Moore on weekend excursions to New York City. Williams never lost the enthusiasm for poetry that Pound and Doolittle had helped spark. His early work includes *Poems* (1909) and *The Tempers* (1913), which Pound helped him publish; he also contributed to Pound's anthology *Des Imagistes* (1914). His characteristic style, with its short free-verse line and simple diction, emerged with the collection *Spring and All* (1923). Like Hart Crane, he took exception to the pessimism of Eliot's early work, even as he found himself influenced by some of Eliot's techniques. His later work includes the experimental, five-volume poem *Paterson* (1946–58), which won the National Book Award, *The Desert Music* (1954), and *Pictures from Brueghel* (1962), which was awarded a posthumous Pulitzer Prize. Williams also wrote short stories, plays, and essays. He exerted a great deal of influence on later developments in free verse, such as objectivism, the Black Mountain School, and the beats.

YVOR WINTERS (1900–1968) was born in Chicago and raised near Pasadena, California. He attended the University of Chicago, the University of Colorado, and Stanford. Winter contracted tuberculosis and moved to a sanatorium in Santa Fe, New Mexico. He taught at the University of Idaho from 1925 to 1927 and at Stanford from 1928 to 1966. Winters became one of the first significant poets of the American West and was a pioneer in the field of teaching creative writing. He provided assistance to the poet J. V. Cunningham, and his students included Edgar Bowers, Thom Gunn, N. Scott Momaday, and Robert Pinsky. In 1926 he married the poet Janet Lewis. Winters's early work, cast in an imagistic free-verse mode influenced by Pound and Williams, includes *The Immobile Wind* (1921), *The Magpie's Shadow* (1922), and *The Bare Hills* (1927). Starting with *The Proof* (1930) and *The Journey* (1931), Winters, in emulation of the Renaissance and modern poets (such as Thomas Hardy and Robert Bridges) he most admired, turned to a severe metrical style. His *Collected Poems* appeared in 1952, and a revised edition in 1960 won the Bollingen Prize. Winters established a reputation as a rigorous but idiosyncratic critic whose principal concerns were with morality, rationality, and evaluation. His major critical studies, *Primitivism and Decadence* (1937), *Maule's Curse* (1938), and *The Anatomy of Nonsense* (1943), were collected in *In Defense of Reason* (1947). Later critical works include *The Function of Criticism* (1957) and *Forms of Discovery* (1967). He also wrote studies of Robinson (1946), Yeats (1960), and Cunningham (1961). Winters gained a reputation as a maverick critic, dismissing many writers with major reputations and promoting lesser-known figures, such as Fulke Greville, Jones Very, and Frederick Goddard Tuckerman. He also published a novella, *The Brink of Darkness* (1947).

JAMES WRIGHT (1927–1980) was born in Martin's Ferry, Ohio. After high school, he served in the army in Japan, then studied under John Crowe Ransom at Kenyon College and under Theodore Roethke at the University of Washington, where he completed his Ph.D. Wright taught at the University of Minnesota, Macalester College, St. Paul, and Hunter College in New York City from 1966 until his death. His first two volumes, written in a formal style indebted to the work of Edwin Arlington Robinson and Thomas Hardy, are *The Green Wall* (1957), which was featured in the Yale Younger Poets series, and *Saint Judas* (1959). His later volumes, starting with *This Branch Will Not Break* (1963), adopt a free-verse style and surrealist imagery influenced by his reading of Spanish and German poets, but his unadorned language, emphasis on natural imagery, elegiac impulse, understanding of despair and defeat, and compassionate tone remained consistent throughout his career. His later books include *Shall We Gather at the River* (1968), *Two Citizens* (1974), *Moments of the Italian Summer* (1976), *To a Blossoming Pear Tree* (1977), and the posthumously published *This Journey* (1982).

ELINOR WYLIE (1885–1928) was born in Somerville, New Jersey, to a prominent family. She married Philip Hichborn in 1906 and bore him a son. Hichborn was diagnosed with acute mental illness the following year, and Elinor (whose maiden name was Hoyt) eloped to England in 1908 with Horace Wylie. They could not marry, however, as Horace's wife would not grant him a divorce. Hichborn committed suicide in 1912, the year that Elinor's first poetry collection, *Incidental Numbers*, was privately printed. In 1916 Horace and Elinor settled in the United States and were finally married after his divorce became final. Wylie's second and most famous collection, *Nets to Catch the Wind*, appeared in 1921 and established her reputation as an elegant miniaturist. In 1923 she became literary editor of *Vanity Fair*, divorced Horace Wylie and married the poet William Rose Benét, and brought out her third collection, *Black Armour*. Her final collections include *Trivial Breath* (1928) and *Angels and Earthly Creatures* (1929), published posthumously. She also wrote several novels. In 1928 Wylie suffered a stroke that paralyzed one side of her face, and she died shortly thereafter, at the age of forty-three, from a second stroke.

Further Reading

Bloom, Harold. *Figures of Capable Imagination*. New York: Seabury Press, 1976.
———. *The Ringers in the Tower: Studies in Romantic Tradition*. Chicago: University of Chicago Press, 1971.
Bogan, Louise. *Achievement in American Poetry*. Chicago: Henry Regnery Press, 1951.
Breslin, James E. B. *From Modern to Contemporary: American Poetry 1945–1965*. Chicago: University of Chicago Press, 1984.
Donoghue, Denis. *Connoisseurs of Chaos: Ideas of Order in Modern American Poetry*. 2d ed. New York: Columbia University Press, 1984.
Elder, John. *Imagining the Earth: Poetry and the Vision of Nature*, 2d ed. Athens: University of Georgia Press, 1996.
Farr, Judith. *The Passion of Emily Dickinson*. Cambridge: Harvard University Press, 1992.
Fussell, Edwin. *Lucifer in Harness: American Meter, Metaphor, and Diction*. Princeton: Princeton University Press, 1973.
Gelpi, Albert. *A Coherent Splendor: The American Poetic Renaissance, 1910–1950*. Cambridge: Cambridge University Press, 1987.
———. *The Tenth Muse: The Psyche of the American Poet*. Cambridge: Harvard University Press, 1975.
Gioia, Dana. *Can Poetry Matter? Essays on Poetry and American Culture*. Saint Paul: Graywolf Press, 1992.
Kenner, Hugh. *A Homemade World: The American Modernist Writers*. New York: Alfred A. Knopf, 1975.
———. *The Pound Era*. Berkeley: University of California Press, 1971.
Kirby-Smith, H. T. *The Origins of Free Verse*. Ann Arbor: University of Michigan Press, 1996.
Lentricchia, Frank. *Modernist Quartet*. Cambridge: Cambridge University Press, 1994.
Lewis, R. W. B. *The American Adam: Innocence, Tragedy, and Tradition in the Nineteenth-Century*. Chicago: University of Chicago Press, 1955.

Matthiessen, F. O. *American Renaissance: Art and Expression in the Age of Emerson and Whitman*. New York: Oxford University Press, 1941.

Miller, Edwin H. *Walt Whitman's Poetry: A Psychological Journey*. New York: New York University Press, 1968.

Nelson, Cary. *Repression and Recovery: Modern American Poetry and the Politics of Cultural Memory, 1910–1945*. Madison: University of Wisconsin Press, 1989.

Parini, Jay, ed. *The Columbia History of American Poetry*. New York: Columbia University Press, 1993.

Pearce, Harvey. *The Continuity of American Poetry*. Princeton: Princeton University Press, 1961.

Perkins, David. *A History of Modern Poetry: From the 1890s to the High Modernist Mode*. Cambridge: Belknap Press Harvard University, 1976.

———. *A History of Modern Poetry: Modernism and After*. Cambridge: Belknap Press Harvard University, 1987.

Plimpton, George, ed. *Poets at Work: The Paris Review Interviews*. New York: Viking, 1989.

Poirier, Richard. *Robert Frost: The Work of Knowing*. New York: Oxford University Press, 1977.

Schwartz, Sanford. *The Matrix of Modernism: Pound, Eliot, and Early Twentieth-Century Thought*. Princeton: Princeton University Press, 1985.

Shucard, Alan, Fred Moramarco, and William Sullivan. *Modern American Poetry: 1865–1950*. Boston: Twayne Publishers, 1989.

Spiller, Robert E., ed. *Literary History of the United States*, 3d ed. London: Macmillan, 1974.

Steele, Timothy. *Missing Measures: Modern Poetry and the Revolt against Meter*. Fayettesville: University of Arkansas Press, 1990.

Stevens, Wallace. *The Necessary Angel: Essays on Reality and the Imagination*. New York: Vintage Books, 1951.

Vendler, Helen. *The Music of What Happens: Poems, Poets, Critics*. Cambridge: Harvard University Press, 1988.

———. *Wallace Stevens: Words Chosen out of Desire*. Knoxville: University of Tennessee Press, 1984.

Waggoner, Hyatt. *American Poets: From the Puritans to the Present*. Rev. ed. Baton Rouge: Louisiana State University Press, 1983.

Wilbur, Richard. *The Catbird's Song: Prose Pieces 1963–1995*. New York: Harcourt, Brace & Co., 1997.

Winters, Yvor. *Edwin Arlington Robinson*. New York: New Directions, 1946.

Title Index

☙⚶❧

Boldfaced page numbers indicate the principal thematic discussion of a poem.

Name Index

Boldfaced page numbers indicate the principal thematic discussion or discussions of a poet's work.

Subject Index

About the Author

ALLAN BURNS is Assistant Professor of English at Southern Illinois University, Edwardsville. His interests include American poetry and American nature writing. His articles and reviews have been published in *American Literary Realism, American Literature, English Studies, The Henry James Review* and *Papers on Language and Literature.*